ECONOMIC INFORMATION, DECISION, AND PREDICTION

SELECTED ESSAYS: VOLUME I

THEORY AND DECISION LIBRARY

AN INTERNATIONAL SERIES
IN THE PHILOSOPHY AND METHODOLOGY OF THE
SOCIAL AND BEHAVIORAL SCIENCES

VOLUME 7

JACOB MARSCHAK

ECONOMIC INFORMATION, DECISION, AND PREDICTION

Selected Essays: Volume I

PART I

Economics of Decision

D. REIDEL PUBLISHING COMPANY

DORDRECHT-HOLLAND / BOSTON-U.S.A.

Library of Congress Catalog Card Number 74–81940

The set of three volumes: ISBN 90 277 0524 0
Volume I: ISBN 90 277 0544 5
Volume II: ISBN 90 277 0545 3
Volume III: ISBN 90 277 0546 1

Published by D. Reidel Publishing Company,
P.O. Box 17, Dordrecht, Holland

Sold and distributed in the U.S.A., Canada and Mexico
by D. Reidel Publishing Company, Inc.
306 Dartmouth Street, Boston,
Mass. 02116, U.S.A.

Printed in The Netherlands by D. Reidel, Dordrecht

CONTENTS

PART I: ECONOMICS OF DECISION

CONTENTS OF VOLUMES II AND III

VOLUME II

PART II: ECONOMICS OF INFORMATION AND ORGANIZATION

VOLUME III

PART III: MONEY AND OTHER ASSETS

FOREWORD

The papers of Jacob Marschak which follow in these volumes are an extraordinary combination of original and fruitful departures in economic and social thought, superb clarity of exposition, and sensitivity to the values of earlier work and even competing traditions. They make us marvel alike at their variety, their quantity, and their quality.

But they do not, even so, fully reflect Marschak's contributions to the development of social science. He has had an unusual influence as one who exercises leadership. In a formal, organizational sense, this role has been manifest in his capacity as Director of the Cowles Commission for Research in Economics, then at the University of Chicago, in that organization's most productive and influential period, and later in his central role in the Western Management Science Institute, at the University of California at Los Angeles. I can speak from first-hand knowledge about the first. His special capacities are, first, the recognition of promising new concepts and of promising young scholars, and, second, getting his colleagues to join him in developing the ideas and involving them fully in the necessary tasks. There was an unusual combination of strength and humility in his methods; a display of force in pushing the work along but a willingness, almost an insistence, on treating even the most junior associate as a fully equal colleague in intellectual development, whose criticism of himself was to be encouraged.

His leadership has been exercised in the absence of formal positions. It appears to me that his aim, in his papers, at least since about 1950, has virtually never been only the presentation of results interesting in themselves and displaying his abilities; the papers have always been aimed to persuade the reader of the intellectual importance of the tasks as well of the rewards they will receive in terms of interesting problems.

The more recent interests of Jacob Marschak have been increasingly deep and broad. They have revolved about the question, how do and should individuals and groups of individuals make decisions? These are issues that have been posed perhaps most sharply by economists and statisticians but clearly cover a far wider domain of social thought; his intended audiences (and actual audiences, for many of the papers presented here originated as lectures or presentations before learned societies) include social psychologists, logicians, biologists, organization theorists, and management scientists.

The interesting problems in decision theory arise under conditions of uncertainty. Bernoulli's expected-utility hypothesis of 1738, designed to explain why individuals bought insurance at actuarially unfair rates and to resolve the St. Petersburg paradox, had been given axiomatic underpinnings by Frank Ramsey and, independently, by John von Neumann and Oskar Morgenstern; and Ramsey had added an axiomatic argument that rational choice under uncertainty had to be based on subjectively-held probabilities, a conclusion again independently arrived at later by Bruno de Finetti and Leonard J. Savage. Marschak was quick to recognize the importance of these hypotheses, for in his pioneering work on the theory of demand for money, he had stressed the importance of the holding of money as a rational response to uncertainty (see especially his important Essay 37), and so was aware of the need for a convenient general theory of behavior under uncertainty. His expositions and developments contributed heavily to acceptance of the new viewpoints and greatly enriched their content. But he was equally interested in the errors that individuals make in choice, their random responses to identical conditions. His series of axiomatic and empirical analyses have clarified greatly the meaning of the alternative hypotheses and have shown clearly the need for models to make sense out of experiments in this field on the borderline of economics and psychophysics.

Most original and most important of all, in my judgment (this may reflect only my own interests, but they have been conditioned by Marschak's work), is the economics of information and organization, the theory of decision-making by collectivities. Not only do human beings have limited knowledge, but they have particular knowledge; the uncertainties of different individuals are not identical, for they are probability distributions conditioned on different sets of signals from the world about them. The distribution of information has implications for the rules by which individuals make decisions; further, like any other distribution of goods, it gives rise to the possibility of making everyone better off by transmitting information, though as Marschak so strongly emphasizes, only at a cost.

The aim of this introduction, like that of a good *apéritif*, should be to arouse the appetite for the feast ahead, not to allay it, and I do not propose to give potted summaries of the works ahead; nothing could replace the style and verve of the original. I cannot refrain, though, from simply calling the reader's attention to the Essays (48 and 49) on measurement in economics, which combine exposition of highly technical methods of economic statistics with deep insights into the epistemology of the social sciences and make these elements all of a piece; and at least the economist should study the remarkable combination of empirical and theoretical reasoning in Essay 47.

No doubt, by the time these volumes appear, Jacob Marschak will have added more of his wide-ranging applications and developments, perhaps to some still further field of human inquiry. We will all remain grateful for the example of rigorous thought illuminating the broad concerns of human individuality and society.

KENNETH J. ARROW

PREFACE

This collection of essays reflects discussions of the last three or four decades, and some changes in the thinking habits of economists. It also reflects a broadening of the author's concept of 'economics'. As time advanced his interests shifted from econometrics and monetary theory to problems of decision, information and organization. The actions considered and their outcomes may, but need not be, inputs and outputs of quantifiable and marketable production factors and products, or their prices. Nowadays, broader 'optimization problems' are pigeonholed as belonging to 'operations research,' 'management science,' 'systems analysis'. They occupy economists, engineers and (to the extent that applied probabilities are involved) statisticians as well. As 'benefit-cost analysis' these tools are also applied to problems of social policy no less than to military or medical planning. There is a promise of cross-fertilization with the evolutionary theories of life science and anthropology. And the decision-theoretical approach has recently taken a foothold in the philosophy of science. Some of the papers in this volume reflect such interdisciplinary efforts, unified by a broadly 'economic' point of view.

A collection of essays is not a book. The reader of a book chapter is familiar with concepts explained in preceding chapters. But an essay should be self-contained. Hence many overlappings occur. Also, a collection of essays portrays the development of ideas and methods over time – a very fast development in the fields whose results are covered here – while in a book not only earlier terminology but also all earlier results may be discarded. Finally, the present essays have been addressed to audiences with different backgrounds, and so they differ in language, some are more expository, others cover more new ground.

I did not attempt to reshape the material of these essays into a unified, fresh-vintage book. Some errors were noticed and corrected. A few (too few!) references were updated. Some cross-references were added. Is the undertaking presumptuous? Or will it provide some convenience, by assembling materials from various sources, not all equally accessible?

The collection is in five parts. A rigid demarcation of their fields was not possible. Some essays could be assigned in a different way. An Introductory Note to each part will indicate some of its relations to other parts. Still, a reader concentrating on a special problem may find the classification useful.

Within each of the five parts, the essays are arranged chronologically, with the date of the first publication given after the title.

Cordial thanks to my co-authors, both for inspiring and working with me in the past and for permitting now this use of our joint product. They are (with ten essay numbers in brackets): William Andrews (47), Kenneth Arrow (19), Gordon Becker (10, 12, 14, 15), H. D. Block (7), Donald Davidson (6), Morris DeGroot (10, 12, 14, 15), Ted Harris (19), Helen Makower (34), Koichi Miyasawa (29). Some of them are better mathematicians than the undersigned (Block, DeGroot, Harris, Miyasawa), others are more skilled experimenters (Davidson, Becker). These and all other co-authors have made distinct contributions. I was also helped and encouraged by other members of research groups in which I was privileged to work: the Oxford Institute of Statistics; the Cowles Commission (later, Foundation) for Research in Economics at the University of Chicago (later at Yale University); the Institute of Industrial Administration, Carnegie-Mellon University; and the Western Management Science Institute, University of California at Los Angeles.

JACOB MARSCHAK

Los Angeles, October 1974

ACKNOWLEDGEMENTS

Essay 1 first appeared in *Econometrica*, Vol. 18, No. 2, pp. 111–141 (April 1950) and is reprinted here by permission of Joseph E. Stiglitz, Reprint Editor.

Essay 2 first appeared in *Proceedings of the Second Symposium on Mathematical Statistics and Probability* (ed. by Jerzy Neyman), pp. 493–506 (1951). Originally published by the University of California Press; reprinted by permission of The Regents of the University of California.

Essay 3 first appeared in *Game Theory and Political Behavior* (ed. by Martin Shubik), pp. 22–32, Doubleday and Co., 1954. It was included in *Game Theory and Related Approaches to Social Behavior* (ed. by Martin Shubik), pp. 95–109, Wiley, New York, 1964; reprinted here by permission of John Wiley and Sons, Inc.

Essay 4 first appeared in *Mathematical Thinking in the Social Sciences* (ed. by Paul F. Lazarsfeld), pp. 166–215, The Free Press, 1954. The volume was re-issued by Russell and Russell, 1964; reprinted here by permission of Macmillan Publishing Co., New York.

Essay 5 first appeared in *Mathematical Models of Human Behavior – Proceedings of a Symposium*, pp. 45–53. Copyright, 1955, by Dunlap and Associates, Inc., Stamford, Conn. Permission granted by J. Fucigna, Executive Vice-President.

Essay 6 (co-author: Donald Davidson) first appeared in *Measurement: Definitions and Theories* (ed. by C. West Churchman and Philburn Ratoosh), pp. 233–269. First published by Wiley, New York, 1959, and reprinted here by permission of John Wiley and Sons, Inc.

Essay 7 (co-author: H. D. Block) first appeared in *Contributions to Probability and Statistics: Essays in Honor of Harold Hotelling* (ed. by I. Olkin, S. G. Ghuryé, W. Hoeffding, W. G. Madow, and H. B. Mann, pp. 97–132 (1960). Reprinted here with the permission of the publishers, Stanford University Press. © 1960 by the Board of Trustees of the Leland Stanford Junior University.

Essay 8 first appeared in *Mathematical Methods in the Social Sciences* (ed. by K. J. Arrow, S. Karlin, and P. Suppes), pp. 312–329 (1960). Reprinted here with the permission of the publishers, Stanford University Press. © 1960 by the Board of Trustees of the Leland Stanford Junior University.

Essay 9 first appeared in *Behavioral Science*, Vol. 9, No. 2, pp. 103–110 (April 1964) and is reprinted here by permission of James G. Miller, M.D., Ph.D., Editor.

Essay 10 first appeared in *Behavioral Science*, Vol. 8, No. 1, pp. 41–55 (January 1963) and is reprinted here by permission of James G. Miller, M.D., Ph.D., Editor.

Essay 11 first appeared in *Management Science*, Vol. 9, No. 4, pp. 517–526 (July 1963) and is reprinted here by permission of The Institute of Management Sciences.

Essay 12 (co-authors: G. M. Becker and M. H. DeGroot) first appeared in *Behavioral Science*, Vol. 8, No. 3, pp. 199–202 (July 1963) and is reprinted here by permission of James G. Miller, M.D., Ph.D., Editor.

Essay 13 first appeared in *Econometrica*, Vol. 31, No. 4, pp. 719–725 (October 1963) and is reprinted here by permission of Joseph E. Stiglitz, Reprint Editor.

Essay 14 (co-authors: G. M. Becker and M. H. DeGroot) first appeared in *Behavioral Science*, Vol. 8, No. 4, pp. 306–311 (October 1963) and is reprinted here by permission of James G. Miller, M.D., Ph.D., Editor.

Essay 15 (co-authors: G. M. Becker and M. H. DeGroot) first appeared in *Behavioral Science*, Vol. 9, No. 3, pp. 226–232 (July 1964) and is reprinted here by permission of James G. Miller, M.D., Ph.D., Editor.

Essay 16 first appeared in *International Encyclopedia of the Social Sciences* (ed. by David L. Sills), Vol. 4, pp. 42–55 (1968) and is reprinted here by permission of the Publisher. Copyright © 1968 by Crowell Collier and Macmillan, Inc.

Essay 17 first appeared in *Induction, Growth and Trade: Essays in Honor of Sir Roy Harrod* (ed. by W. A. Eltis, M. FG. Scott and J. N. Wolfe), pp. 38–54, Clarendon Press, Oxford, 1970. © Oxford University Press, 1970. Reprinted by permission of the publishers.

Essay 18 is to be included in a forthcoming Volume in Honor of Ralph W. Gerard (ed. by R. Grenell) and is here printed by permission.

RECENT PUBLICATIONS BY THE AUTHOR

A list of publications by the author for 1923–71 will be found in *Decision and Organization, a Volume in Honor of Jacob Marschak* (ed. by C. B. McGuire and R. Radner), pp. 337–41, North-Holland Publishing Co. For the subsequent years add:

1972

'Optimal Systems for Information and Decision', in *Techniques of Optimization* (ed. by A. V. Balakrishnan), pp. 355–70 (*Selected Essays*, 32).

'Interdisciplinary Discussion on Mathematics in Behavioral Sciences', in *Festschrift fuer Walter G. Waffenschmidt* (ed. by H. J. Niedereichholz), pp. 127–32, Verlag A. Hain (*Selected Essays*, 55).

1973

'Limited Role of Entropy in Information Economics', *5th Conference on Optimization Techniques*, Part II (ed. by R. Conti and A. Ruberti), pp. 264–71. (Revised, in *Theory and Decision*, Vol. 5, pp. 1–7).

'Intersubjektive Wahrscheinlichkeit', *Heidelberger Jahrbuecher*, Vol. 17, pp. 14–26.

1974

'Prior and Posterior Probabilities and Semantic Information', in *Information, Inference and Decision* (ed. by G. Menges), pp. 167–80. Theory and Decision Library, Vol. 1, D. Reidel.

'Information, Decision and the Scientist', *Pragmatic Aspects of Human Communication* (ed. by C. Cherry), pp. 145–78. Theory and Decision Library, Vol. 4, D. Reidel.

'Optimal Organization: Analytiker möchten sich mit Praktikern verständigen', *Zeitschrift fuer Betriebswirtschaftliche Forschung*, Vol. 26, pp. 283–97.

'Value and Cost of Information', in *Production Theory* (ed. by W. Eichhorn, R. Henn, O. Opitz and R. W. Shephard), pp. 335–58, Springer.

'Economics of Organizational Forms', *Proceedings of Conference on Man and Computer* (ed. by M. Marois), North-Holland Publishing Co.

1975
'Personal Probabilities of Probabilities', (with K. Borch, H. Chernoff, M. DeGroot, R. Dorfman, W. Edwards, T. S. Ferguson, K. Miyasawa, P. Randolph, L. J. Savage, R. Schlaifer, R. L. Winkler). *Theory and Decision*, Vol. 6.

PART I

ECONOMICS OF DECISION

INTRODUCTORY NOTE

The author's work on economics of decision, the subject of Part One of Selected Essays, has, in fact, started with studies of optimal balance sheets and of liquidity, covered in Part Three. Under uncertainty, to choose between decisions is to choose between 'prospects': the probability distributions of outcomes. In some of those earlier writings (Essays 33,34) it was deemed useful to express each distribution of monetary yields by its moments and to associate these with words of common usage (lucrativity, risk, long odds), an approach that has later proved, at the hands of H. Markowitz (1959), computationally convenient. If expected utility is maximized such description of decision presupposes a polynomial utility function of money, an assumption later discarded, for good reasons, by J. W. Pratt (1964) and K. Arrow (1965). However, expected utility came later. Thus in the analysis of liquidity under uncertainty (Essay 35) the principle of 'minimax regret' was used. This and various other competing principles were surveyed by R. Radner and J. Marschak (1954). Expected utility (of decisions with outcomes not necessarily monetary or numerical) is introduced in Essay 1 of Part One on the lines of J. von Neumann and O. Morgenstern (1944), with only 'objective' probability considered. Personal probabilities of F. Ramsey (1926), B. de Finetti (1937), L. J. Savage (1954) came in later, in Essays 3, 4, 15; the 'intersubjective' nature of 'objective' probabilities and their relation to observable frequencies is treated in Essay 17 and the author's Heidelberg paper (1973), and more rigorously in Chapter 2 of the *Economic Theory of Teams* (Marschak and Radner 1972). A 'Round Robin' on 'Personal Probabilities of Probabilities' was initiated by the author who later added some further comments in the publication (1974).

Models of actual behavior (Essays 9, 15), in particular 'stochastic' ones (Essays 6–8, 10, 12, 14) acknowledge limitations of men's 'rationality'. To ignore those limitations is not economical.

REFERENCES

Arrow, K. J. (1965), Lecture 2 in *Aspects of the Theory of Risk-Bearing*, Helsinki, Yrjö Johnssonin Säätio. Republished as Chapter 3 of Essays in the *Theory of Risk-Bearing*, Markham Publishing Co., Chicago 1971.

De Finetti, B. (1937), 'La prévision, ses lois logiques, ses sources subjectives'. Republished in English, with some revisions, in *Studies in Subjective Probabilities* (ed. by H. E. Kyburg and H. Smokler), J. Wiley, New York, 1964.

Markowitz, H. (1959), *Portfolio Selection*, Cowles Foundation Monograph, 16, New York, J. Wiley.

Marschak, J. (1973), Intersubjektive Wahrscheinlichkeit, *Heidelberger Jahrbuecher*, **17**.

Marschak, J. and Others (K. Borch, H. Chernoff, M. H. DeGroot, R. Dorfman, W. Edwards, T. S. Ferguson, K. Miyasawa, P. Randolph, L. J. Savage, R. Schlaifer, R. L. Winkler) (1974). 'Personal Probabilities of Probabilities', *Theory and Decision*, **6** (forthcoming).

Marschak, J. and Radner, R. (1972), *Economic Theory of Teams*, Yale University Press.

Pratt, J. W. (1964), 'Risk Aversion in the Small and in the Large', *Econometrica*, **32**, 122–136.

Radner, R. and Marschak, J. (1954), 'Note on Some Proposed Decision Criteria,' in *Decision Processes* (ed. by R. M. Thrall *et al.*), pp. 61–68, Wiley, New York.

Ramsey, F. P. (1926), 'Truth and Probability', republished in *Foundations of Mathematics and Other Logical Essays*, Humanities Press, New York, 1950.

Savage, L. J. (1954), *The Foundations of Statistics*, J. Wiley. Revised edition, Dover Publications, 1972.

Von Neumann, J. and Morgenstern, O. (1944), *Theory of Games and Economic Behavior*, esp. Appendix added in the 1948 edition.

1

RATIONAL BEHAVIOR, UNCERTAIN PROSPECTS, AND MEASURABLE UTILITY*

(1950)

ABSTRACT. After introducing some basic concepts and three postulates on rational choice, it is proposed to show that if the economists' theory of assets is completed by a fourth postulate on rational choice, then utility can be defined as a quantity whose mathematical expectation is maximized by the rational man. In this sense, utility is 'measurable' and 'manageable'. These results are inspired by von Neumann's and Morgenstern's discussion of utility in *Theory of Games and Economic Behavior*; an attempt is made to sketch some relations between their approach and the present one, It is shown in conclusion that while gambling is compatible with the four postulates, the 'love of danger' is not: and a property of the maximum mathematical expectation of utility is conjectured.

I. SOME BASIC CONCEPTS

1. *Rational Behavior: Description and Advice*

The theory of rational behavior is a set of propositions that can be regarded either as idealized approximations to the actual behavior of men or as recommendations to be followed.

This can be shown in the following proposition: "The rational man does not make logical and arithmetical errors." Or, to give three particular examples: "if $x=2$ and $y=0.005$, the rational man concludes that $xy=0.01$"; "if all A are B, the rational man concludes that all non-B are non-A, but he does not conclude that all B are A"; "if P follows from Q, he concludes that non-Q follows from non-P, but he does not conclude that Q follows from P." Now, a large proportion of people, especially when in a hurry to answer and to act, are apt to disobey those rules. Living men and women are apt to misplace their decimal points; they often conclude from the part to the whole; and they are not above confusing a sufficient condition with a necessary one. That is, they do not behave rationally. What is, then, the use of setting up the above propositions of arithmetic and logic? The use is twofold: to describe approximately the behavior of men who, it is believed, cannot be 'all fools all the time', and to give advice on how to reach 'correct' conclusions. These two aspects of the rules of logic and arithmetic can be called, respectively, the descriptive and the recommendatory aspect.

As an approximative description of actual behavior, the rules of logic and arithmetic may be regarded as hypotheses on the psychology of reasoning and calculating: hypotheses whose predictive power ('predict how many people of a certain age-group, etc., will make a certain kind of error') is susceptible of empirical tests. Viewed from their recommendatory aspect, as advice on how to reach 'correct' conclusions, the rules of logic and arithmetic are susceptible only to the test of internal consistency; in fact, the aggregate of these rules (including the rule of internal consistency itself) can be regarded as nothing but the definition of 'correctness' of conclusions.

Note, however, that 'correct' conclusions are often regarded as having, in addition, a 'utilitarian' virtue. The results of decisions based on 'correct' conclusions are, in some sense, 'preferable' to results of decisions based on incorrect ones. It is 'advisable' to follow the rules of logic and arithmetic. In dealing with his environment ('nature', which includes 'society') a man who often makes mistakes in his inferences and his sums is, in the long run, apt to fare less well than if he had been a better logician and arithmetician. Thus concepts of 'welfare' and of 'long run', or of utility and mathematical expectation, become involved. If advisable decisions must obey rules of logic and arithmetic, they are not themselves defined by those rules alone. The fulfillment of rules of conventional logic and arithmetic is a necessary but not a sufficient condition for a decision to be advisable. We need additional definitions and postulated rules, to 'prolong' logic and arithmetic into the realm of decision. We shall define rational behavior as that which follows those rules, in addition to the rules of logic and arithmetic. It will be seen (an experience common in logic and mathematics) that alternative sets of postulated rules may or may not lead to different implications.

Again (as in the case of the logico-arithmetical rules in the narrower sense) these postulates, and their implications, can be used in two ways: they can be conceived as approximate descriptions of actual behavior or they can be regarded as rules of behavior to be followed. Both the descriptive and the recommendatory aspects have practical use. For example, a government (or a firm) has to (a) choose the advisable course of its own responses to environment and (b) know, as a part of its environment, something about the actual behavior of tax-payers, consumers, competitors, etc.

Rational behavior is also called the behavior of a rational man. For brevity, we shall speak of 'the man,' to cover the rational consumer, the rational firm, the rational government, etc.

2. *Complete Information*

We have further to distinguish between two cases: the case when the man thinks he knows certain relevant probability distributions, and the case when the man does not think so. We call the former case *complete information*, and the latter, *incomplete information*.[1] The theory of rational behavior under incomplete information is not presented here. It would be related to the studies on the rationale of sampling, started by Neyman and Pearson [1] and developed particularly by A. Wald, e.g. [1, 2]. The case of complete information can (but need not) be represented as a limiting one: it is approached as the number of observations which have been made by the man increases. Alternatively, one can think of the probabilities used in the man's decisions as 'degrees of belief' not related to specific samples in any simple way, yet obeying the usual axioms on probabilities.

A special case of complete information is that of *certainty*: in this case all probabilities have values 0 or 1.

3. *Future Histories x; Commodity Space X*

At a given point of time the man considers a sequence of, say, τ future time intervals, up to a certain time point called horizon. The amounts of each commodity consumed during each interval and the stocks of various kinds available at the horizon point define one of the mutually exclusive 'future histories'. Each such history can be represented by a point x in the 'commodity space' X. Since, for the more remote future, the man may have a coarser classification of goods than for the immediate future (a point emphasized by Koopmans [1]), some commodities, or commodity groups, may have to be entered identically as zeros for some time intervals or for the horizon point; hence the dimensionality of X at most equals $\gamma(\tau+1)$, where γ is the number of commodities ever to be entered.

One can also interpret each point x more narrowly, as the development of a particular 'venture' ('play'), disregarding all other aspects of a man's future. Thus, a firm owner's choice between various uses of cash profits in his personal plans of consumption may be considered irrelevant (this diminishes γ); only the near future is considered (this makes τ small); and attention is paid only to a particular shop or ship, patent or contract. Note, however, that even if one is concerned only with a single money wager, the number of alternative points x (here the alternative amounts of money gains) may be large.

Inasmuch as the man may treat time and the amounts of goods as both discrete and bounded, we shall assume the number of points x finite, though, of course, as large as we like. We shall enumerate these points as $x^{(0)},..., x^{(\nu)}$.[2]

4. *Prospects a; domain A*

We call a prospect a the vector (the distribution) of the probabilities $a_0,..., a_\nu$, assigned respectively to all the mutually exclusive histories $x^{(0)},..., x^{(\nu)}$. We can write $a=a(x)$, where x is a random vector.[3] We have

$$(4.1) \qquad \sum_{\mu=0}^{\nu} a_\mu = 1, \quad a_\mu \geqslant 0, \quad (\mu = 0,..., \nu).$$

Accordingly, we can represent each prospect by a point $a=(a_1,..., a_\nu)$ in the domain A of the Euclidian ν-space defined by the condition that A consists of all points a such that for every a,

$$(4.2) \qquad \sum_{\mu=1}^{\nu} a_\mu \leqslant 1, \quad a_\mu \geqslant 0, \quad (\mu = 1,..., \nu);$$

we define a_0:

$$(4.3) \qquad 0 \leqslant a_0 = 1 - \sum_{\mu=1}^{\nu} a_\mu \leqslant 1.$$

Note that A is an infinite set regardless of whether ν is or is not infinite, because each probability can take all real values from 0 to 1 subject only to the restriction (4.1).

If a prospect promises one particular history, say $x^{(\mu)}$, $(\mu=0,..., \nu)$, with certainty, we call it a *sure prospect* and denote it by $a^{(\mu)}$. Prospects which are not sure are called uncertain.

5. *Geometric Presentation*: *Boundary and Interior of A*

In Figure 1, $\nu=2$, and the sure prospect $a^{(0)}$ is chosen as the origin. The two other sure prospects $a^{(1)}$, $a^{(2)}$, lie on the two axes, each at unit distance from the origin. The lengths of segments $\overline{am}=a_0$, $\overline{an}=a_1$, $\overline{ap}=a_2$, indicate the component probabilities of the uncertain prospect a; and $a_0+a_1+a_2=1$.[4] All points in or on the rectangular isosceles triangle $a^{(0)}a^{(1)}a^{(2)}$ constitute the domain A, as defined by (4.2). For any ν, the sure prospect $a^{(0)}=(0,\ldots,0)$ is at the origin; while any other sure prospect, $a^{(\mu)}$, $\mu=1,\ldots,\nu$, will be at some other corner of the domain A; $a^{(\mu)}$ is a unit vector: each of its ν components $a_\pi^{(\mu)}$ $(\pi=1,\ldots,\nu)$ is 1 or 0 according as $\pi=\text{or}\neq\mu$. Any prospect a for which at least one component is zero, lies on the boundary of A. Any prospect not on the boundary of A is called an interior point.

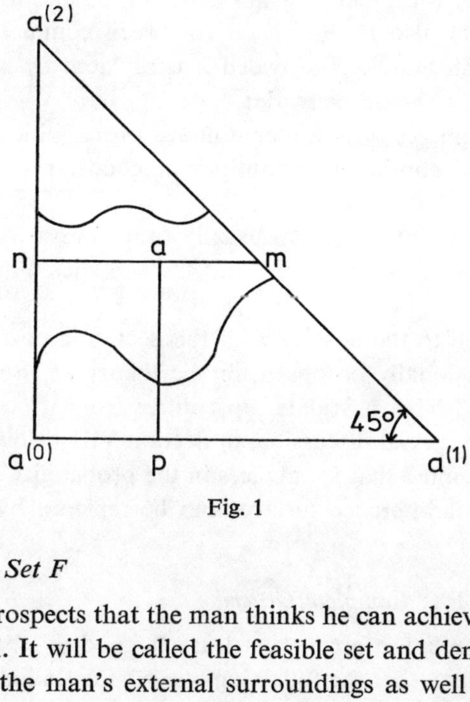

Fig. 1

6. *The Feasible Set F*

The set of all prospects that the man thinks he can achieve by his actions is a subset of A. It will be called the feasible set and denoted by F. It is determined by the man's external surroundings as well as his own endowment: the technology of his farm or factory, his ability to borrow, the market conditions, etc. Set F is not dependent on the man's 'tastes', to be defined in Section 8 below. In Figure 1, set F is indicated by the area bounded by, and including, the curved line and segments of axes. We shall always assume F to be a closed set.

II. THREE POSTULATES ON CHOICE

7. *Commodity Space X and Probability Space A*

The economic theory of choice was originally applied to alternative bundles of commodities, each promised with certainty, or to alternative combinations of this year's, next year's, third year's... flows of money (Fisher [2]) or of some other single commodity, again promised with certainty. We have called the set of such alternatives the space X. To treat uncertain prospects we have introduced the domain A of the ν-dimensional probability space, $\nu+1$ being the number of points in the commodity space X. The propositions (postulates, definitions, and derived propositions) on choice, formulated in this Part for points in the probability space, hold good also for the choice between commodity bundles or sequences of such bundles,[5] provided A is replaced by X. However, the following remarks should be made:

(1) The coordinates of A are continuous probabilities; if coordinates of X represented continuous quantities of goods, ν would be infinite. But see note 2.

(2) While the points in X are usually (not always) required to have nonnegative coordinates, the points in A are restricted more strongly by (4.2).

(3) In addition to the postulates of this section a postulate of 'monotonicity' is occasionally proposed for the theory of choice in the commodity space X. This postulate must differ from its counterpart in A and will deserve special discussion, in Section VIII below.

(4) It will be noted that for choices in the probability space, Postulate III introducing indifference surfaces can be replaced by a weaker one, III′ or III*.

8. POSTULATE I: *Complete Ordering*

One assumes a relation $\mathfrak{g}$ (read 'at least as good as') between elements a, b, c... of A, such that the following two postulates hold: Postulate Ia: *For any two a, b, at least one of the following holds*: $a\mathfrak{g}b$, $b\mathfrak{g}a$ (*comparability*). Postulate Ib: $a\mathfrak{g}b$, $b\mathfrak{g}c$ *together imply* $a\mathfrak{g}c$ (*transitivity*). Ia and Ib together state that $\mathfrak{g}$ is a *complete ordering* of A.

We define *tastes* by attaching the values 'true', 'false', to the statements $a\mathfrak{g}b$ applied to all pairs of points in A.

The *preference* and *indifference* relations, $\mathfrak{p}$ (read 'preferred to' or 'better than') and $\mathfrak{i}$ (read 'indifferent to' or 'equivalent to'), are defined as follows:

$$a\mathfrak{p}b \text{ means } a\mathfrak{g}b \text{ and not } b\mathfrak{g}a,$$
$$a\mathfrak{i}b \text{ means } a\mathfrak{g}b \text{ and } b\mathfrak{g}a,$$

where a, b are real vectors, and $a=b$ means, as usual, $a_\mu = b_\mu$, $\mu = 1, \ldots, \nu$. It follows from the above postulates and definitions that $a=b$ implies $a\mathfrak{i}b$; $a\mathfrak{i}b$ implies $b\mathfrak{i}a$; and that $\mathfrak{i}$ and $\mathfrak{p}$ are transitive relations.

9. *Indifference Sets; Utility Indices; Utility Function*

For any a, we define its indifference set $J(a)$ as follows: $J(a)$ consists of all b's such that $b\mathfrak{i}a$. It follows that every a breaks up the set A into the following three pairwise disjunct subsets: $J(a)$; the region of all b's such that $b\mathfrak{p}a$; the region of all c's such that $a\mathfrak{p}c$.

It follows that the indifference sets can be uniquely arranged into a sequence. If a real number $u(a)$ is assigned to the indifference set $J(a)$, one can assign to any indifference set $J(b)$ a real number $u(b)$ such that $u(a) \geqslant u(b)$ means $a\mathfrak{g}b$. It follows that

$$u(a) > u(b) \text{ means } a\mathfrak{p}b,$$

and

$$u(a) = u(b) \text{ means } a\mathfrak{i}b.$$

The numbers $u(a), u(b), \ldots$ are called utility indices or, briefly, utilities; and the function u on set A, a utility function. The class of all utility functions will be denoted by U.

A function $\phi(z)$ is said to be monotonically increasing if $\phi(z_1) > \phi(z_2)$ for $z_1 > z_2$. Let $u(a)$ be a utility function. Then $\phi[u(A)]$ is a utility function if and only if ϕ is a monotonically increasing function.

10. *Maximizing Utility*

Define a subset F' of the feasible closed set F (Section 6 above) as follows: if d and b are in F' and if c is in F but not in F' then $d\,\mathfrak{i}\,b\mathfrak{p}c$. The set F' consists of the 'best feasible' prospects; and since F is closed, F' must contain at least one element (Arrow [1]). We study the case when F' has only one element (the best feasible prospect). Let u be a utility function. Then, under conditions just stated, $u(c) < u(b) = u(d) = \max\, u(a)$

over all a in F. To say that a certain function u is a utility function means that $u(a)$ is maximized with respect to a, subject to the condition that a is in the feasible set F.

11. *Internal and External Averages*

Let r be a real number, $0<r<1$. Then $b=ra+(1-r)\,c=\{[ra_0+(1-r)\,c_0], \ldots, [ra_\nu+(1-r)\,c_\nu]\}$ will be called an internal average of a and c; it is represented by a point on the straight line segment $\overline{ac}$. Let q be a real number, $q>1$. Then $d=qa+(1-q)\,c$ is called an external average of a and c and lies on the continuation of $\overline{ac}$ beyond a. Obviously, a is an internal average of d and c, with $q=1/r$.

12. POSTULATE II: *If* $a\mathfrak{p}b\mathfrak{p}c$, *then there exists* r, $0<r<1$, *such that* $b\mathfrak{i}[ra+(1-r)\,c]$. (*Continuity* of the preference relation.)

13. POSTULATE III: *For any* a *and* r, $0<r<1$, *there exists a prospect* b *such that not* $a\mathfrak{i}[ra+(1-r)\,b]$

That is, the neighborhood of any point a contains at least one point b in A which is not equivalent to a.

14. *Indifference Surfaces*

Postulates II and III imply together that the indifference set $J(a)$ forms a boundary between two regions of A: one containing all b's such that $b\mathfrak{p}a$; the other containing all c's such that $a\mathfrak{p}c$. In this case, $J(a)$ has one dimension less than the space, that is, $\nu-1$ dimensions, and is called an indifference surface. [Note that in special cases, e.g., for some points a on the boundary of A, the set $J(a)$ may have $<\nu-1$ dimensions: a may have either no b's ($b\mathfrak{p}a$) or no c's ($a\mathfrak{p}c$) in its neighborhood.] In any case, no two distinct indifference sets $J(a)\neq J(b)$ may intersect, since by the definitions in Section 8, $a\mathfrak{p}b$ is inconsistent with $a\mathfrak{i}b$.

15. Postulate III and its implication that indifference sets are, in general, surfaces forms an interesting link with tradition. But for the present purposes it can be replaced by one of the following two weaker postulates suggested, respectively, by Abraham Wald and Herman Rubin.

POSTULATE III*: *There exist two prospects* a *and* b *in the interior of* A *such that* $a\mathfrak{p}b$ *or* $b\mathfrak{p}a$.

POSTULATE III′: *There exist at least four distinct indifference sets.*

III. THE THEORY OF ASSETS

16. The theory of assets pointed out that the man chooses between achievable probability distributions. This proposition was just stated in Section 10. However, with exceptions that will be stated below, past writings on the theory of assets[6] did not represent each prospect by a point in the space of probabilities of mutually exclusive 'histories' x. They considered instead the joint probability distribution of the $\gamma(\tau+1)$ quantities of each commodity at each point of time (see Section 3). Each 'cell' of such a joint distribution corresponds to some history x. To a given distribution $a(x)$ of the histories x corresponds one joint probability distribution of the alternative commodity-amounts at various points of time. The latter distribution can be characterized by certain parameters, and writers on the theory of assets represented each prospect by a point in the space of these parameters; call this space P. For example, if only one commodity – say, money income – and one point of time are considered, so that the alternative histories x differ only by the amounts of money income, each prospect can be characterized by the mean, the variance, the skewness, etc., of the probability distribution of income; if more than one commodity or time-point is considered, say $\gamma(\tau+1)=\varepsilon$ quantities, each prospect may be characterized by ε means, ε variances, $\varepsilon(\varepsilon-1)/2$ correlations, etc. Each distribution parameter was regarded as being a 'good' (or possibly a 'bad') in the eyes of the man. Accordingly, each distribution was regarded as a bundle of 'commodities', subject to postulates which are analogous to Postulates I–III above. Tastes were described by indifference surfaces drawn in the parameter space P, and the empirical properties of these surfaces were discussed. For example, the risk-aversion (risk-discount), i.e., the rate of substitution between the mean and the variance of income, expressed by the relevant slope of an indifference surface, was stated to be positive. Opportunities were defined as a region of the space P (analogous to our region F of A). The boundary of this region – the 'opportunity surface' – was derived from the individual's initial possession of assets (physical goods and positive or negative claims), the prices or other conditions in the market of the assets (perfect or otherwise), and the production conditions. With opportunities

and tastes defined in the space of distribution parameters, the old theory of assets defined rational decision analogously to Section 10. (If all functions are well behaved, this will correspond to choosing the point of tangency between the opportunity surface and an indifference surface.) From here, the theory explained the market prices of assets in the same way in which prices of production factors are determined from the indifference maps of individuals, their initial possession of production factors, and the production functions for final goods. It also claimed to explain the determination of optimal balance sheets and plans, in the way the ordinary theory determines the equilibrium flows of consumption.

17. It was pointed out by Tintner[7] that the utility index might be considered, not as a function of distribution parameters but as a functional of the distribution function itself. This is tantamount to the use of the domain of probabilities, A, as in Part I above. To become more than a change in notation, this suggestion will need an additional postulate (Part IV). With the help of such a postulate, it will be shown in Part V that indifference sets in the A-space must be parallel hyperplanes. This will, in turn, imply the possibility of defining utility functions determined up to linear transformations. It will also imply that such a utility index of an uncertain prospect $a \equiv (a_0, \ldots, a_\nu)$ equals its 'expected utility', defined as the average of the utility indices of the sure prospects $a^{(0)}, \ldots, a^{(\nu)}$, weighted with the probabilities $a_0, \ldots, a_\nu$. This should also help to revise the theory of determination of optimal plans, defined as rational balance sheets or rational strategies.[8]

18. *The Mean vs Other Parameters*

It has been common among economists to insist that the means of the amounts of commodities are not the only parameters of their joint distribution that are relevant to the man's decisions, and possibly not the most important ones, and attempts were made to specify which additional, or alternative, parameters – e.g., the higher moments[9] – should be considered. These writers, e.g., Marschak [2], Tintner [1], often failed to make clear that the statement "the average *amounts of goods* are not alone relevant to the man's decision" does not contradict the statement that the average *utility* is maximized by him. The latter proposition permits, in fact, to relate 'risk-aversion', 'advantage of diversification', and similar concepts of the older asset theory to the properties of the utility function of sure prospects.[10]

IV. FOURTH POSTULATE ON CHOICE BETWEEN PROSPECTS

19. POSTULATE IV_1: *If* $a \mathrm{i} a'$ *and* $0<r<1$, *then* $a \mathrm{i}\, [ra+(1-r)\, a']$.

In words: If prospect *a* is equivalent to another prospect, *a'*, then the prospect of obtaining either *a* or *a'* with certainty is equivalent to each of them. To illustrate this postulate, we can first interpret *a, a'* as sure prospects (Section 4 above), that is, as two mutually exclusive future sequences of events or, still simpler, as two mutually exclusive bundles of commodities. Suppose a man is indifferent as between a car and a $1000 bill. Then he should be also indifferent as between a car, a $1000 bill, and the ticket to a lottery in which the changes of winning a car or a $1000 bill are, respectively, 0.2 and 0.8, say. The same applies if, for a car and $1000, we substitute securities, or patents, or lottery tickets, etc., promising, respectively (if combined with the man's other assets), prospects such as those defined in Part I.

POSTULATE IV_2: *Let* a, a', b, *be three distinct prospects*; *let* $c=ra+$ $+(1-r)\, b$, *and* $c'=ra'+(1-r)\, b$, *where* $0<r<1$; *then* $a' \mathrm{i} a$ *implies* $c' \mathrm{i} c$.

In words: If two prospects *a* and *a'* are equivalent, then the prospect of having *a* or *b* with probabilities r, $1-r$, and the prospect of having *a'* or *b* with the same respective probabilities r, $1-r$, are equivalent. For example, suppose a $1000 bill and a car are equivalent. Compare two lottery tickets, one promising a $1000 bill or a house with probabilities 0.9 and 0.1, the other promising a car or a house, also with probabilities 0.9 and 0.1. Then there is no reason to prefer one of the two lottery tickets to the other.

For the geometry of these postulates see Figure 2, where $a' \mathrm{i} a$ and $\overline{a'a} \parallel \overline{c'c}$. Then by IV_1, the internal average $m \mathrm{i} a$; and by IV_2, $c' \mathrm{i} c$.

POSTULATE IV: *If* $a' \mathrm{i} a$ *and* $0<r<1$, *then for any* b, $[ra'+(1-r)\, b]$ $\mathrm{i}\, [ra+(1-r)\, b]$. This postulate summarizes IV_1 (for $b=a$) and IV_2 (for $b \neq a$).

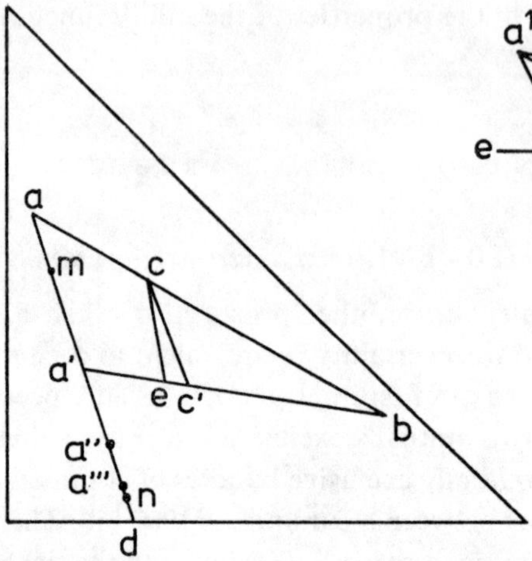

Fig. 2

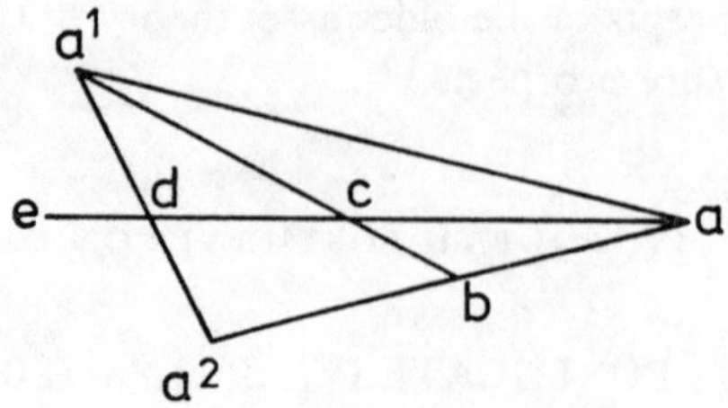

Fig. 3

20. While IV_1 states that the interval average (see Section 11 above) of two equivalent prospects is equivalent to them, the following lemma, implied in IV_1 and IV_2, extends this statement to external averages though under a restriction:

LEMMA 1: *If* $a\,\mathrm{i}\,a'$, *and an interior point* p *is collinear with* a, a', *then* $p\,\mathrm{i}\,a$.

Proof: Suppose p is between a and a': for example, $p=m$ in Figure 2; then the proposition follows directly from Postulate IV_1. Suppose now a' is between p and a: for example $p=n$ in Figure 2. Then continue the line $\overline{a'n}$ till its intersection d with the boundary of the domain. Define s, $0<s<1$, by the equation $a'=sd+(1-s)\,a$. Define $a''=sd+(1-s)\,a'$. Then $a\,\mathrm{i}\,a'$ implies, by IV_2, $a''\,\mathrm{i}\,a$. Define next $a'''=sd+(1-s)a''$, $a''''=$ $=sd+(1-s)\,a'''$, etc. By applying IV_2 successively, every point a'', a''', a'''',... is shown to be in $J(a)$; and by IV_1 any point between a and a',..., a'''',... is also in $J(a)$. Therefore, since the distances $\overline{da'}$,..., $\overline{d''''}$,... approach zero, any point on the segment $\overline{ad}$ is in $J(a)$ except possibly d itself.

V. LINEAR UTILITY FUNCTIONS OF PROSPECTS

21. Part V will develop the implications of our four postulates. A particularly simple system of indifference sets – a family of parallel planes – will be shown to represent tastes with regard to prospects. It will then be proved that there exists a class of linear utility functions of prospects, and that the 'expected values' (properly defined) of such functions are maximized over the feasible set of prospects by the rational man (defined as one who follows the rules of logic and arithmetic and the four postulates of Part IV).

THEOREM 1: *The indifference sets $J(a)$ are parallel hyperplanes of $\leqslant \nu-1$ dimensions. For any interior a, $J(a)$ has $\nu-1$ dimensions.* This theorem will be derived from Postulates I, II, III*, IV; the results[11] would of course be valid if III* were replaced by a stronger Postulate III. (If, instead of Postulate III*, we admitted the stronger Postulate III and hence the existence of indifference hypersurfaces, Postulate IV would imply immediately that these surfaces must be parallel hyperplanes.)

To give a general idea of the proof we first confine ourselves to $\nu=2$ and to the interior of A only, and show that then (1) all indifference sets are straight lines and (2) all these lines are parallel. The general case will then be introduced in Section 22:1.

21:1. We first show that if three interior points a^1, a^2, a^3, are equivalent they must be collinear.[12] For suppose that, on the contrary, they are the vertices of a triangle, as in Figure 3. Then, by Lemma 1, any b on the triangle, any c within the triangle, and any interior point e outside the triangle are in $J(a^1)$; and this contradicts III*. Conversely, any interior point on the straight line containing a^1 and a^2 is in $J(a^1)$; this follows from Lemma 1.

21:2. Figure 2 shows that if $J(a)$ and $J(c)$ are straight lines containing the segments $\overline{aa'}$ and $\overline{cc'}$, then $\overline{aa'} \parallel \overline{cc'}$. For suppose that the line drawn through c parallel to aa' meets ba' in e. Then by IV_2, eic; and since cic', the points c, c', e, must be collinear, as shown in 21:1. Hence e must coincide with c'.

22:1. To prove for the whole domain A, of any dimension ν, that each set $J(a)$ is a hyperplane of $\leqslant \nu-1$ dimensions (of exactly $\nu-1$ dimensions if a is in the interior of A), Abraham Wald suggested the following set of lemmas. Denote by a' an interior point;[13] denote by $J'(a')$ the set of all interior points in $J(a')$.

22:2. LEMMA 2: *For any interior point a', the set $J'(a')$ consists of all the interior points of a hyperplane, $H(a')$ of $\leqslant \nu-1$ dimensions.* This follows from Lemma 1, as in 21:1, by proving that the vertices of a $(\nu+1)$-hedron cannot be equivalent, and that any interior point contained in the same hyperplane with ν equivalent points is equivalent to them.

22:3. LEMMA 3: *For any interior point a', $J(a')$ consists of $J'(a')$ and the intersection of $H(a')$ with the boundary of A.* To prove this, consider b'', a point on the boundary of A, and show that b'' is in $J(a')$ if, and only if, b'' is on the hyperplane $H(a')$.
22:3:1. *Necessity*: Suppose b'' is in $J(a')$ but not in $H(a')$. Then any interior point c' on the segment $\overline{b''a'}$ is not in $H(a')$; but on the other hand, by IV, c' is in $J(a')$ and hence in $J'(a')$ and, by Lemma 2, in $H(a')$. Because of this contradiction, b'' must be in $H(a')$.
22:3:2. *Sufficiency*: To show that if the boundary point b'' is on the hyperplane $H(a')$ it is also in the indifference set $J(a')$, distinguish three cases: (1) there exist two interior points c', d', such that $c' \mathfrak{p} a' \mathfrak{p} d'$; (2) thre is no interior point c' such that $c' \mathfrak{p} a'$; (3) thre is no interior point d' such that $a' \mathfrak{p} d'$.

In Case (1), by Lemma 2, neither c' nor d' is in $H(a')$. Suppose first $\overline{(1\alpha)}$: that $b'' \mathfrak{p} a'$; then $b'' \mathfrak{p} a' \mathfrak{p} d'$, and, by Postulate II, there exists a point e' on segment $\overline{b''d'}$ such that e' is in $J(a')$; by Lemma 2, e' is in $H(a')$. But on the other hand, since b'' is in $H(a')$ while d' is not, e' on segment $\overline{b''d'}$ cannot be in $H(a')$. Because of this contradiction, the assumption (1α) that $b'' \mathfrak{p} a'$ is false; so is, by symmetry, the assumption (1β) that $a' \mathfrak{p} b''$. Hence $a' \mathfrak{i} b''$.

In Case (2) there exists, by III*, an interior point d' such that $a' \mathfrak{p} d'$; and, by Lemma 2, d' is not in $H(a')$. Suppose first $\underline{(2\alpha)}$: that $b'' \mathfrak{p} a'$. Then $b'' \mathfrak{p} a' \mathfrak{p} d'$, and, by II, there exists an interior point e' on segment $\overline{b''d'}$ such that e' is in $J(a')$ and hence, by Lemma 2, in H(a'). But on the other hand, since b'' is in $H(a')$ while d$'$ is not, e' is not in $H(a')$. Because of this contradiction, the assumption $b'' \mathfrak{p} a'$ must be false.

Suppose next (2β): that $a' \mathfrak{p} b''$; and consider separately three subcases: $(2\beta\alpha)$: $d' \mathfrak{p} b''$; $(2\beta\beta)$: $b'' \mathfrak{p}\ d'$; $(2\beta\gamma)$: $b'' \mathfrak{i} d'$. In $(2\beta\alpha)$, $a' \mathfrak{p} d' \mathfrak{p} b''$ and hence, by II, there is a point e' on $\overline{a''b'}$ such that $e' \mathfrak{i} d'$; but then, since both a' and b'' are in $H(a')$, e' is in H(a'), while [as stated at the beginning of Case (2)] its equivalent d' is not in $H(A')$. This contradicts Lemma 2; hence $(2\beta\alpha)$ is impossible. Subcase $(2\beta\beta)$ is also impossible: for then $a' \mathfrak{p} b'' \mathfrak{p} d'$ so that, by II, there exists a point e' on $\overline{a'd'}$ such that $e' \mathfrak{i} b''$ and e' is not in $H(a')$. Let $f' = re' + (1-r)\,a'$; $g' = rb'' + (1-r)\,a'$; $0 < r < 1$. Then, by IV, $f' \mathfrak{i} g'$. But, by Lemma 2, this is impossible since g' is in $H(a')$ (because b'' is), while f' is not in $H(a')$ (because e' is not). There remains subcase $(2\beta\gamma)$: $b'' \mathfrak{i} d'$. This is also impossible since then $rd' + (1-r)\,a' \mathfrak{i} rb'' + (1-r)\,a'$, $0 < r < 1$; yet the point to the right of $\mathfrak{i}$ is, and that to the left is not, in $H(a')$, thus contradicting Lemma 2.

Thus cases (2α): $b'' \mathfrak{p} a'$, and (2β): $a' \mathfrak{p} b''$, are both impossible. There remains (2γ): $b'' \mathfrak{i} a'$.

In Case (3), by a proof similar to that of Case (2), one shows again that $b'' \mathfrak{i} a'$.
22:4. LEMMA 4: *If $b \mathfrak{p} a$, $0 < r < 1$, and $c = ra + (1-r)\,b$, then $b \mathfrak{p} c \mathfrak{p} a$.*

Proof: Since b, c, a, are collinear, it follows from Lemmas 2 and 3 that neither $a \mathfrak{i} c$ nor $b \mathfrak{i} c$ holds. If $a \mathfrak{p} c$ then by II the segment bc has an interior point d such that $a \mathfrak{i} d$. But this is impossible since, by IV, $b \mathfrak{p} a$ would then be false. One shows similarly that $c \mathfrak{p} b$ is impossible. Hence $b \mathfrak{p} c \mathfrak{p} a$.

By Lemmas 2 and 3 the indifference set $J(a')$ containing an interior point a' is a hyperplane, $H(a')$. We shall now prove
22:5. LEMMA 5: *If c is an interior point, $J(c)$ is a hyperplane of dimension* $= \nu - 1$.

Proof: Suppose the set $J(c)$ [identical with $H(c)$] has $\nu - \alpha > 0$ dimensions, and $\alpha > 0$. Then $H(c)$ is determined by α independent linear equations. If $\alpha > 1$, we can choose a 2-dimensional plane K through c that is determined by $\nu - 2$ independent equations such that, when combined with the α independent equations of $H(c)$, they give ν independent equations determining c; that is, K and $H(c)$ intersect in a unique point c. But if $\alpha = 1$, the intersection of $H(c)$ with any 2-dimensional plane is determined by at most $1+\nu-2=\nu-1$ independent equations, and hence has at least one dimension. We shall now show that $\alpha>1$ contradicts our previous lemmas. For if c is the only point common to both $H(c)$ and K, then, by Lemma 2, for no point a in K, distinct from c, is $a\,\mathfrak{i}\,c$. Choose three noncollinear points a^1, a^2, a^3, in K such that c is in the interior of the triangle $a^1a^2a^3$ (see Figure 3), Let $a^1\mathfrak{p}c$; then $a^2\mathfrak{p}c$, $a^3\mathfrak{p}c$; for if (for example) $c\mathfrak{p}a^2$ held, then by Postulate II, there would be a point d on segment $\overline{a^1a^2}$ such that $d\,\mathfrak{i}\,c$; but this is impossible since the plane K has only one point in common with $H(c)$. Hence either $a^i\mathfrak{p}c$ $(i=1,2,3)$ or $c\mathfrak{p}a^i$ $(i=1,2,3)$. The line a^1c intersects the segment $\overline{a^2a^3}$ in b, an internal average of a^2 and a^3. Hence $a^i\mathfrak{p}c(i=1,2,3)$ implies $b\mathfrak{p}c$ because both $a^2\mathfrak{p}c$ and $a^3\mathfrak{p}c$, and because either $a^2\mathfrak{i}a^3$ (in which case Lemma 1 applies) or not $a^2\mathfrak{i}a^3$ (in which case Lemma 4 applies); but by the same Lemma 4, $a^i\mathfrak{p}c$ $(i=1,2,3)$ implies $c\mathfrak{p}b$ because $a^1\mathfrak{p}c$. Hence the assumption $a^i\mathfrak{p}c$ was false. The assumption $c\mathfrak{p}a^i$ leads (by symmetry) to a similar contradiction; and $a^i\mathfrak{i}c$ was already ruled out. Hence the assumption $\alpha>1$ was false, and the lemma is proved.

22:6. LEMMA 6: *If a is on the boundary of A, J(a) is a hyperplane of* $\leqslant \nu-1$ *dimensions.* For, if $J(a)$ contains an interior point a', $J(a)=J(a')=H(a')$ has $\nu-1$ dimensions by Lemma 5. If $J(a)$ contains boundary points only, then $J(a)$ is a hyperplane of $\leqslant\nu-1$ dimensions (facet, edge,...) forming part of the boundary of A.

23. To prove Theorem 1 (Section 2:1 above), it remains to be shown that all the indifference hyperplanes are parallel. This is done by the same reasoning as in 21:2, except that the lines $\overline{aa'}$, $\overline{cc'}$, $\overline{ce}$, have to be regarded as the intersections of the plane of the page with hyperplanes of dimension $\leqslant\nu-1$.

24. THEOREM 2: *If prospects* $a^1, a^2, a^3, \ldots$ *lie on a straight line in this order, and if* $h>i$ *and* $j>k$, *then* $a^h\mathfrak{i}a^i$ *implies* $a^j\mathfrak{i}a^k$, *and* $a^h\mathfrak{p}a^i$ *implies* $a^j\mathfrak{p}a^k$.[14] This follows immediately from the above lemmas.

25. Since all indifference sets J are parallel hyperplanes (Figure 4 for $\nu=2$), we can write an equation for any $J(a)$. Choose any sure prospect, e.g., $a^{(0)}$, as the origin, and let $d[a;a^{(0)}]$ be its distance from the plane $J(a)$ which contains the point a with the coordinates $a_1,\ldots,a_\nu$. Then

$$(25.1)\qquad d[a;a^{(0)}]=\sum_1^\nu k_\mu a_\mu,\ \sum_1^\nu (k_\mu)^2=1,$$

where k_μ $(\mu=1,\ldots,\nu)$ are real numbers (direction cosines) characteristic of $J(a)$ but independent of a and of $a^{(0)}$. In particular, if $a^{(\mu)}$ is another sure prospect, its coordinate a_π^ν $(\pi=1,\ldots,\nu)=\delta_{\pi\mu}$, i.e., equals 1 when $\pi=\mu$ and 0 otherwise. Therefore the distance of $J[a^{(\mu)}]$ from $a^{(0)}$, $d[a^{(\mu)}:a^{(0)}]=\sum_{\pi=1}^\nu a_\pi^{(\mu)}k_\pi=\sum_{\pi=1}^\nu \delta_{\pi\mu}k_\pi=k_\mu$. If, in addition, we define

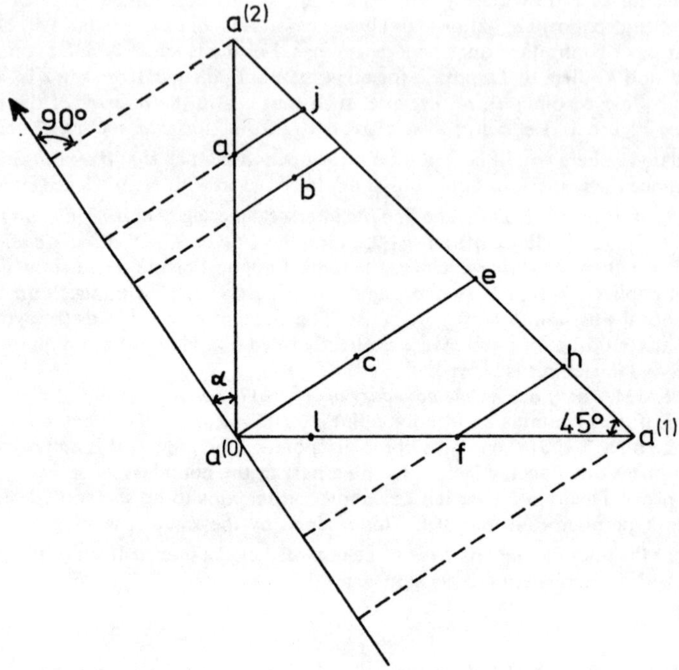

Fig. 4

$k_0 \equiv 0 = d[a^{(0)}; a^{(0)}]$, we have

$$(25.2) \qquad d[a^{(\mu)}; a^{(0)}] = k_\mu, \quad (\mu = 0, \ldots, \nu).$$

If the origin is changed from $a^{(0)}$ to $a^{(\mu)}$, the distance of each indifference hyperplane from the origin is changed by the same constant k_μ. We can therefore replace $d[a; a^{(0)}]$ by the shorter symbol $d(a)$ with the understanding that $d(a)$ is determined up to an additive constant which depends on the arbitrary origin $a^{(0)}$. For further brevity, we shall write

$$(25.3) \qquad d[a^{(\mu)}] \equiv d^{(\mu)}, \quad (\mu = 1, \ldots, \nu).$$

In this notation, and by (25.2), the equation (25.1) of an indifference plane $J(a)$ becomes

(25.4) $$d(a) = \sum_0^{\nu} a_\mu d^{(\mu)}.$$

26. We shall now show that the distance function $d(a)$ can be used as a utility function, as defined in Section 9 above. For this, we first prove the following lemma.

LEMMA 7: *If* $a \mathfrak{p} b \mathfrak{p} c$, *then either* $d(a) > d(b) > d(c)$ *or* $d(a) < d(b) < d(c)$.
Proof: By Postulate II there exists $b' = ra + (1-r)\,c$, $0 < r < 1$, such that b' is in $J(b)$. For each component of b', $b'_\mu = ra_\mu + (1-r)\,c_\mu$, $\mu = 0, \ldots, \nu$. Hence, by (25.4),

$$d(b) = d(b') = \sum b'_\mu d^{(\mu)} = r \sum a_\mu d^{(\mu)} + \\ + (1-r) \sum c_\mu d^{(\mu)} = rd(a) + (1-r)\,d(c),$$

thus proving the lemma: the plane $J(b)$ lies between the planes $J(a)$ and $J(c)$.

We can always define the positive direction for distances in such a way that the first and not the second alternative of Lemma 7 holds. We then have for any two prospects a, b:

(26.1) $d(a) > d(b)$; $d(a) < d(b)$; $d(a) = d(b)$;
according as $a \mathfrak{p} b$; $b \mathfrak{p} a$; $a \mathfrak{i} b$.

Recalling the definitions in Section 9, we can therefore state as proven the following theorem.

THEOREM 3. *If positive direction is defined by* (26.1), *then the distances* $d(a)$, $d(b)$,... *of the planes* $J(a)$, $J(b)$,... *from the origin* $a^{(0)}$ *form a set of utility indices.*

27. Other statements of Theorem 3 are the following:

The distance function $d(a)$ *is a utility function.*

The man maximizes $d(a)$ *over the feasible set* F.

There exist $\nu + 1$ *numbers* $k_1, \ldots, k_\nu$, *and* $k_0 = 0$, *such that for any a,b,* $\sum_0^\nu k_\mu a_\mu >$, $<$, *or* $= \sum_0^\nu k_\mu b_\mu$, *according as* $a \mathfrak{p} b$, $b \mathfrak{p} a$, *or* $a \mathfrak{i} b$.

The indifference sets in the space of prospects are parallel planes stacked up in the order of the man's preferences.

28. On the 'indifference map' in Figure 4, the arrow indicates positive

direction from the origin $a^{(0)}$. As always (compare with Figure 1), $\overline{a^{(0)}a^{(1)}} = \overline{a^{(0)}a^{(2)}} = 1$. Further, in this example

$$
\begin{aligned}
(28.1) \quad & a^{(2)}\,\mathfrak{p}\,a\,\mathfrak{p}\,b\,\mathfrak{p}\,a^{(0)}\,\mathfrak{i}\,c\,\mathfrak{p}\,f\,\mathfrak{p}\,a^{(1)}; \\
& 0 < \alpha < \pi/2; \quad d^{(2)} = \cos\alpha > d(a) = \overline{aa^{(0)}}\cos\alpha > d(b) > \\
& \quad > d^{(0)} = 0 = d(c) = d(e) > d(f) = -\overline{fa^{(0)}}\sin\alpha = \\
& \quad = d(h) > d^{(1)} = -\sin\alpha, \quad \text{etc.}
\end{aligned}
$$

Note that the scale unit is determined by the fact that for any a, $\sum_0^{\nu} a_\mu = 1$, while the origin is fixed by choosing $d^{(0)} = 0$.

29. Theorems 1 to 3 are derived from Postulates I, II, III*, and IV on *rational* behavior. They cannot be tested by observation. But we can sketch out the following statements on *actual* behavior which, in principle, can be so tested:

(1) "Faced with a varying set of feasible prospects, Mr. Smith makes decisions which, with a probability p, do not deviate by more than a preassigned distance from the decisions consistent with Theorem 3." For example, with $\nu = 2$, let $a^{(0)}$, $a^{(1)}$, $a^{(2)}$ be the prospects of a sure life income of, respectively, \$2000, \$5000, and \$20000. The varying sets of feasible prospects can consist of various pairs or triplets, etc., of points marked in Figure 4. A set of decisions of Mr. Smith is inconsistent with the four postulates whenever it is inconsistent with relations (28.1), after fixing $d^{(0)} = 0$. A set of decisions indicating that there is no angle α such that $d^{(2)} = \cos\alpha$, $d(f) = -\overline{fa^{(0)}}\sin\alpha = d(h)$, would indicate deviations from rationality as defined by the postulates. The procedure of testing whether Smith is 'tolerably rational', i.e., whether p exceeds a certain limit, is a statistical one; so is the procedure of estimating the parameters of the indifference map (in our example, the angle α). The difficulties are obvious and stem from the economist's inability to make experiments. If Smith is made to answer questions on his decisions when faced with hypothetical sets of feasible prospects, the answers may involve a bias (and not merely a random deviation) when compared with his actual behavior. If, on the other hand, the sets of feasible prospects are those that have actually faced him in his life, they may not yield themselves to convenient simplification; moreover, Smith may have changed his tastes in the course of his life, although they had remained

consistent during each of several shorter periods. Some of these difficulties are obviated, but replaced by others, if the following hypothesis is tested:[15]

(2) "At least a fraction q of the buyers and sellers of real estate, securities, insurance policies, and other assets are tolerably rational (in the sense defined above); and the numbers characterizing their indifference maps (viz., their respective angles α, in the example of Figure 4) have such and such a frequency distribution."

30. The μth sure prospect can be denoted both as $a^{(\mu)}$ and as $x^{(\mu)}$; its utility will be denoted by

(30.1) $\quad u^{(\mu)} \equiv u\,[a^{(\mu)}] \equiv u\,[x^{(\mu)}].$

$x^{(\mu)}$ is a particular value of the random vector x, and $u^{(\mu)}$ is a particular value of the random scalar $u(x)$. The expected value of $u(x)$ given the distribution $a(x)$ can be written[16] as

(30.2) $$\mathscr{E}u(x)\mid a(x) \equiv \sum_{\mu=0}^{\nu} u\,[x^{(\mu)}]\,a_\mu \equiv \sum_{\mu=0}^{\nu} u^{(\mu)} a_\mu \equiv \mathscr{E}u \mid a;$$

in the last form no dummy variables (x, μ) appear, thus making clear that the quantity in question depends only on the utility function u and the distribution ('prospect') a. The quantity $\mathscr{E}u|a$ can be regarded as the result of an operation which is performed upon the function u and depends on a; or as the result of an operation which is performed upon the prospect a and depends on u. According to the emphasis needed we may call $\mathscr{E}u|a$ the 'expected value of the utility function u', as well as the 'expected utility for a'.

31. In this notation and by Theorem 3, the distance function (25.4) has the following properties: $d(a)$ is a utility function; and $\mathscr{E}d|a=d(a)$. Consequently, $\mathscr{E}d|a$ is a utility function. That is, the man maximizes the expected value of utility function d. In Section 9 above, we have defined U, the class of utility functions. Now define a subclass V of U, consisting of all functions v with the following properties:

(α_1) $\quad \mathscr{E}v|a$ is in U,
(α_2) $\quad \mathscr{E}v|a$ is in V,

and

(α_3) $\mathscr{E}v \mid a = v(a)$.

Note that property (α_3) would suffice to define V, since (α_3) implies (α_2), and (α_2) implies (α_1). We have just shown that V contains at least one element, viz., the distance function d: it satisfies (α_3). We shall now prove the following theorem.

32. THEOREM 4: *V consists of all linear increasing functions of d.* That is, a function v is in V if and only if there exist two numbers l, m ($m>0$) such that for any a

(β) $v(a) = l + md(a)$.

Proof: Sufficiency: If (β) is true, then by (25.4) and the definitions (30.2),

$$\mathscr{E}v \mid a = \sum v^{(\mu)} a_\mu = l + m \sum d^{(\mu)} a_\mu = l + md(a) = v(a).$$

Thus (β) implies all three α-properties in Section 31.

Necessity: Suppose (α_1), the weakest of those three properties, is true. Then since both $\mathscr{E}v \mid a$ and $d(a)$ are in U, there exists a monotone increasing function ϕ, such that

$$\mathscr{E}v \mid a = \phi\,[d(a)] \equiv \phi d(a) \tag{32.1}$$

(omitting brackets after ϕ for brevity). Put $a = a^{(\mu)}$. Then, since $\mathscr{E}v \mid a^{(\mu)} = v^{(\mu)}$, we have, by (32.1), $v^{(\mu)} = \phi d^{(\mu)}$; $\phi d(a) = \mathscr{E}v \mid a = \sum a_\mu v^{(\mu)} = \sum a_\mu \phi d^{(\mu)}$; thus

$$\begin{cases} \sum a_\mu \phi d^{(\mu)} - 1 \cdot \phi d(a) = 0\,; & \\ \sum a_\mu d^{(\mu)} - 1 \cdot d(a) = 0 & \text{[by (25.4)];} \\ \sum a_\mu \cdot 1 - 1 \cdot 1 = 0 & \text{[by (4.1)].} \end{cases} \tag{32.2}$$

The three equations (32.2) form a homogeneous linear system identical in $a_0, \ldots, a_\nu, -1$. Hence the rows

$$\begin{array}{c} \phi d^{(0)}, \ldots, \phi d^{(\nu)}, \phi d(a) \\ d^{(0)}, \ldots, \phi d^{(\nu)}, \phi d(a) \\ 1, \ldots, 1, 1 \end{array}$$

are linearly dependent. Therefore ϕ is a linear function,

$$\phi d(a) = l + md(a)\,;$$

and $m>0$ since ϕ was already stated to be an increasing function. Thus (α_1) implies (β); and since (β) was shown (in the sufficiency proof) to imply (α_2) and (α_3), the proof is complete.

33. Thus V consists of all increasing linear functions of the probabilities $a_0, \ldots, a_\nu$:

$$(33.1) \qquad v(a) = l + m \sum a_\mu d^{(\mu)}.$$

We shall call the function $v(a)$ a *linear utility function* and the scalar $v(a)$ a *linear utility index* of prospect a. If Figure 4 represents an indifference map, and the utility index is measured perpendicularly to the plane of the page, then any plane whose intersection with the plane of the page is parallel would represent some element of V, or its negative.

The simplest linear utility function is the distance function $d(A)$ itself. In this case $l=0$, $m=1$. The distance function is a linear utility function unique up to an additive constant that depends on the choice of the origin such as $a^{(0)}$.

34. Immediately from (33.1) we obtain the well-known property of linear functions summarized in

THEOREM 5: *Let prospect a be a linear combination of ρ prospects, $b^1, \ldots, b^\rho$: $a = \sum_1^\varrho r_\pi b^\pi$. If v is a linear utility function, then and only then*

$$(34.1) \qquad v(a) = \sum_1^\varrho r_\pi v(b^\pi).$$

In particular, if a is an average, $a = r_1 b^1 + r_2 b^2$, $r_1 + r_2 = 1$,

$$(34.2) \qquad v(a) = r_1 v(b^1) + r_2 v(b^2)$$

and

$$(34.3) \qquad \frac{v(b^1) - v(a)}{v(a) - v(b^2)} = \frac{r_2}{r_1}.$$

Moreover, since $a = \sum_0^\nu a_\mu a^{(\mu)}$, we obtain again the property (α_3) in (31):

$$(34.4) \qquad v(a) = \sum_0^\nu a_\mu v^{(\mu)} = \mathscr{E} v \mid a \equiv \mathscr{E} v(x) \mid a(x).$$

35. On the other hand, the following property is not exclusive to linear utility functions: *If* v_1 *and* v_2 *are two linear utility functions, then there exist two numbers* l, m ($m>0$) *such that for any prospect* a,

(35.1) $$v_2(a) = l + mv_1(a).$$

That is, v_1 and v_2 are (increasing) linear transforms of each other; or, in other formulations, the function v is unique up to a linear transformation or up to two linear coefficients. This property follows from (33.1) but is obviously possessed also by any class W consisting of utility functions w such that for any a

(35.2) $$w(a) = l + m\phi_w d(a),$$

where $m>0$, and ϕ_w is a monotone increasing function, *not necessarily linear*; for example, ϕ_w may be the cubic function.

36. Another property which follows from (33.1) yet is possessed by certain classes of nonlinear utility functions is this: *If* v_1 *and* v_2 *are two linear utility functions, then*

(36.1) $$v_2(a) - v_2(b) = m[v_1(a) - v_1(b)],$$

where m *is a positive constant independent of* a, b. That is, the difference between the linear utilities of two prospects is unique up to a proportionality factor. This property follows from the property (35.1), and is therefore also shared by a class of nonlinear utility functions such as W defined in (35.2).

VI. MEASURABILITY AND MANAGEABILITY

37. The question has been often asked whether utility is 'measurable in the sense in which temperature is'.[17] Because temperature readings are nothing but distances (or angles or volumes depending on the design of the thermometer), and in order to avoid discussing the relation between the absolute and other scales of temperature, I prefer comparison with altitudes. The altitude of a point on the earth's surface is unique up to two constants (one positive) depending on the origin, such as the sea level, and the unit, such as the meter. The linear utility index of a prospect is also unique up to two constants (one positive), l and m in (33.1). In

this sense, altitudes expressed in meters, and linear utility indices, are equally strictly measurable.

38. This property they share, however, with altitudes expressed in cubes of their meter measurements, and with utility indices obtained from linear ones by substituting, say, $[d(a)]^3$ for $d(a)$; see Section 35. The property of being unique up to two constants is weaker than certain other properties of linear utility functions, for example, the property (34.4) of expected values of linear utility indices.

Numbers of meters, and not cubes of those numbers, are used in measuring altitudes because this simplifies certain important operations. One derives the altitude of point Y in meters from the altitude of point Z in meters and from the number of meters contained in the upward horizontal projection of the line connecting the two points, by forming an algebraic sum of the latter two numbers. If cubes of those numbers were used instead, one would have to cube the sum of two cube roots, a more complicated operation.

Money amounts are unique up to one positive proportionality factor depending on the currency unit. Their logarithms are also determined up to a single constant, an additive one. For additive operations, dollars are more manageable than logarithms. But the latter may be preferable when, as in constructing graphs of hyperinflation, one is interested in ratios; just as (I understand) it is convenient to use logarithms of time in discussing radioactive disintegration.

39. Thus, linear utility indices of prospects share with altitudes expressed in units of length not only the particular kind of measurability (viz., up to two constants, one positive) but also the 'manageability' with respect to certain, viz., linear, operations. In the case of utility indices of prospects, a particularly important kind of linear operations is the forming of averages as in (34.2), and especially the forming of expected values as in (34.4). For no other but linear utility indices is it true that the utility of a distribution (a prospect) is equal to the expected value of utilities of sure prospects, computed on the basis of that distribution.[18]

40. In Part V implications were derived from our four postulates on rational behavior. These results can be stated in two equivalent forms:

(α) The indifference surfaces in prospect space are linear and parallel (Theorem 1).

(β) There exist linear utility functions of prospects, with certain convenient properties (Theorems 3–5).

We have just shown that (α), (β) – and therefore our four postulates – are sufficient to derive measurable and manageable (in the defined sense) utility functions. To see whether these postulates are also necessary, we shall weaken (α) and study the implications. Suppose then that the indifference sets were not parallel planes [cf. (25.1)],

$$(40.1)\qquad \sum_{0}^{\nu} k_\mu a_\mu = d(a), \quad k_0 = 0,$$

but would satisfy, instead, a more general equation

$$(40.2)\qquad \sum_{0}^{r} k_\mu \psi(a_\mu) = d_\psi(a), \quad k_0 = 0, \quad k_\mu \geqslant 0, \quad (\mu = 1, \ldots, \nu),$$

where $d_\psi(a)$ is the utility index (a 'generalized distance') of $J(a)$, and ψ is a monotone increasing function such that $\psi(0)=0$, $\psi(1)=1$. [For example, if $\psi(z)=z^2$, then indifference surfaces are concentric ellipsoids.] Equation (40.2) is consistent with our postulates, except Postulate IV [unless $\psi(z)=z$]. Statements analogous to those in Section 25 and Section 26 would hold. Putting $a=a^{(\mu)}$, (40.2) becomes

$$(40.3)\qquad k_\mu = d_\psi[a^{(\mu)}] \equiv d_\psi^{(\mu)},$$

say; substituting in (40.2), we find that the set $J(a)$ is defined by the utility index

$$(40.4)\qquad d_\psi(a) = \sum_{0}^{\nu} \psi(a_\mu)\, d_\psi^{(\mu)}.$$

Define the operator $\mathscr{E}_\psi$ by

$$(40.5)\qquad \mathscr{E}_\psi u \mid a \equiv \mathscr{E}_\psi u(x) \mid a(x) \equiv \sum_{0}^{\nu} \psi(a_\mu)\, u[a^{(\mu)}];$$

this is a generalization of the operator $\mathscr{E}$, each probability a_μ being replaced by its transform $\psi(a_\mu)$. Then, by (40.4),

$$(40.6)\qquad d_\psi(a) = \mathscr{E}_\psi d_\psi \mid a.$$

Now, in analogy to the class V in Section 31, define a class V_ψ consisting of all utility functions v_ψ such that, for any a, $v_\psi(a) = \mathscr{E}_\psi v_\psi | a$. Then V_ψ consists of all products of the 'generalized distance' with arbitrary (and positive) constants, m. For, if $v_\psi = md_\psi$, the definition (40.5), with v_ψ substituted for u, implies $\mathscr{E}_\psi v_\psi | a = v_\psi(a)$. Conversely, if v_ψ is in V_ψ, and if ϕ is an unknown monotone function such that $\phi d(a) \equiv \phi\,[d(a)] = \mathscr{E}_\psi v_\psi a$, we obtain a system analogous to (32.2) but with only two instead of three equations (since the transforms of probabilities need not add up to unity):

$$(40.7)\qquad \begin{aligned} \sum_\mu \psi(a_\mu)\, \phi d_\psi^{(\mu)} &= \phi d_\psi(a), \\ \sum_\mu \psi(a_\mu)\, d_\psi^{(\mu)} &= d_\psi(a). \end{aligned}$$

We see that if Postulate IV were replaced in such a way as to lead to (40.2) instead of (40.1), it would be possible to define a utility function $v_\psi(a)$ unique up to a proportionality factor. Thus $v_\psi(a)$ is even more strictly 'measurable' than the function $v(a)$ derived with the aid of Postulate IV. In this sense, the virtue of that postulate does not consist in the 'measurability' of the function $v(a)$. Rather, it consists in the 'manageability' of $v(a)$, in the sense of property (34.4). In the case of the utility function $v(a)$ the expected value $\mathscr{E}v | a \equiv \sum v^{(\mu)} a_\mu$ is maximized; while in the case of the function $v_\psi(a)$, not the expected value, but a more complicated, usually nonlinear, expression $\mathscr{E}_\psi v_\psi | a \equiv \sum_\mu v_\psi^{(\mu)} \psi(a_\mu)$ is maximized.

41. This opens the question (to be taken up again in Part VIII) of still further, or of alternative, generalizations of (40.1) and, consequently, of the appropriate generalization of underlying postulates. Each such generalization would possibly define a nonlinear analogon – say $\mathscr{E}_*$ – of the operation $\mathscr{E}$ and an analogon – say V_* – of the linear subclass V of utility functions. V_* may be empty or consist of one element only, or of two or more functions which are, possibly nonlinear, transforms ϕ_* of each other. The possible nonlinearity of the operations $\mathscr{E}_*$ and ϕ_* that replace the operations $\mathscr{E}$ and ϕ of Section 30 will render the utility functions of prospects less 'manageable'. One might call them less 'measurable' if ϕ_* involved more parameters than ϕ; but in Section 40 we just had a case where the opposite was true.

VII. COMPARISON WITH VON NEUMANN AND MORGENSTERN

42. The word prospect is occasionally used in the *Theory of Games and Economic Behavior* (e.g., on top of page 18) essentially in the same sense as in this paper (see also Hicks [2]). More often the authors speak of a 'combination of events'. We call a prospect the probability distribution of the time sequences of all combinations of commodities (or, in fact, of any kinds of events), while von Neumann and Morgenstern take examples involving two or three commodities at one time point only. Since our time sequences are by necessity mutually exclusive, no confusion can arise in our formulations as to the effect of complementarity upon the choices. If proper wording is used, this is not an essential difference.

43. *Verbal Presentation: Utility Differences*

In the verbal presentation (Section 3.3) of the *Theory of Games*, the authors use as a behavior postulate the equivalent of our (34.3). In the present paper, on the other hand, (34.3) was derived from four postulates on rational behavior. Von Neumann and Morgenstern (in their verbal presentation) do not have Postulate IV but seem to have what amounts to Postulates I and II.

Our decision to introduce Postulate IV, rather than to start with (34.3) as a behavior postulate, is dictated by the desire to avoid behavior postulates which are neither immediately plausible nor show themselves as approximated by easily observable action. Postulates I and III* state essentially that man chooses between prospects; and we see men actually making choices – determining the balance sheet by buying or selling, or by abstaining from buying and selling, assets. Postulate II excludes discontinuities. Postulate IV is also a very weak (i.e., very plausible) one; it merely rules out behavior of a kind which most people would call absurd. The statement (34.3), on the other hand, is neither immediately plausible nor is it amenable to easy observation. True, a person when interviewed may make comparisons between two utility differences, but the comparison does not show itself in any choice except in the choice to answer a certain question in a certain way. However, H. Chernoff pointed out that such a check of utility comparison by an actual choice could be made in the following situation. According to L. J. Savage, the rational strategy in a one-person game under complete ignorance of circumstances might be defined as one that results in minimaxing 'regret', i.e., the difference between the utility actually realized and the utility that would have been realized if all circumstances were known. (See Marschak [6a] where this postulate was used.) That is, the strategy must be chosen so that even under circumstances which yield for this strategy a regret not smaller than under any other circumstances, this regret is not larger than for any other strategy.[19] Thus, a rational man playing the one-person game under ignorance of future circumstances has to base his choices on comparing differences between utilities.

44. *Mathematical Presentation: The Chain of Implications*

In their mathematical presentation, the authors of the *Theory of Games* do not actually make use of a behavior postulate on utility differences.[20] The behavior postulates used are set up in their Section 3.6, and we shall refer to them presently. An extensive appendix published in the second edition of the book shows that these postulates result in propositions (3:1:a) and (3:1:b) of the text (Section 3.5). The second of these implies, and is implied by, the linearity of what we called the utility functions of prospects, and appears thus equivalent to our Theorems 1–5. From this, the 'measurability' of utility is derived in (3:5:b) and (3:6) of the *Theory of Games*, in the sense that utility is unique up to a linear transformation: a property weaker than the preceding one, as shown in this paper (Sections 35–41 above).

44.1. *The axioms.* The difference between the presentation in this paper and in the *Theory of Games* thus boils down to the difference between our Postulates I–IV, and the group of axioms (3:A), (3:B), (3:C), of the *Theory of Games.*[21] The 'entities' u, v, of the *Theory of Games* correspond to the various indifference sets – say J, J', in the present paper. The symbol $>$ defined in the authors' (3:A) is related to our $\mathfrak{p}$ as follows: if J contains a and J' contains a', and J, J' are distinct, we say $a \mathfrak{p} a'$ or $a' \mathfrak{p} a$; Von Neumann and Morgenstern say (replacing J, J' by u, v) $u>v$ or $v>u$. Moreover, $u=v$ corresponds to $J=J'$. As to the symbol $+$, and the operation $\alpha u+(1-\alpha)\ v=w$, the authors define it implicitly by the axioms (except that α is a real scalar, $0<\alpha<1$, identical with our r); while we use the symbol $+$ and the operation $ra+(1-r)a'$ in their usual meaning (addition, multiplication) as applied to the real vectors a, a'

and the scalar r. However, select element a from J, and a' from J'. Then the following operation on indifference sets can be defined: $rJ+(1-r)J'$ means $J[ra+(1+r)a']$. With this interpretation Axioms (3:A) and (3:B) of the *Theory of Games* will follow (with u, v, α replacing J, J', r) if the indifference sets are parallel hyperplanes, i.e., if our Postulates I, II, III*, and IV are fulfilled. In particular, the axiom (3:C:b) can be rendered as follows: "Let $0<r<1$, $0<q<1$; let a, b, c, e be prospects such that $b=ra+(1-r)\,e$, $c=qb+(1-q)\,e$. Then $c\,\mathfrak{i}\,[qra+(1-qr)\,e]$." This 'double mixing' is indeed implied in Postulate IV, as a succession of two single mixings discussed there.

I hesitate to say which (if any) is the stronger system of axioms. I find it easier to translate Postulate IV immediately into the language of observable decisions – see the examples in Section 19 above – than to do so with von Neumann and Morgenstern's (3:C:b), whether stated as it is in terms of entities not susceptible to ordinary arithmetical operations, or restated in the form I have just suggested. To use a phrase of von Neumann and Morgenstern, the approach used here seems to be more 'transparent', and its postulates have a more 'immediate intuitive meaning by which [their] appropriateness may be judged directly'.

44.2. *The proofs.* As already mentioned in Section 44, a part of the route, the part after establishing the proposition on the linearity of (certain) utility functions, is common to both presentations. But the previous part of the route, between the axioms and that proposition, is different. The present author does not claim to improve upon the minutiousness and rigor of the appendix to the second edition of the *Theory of Games*. The present paper consists essentially in applying the technique of indifference curves – as stated in our Postulates I –III– to prospects which are not sure. When Postulate IV is added, this technique yields in a simple way the Neumannian results. These are also obtained if III is replaced by a weaker Postulate III* (or III′).

VIII. LOVE OF DANGER INCOMPATIBLE WITH THE FOUR POSTULATES

45. THEOREM 6: *If* $a\,\mathfrak{p}\,b$ *and* $c=ra+(1-r)\,b$, *then* $a\,\mathfrak{p}\,c$ *for* $r>1$, $c\,\mathfrak{p}\,a$ *for* $r<1$. (That is, a is preferred to every point between a and b and to

every point on the prolongation of the segment ab beyond b; and every point on the prolongation of that segment beyond a is preferred to a.) This property of prospects follows directly from Theorems 2 or 4. In Figure 4, take any three points on a straight line not parallel to the indifference lines (planes)! The property may be called the monotonicity of the utility function of prospects $u(a)$, on the space A. It is different from the monotonicity assumption sometimes made for the utility function of commodities – say, $w(x)$ on the space X. This assumption is stated formally as follows (cf. Arrow [1]):

It is always possible to define final goods $x_1, \ldots, x_\varepsilon$ in such a way that if $x^{(\alpha)} \equiv (x^{(\alpha)}{}_1, \ldots, x_\varepsilon{}^{(\alpha)})$ and $x^{(\beta)} \equiv (x_1{}^{(\beta)}, \ldots, x_\varepsilon{}^{(\beta)})$ and if $x_\gamma{}^{(\alpha)} \geqslant x_\gamma{}^{(\beta)}$ for all γ and $x_\delta{}^{(\alpha)} > x_\delta{}^{(\beta)}$ for some $\delta\,(\gamma, \delta = 1, \ldots, \varepsilon)$, then $x^{(\alpha)}\, \mathrm{p}\, x^{(\beta)}$.

That is, the addition of any final 'good' to (or subtraction of any final 'bad' from) a bundle of commodities (a history, a sure prospect) increases the utility of the bundle. More precisely, this assumption is taken to be valid not over the whole space X but only over a so-called effective region of it,[22] outside of this region the man is saturated with one or more of the 'goods', so that 'goods' become 'bad' or at least indifferent.

Obviously this form of monotonicity cannot apply to the prospect space A, because of restriction (4.1): it is impossible to increase the probability of one of the histories, say, the probability a_μ of $x^{(\mu)}$, without decreasing the probability of at least one of the other histories. Also, it would be impossible to classify each history – possibly a whole course of life – as either 'good' or 'bad' in the way we classify single final commodities such as bread and leisure or labor and sickness. The monotonicity assumption for commodities says: "The more of a good thing the better. If opportunities are unlimited, increase the quantity of every good thing until it ceases to be a good thing." The monotonicity assumption for prospects says: "If one alternative is better than another, increase the probability of the former at the expense of the latter.[23] If opportunities are unlimited, choose the prospect that promises the best history with 100% probability": the corner $a^{(2)}$ in Figure 4.

The monotonicity assumption for commodities is usually stated as an independent postulate or as the definition of the effective region. The monotonicity assumption for prospects (Theorem 6) follows from Postulates I, II, III (or III* or III′), and IV.

46. If our four postulates define rational behavior, the following actual behavior is not rational: many men, not at all bent on suicide, are enthusiastic mountain climbers and are elated, not (or not only) by exercise and scenery but by the very danger, in the following sense. Suppose the probability of fatal accident is 5%. The climber may prefer a survival chance of 95% to one of, say, 80% *but also* to one of 100%! The utility index of prospects reaches in this case its maximum at a point which is not a corner of domain A. (If in Figure 4, $a^{(0)}$ and $a^{(2)}$ are two ways of continuing to live, and $a^{(1)}$ is death, the highest utility will be not at $a^{(0)}$ or $a^{(2)}$ or a but, say, at j or l or b.)

47. Such behavior contradicts the monotonicity Theorem 6, and therefore at least one of our postulates. It is, therefore, in general inconsistent with the existence of linear utility functions for prospects. It also follows that the lover of danger does not, in general, maximize the expected value of the utility index. Not for him the linear utility functions of prospects, and the measurable and 'manageable' (Part VI) utility indices. Love of danger in this sense may very well be present also in what is usually considered economic decisions. The danger of loss including ruin, though probably shunned in the conservative code or cant of business, has quite possibly added to the zest and desirability of many an historically important venture, in the career of the leaders of mercenary armies, in the financing of great geographic discoveries or, closer to our time, in the financing of inventions and theater plays, and in stock and commodity speculation.

48. The 'love of danger' defined as nonmonotonicity of the utility function for prospects is to be carefully distinguished from the phenomenon alluded to in Part III: whether high variance of random income (or of the random quantity of any commodity) is or is not desirable depends on whether the marginal utility of mean income (or commodity) happens to be increasing rather than decreasing. Neither a positive nor a negative sign of the 'risk-discount' contradicts the monotonicity of the utility function for prospects (nor, of course, the monotonicity assumption for goods).[24]

The statement 'a man may desire to gamble' has thus two meanings.

If it means that the sign of the risk-discount is indefinite, the statement is consistent with rational behavior as defined by the four postulates. (In fact, it is well explained by implications from these very postulates.) If it means, however, that the man 'loves danger' so that his utility function of prospects is not monotonic along a straight line in space *A*, drawn at an angle to the indifference planes, then the statement is not consistent with the four postulates. Should one revise the postulates of rational choice in order to be able to include love of danger under rational behavior, then it would probably become impossible to attain manageable utility indices in the sense of Part VI. As indicated in Section 41, the operation of maximizing expected value would have to be replaced by a more general or more unwieldy one. The alternative is to stamp love of danger as nonrational, on a par with, say, the behavior of a man who prefers *a* to *b* and *b* to *c* and yet prefers *c* to *a* (denial of transitivity Postulate I); or a man to whom a car and a $1000 bill are equivalent and who yet prefers one of these things to a lottery ticket promising with certainty that either the one or the other thing will be obtained (denial of Postulate IV_1).

49. At this point we can only hint at what is probably the most important virtue of the advice to maximize expected utility and, hence, of the behavior postulates implied in this advice. We conjecture that, for a large class of distribution functions and utility functions, the following proposition is true: if every action is chosen in such a way as to maximize the expected utility, then, as the number of such actions is increased, the probability that the achieved utility differs from the maximum achievable utility by an arbitrarily small number, approaches unity. If this proposition is true, and if the logic of rational behavior is used as a tool of advice (see Section 1 above), it is best to exclude love of danger as irrational. If, on the other hand, rational behavior is used as an approximation hypothesis for the study of actual behavior, then again, love of danger may be considered as a departure from rationality. It is then a matter of empirical psychology and is important to economics in the same way in which inconsistency (intransitivity) of preferences, inability to measure, to imagine, to remember, are important. We treat it in the same way that we treat the fact that people make mistakes of arithmetic and infringe upon the rules of conventional logic.

NOTES

* Based on a Cowles Commission Discussion Paper, Economics No. 226 (hectographed), July, 1948, and a paper presented at the Madison Meeting of the Econometric Society, September, 1948, Marschak [4].

Acknowledgements are due to various present and former members of the Cowles Commission staff, especially Kenneth J. Arrow, Herman Chernoff, Nathan J. Divinsky, Clifford Hildreth, and Herman Rubin; to Leonard J. Savage, The University of Chicago and to Abraham Wald, Columbia University.

1 Uncertainty in Knight's [1] sense is presumably identical with incomplete information See also Marschak [5]; and Hart [1, 2].

2 The case of a possibly infinite ν has been treated by Rubin [1] with results substantially unchanged. The choice between ν finite or infinite is one of mathematical elegance rather than realism sugar is retailed by the pound, interests accrue daily, and horizons are limited.

3 We use letters $x, a, b, c, \ldots,$ with or without superscripts for vectors, and $a_1, \ldots, a_\mu, \ldots, a_\nu$, for components of a. The letters $q, r, \ldots,$ denote scalars. A line connecting two points is denoted thus: $\overline{ab}$. Capital letters A, F, J, U, V, X, are used for sets or classes

4 A more symmetrical but less familiar presentation would measure a_0, a_1, a_2 as the distances of a point a from each of the sides of an equilateral triangle.

5 Such propositions were discussed by Frisch [1, 2], Wold [1], Allen [2], Lange [1, 2], Samuelson [1], Arrow [2], and others.

6 Fisher [1], Appendix to Chapter XVI, p. 10. Pigou [1], Appendix 1. Hicks [1, 2]. Makower and Marschak [1]. Marschak [1, 2, 3]. This list is incomplete. See also note 9.

7 Tintner [1, 2, 3]; see also Hurwicz [1].

8 Marschak [7].

9 As a rival to the mean, the mode was suggested by Lange [3], As a measure of riskiness the standard deviation was suggested by I. Fisher [1] as early as 1906. This is in line with the actuarial theory of an individual insurance policy; Cramér [1], Part II. Another important parameter is the probability that a certain variable (cash reserve, annual profit, etc.) fall below a constant, for example, below zero. This occurs in the theory of the total risk of an insurance company: Cramér [1], Part III. According to a verbal communication of H. Somers, this may also be the meaning of a suggestion made by Fellner [1]. Unlike those of Cramér, the suggestions of Lange, Fellner, and other economists often intend to describe actual rather than advisable behavior (see Section 1, above).

10 See Marshall [1], Menger [1], Friedman and Savage [1], Marschak [4,7].

11 Rubin [1] has used Postulate III′ instead of III or III*. His proof applies to ν finite or infinite.

12 Superscripts indicate sure prospects only if in parentheses: $a^{(1)}$ not a^1; see Section V.

13 We shall denote interior points by single, boundary points by double, primes through Sections 22:1–22:4.

14 We shall encounter this theorem in Part VIII when discussing the 'monotonicity of utility functions of prospects'.

15 See in particular Friedman and Savage [1], Section 6; Vickrey [1]; and Törnqvist [1].

16 Henceforth all summations over μ will be from 0 through ν.

17 Allen [2], Lange [1], von Neumann and Morgenstern [1].

18 Compare Arrow [2], Chapter II, Section 1.

19 Contrast this with the two-person zero-sum game. There the rational player obtains the minimax utility, not the minimax difference between two utilities. (Von Neumann and Morgenstern [1], Sections 3–15.)
20 For sure prospects, R. Frisch [1] derived utility increments measurable up to a proportionality factor, by introducing postulates on the individual's choice between small displacements occurring in two different points of the commodity space.
21 We reprint these axioms from Section 3.6.1 (p. 26) of the *Theory of Games*; "*3.6.1.*., consider a system U of entities $u, v, w, \ldots$. In U a *relation* is given, $u > v$, and for any number α, $(0 < \alpha < 1)$, an *operation*

$$\alpha u + (1 - \alpha)\, v = w.$$

These concepts satisfy the following axioms:
(3:A) *$u > v$ is a complete ordering of U.*
This means: Write $u < v$ when $v > u$. Then:
(3:A:a) For any two u, v one and only one of the three following relations holds:

$$u = v,\ u > v,\ u < v.$$

(3:A:b) $u > v$, $v > w$ imply $u > w$.
(3:B) *Ordering and combining.*
(3:B:a) $u < v$ implies that $u < \alpha u + (1 - \alpha) v$.
(3:B:b) $u > v$ implies that $u > \alpha u + (1 - \alpha) v$.
(3:B:c) $u < w < v$ implies the existence of an α with

$$\alpha u + (1 - \alpha)\, v < w.$$

(3:B:d) $u > w > v$ implies the existence of an α with

$$\alpha u + (1 - \alpha)\, v > w.$$

(3:C) *Algebra of combining.*
(3:C:a) $\alpha u + (1 - \alpha)\, v = (1 - \alpha)\, v + \alpha u.$
(3:C:b) $\alpha[\beta u + (1 - \beta)\, v] + (1 - \alpha)\, v = \gamma u + (1 - \gamma)\, v$
where $\gamma = \alpha\beta$."
On what follows, I had the privilege of consulting Abraham Wald.
22 Allen [1], H. Wold [1].
23 This verbal proposition is easiest to visualize in the special case when the alternatives considered are sure prospects. Theorem 6 is more general since it holds for all prospects.
24 To show this, expand $\mathscr{E}u(x)$ about the mean of x, where $x =$ income.

BIBLIOGRAPHY

Allen, R. G. D. [1] 'The Nature of Indifference Curves', *Review of Economic Studies* 1 (February, 1934) 110–121; [2] 'Note on the Determination of the Utility Function', *Review of Economic Studies* 2 (February, 1935) 155–158.

Arrow, K. J. [1] 'The Determination of Many-Commodity Preference Scales by Two-Commodity Comparisons', *Cowles Commission Discussion Paper* (hectographed), and to be published; [2] *Social Choice and Individual Values*, Cowles Commission Monograph No. 12, New York: John Wiley and Sons, forthcoming.

Cramér, H. [1] 'On the Mathematical Theory of Risk', *Försäkringsaktiebolaget Skandias Festkrift*, Centraltryckeriet, Stockholm, 1930, pp. 7–84.

Fellner, W. [1] *Monetary Policies and Full Employment*, University of California Press, Berkeley and Los Angeles, 1946, pp. 152–167.

Fisher, I. [1] *The Nature of Capital and Income*, The Macmillan Co., New York and London, 1906, 427 pp.; [2] *The Theory of Interest as Determined by Impatience to*

Spend Income and Opportunity to Invest It, The Macmillan Co., New York, 1930, 550 pp.

Friedman, M. and Savage, L. J. [1] 'The Utility Analysis of Choices Involving Risk', *Journal of Political Economy* **56** (August, 1948) 279–304.

Frisch, R. [1] 'Sur un problème d'économie pure', *Norsk Matematisk Forenings Skrifter*, Series 1, No. 16, 1926, pp. 1–40; [2] 'General Choice Field Theory', *Report of Third Annual Research Conference on Economics and Statistics, Colorado Springs*, Cowles Commission for Research in Economics, 1937, pp. 64–69.

Hart, A. G. [1] 'Anticipations, Uncertainty, and Dynamic Planning', *Journal of Business* **13** (October, 1940) (*Studies in Business Administration* **11**, No. 1, 98 pp.); [2] 'Risk, Uncertainty and the Unprofitability of Compounding Probabilities', *Studies in Mathematical Economics and Econometrics, in Memory of Henry Schultz* (ed. by O. Lange, F. McIntyre, T. O. Yntema), The University of Chicago Press, Chicago, 1942, pp. 110–118.

Hicks, J. R. [1] 'The Theory of Uncertainty and Profit', *Economica* (May, 1931), 170–189; [2] 'Application of Mathematical Methods to the Theory of Risk' (abstract), *Econometrica* **2** (April, 1934) 194–195; [3] 'A Suggestion for Simplifying the Theory of Money', *Economica*, New Series, Vol. 2 (February, 1935) 1–19.

Hurwicz, L. [1] 'Theory of Firm and of Investment', *Econometrica* **14** (April, 1946) 109–136; especially pp. 131–135.

Knight, F. H. [1] *Risk, Uncertainty, and Profit*, Houghton Mifflin Co., Boston and New York, 1921, 381 pp.

Koopmans, T. C. [1] 'Utility Analysis of Decisions Affecting Future Well-Being' (abstract), *Econometrica* **18** (April, 1950) 174–175.

Lange, O. [1] 'The Determinateness of the Utility Function', *Review of Economic Studies* **1** (June, 1934) 218–225; [2] *Review of Economic Studies* **2** (October, 1934) 75–77; [3] *Price Flexibility and Unemployment*, Cowles Commission Monograph No. 8, Principia Press, Bloomington, Ind., 1944, Chapter VI.

Makower, H. and Marschak, J. [1] 'Assets, Prices and Monetary Theory', *Economica*, New Series, **5** 1938) 261-268.

Marschak, J. [1] 'On Investment' (hectographed and privately circulated), 1935; [2] 'Utilities and Probabilities in Human Choice', *Report of Third Annual Research Conference on Economics and Statistics, Colorado Springs*, Cowles Commission for Research in Economics, 1937, pp. 79–82; [3] 'Money and the Theory of Assets', *Selected Essays*, 33; [4] 'Measurable Utility and the Theory of Assets' (abstract), *Econometrica* **17** (January, 1949) 63–64; [5] 'Von Neumann's and Morgenstern's New Approach to Static Economics', *Journal of Political Economy* **54** (April, 1946) 97–115; [6] 'The Role of Liquidity under Complete and Incomplete Information', *Selected Essays*, 39; [7] 'Optimal Investment of a Firm' (abstract), *Econometrica* **18** (April, 1950) 176–177.

Marshall, A [1] *Principles of Economics*, Macmillan and Co., London, 1920, Mathematical Appendix, Note IX.

Menger, K. [1] 'Das Unsicherheitsmoment in der Wertlehre', *Zeitschrift für Nationalökonomie* **5** (1934) 459–485.

Neumann, J. von and Morgenstern, O. [1] *Theory of Games and Economic Behavior*, Second Edition, Princeton University Press, Princeton, 1947, 641 pp.

Neymann, J. and Pearson, E. S. [1] 'Contributions to the Theory of Testing Statistical Hypotheses', *Statistical Research Memoirs* **1** (June, 1936).

Pareto, V. [1] *Manuel d'Economie Politique*, Second Edition, Giard, Paris, pp. 572–578.

Pigou, A. C. [1] *The Economics of Welfare*, Macmillan and Co., London, 1920, 176 pp.

Rubin, H. [1] 'An Axiom System for Measurable Utility' (unpublished).

Samuelson, P. A. [1] 'The Numerical Representation of Ordered Classifications and the Concept of Utility', *Review of Economic Studies* **6** (October, 1938) 65–70.

Tintner, G. [1] 'The Theory of Choice Under Subjective Risk and Uncertainty', *Econometrica* **9** (July–October, 1941) 298–304; [2] 'The Pure Theory of Production under Technological Risk and Uncertainty', *Econometrica* **9** (July–October, 1941) 305–312; [3] 'A Contribution to the Nonstatic Theory of Production', *Studies in Mathematical Economics and Econometrics, in Memory of Henry of Henry Schultz* (ed. by O. Lange, F. McIntyre, T. O. Yntema) The University of Chicago Press, Chicago, 1942, pp. 92–109.

Törnqvist, L. [1] 'On the Economic Theory of Lottery Gambles', *Skandinavisk Aktuarietidskrift* **28**, Nos. 3–4 (1945) 228–246.

Vickrey, W. [1] 'Measuring Marginal Utility by Reactions to Risk', *Econometrica* **13** (October, 1945) 319–333.

Wald, A. [1] 'Statistical Decision Functions Which Minimize the Maximum Risk, *Annals of Mathematics* **46** (April, 1945) 265–280; [2] 'Statistical Decision Functions', *Annals of Mathematical Statistics* (June, 1949) 165–205.

Wold, H. [1] 'A Synthesis of Pure Demand Analysis, Part II', *Skandinavisk Aktuarietidskrift* **26** (1943) 220–263.

2

WHY 'SHOULD' STATISTICIANS AND BUSINESSMEN MAXIMIZE 'MORAL EXPECTATION'?

(1951)

1. Introduction

1.1. The word 'should' in the title of this paper has the same meaning as in the following sentences: "In building a house, why should one act on the assumption that the floor area of a room is the product and not the sum of its length and width?"; "If all *A* are *B* and all *B* are *C*, why should one avoid acting as if all *C* were *A*?" People may often act contrary to these precepts or norms but then we say that they do not act reasonably. To discuss a set of norms of reasonable behavior (or possibly two or more such sets, each set being consistent internally but possibly inconsistent with other sets) is a problem in logic, not in psychology. It is a normative, not a descriptive, problem.

1.2. The phrase 'moral expectation' stems from the early students of probability who applied probabilities in their study of reasonable behavior of players in games of chance. Let the 'prospect' *P*, that is, the probability distribution $P(X)$ of a random 'outcome' *X*, depend upon a man's decision ('strategy') *S*:

$$(1.2{:}1)\quad P = P(X) = P(X; S).$$

Let the set $\mathscr{X}$ of all possible outcomes *X* be completely ordered by a relation $\mathfrak{g}$ ('read: as good as or better than'). Define a scalar function $u(X)$ on the set $\mathscr{X}$ as follows: for any pair, X_1 and X_2, in $\mathscr{X}$,

$$(1.2{:}2)\quad u(X_1) \geqq u(X_2) \quad \text{if} \quad X_1 \,\mathfrak{g}\, X_2 .$$

Then $u(X)$ is called the utility of *X*. It is a random variable whose distribution depends on the distribution *P* and hence on the strategy *S*. Its expected value,

$$(1.2{:}3)\quad Eu(X) \,|\, P(X; S) = \mu_u(S), \quad \text{say},$$

is called the moral expectation of X. Define a space $\mathcal{S}$ whose elements S represent possible strategies. The title of the paper asks whether it is reasonable always to choose as one's strategy an element S^* of $\mathcal{S}$ whenever

$$(1.2{:}4) \quad \mu_u(S^*) > \mu_u(S')$$

where S' is any element of $\mathcal{S}$ distinct from S^*.

1.3. The 'precept', always (that is, for any space $\mathcal{S}$) to maximize moral expectation, leads to inconsistent results unless all the utility functions considered are linear transforms of each other (in which case utility is sometimes said to be 'measurable'). This can be easily shown for the case of discrete probability distributions. Suppose X can only take values $X_0, \ldots, X_N$, and denote the corresponding probabilities by $p_0, \ldots, p_N$. Let u and v be two utility functions as defined in (1.2:2), and suppose the space $\mathcal{S}$ is such as to include a strategy for every distribution. In particular, let S' result in probabilities $p'_0, \ldots, p'_N$; and S^* in $p^*_0, \ldots, p^*_N$. Suppose that, following the 'precept,' S^* is not chosen in preference to S'; that is, by (1.2:4),

$$(1.3{:}1) \quad \mu_u(S^*) \leqq \mu_u(S'); \qquad \mu_v(S^*) \leqq \mu_v(S').$$

Suppose, in addition, that neither is S' chosen in preference to S^*. Then (1.3:1) becomes

$$\mu_u(S^*) = \mu_u(S'); \quad \mu_v(S^*) = \mu_v(S');$$
$$\sum_0^N (p^*_n - p'_n) \cdot u(X_n) = 0 = \sum_0^N (p^*_n - p'_n) \cdot v(X_n) = \sum_0^N (p^*_n - p'_n) \cdot 1 .$$

This must remain true for prospects such that $p^*_n \neq p'_n$ for $n \leqq 2$ and $p^*_n = p'_n = 0$ for $n > 2$. Then the three equations

$$\sum_0^2 (p^*_n - p'_n) \cdot u(X_n) = \sum_0^2 (p^*_n - p'_n) \cdot v(X_n) = \sum_0^N (p^*_n - p'_n) \cdot 1$$

form a homogeneous linear system in the three $(p^*_n - p'_n)$, $n = 0, 1, 2$. Hence the $u(X_n)$, $v(X_n)$, 1 are linearly dependent, for any three arbitrarily chosen values of n. Therefore, there exist α, β such that

$$v(X_n) = \alpha + \beta u(X_n), \quad n = 0, \ldots, N.$$

The linear dependence of the utility functions follows thus from the linear nature of the operator E in (1.2:3). The following illustration may be useful. Suppose $\mathscr{X}$ consists of three alternative sums of money: \$−1, 0, 1. Let $w = M(u)$ and $v = L(u) = 1 + 2u$ be, respectively, a nonlinear and a linear monotone increasing transform of a utility function $u(X)$. Let S' and S'' be two strategies resulting, respectively, in two different probability distributions of X, $P'(X)$ and $P''(X)$. In Table I the moral expectations,

TABLE I

X	u	w	v			$P'(X)$	$P''(X)$
−1	−2	−1	−3			$\frac{1}{2}$	0
0	0	0	1			0	1
1	1	2	3			$\frac{1}{2}$	0
$\mu(S') =$	$-\frac{1}{2}$	$\frac{1}{2}$	0	EX	=	0	0
$\mu(S'') =$	0	0	1	$E(X - EX)^2$	=	1	0
Best $S =$	S''	S'	S''				

$\mu(S')$ and $\mu(S'')$, are computed for the three different utility functions, u, w and v. Thus, of the two strategies S' and S'', S'' (resulting in a smaller variance of X) is chosen when the utility function is u or the linear transform v of u. But when the utility function is the nonlinear monotone transform w of u, a different strategy may be chosen – although the man maximizes his moral expectation.

1.4. Pascal's [9] immortality wager was an early application of the precept to maximize moral expectation. Essentially, Pascal made four propositions, with the first three of which we shall not quarrel. *First*, assume that, since chances for and against immortality are unknown, they are equal. *Second*, assume that, if there is immortality, then good life is followed by eternal bliss and bad life by eternal damnation. Regard these two sequences as outcomes X_1' and X_1'', respectively, and denote the outcomes 'good life followed by nothing' and 'bad life followed by nothing' by X_2' and X_2'', respectively. Consider 'good life' and 'bad life' as two strategies, S' and S''. In effect, Pascal computes the following two expected values:

$$\mu_u(S') = \tfrac{1}{2}u(X_1') + \tfrac{1}{2}u(X_2'),$$
$$\mu_u(S'') = \tfrac{1}{2}u(X_1'') + \tfrac{1}{2}u(X_2'').$$

Hence,

$$\mu_u(S') > \mu_u(S'') \quad \text{if} \quad u(X_1') - u(X_1'') > u(X_2'') - u(X_2').$$

For Pascal, the difference between the advantages of eternal bliss (following a short period of possibly tedious good life) and the disadvantages of eternal damnation (following a short though possibly not unpleasant bad life) exceeds the difference between the possible pleasures of sin and the possible inconveniences of virtue. These valuations (the utility function u) can be regarded as his *third* proposition and may be accepted. We shall be concerned with his *fourth* proposition: that, because $\mu_u(S')$ exceeds $\mu_u(S'')$, it is reasonable to choose S'.

1.5. In the particular case when the space $\mathscr{X}$ of outcomes consists of alternative sums of money (as in 1.3, table), the moral expectation of the gain, $Eu(X)$, is contrasted with its 'mathematical expectation', EX, which also depends on S. In the Petersburg game, there exists a strategy S', say, which makes EX infinite, yet a reasonable player would not choose S'. To explain the paradox, Daniel Bernoulli stated that a reasonable man maximizes $Eu(X)$ and not EX and that the function $u(X)$ has certain properties. See Menger [7].

1.6. In Section 2 of this paper, the precept to maximize $Eu(X)$ will be related to problems facing statisticians and businessmen and, in fact, to human decisions in general. Section 3 gives as a necessary condition for the precept a postulate which may be called the *Postulate of Substitution between Indifferent Prospects*. In an earlier paper [4], this postulate (jointly with certain other postulates) was shown to be a sufficient condition for the precept of maximizing $Eu(X)$, valid for a non-empty class of utility functions, each element of which is a linear transform of any of the others. This postulate appears, thus, to be logically equivalent to the moral expectation precept (provided the other postulates are admitted). It is also possibly equivalent to certain postulates of von Neumann and Morgenstern [8]. For a comparison, see [4, Section 7]. Finally, it is also equivalent to a postulate which Samuelson [11] recently formulated very succinctly and which he proposed to call *Special Independence Assumption*. A comparison between the postulate and the economist's concept of 'independence between consumption goods' is contained in Section 3 of the present paper.

1.7. In Section 4 a very rough outline of a different approach will be attempted. A rule of *Long Run Success* is formulated ('in the long run, it pays to be reasonable') by considering a strategy as a sequence of rules of action to be taken in response to future situations. It seems that the rule of Long Run Success is not equivalent to the precept to maximize moral expectation unless some further conditions are imposed upon the utility functions. No definitive results are available so far.

1.8. Note that the space $\mathscr{S}$ of strategies can be conceived as including among its elements, strategies consistent with the ordinary rules of logic and mathematics, and strategies not consistent with these rules. The distribution P of outcomes X and, therefore, the quantity $Eu(X)$ will depend on whether the decision maker is a good or a bad logician and arithmetician, on what kind of geometry he applies, etc. This kind of justification of a set of behavior norms including norms of thinking and counting was, I believe, occasionally attempted by pragmatist and evolutionary writers with some rule of long run success in mind: "If you act on the assumption that 2 times 2 equals 5, you (or your tribe or species) will, in some sense, fare worse in the long run than if you act on the assumption that 2 times 2 equals 4."

2. Some concrete cases

2.1. In recent years, the theory of statistical inference has taken a remarkably 'economic' turn. In choosing a rule for making observations (the design of a sample), money cost (C) is subtracted from what may be called the gross gain (G) derived by the statistician or his 'employer' from the knowledge acquired from the observations. G is conceived as a sum of money and is, in a simple case, the larger the smaller the error of the estimation based on the sample. The money sum $G-C=X$ is thus the outcome of the statistician's decision to choose a certain sample design. X is called the net gain or profit. X is to be maximized with respect to the variable under the statistician's control, that is, with respect to the design of the sample.

2.2. In a particular case when the sample designs under consideration differ only with respect to the size of the sample (number of observations) S, the best value $S=S^*$ must satisfy the approximate rule,

$$\frac{dG}{dS}=\frac{dC}{dS},$$

(provided G and C can be approximated by differentiable functions of S). This is the familiar rule of the economists: to equalize the marginal monetary product and the marginal monetary cost of the 'input' S. More generally one defines the space $\mathscr{S}$ of all possible sample designs and maximizes the scalar function $X(S)$ over this space.

2.3. However, the profit X is a random scalar since the gross gain G depends on the values that the observed random variables happen to take. (In addition, the cost C, too, may depend on observed values, as for example, when C depends on the location of individuals that happen to fall into a social survey sample or when the number of observations depends on observed values as in sequential sampling.) One cannot maximize the random variable X but one can maximize some quantity depending on its distribution, for example, its mean EX.

2.4. Both concepts, the sample design and the monetary profit, can be replaced by wider ones. As regards the first: the statistician can recommend not only the rule of making observations but also the decision to be taken after having collected them. This decision may be the choice of an estimate or of a hypothesis. More generally, it may be any decision that will influence the probability distribution of the gross gain G, for example, the decision to buy a certain quantity of a commodity. Generalizing the notation of 2.2, one defines $\mathscr{S}$ as the space of all possible 'strategies' S, each strategy being a certain rule for making observations *and* for taking decisions on the basis of these observations. The distribution of the random profit X – to be denoted by $P(X)$ – will depend on S and on the true distribution F of the observables. We can write

$$(2.4{:}1)\quad P(X) \equiv P(X;\, S, F), \qquad EX \equiv EX\big|(S, F) \equiv \mu_X(S, F), \quad \text{say}.$$

(In the simple case of 2.1, X depended on the estimation error, that is, the difference between a point estimate and the true value of the estimated parameter of the distribution of observables. This was obviously a special case of the one now stated.) The negative of the function μ_X just defined is identical with Wald's [12] 'risk function', with two differences: first, Wald always has $G \geqq 0$ (regarding $-G$, the 'loss suffered by the statistician', as a nonpositive quantity) – a trivial difference; second, Wald does not necessarily regard G, C and X as monetary quantities and presumably accepts the generalization that we are going to make now.

2.5. With the 'statistician' taking over entrepreneurial decisions, it becomes necessary to reconsider what is of concern to the businessman. To begin with, 'A full purse is not as good as an empty one is bad'. There exists a certain quantity K (possible zero) which depends on the firm's reserves and is such that, if $X \leqq K$, the firm is bankrupt and must be dissolved. It is reasonable that the probability of the occurrence of this situation should be made as small as possible. This objective may not be reached if the strategy chosen maximizes EX. On the other hand, suppose the firm tries to maximize the expression $Eu(X)$, where the 'utility function' $u(X)$ is defined as follows:

$$(2.5{:}1) \quad \begin{aligned} u(X) &= -v \quad \text{when} \quad X \leqq K, \\ u(X) &= X \quad \text{when} \quad X > K, \end{aligned}$$

where v is a positive constant. Let the probability density function of X, $X \neq K$, for a given strategy S be $p(X; S)$. Then the expected value of $u(X)$ given S is

$$(2.5{:}2) \quad Eu(X; S) = -\alpha(v + \beta) + \beta,$$

where

$$\alpha = \int_{-\infty}^{K} p(X; S)\, dX = \text{probability of bankruptcy},$$

$$\beta = \frac{\int_K^\infty X p(X; S)\, dX}{\int_K^\infty p(X; S)\, dX}$$

$$= \text{profit averaged over all cases other than bankruptcy.}$$

Both α and β depend on S, and β is usually nonnegative. It follows from (2.5:2) that, for a given β, the firm's moral expectation is the larger the smaller is α, the probability of bankruptcy. The maximization of $Eu(X)$ would thus seem to describe reasonable behavior better than the maximization of EX.

2.6. Another example of the utility function of a random sum of money and of the effect of properties of this function upon the choice of strategy was given in Table I. A much discussed case has been that of a function $u(X)$ that is differentiable at least twice. If $u'(X)>0$ and $u''(X)<0$ for all values of X (the case of "decreasing and positive marginal utility of income"), then the individual who maximizes $Eu(X)$ will prefer, given the value of the mean profit EX, a prospect with a low variance to a prospect with a high variance of X. This is seen by expanding $Eu(X)$ into a Taylor series. See [6] and, for a somewhat more general case, [2].

2.7. More generally, the businessman is concerned not with a scalar quantity but with a vector: with the sequence of profits to be earned in successive years, the more distant ones being possibly of less import to the firm's decision (even if the joint probability distribution of the sequences is known exactly) than the more immediate ones; or, if he is a farmer, with a set of quantities earned, respectively, in the form of food, housing accommodation, etc. The fact that nonmonetary earnings and future earnings of any kind can be converted into current money at prices and interest rates prevailing in (perfect) markets does not dispose of the complication since these prices and interest rates themselves have to be explained by the strategies of the people that transact in these markets. However, the generalization from a scalar to a vector $X=\{x_i\}$ does not present difficulties. In particular, if $u(X)$ is twice differentiable, the results mentioned in 2.6 are easily generalized. Write vector

$$\mu \equiv \{Ex_i\}$$

and matrix

$$\sigma \equiv \|\sigma_{ij}\| \equiv \|E(x_i - \mu_i)(x_i - \mu_j)\| .$$

Then, if

$$u_{ij} = \frac{\partial^2 u}{\partial x_i \partial x_j}$$

exists for all i, j, we have by expanding about μ,

$$Eu(X) = u(\mu) + \tfrac{1}{2} \sum_{i,j} u_{ij}\sigma_{ij} + \cdots .$$

It follows that if $u_{ii}<0$ (decreasing marginal utility of the ith kind of commodity earned or of the ith year's money profit), then the individual will try to make the variance σ_{ii} as small as possible, given the other elements of μ and σ. A high correlation between the ith and the jth elements of the profit vector will be feared if $u_{ij}<0$ (the case of goods with negative complementarity); a high correlation between i and j will be desired if $u_{ij}>0$ (the case of positively complementary goods).

2.8. Note that the definition of complementarity just used is only possible because, as a corollary of the requirement to maximize moral expectation $Eu(X)$, all utility functions form a group of linear transforms. If a nonlinear transform of $u(X)$ – say the function $w(X)=f[u(X)]$, $f'>0$ – were admitted as a utility function, then, since a positive u_{ij} might be consistent with a negative w_{ij}, the sign of complementarity as just defined could not be ascertained.

2.9. In [5], the desirability of large or small variances of, or correlations between, inputs (production factors) of various kinds was studied on lines similar to 2.7. Rational advantages of 'pooling the risks' and of either specialization or diversification of production (depending on the sign of complementarity between factors of production) can be derived –always assuming that it is rational to maximize $Eu(X)$.

2.10. Certain things desired by the businessman – such as power or social position or reputation – are not quantities at all. It is therefore necessary to generalize further the concept of what is being maximized. This generalization was presented in 1.2. If the space $\mathscr{X}$ of 'outcomes' and the space $\mathscr{S}$ of strategies are defined, this permits us to take care of all human decisions, transcending conventional economics and including the private man's choice of profession or wife, the legislator's choice of election tactics or national policies or military and administrative decisions. This is of some interest to statisticians who, after all, are not all employed by profit making organizations.

2.11. Our question is, then, whether the following rule is reasonable: always choose a strategy S^* so as to obtain a prospect (a probability distribution)

$$P(X) \equiv P(X; S^*, F),$$

for which

$$\mu_u(S^*, F) \equiv Eu(X) \,|\, (S^*, F)$$

is larger than or equal to

$$\mu_u(S', F) \equiv Eu(X) \,|\, (S', F),$$

for any S'; where the scalar function $u(X)$ is defined over the space $\mathscr{X}$ of outcomes, S^* and S' are elements of the space $\mathscr{S}$ of strategies and F is the true distribution of the observables. In general, F is not (or not completely) known – in the case of the statistician as well as in the case of any other decision makers. The economist F. H. Knight [3] called the case of unknown F 'presence of uncertainty' and the case of known F (as in games of chance) 'presence of risk'. This terminology has been widely accepted among economists although it is not in line with general scientific usage of the word uncertainty. It would be better to speak of 'incomplete' versus 'complete' information. For the purpose of this paper, it is sufficient to deal with the case of complete information, that is, to assume F known. It is of no relevance to us here whether, in the case of F unknown, probabilities of the several alternatives have to be assumed equal before maximizing $\mu_u(S, F)$ with respect to S as was done by Pascal (1.4 above), or whether, following Wald and the authors of the *Theory of Games*, one should assume the least favorable distribution F, that is, minimize $\mu_u(S, F)$ with respect to F before maximizing it with respect to S. It is the latter, the maximization of μ_u with respect to S, that concerns us here: a problem common to the case of complete and to that of incomplete information and arising with Pascal as with Wald.

3. THE RULE OF SUBSTITUTION BETWEEN INDIFFERENT PROSPECTS

3.1. In [4], a certain set of behavior postulates, numbered I–IV, was shown by the author to imply the proposition that there exists a class of utility functions, linear transforms of each other, and such that for every utility function the expected value of utility is maximized. We shall presently restate these postulates and show that, if postulates I–III (which appear rather mild) are accepted, then postulate IV follows from the condition that $Eu(X)$ is maximized. A joint result of the two papers is, then, that under certain weak conditions, postulate IV and the rule of maximizing moral expectation are equivalent. Postulate IV will be called the 'rule of substitution between indifferent prospects'.

3.2. As in [4], we define a space $\mathscr{P}$ of prospects P (=probability distributions) for the case that the space $\mathscr{X}$ of outcomes consists of a finite number of elements, $X_0, X_1, \ldots, X_N$. (The case of N infinite was discussed by Rubin in [10] for the problem of [4].) Regard the probability that the particular outcome X_n will occur, $p(X_n)$, as a coordinate of the point P in the Euclidean N-space, $n=1,\ldots, N$. Since

$$(3.2{:}1)\quad 0 \leqslant \sum_{n=1}^{N} p(X_n) = 1 - p(X_0) \leqslant 1\,,$$

the space $\mathscr{P}$ of prospects is the domain of the N-space bounded by and including the surface of an $(N+1)$-hedron whose vertices are the origin $(0, 0,\ldots, 0)$ and the ends $(1, 0, 0,\ldots, 0)$, $(0, 1, 0,\ldots, 0)$,..., $(0, 0, 0,\ldots, 1)$ of the N unit vectors. These vertices represent the 'sure' prospects, each promising with certainty one particular outcome. Sure prospects will be denoted by $P^{(0)}, P^{(1)},\ldots, P^{(N)}$. Using letters $P, Q, R,\ldots$ for prospects in general, we state the following postulates:

I. *The space $\mathscr{P}$ is completely ordered by the relation* $\mathfrak{g}$ (read 'as good as or better than'). Note: Whenever $P\mathfrak{g}Q$ we shall also write $u(P) \geqq u(Q)$. This defines a scalar 'utility function' $u(P)$ on the space $\mathscr{P}$. It is related in a simple way to the function $u(X)$ on the space $\mathscr{X}$, defined in 1.2 above, that is, we have $u(X_n) = u(P^{(n)})$, $n=0, 1,\ldots, N$, by definition. Furthermore, whenever $P\mathfrak{g}Q$ and not $Q\mathfrak{g}P$, we write $P\mathfrak{p}Q$ (read 'P preferred to Q') and have $u(P) > u(Q)$. Whenever $P\mathfrak{g}Q$ and $Q\mathfrak{g}P$, we write $P\mathfrak{i}Q$ (read 'P and Q are indifferent') and have $u(P) = u(Q)$.

II. $\mathfrak{g}$ *is continuous*, that is, if $P\mathfrak{g}Q\mathfrak{g}R$, then there exists a number r, $0 \leqq r \leqq 1$, such that if $Q' = rP + (1-r)\,R$ then $Q\mathfrak{i}Q'$. Note: We are using the symbols for addition, multiplication and equality in their ordinary meaning. Q' is the result of ordinary multiplication and addition performed on two vectors, P and R. Geometrically, Q' is a point on a straight line connecting P and R.

III. *There exist P and Q not on the boundary of $\mathscr{P}$, such that not $P\mathfrak{i}Q$.* Note: This is postulate III* of [4]. We refer to [4] for an alternative postulate and for a stronger one.

IV. *If* $P \mathfrak{i} Q$ *and* $0<r<1$ *and if* $P'=rR+(1-r)P$ *and* $Q'=rR+(1-r)Q$, *then* $P' \mathfrak{i} Q'$. Note: P' is the prospect of having either prospect P or prospect R with certain probabilities, $1-r$ and r. Q' is the prospect of having either Q or R also with probabilities $1-r$ and r. Postulate IV states that if P and Q are indifferent, so are P' and Q'. In a special case P and P' may coincide [4, postulate IVa]. Also, P or Q or R may be sure prospects.

3.3. In the language of the last section – see note to postulate I – the rule of maximizing $Eu(X)$ can be stated thus [writing for brevity $u(P^{(n)})=u^{(n)}$, which is independent of the prospects considered, and $P(X_n)=p_n$, $Q(X_n)=q_n$, etc.].

PROPOSITION 1. $Q \mathfrak{g} R$ *if and only if* $\sum_0^N u^{(n)} q_n \geqq \sum_0^N u^{(n)} r_n$.

We shall prove that this rule implies

PROPOSITION 2. *If* $P \mathfrak{p} Q \mathfrak{p} R$ *then the indifference sets* $J(P)$, $J(Q)$, $J(R)$ *are segments of three parallel* $(N-1)$*-dimensional hyperplanes, contained in* $\mathscr{P}$ *and stacked in the order* P, Q, R, *or its reverse*, where for any prospect P the indifference set $J(P)$ is defined as consisting of all prospects P' for which $P' \mathfrak{i} P$.

In fact, if $P \mathfrak{p} Q \mathfrak{p} R$ then, by the definition of the relations $\mathfrak{p}$ and $\mathfrak{i}$, proposition 1 implies that

$$(3.3:1) \quad \sum_0^N u^{(n)} p_n > \sum_0^N u^{(n)} q_n > \sum_0^N u^{(n)} r_n .$$

If, in addition, $P \mathfrak{i} P'$, $Q \mathfrak{i} Q'$ and $R \mathfrak{i} R'$, proposition 1 requires that

$$\sum_0^N u^{(n)} p_n = \sum_0^N u^{(n)} p'_n = a^* \quad \text{say,}$$

$$\sum_0^N u^{(n)} q_n = \sum_0^N u^{(n)} q'_n = b^* \quad \text{say,}$$

$$\sum_0^N u^{(n)} r_n = \sum_0^N u^{(n)} r'_n = c^*, \quad \text{say;}$$

where $a^*>b^*>c^*$. Write $v^{(n)}=u^{(n)}-u^{(0)}$, $n=1, 2, \ldots, N$. Then the above equations become upon replacing p_0 by $1-\sum_1^N p_n$, etc. and upon replacing $a^*-u^{(0)}$ by a, etc.

$$\text{(3.3:2)}\quad \sum_1^N v^{(n)} p_n = \sum_1^N v^{(n)} p'_n = a\,,$$

$$\sum_1^N v^{(n)} q_n = \sum_1^N v^{(n)} q'_n = b\,,$$

$$\sum_1^N v^{(n)} r_n = \sum_1^N v^{(n)} r'_n = c\,.$$

The last two terms in the first line of (3.3:2) give the equation of a $(N-1)$-dimensional hyperplane which contains all P' such that $P'\,\mathfrak{i}\,P$. This hyperplane is therefore identical with the indifference set $J(P)$. Similarly, the other two lines in (3.3:2) provide the equations for the hyperplanes $J(Q)$ and $J(R)$. The three hyperplanes are parallel, each having the N direction cosines proportional to $v^{(n)}$, $n=1, 2, \ldots, N$. The distances of the three hyperplanes from the origin are proportional to a, b and c, respectively. Hence they are stacked in the order P, Q, R or its reverse.

3.4. Proposition 2 implies, in turn, postulate IV, provided postulates I–III are granted. In fact, in the notation used in the statement of postulate IV, prospects P and Q must both lie on $J(P)$, one of the parallel indifference planes revealed in proposition 2. Moreover, the indifference planes $J(P')$ and $J(Q')$ must be parallel to $J(P)$. On the other hand, P' and Q' must both lie on a plane parallel to $J(P)$ because $r=\overline{PP'}/\overline{PR}=$ $=\overline{QQ'}/\overline{QR}$. And since in an Euclidean space there is only one plane through P' parallel to $J(P)$, we have $P'\,\mathfrak{i}\,Q'$.

The reasoning of this and the preceding sections presupposes the validity of postulates I–III. Postulate I excludes the case in which neither $P\,\mathfrak{g}\,Q$ nor $Q\,\mathfrak{g}\,P$ and this would rule out the existence of a function $u(P)$ on $\mathscr{P}$. Postulate II excludes the possibility of 'holes' in the indifference planes. Postulate III excludes the possibility that the whole interior of $\mathscr{P}$ might form a single indifference set.

We conclude that, given postulates I–III, postulate IV is not only a sufficient condition for proposition 1 (as was shown in [4]), but also a necessary condition. Thus, the two are equivalent, provided postulates I–III are granted. Postulates I–III seem indeed weak enough as a description of reasonable behavior. Postulate IV also seems reasonable to me and some further remarks in 3.5 may convince others. If, in addition, this postulate is taken to be intuitively more convincing than its logical equivalent, proposition 1, then the question asked in the title is answered.

3.5. In the discussion of the theory of choice between prospects, confusion seems to arise through the use of an ambiguous word, 'combination'. This word naturally expresses the operation '*and*', as in '*A and C*'. But it has also been applied to express the relation '*either–or*', as in '*either A or C*, with probabilities r and $1-r$'. Since prospects are always mutually exclusive, they cannot be 'combined' into an object of choice such as 'prospect A *and* prospect C' to be chosen in preference to another 'combination' such as 'prospect B *and* prospect C'. But they can be 'combined' in a different sense, namely, the combination 'either A or C, with probabilities r and $1-r$' can be formed and may be chosen in preference to the combination 'either B or C, with probabilities q and $1-q$'. Suppose, on the other hand, that A, B, C are objects that are not mutually exclusive. For example, A=country house, B=city house, C=car. Then the following rule of behavior would *not* be reasonable: "If I like A as well as I like B, then I like *A and C* as well as I like *B and C*." Such a rule would neglect the possibility that a car has more use in the country than in the city. But such a rule is *not* our postulate IV. The latter says, rather: "Call P the prospect of having the country house A and having, in addition, certain other things which will be held constant throughout the comparisons and which we shall call D; call Q the prospect of having the city house B and D. Then, if I like P as well as I like Q, I like the prospect of having either P or R as well as I like the prospect of having either Q or R, provided the odds are the same in each case." This is reasonable. The fact that the car is of better use when possessed jointly with a country house than when possessed jointly with a city house has no bearing on the choice between the prospects discussed, of which *none promises the joint possession of a car and a house*. To exclude more completely from our mind the logically illegitimate picture of a joint occurrence of mutually exclusive events, postulate IV might be illustrated most simply as follows: P=the career of a professor, Q=the career of a church minister, R=the career of a bus driver. Or, imagine that you have to choose between drawing from one or another of two urns; in each of them, 20 per cent of all tickets are inscribed 'car'; the remaining 80 per cent are inscribed 'country house' in the first urn and are inscribed 'city house' in the second urn. If you are indifferent between city house and country house, will you prefer one urn to the other, knowing that if you do get a car in any of the lotteries you will *not* get a house with it? The same applies naturally when P, Q and R are themselves nonsure prospects; for example, if they are tickets to three different lotteries.

3.6. It may be useful to refer to the notation of 2.7 where the outcome X was a joint occurrence of quantities $x_1, x_2, \ldots$ and was regarded as a vector $\{x_i\}$. The utility of X (or, in the language of prospects, the utility of the sure prospect that X occurs with certainty) is denoted by $u(x_1, x_2, \ldots)$. Disregard, as being kept constant, all x_i for $i>3$. We say that commodity 3 is more complementary with commodity 1 than with commodity 2, over some defined intervals, if

$$(3.6{:}1) \quad u(x_1 + h_1, x_2, x_3) = u(x_1, x_2 + h_2, x_3)$$

and

$$u(x_1 + h_1, x_2, x_3 + h_3) > u(x_1, x_2 + h_2, x_3 + h_3),$$

where the h_i are positive. This definition of complementarity is in accord with the one used in 2.7 for the case when the x_i are continuous and u is twice differentiable. This is seen by expanding the function u into a Taylor series about x_1, x_2, x_3, and inserting into (3.6:1). On the other hand, in our example of the car and the two different houses, the three x_i can take the values 0 and 1 only. If, in the continuous case, the cross derivative $u_{13}=0$ or if in the general case

$$u(x_1, x_2, x_3 + h_3) - u(x_1, x_2, x_3) = u(x_1 + h_1, x_2, x_3 + h_3) - \\ + u(x_1 + h_1, x_2, x_3),$$

we say that there is no complementarity (positive or negative) between commodities 1 and 3 or that the two are 'independent'. As stated in 2.8, these definitions presuppose that utility functions are linear transforms of each other.

To apply this concept to the choice between prospects, remember that we have then, as the argument of the utility function, not the vector of quantities of commodities but the probabilities of mutually exclusive events, $p_1, \ldots, p_N$ where, in particular, p_1 may be the probability that the vector of commodity quantities has a certain value and p_2 may be the probability that this vector has another value. It would be misleading to say that postulate IV asserts 'independence' (in the sense just stated) between any objects of choice themselves: the prospects $P, Q, \ldots$ are not (as the commodity quantities $x_1, x_2, \ldots$ are) coordinates of the space in which the indifference surfaces are drawn.

3.7. On the other hand, the probabilities $p_1, \ldots, p_N$ are indeed 'independent', in the sense that, if the precept of maximizing expected utility is always followed, then

$$\frac{\partial^2 u(p_1, p_2, \ldots, p_N)}{\partial p_m \partial p_n} = 0, \quad m, n = 1, \ldots, N,$$

because u is linear in its continuous argument, the vector $\{p_i\}$.

4. The Rule of Long Run Success

4.1. We shall now outline tentatively another proposition which may under certain conditions be implied by the rule of maximizing moral expectation and which appears (like postulate IV) intuitively more convincing than the rule itself.

For an integer $T>0$, define a space $\mathscr{X}_{(T)}$, whose element $X_{(T)}$ represents a possible time sequence of situations $x_0, x_1, \ldots, x_T$ (for example, a sequence of annual profits or of balance sheets). Define a utility function $u_T(X_{(T)})$ such that if $X'_{(T)}$ and $X''_{(T)}$ are in $\mathscr{X}_{(T)}$, and $X'_{(T)} \mathrel{\mathrm{g}} X''_{(T)}$ then $u_T(X'_{(T)}) \geqq u_T(X''_{(T)})$. Define a closed space $\mathscr{S}$, whose element S_T represents a possible strategy, defined as a sequence of functions, $s_0, s_1, \ldots, s_{T-1}$, where $s_t = s_t(x_0, x_1, \ldots, x_t)$. Thus S_T is a sequence of rules of how to respond at given times to a given sequence of past situations. Now define the probability that the strategy S_T^* will be at least as successful as S_T':

$$(4.1{:}1) \quad Pr\{[u_T(X_{(T)}; S_T^*) \geqq u_T(X_{(T)}; S_T')]\} = \pi_T(S_T^*, S_T'), \quad \text{say.}$$

Now let T increase and consider sequences such as

$$\mathscr{S}^* = (S_1^*, S_2^*, \ldots), \qquad \mathscr{S}' = (S_1', S_2', \ldots), \quad \text{etc.}$$

Suppose that there exists a limit

$$\lim_{T\to\infty} \pi_T(S_T^*, S_T') = \pi(\mathscr{S}^*, \mathscr{S}'), \quad \text{say},$$

for any two sequences $\mathscr{S}^*$ and $\mathscr{S}'$ and suppose that this limit

$$(4.1{:}2) \quad \pi(\mathscr{S}^*, \mathscr{S}') = 1 .$$

Then the rule of long run success requires that the sequence $\mathscr{S}^*$ be chosen [or, if two or more values $\mathscr{S}^*$ exist that satisfy (4.1:2), one of them must be chosen]. This corresponds to the common sense definition, 'The best policy is the one that succeeds in the long run'.

4.2. We should like to know conditions under which the rule of maximizing moral expectation implies that the rule of long run success is satisfied. As a mere example that may start a discussion among those better qualified, we shall impose a (probably unnecessarily strong) condition upon the sequence of utility functions,

$$u_1(x_1), u_2(x_1, x_2), \ldots, u_T(x_1, x_2, \ldots, x_T)$$

with means

$$Eu_1, Eu_2, \ldots, Eu_T$$

and variances

$$\sigma_1^2, \sigma_2^2, \ldots, \sigma_T^2 .$$

We do not assume the successive random variables $u_1, u_2, \ldots$ to be independent statistically. But we make the assumption that the variance σ_T^2 tends to zero as $T \to \infty$. Then u_T converges in probability to Eu_T. Therefore the difference,

$$u_T(X_{(T)}; S_T^*) - u_T(X_{(T)}; S\text{x}),$$

converges in probability to

$$Eu_T(X_{(T)}; S\text{x}) - Eu_T(X_{(T)}; S_T') .$$

(See, for example, [1, especially pp. 253–255].) This difference is non-negative if the rule of maximizing moral expectation is followed, that is, if for every T a strategy S_T^* is chosen satisfying

$$Eu_T(X_{(T)}; S_T^*) \geqq Eu_T(X_{(T)}; S_T'),$$

where S_T' is another strategy in $\mathscr{S}_T$. Then

$$\pi(\mathscr{S}^*, \mathscr{S}') = 1$$

for every $\mathscr{S}'$ and the rule of long run success is satisfied.

We have used here, merely to illustrate the proposed approach, a crucial assumption that is hardly plausible: that the variance of the utility function of outcomes over a horizon T, tends to zero as the horizon increases. This assumption is also unnecessarily strong as it proves more than is required: for the limiting probability $\pi(\mathscr{S}^*, \mathscr{S}')$ to be equal to 1, it is not necessary that each of the two compared utilities converge separately to its respective expected value.

An alternative assumption might be that of statistical independence between utility functions over successive horizons, that is, between $u_1(x_1), u_2(x_1, x_2), \ldots$. But this is even less reasonable. It is possible that no plausible conditions exist under which the rule of maximizing moral expectation implies the rule of long run success as defined.

5. Summary

The rule of maximizing the expected value of utility was shown to imply that utility functions of prospects (that is, of alternative distributions of outcomes of strategies) are linear transforms of each other and are linear in the probabilities of outcomes. The rule is equivalent to the postulate that indifferent prospects are substituted for each other – provided certain other, weak postulates are granted. Finally, an attempt was made to relate the rule of maximizing the expected value of utility to a rule of aiming at a long run success. This required redefining outcomes, strategies and utilities as time sequences. The strategies discussed included those of statisticians and businessmen and can be conceived to include human decisions in general. At no point was it claimed that reasonable behavior is actually practiced by men: the paper is a study in consistent sets of norms, not an empirical study.

BIBLIOGRAPHY

[1] H. Cramér, *Mathematical Methods of Statistics*, Princeton University Press, Princeton, 1946.

[2] M. Friedman and L. J. Savage, 'The Utility Analysis of Choices Involving Risk', *J. of Political Economy* **56** (1948), 279–304.

[3] F. H. Knight, *Risk, Uncertainty, and Profit*, Houghton Mifflin, Boston and New York, 1921.

[4] J. Marschak, 'Rational Behavior, Uncertain Prospects, and Measurable Utility', *Selected Essays*, 1.

[5] J. Marschak, 'Optimal Investment of a Firm', *Selected Essays*, 39.

[6] A. Marshall, *Principles of Economics*, Macmillan, London, 1920. See Mathematical Appendix, Note IX.

[7] K. Menger, 'Das Unsicherheitsmoment in der Wertlehre', *Zeitschrift fuer Nationaloekonomie* **5** (1934), 459–485.

[8] J. von Neumann and O. Morgenstern, *Theory of Games and Economic Behavior*, 2nd ed., Princeton University Press, Princeton, 1947.

[9] B. Pascal, 'Article II: Qu'il est plus avantageux de croire que de ne pas croire ce qu'enseigne la religion chrétienne', *Pensées*, Garnier Frères, Paris, after the edition of 1670.

[10] H. Rubin, *Axiom System for Measurable Utility*, unpublished.

[11] P. A. Samuelson, *Measurement of Utility Reformulated*, unpublished.

[12] A. Wald, 'Statistical Decision Functions', *Annals of Math. Stat.* **20** (1949), 220–263.

3

SCALING OF UTILITIES AND PROBABILITIES

(1954)

One strategy is better than another if it brings the player more. More of what? Clearly, one uses some criterion of 'utility', of something that is being maximized. Moreover, since the opponent's response or the future in general is uncertain, the player does not know a unique result of his strategy but rather expects various possible results, some with greater, some will smaller degrees of belief or '(subjective) probabilities'.

If utilities and probabilities could be merely ranked (like degrees of patriotism) but not also scaled (like degrees of temperature), the theory of games could say rather little. Accordingly, von Neumann and Morgenstern revived the eighteenth century concept of a player who is concerned with his subjective status (so called 'moral wealth' – the modern 'utility'), a number which, under uncertainty, is a random one, and whose average (the 'moral expectation' – the modern 'expected utility') the player tries to maximize. A lively discussion developed.[1] The most elegant restatement of the relevant postulates of rational behavior and a rigorous proof of the implied 'Bernoulli theorem' was given by Herstein and Milnor.[2] In this discussion, the necessarily subjective nature of the probabilities was somewhat neglected. But this latter aspect (actually also traceable back to the eighteenth century) was revived by Ramsey and De Finetti and in L. J. Savage's *Foundations of Statistics*.[3]

The following exposition tries to appeal to the reader's intuition and cater to his laziness more than it would be permissible in a mathematical paper. A proof is merely sketched. It may be added, however, that the substance of the proof, too, is simpler than in my earlier papers on the subject.[4]

I shall often use the second person pronoun. In discussing rational behavior as in discussing logic, appeal is made to the reader's reasonable self: given time to think, how would you decide? I don't deal with another, quite a different question (as different as psychology is from logic): how often do you decide hurriedly and foolishly?

I. THE CASE OF THREE OUTCOMES

Suppose you, the reader, have to choose between two decisions (actions): to build or not to build a bomb-proof shelter for yourself and your family. To make the example drastic, let us suppose that you are rich but that the shelter would cost you practically the whole of your fortune; and that such a shelter is both indispensable and sufficient for life preservation in the case of war. Thus your two alternative decisions and the two alternative states of the world (war or peace) combine into the following 'payoff matrix':

Decisions	States of World	
	Peace	War
Build shelter	Alive and poor (r_2)	Alive and poor (r_2)
Don't build shelter	Alive and rich (r_3)	Dead (r_1)

This is oversimplified indeed. Especially, we have neglected the difference between being alive and poor in peace, and being alive and poor in war (with shelterless neighbors dead). I need this particular simplification in order to have in my example just three possible outcomes. This will be a convenient introduction to more complicated cases. The three outcomes, or results, I have denoted by r_1='dead'; r_2='alive and poor'; r_3='alive and rich'. I suppose you prefer r_3 to r_2 and r_2 to r_1. This ranking of results is sufficient to determine your choice of action if you are certain about the future. If you are certain that there will be war, you choose to build the shelter (because you prefer r_2 to r_1); if you are sure that there will be peace, you choose not to build the shelter (because r_3 is better than r_2).

But suppose you do not know whether there will be war or peace. Yet you have to take a decision! You will still choose not to build a shelter if your *degree of belief* in peace and your *degree of preference* for wealth relative to survival are sufficiently large. (Note that we now speak of degrees and not of mere ranks! Summer is warmer than spring, and spring is warmer than winter: this is ranking; but we can also measure degrees of temperature in each of the three seasons.)

The statement I have just made, about the degrees of your beliefs and preferences that will make you decide not to build a shelter though you are uncertain about the future, must be made more precise. Denote the degrees of belief (also called subjective probabilities) that you assign to peace and war, respectively, by p and $1-p$. Calibrate your thermometer of preferences, or 'utilities' as follows: assign utility zero to the worst of the three outcomes, and utility one to the best. Thus

$$u(r_1) = 0\,; \qquad u(r_3) = 1\,.$$

Then, since r_2 is better than r_1 and worse than r_3,

$$0 < u(r_2) < 1$$

Subject to these inequalities, you are still free to assign any number $u(r_2)$ to the outcome r_2. I now suggest that you can, without incurring any logical contradiction, determine the number $u(r_2)$ in such a way as to satisfy the following principle: "*of any two decisions, the one you (the reader) choose is the one that, in your opinion, results in the higher, or at least not lower, average utility.*" The average utility that results from the decision 'don't build' is defined as the weighted average of $u(r_3)$ and $u(r_1)$, the weights being the corresponding degrees of belief, which we have denoted above by p and $1-p$, respectively. Thus the average utility that results from 'not building shelter' is

$$(1) \qquad u(r_3)\cdot p + u(r_1)\cdot(1-p) = 1\cdot p + 0\cdot(1-p) = p$$

On the other hand, the average utility that results from the decision 'to build' is

$$u(r_2)\cdot p + u(r_2)\cdot(1-p) = u(r_2)$$

Now, suppose you have chosen to build. According to the above principle of choosing in favor of the decision that results in the higher average utility, your actual choice will imply that, in your opinion [and still using the scale where one had fixed $u(r_3)=1$ and $u(r_1)=0$],

$$u(r_2) \geqslant p$$

On the other hand, if you had chosen not to build, the above principle would imply [still using the same scale]

$$u(r_2) \leqslant p$$

You can now perform on yourself a mental experiment, by varying the number p and asking: "with this degree of belief into persistence of peace, do I still prefer to build (or not to build)?" You may come close enough to a value of p, at which you will be *indifferent* between building and not building. Call this hypothetical value: $p = p_0$. Then both statements are true: $u(r_2) \geqslant p_0$ and $u(r_2) \leqslant p_0$. That is

$$u(r_2) = p_0$$

You have now attached numerical utilities to all three outcomes considered. You have also attached numerical average utilities to the two alternative decisions, to build and not to build. Call these two decisions (actions) a_1 and a_2, respectively. Thus

$$u(r_1) = 0 \,; \qquad u(r_2) = p_0 \,; \qquad u(r_3) = 1 \,;$$
$$\text{average utility if } a_1 \text{ is taken} = p_0$$
$$\text{average utility if } a_2 \text{ is taken} = p$$

Remember that p is your actual degree of belief in peace; while p_0 is that degree of belief in peace that would make you indifferent between the two decisions. If you have decided to build, this implies that, in your opinion, $p \geqslant 0_0$. If you have decided not to build, this implies that, in your opinion, $p \leqslant p_0$.

We have had occasion to discuss your preferences between results (for example, better to be alive and poor than to be dead: choice between r_2 and r_1) as well as between decisions (better to build than not to build: choice between a_1 and a_2). It is thus natural to extend the concept of utility accordingly, and speak, not only of a utility of a result, but also of a utility of a decision. In fact a 'result' can be regarded as a special case of a 'decision,' viz., a decision which can have only one result. Such was in fact the decision a_1 in our example; its unique result was r_2. Accordingly we might simply assign to it the utility $u(a_1) = u(r_2)$. On the other hand, decision a_2 is identified with a bundle of results (r_3 and r_1), each with a respective degree of belief (p and $1-p$). We can call such a bundle a 'prospect': it is a (subjective) probability distribution of results, a lottery. A prospect promising – as in the case of a_1 – a single result, may be called a sure prospect. It is, in fact, *also* a (subjective) probability distribution, with one of the results having probability one. Thus, when you compared the two decisions, you did, in fact, compare the following two probability distributions (or prospects).

Decision:	Probability of		
	r_1	r_2	r_3
a_1	0	1	0
a_2	$1-p$	0	p

One can say that, of two decisions (or of two corresponding prospects), you have chosen the one with a higher, or at least not lower, utility. If you choose a_1, then $u(a_1) \geqslant u(a_2)$. The principle of choosing the decision that results in a higher average utility can, then, be rephrased as follows: "the utility of a decision is the higher, the higher the average utility resulting from it." It will therefore not contradict this principle if you simply equate $u(a_1)$ and $u(a_2)$ with the corresponding average utilities. That is

$$u(a_1) = p_0\,; \qquad u(a_2) = p$$

You have thus scaled the utilities of prospects, sure as well as non-sure ones:

$$u(r_1) = 0\,; \quad u(r_2) = u(a_1) = p_0\,; \quad u(a_2) = p\,; \quad u(r_3) = 1$$

It will prove more convenient to use a notation that unifies the sure and non-sure prospects, by listing the alternative results and their corresponding probabilities. In this notation, the equations just given become

$$\begin{aligned} &u(r_1, r_2, r_3;\, 1, 0, 0) = 0\,; \\ &u(r_1, r_2, r_3;\, 0, 1, 0) = u(r_1, r_2, r_3;\, 1 - p_0, 0, p_0) = p_0 \\ &u(r_1, r_2, r_3;\, 1 - p, 0, p) = p\,; \\ &u(r_1, r_2, r_3;\, 0, 0, 1) = 1 \end{aligned}$$

It is easily checked that each of these equations satisfies the principle 'utility of a prospect equals its average utility', i.e., the average of the utilities of the component outcomes (sure prospects) promised by the prospect in question.

Note that the zero and the unit of the scale of utilities were chosen arbitrarily, by assigning utility 0 to the worst, and utility 1 to the best of the results considered. To this extent, the scale is arbitrary, just as is a temperature scale. If, for example, we had to put $u(r_1) = -10$ and $u(r_3) = +100$, the principle of choosing the decision with the higher average utility would yield [compare equations (1)]:

$$u(r_3) \cdot p + u(r_1) \cdot (1 - p) = 100 \cdot p - 10 \cdot (1 - p) = 110p - 10$$

as the average utility for the decision a_2; the latter we have also denoted by $(r_1, r_2, r_3; 1-p, 0, p)$. Thus if, as before, p_0 denotes the probability of peace that would make you indifferent between the two actions, our new scale will be (using both of the suggested notations):

$$\begin{aligned}
u(r_1) &= u(r_1, r_2, r_3; 1, 0, 0) = -10; \\
u(r_2) &= u(a_1) = u(r_1, r_2, r_3; 0, 1, 0) = u(r_1, r_2, r_3; \\
&\qquad\qquad 1 - p_0, 0, p_0) = 110p_0 - 10; \\
u(a_2) &= u(r_1, r_2, r_3; 1 - p, 0, p) = 110p - 10; \\
u(r_3) &= u(r_1, r_2, r_3; 0, 0, 1) = 100
\end{aligned}$$

We see that, to convert from the old to the new utility scale, one has to perform a 'linear transformation': that is, to multiply by a constant (110) and to add a constant (−10); just as we do in converting from Fahrenheit degrees to centigrades or from altitudes measured in feet over Lake Michigan level to altitudes in meters over sea level. In this sense, the utility scale that interprets your choices among decisions is 'determinate up to an arbitrary linear transformation'. (Even, measurements of geometrical distances or of physical weights are determinate up to an arbitrary linear transformation, although in those cases only the multiplying constant is arbitrary: the 'unit of measurement'.)

So far, we have treated a case in which only three alternative outcomes (r_1, r_2, r_3) are possible. What have we shown? We have shown that your decisions are consistent with a scale of utilities that satisfies the following principle: *choose the decision that results, on the average, in the highest utility.* After fixing arbitrarily the utilities of two of the outcomes (assigning a higher utility to the better one), the application of this principle results in a definite utility number for the third outcome, and also in definite utility numbers for all prospects that promise the three outcomes with pre-assigned probabilities.

II. THE GENERAL CASE: BERNOULLI NORM

Let us now relax the strait jacket of 'three outcomes only'. Let there be any (finite) number of outcomes, also called 'sure prospects'. Let us generalize even further, by considering prospects which promise, with preassigned probabilities, not only certain outcomes, but possibly also prospects. The case where a prospect is a lottery promising certain outcomes rather than a lottery promising certain lotteries is clearly a special one, with certain probabilities shrinking to zeros.

So far, the letters a_1, a_2 stood for decision or action, and each corresponded to a certain prospect. We shall continue to denote prospects by $a_1, a_2, \ldots$, but it will be convenient also to use the subsequent letters of the alphabet ($b, c, \ldots$) and also x. For probabilities, we shall use, as before, p; but q and π will also be needed.

I want to convince the reader that it will be possible for him to set up a scale of his utilities of all prospects, sure and otherwise, this scale satisfying the following property: if a prospect x is a lottery promising the prospects $a_1, a_2, \ldots, a_n$ with subjective probabilities $\pi_1, \ldots, \pi_n$, then

$$(2) \qquad u(x) = \sum_{1}^{n} u(a_1)\, \pi_1$$

That is, again: the utility of a prospect should equal the average of promised utilities.

If it is possible to interpret your behavior as satisfying (2), we shall say that you obey the 'Bernoulli Norm': see 'Historical Note', below.

The technical term for 'average of values of a variable, weighted by probabilities of their occurrences' is 'mathematical expectation' of that variable, or, more briefly its 'expected value'. The expression on the right-hand side of (2) is, then, the 'expected value of utility of the prospect x', or, still more briefly, 'expected utility of x'. What we try to show is: there exists a numerical scale of utility for all prospects, with the following property: the utility of a prospect equals its expected utility. Since you will decide in favor of a prospect with higher utility in preference to one with lower utility, you will choose a decision that maximizes the utility of a prospect; and, by the principle just mentioned (and that we are going to prove), this implies that you maximize the expected utility of a prospect.

Let a and b be two prospects (either sure or uncertain) facing the reader, and let him regard b as better than a. Consider the following classes of prospects:

1. a and b
2. all prospects that promise a or b
3. all prospects that are not better than b and not worse than a [Obviously (1) and possibly (2) are included in (3).]
4. all prospects that are better than b
5. all prospects that are worse than a.

The utilities in class (1) will be assigned arbitrarily, except for the condition that a is worse than b. We put $u(a)=0$, $u(b)=1$. [If classes (4) and (5) were empty, a might stand for 'agony' and b for 'bliss'!]

The utilities in class (2) will all lie between (and excluding) 0 and 1, for the following reason: Let a lottery c promise b if a possible event s happens, and a if it does not happen. Therefore, if you acquire c and s happens, you get something better than a; while if s does not happen you get a. Hence c is better than a. Similarly, c is worse than b. For, if you acquire c and s happens you get b; but if s does not happen you have something worse than b. Hence $u(a)<u(c)<u(b)$ and therefore $0<u(c)<$ <1, i.e., $u(c)$ is some proper fraction.

Moreover compare two lotteries in class (2): c_1 and c_2, where c_i promises b if the event s_i happens. Let p_i be the probability of s_i and suppose $p_1<p_2$. Then $u(c_1)<u(c_2)$, for the following reason. The lottery c_2 promises b with larger probability than does lottery c_2; but with smaller probability than does a direct offer of b. Therefore c_2 can be conceived of as a lottery that promises c_1 and b with certain probabilities.[5] Hence, by a reasoning similar to the one made before, c_2 must be better than c_1 and worse than b.

It follows that you will rank the utilities of the various prospects in class (2) by assigning increasing proper fractions as the probability p of getting b increases.

It is permissible therefore to choose as the utility number for a lottery the fraction p if the lottery promises b with probability p. We have thus scaled all prospects of class (2), and this scale fits with the boundary values $u(a)=0$ and $u(b)=1$, since a and b can themselves be called lotteries, with $p=0$ and $=1$, respectively.

Before proceeding to the remaining classes of prospects, let us satisfy ourselves that our scale, so far, has the desired property. Let a prospect x

be a lottery promising prospects [belonging to classes (1) and (2)] $c_1, \ldots, c_n$ with probabilities $\pi_1, \ldots, \pi_n$. Show that

$$(3) \qquad u(x) = \sum_1^n \pi_i u(c_i)$$

To prove (3), we replace $u(x)$ by the probability with which the lottery x promises b. This probability is compounded from $p_1, \ldots, p_n$, where p_i is the probability with which c_i promises b. Hence $u(x) = \sum_1^n \pi_i p_i$. But we have seen that $u(c_i) = p_i$. Hence (3) is true.

Consider now the class (3) of prospects. It includes class (1); and we have seen that it also includes class (2); but it includes more. We have covered those of the members of (3), that are a or b or lotteries promising a or b; and we were able to assign to each of these lotteries a utility p equal to the probability with which that lottery promises b. Of course, p ranges from 0 (the utility of a itself) to 1 (the utility of b itself). Now the utility of any member of class (3) must lie between 0 and 1 since it consists of prospects that are not better than b and not worse than a. Hence, any member of class (3) – say, d_1 – that is not a lottery promising a or b has a utility that is equal to that of one of those lotteries – call it c_1 – i.e., to some p, $0 \leqslant p \leqslant 1$. If we now form a lottery y that promises various members $d_1, \ldots, d_n$ of class (3) with probabilities $\pi_1, \ldots, \pi_n$, then y has the same utility as the lottery x considered in Equation (3). For, the event s_1 (with probability π_1) will give the subject the prospect d_1 if he had chosen y; and the prospect c_1 if he had chosen x. And so for $s_2, \ldots, s_n$. But since we have seen each d_i to have the same utility as the corresponding c_i (this utility being equal to the probability with which c_i promises b), it follows that the subject is indifferent between y and x. Thus (3) is extended to all members of the class (3), since $u(y)$ can replace $u(x)$ and each $u(d_i)$ can replace $u(c_1)$.

This would complete the proof if we could assume that there exists for each subject a worst and a best prospect, 'agony' and 'bliss' (a and b). If this is not the case, i.e., utility is not bounded and classes (4) and (5) are not empty, Equation (3) still holds good. To show this, it suffices to pick the worst and the best prospect – say, a' and b' – among those composing the particular lottery x [i.e., a' and b' will be among the $c_1, \ldots, c_n$ in (3)], and use a' and b' in the same way in which a and b were treated previously; i.e., create a new scale of utilities – say, u' – with

$u'(a')=0$, $u'(b')=1$, $u'(a)=p<q=u'(b)$, where p and q are certain probabilities; a and b having, respectively, the same utilities as certain two lotteries, each promising a' or b'. We see by former reasoning, that in terms of this new scale, (3) will be valid, that is

$$(4) \qquad u'(x) = \sum \pi_1 u'(c_1)$$

But this latter equation remains valid also if the function u' is replaced by any linear transform of it, $\alpha u' + \beta$ (this can be easily verified by substitution). Now, the functions u' and u are, in fact, linear transforms of each other, with (for any c) $u'(c)=(q-p)\,u(c)+p$ [i.e., the scale u' is obtained from the scale u by shifting the origin by p and multiplying the utility unit by $q-p$]. Hence the validity of (4) entails the validity of (3) for any prospects,[6] i.e., the validity of (2).

III. HISTORICAL NOTE

Suppose that you apply the utility scale just described to various amounts of monetary wealth, and discover that, for you, the utility can be regarded as proportional to money amount. Should your tastes happen to be of this kind then (since you have agreed that your choices are as described by the Bernoulli Norm and you therefore maximize the mathematical expectation of utility) you are a maximizer of the mathematical expectation of monetary wealth. And remember that this mathematical expectation was computed on the basis of your subjective probabilities.

Now, the idea that a consistent decision-maker chooses a bet that gives him the maximum expected monetary wealth, computed on the basis of his subjective probabilities, can be traced back to Thomas Bayes (eighteenth century). Daniel Bernoulli who lived in that same century was not so clear about the subjective nature of the probabilities that can be said to underline human choice. He assumed people to know the true odds in a game, and neglected the case when a man has no sufficient theory or no large sample to compute the odds with precision. But, on the other hand, Bernoulli was emphatic (as Bayes was not: remember that Bayes dealt with money instead of utilities) about the subjective nature of preferences. Unless your tastes are of a peculiar character, utilities are not proportional to money amounts (and moreover they can and should be attached to many other objects of choice besides money!), and one must be careful to state that the consistent decision-maker maximizes his expected utility, not his expected monetary wealth. This is what we called the Bernoulli Norm. In stating it, we did describe the probabilities used as subjective and called them sometimes degrees of belief. But we did not say how they too (like the equally subjective utility numbers) can be derived as characterizing a consistent decision-maker's behavior. This was done by the late Frank Ramsey in 1926, and more recently by De Finetti and by L. J. Savage. Their approach will be outlined in our concluding section.

IV. THE RAMSEY NORM

I shall now try to convince you that your decisions, if consistent, can be interpreted in the following manner: there exist utility numbers, attached to outcomes of your actions, and there exist degrees of belief, attached to the future states of the world, with the following property: if for each of your possible actions the expected utility (i.e., the mathematical expectation of utility of outcomes) were computed on the basis of your degrees of belief, then the action chosen by you would be the one with the highest expected utility. We may call this the Ramsey Norm.

Imagine that the following eight actions $a_1, \ldots, a_8$ will have one of the two outcomes, Death (D) or Life (L), depending on whether the world will be in the state s_1 or s_2 or s_3 (mutually exclusive), as shown in the following table which, as you can convince yourself, exhausts all possible triplets of L- and D-symbols:

	States of World			Group
Actions	s_1	s_2	s_3	
a_1	D	D	D	1
a_2	L	D	D	2
a_3	D	L	D	2
a_4	D	D	L	2
a_5	D	L	L	3
a_6	L	D	L	3
a_7	L	L	D	3
a_8	L	L	L	4

I assume that you prefer Life to Death. Then you will prefer a_8 to a_7 because a_8 has a better outcome that a_7 in state s_3, and the same outcome as a_7 otherwise. By this reasoning, you will prefer the action a_8 to any of the actions in group 3; you will prefer any action in 3 and any one in 2 to the action a_1.

Now suppose, in addition, that you happen to be indifferent between a_2, a_3, and a_4. If this is the case we shall say that your degrees of belief in the occurrence of each of the states s_1, s_2, s_3 are $\frac{1}{3}, \frac{1}{3}, \frac{1}{3}$; and we shall assign to the occurrence of the state s_1 *or* s_2 (and similarly: of the state s_1 *or* s_3; and s_2 *or* s_3) the degree of belief $\frac{2}{3}$. Moreover: would it be reasonable for you to be indifferent within group 2 and not to be indifferent within group 3? Would this not mean that you grant the three possible future states of the world an equal degree of belief as long as rewards or punishments are attached to them in a certain way, but revise your beliefs when the rewards and punishments are interchanged? This would be unreasonable.

We thus have:

$$u(a_1) < u(a_2) = u(a_3) = u(a_4) < u(a_5) = u(a_6) = u(a_7) < < u(a_8).$$

We now proceed to scale these utilities. We are free to fix the utility of Life (like the utility of 'bliss' in an earlier part of the paper) at 1, and the utility of Death at 0. Then the utilities of prospects will also fall in their places, being equal to the probability of Life as promised in a given prospect. That is, we obtain $u(a_1)=0$; $u(a_8)=1$; $u(a_2)=u(a_3)=u(a_4)=\frac{1}{3}$; $u(a_5)=u(a_6)=u(a_7)=\frac{2}{3}$. We shall find as before that this utility scale is consistent with your being a maximizer of expected utility.

Thus, not only your utilities but also your degrees of belief can be derived from your behavior – including the indifference which you have shown in choosing within group 2 of actions (and also – as consistency required – within the group 3 of actions).

We have thus shown that it was possible to interpret your choices as consistent with the existence of utilities and subjective probabilities and with the maximization of expected utility. Granted that the example was a special one. It can be easily extended to n (instead of 3) states of the world, and degrees of belief $0, 1/n, 2/n, \ldots, (n-1)/n, 1$ can then be defined – if one can catch you as being indifferent within a certain group of decisions.

How to arrange for a demarcation of states of the world that would make this possible requires a more complete and rigorous logical analysis. (This has been done by L. J. Savage.) Here we have had to content ourselves with a mere sketch.

NOTES

1 For example, at the colloquium on risk in econometrics, held in 1952; its Proceedings published by the Centre National de la Recherche Scientifique, Paris, 1953.

2 I. N. Herstein and John Milnor, 'An Axiomatic Approach to Measurable Utility', *Econometrica*, 1953.

3 John Wiley and Sons, 1954.

4 *Selected Essays*, 1, 2.

5 Let these probabilities be q and $1-q$, respectively, q is easy to find (though it is not really necessary for our purpose) by posing

$$q \cdot p_1 + (1 - q) \cdot 1 = p_2$$

since p_2, the chance of obtaining b, must be equal to the chance (in the new lottery) of getting it by virtue of having gotten c_1, *plus* the chance of getting it directly. We have $q = (1 - p_2)/(1 - p_1)$.

6 With $u(a) = 0$ and $u(b) = 1$, the utility $u(e)$ of a member of class (4) and the utility $u(f)$ of a member of class (5) are easily shown to be

$$u(e) = \frac{1}{q} > 1; \quad u(f) = 1 - \frac{1}{r} < 0$$

where q and r are probabilities defined as follows: the subject is indifferent between b and a lottery promising e or with respective probabilities q and $1-q$; and he is indifferent between a and a lottery promising f or b with respective probabilities r and $1-r$. It is easily verified that with these definitions,

$$u(e) \cdot q + u(a) \cdot (1 - q) = u(b)$$

and

$$u(f) \cdot r - u(b) \cdot (1 - r) = u(a)$$

4

PROBABILITY IN THE SOCIAL SCIENCES

(1954)

I. PROBABILITIES AND THE NORMS OF BEHAVIOR

Recently,[1] the U.N. forces in Korea faced the choice between two decisions: (I) to cross the 38° parallel or (II) not to cross it. Their commanders did not know whether, if the parallel were crossed, the Chinese adversary would or would not answer by counter-attacking in superior power, from across Korea's Northern border. In the language of current newspapers, our officers did not know whether the Chinese did or did not have 'aggressive intentions'. This is a vague term. The following table gives, however, an implicit definition that is precise enough. The intentions of the adversary are defined by their results, as follows:

TABLE I.1

Chinese behavior	Our behavior (I) Cross the parallel	 (II) Don't cross the parallel
(a) 'aggressive'	U.N.Losses	Stalemate
(b) 'non-aggressive'	U.N.Gains	Stalemate

We shall assume that, from the U.N. point of view, gains are preferable to stalemate, and stalemate is preferable to losses. We shall use the phrase 'probability is equal to one' as equivalent to 'it is certain'. Now suppose the probability of the Chinese being 'non-aggressive' is one. Then policy (I) produces a result (gains) preferable to the result (stalemate) of policy (II). The U.N. commander 'should' choose (I). If the probability of (b) were not one but zero – i.e., if the probability of (a) were one – he 'should' choose (II). Thus if we know that our commander was sure (rightly or wrongly) of his opponent's intentions and has done what he 'should' have done, then his opinion about those intentions – his assignment of probabilities to (a) and (b) – would be revealed by this action.

A similar inference from action to opinion, under the assumption that the acting person is doing what he 'should' be doing, can be made also in a more general case: namely, in the case when our commander is not necessarily sure as to the adversary's intentions, and thus associates them with probabilities that are not necessarily 1 or 0 but may be intermediate between 1 and 0. Such fractional probabilities we have not yet defined. Yet you have no doubt acted on the basis of judgments such as 'an assertion is almost certain to be true' (='is very probable'), 'almost certain to be untrue' (=has small probability), 'as likely as not to be true' (=has probability $\frac{1}{2}$).

Let us look into this more carefully. To avoid terminological confusion, let us call the probabilities assigned by our commander to the alternatives (a) and (b), his 'subjective probabilities'. We are not interested at present in how they originate – whether the commander derived them from some systematic observations, or based them on some vague experience, or even possibly on mere prejudice. We shall explore, instead, *whether these subjective probabilities can be defined in terms of his action.* The suspicion that this can be done is suggested by the following. Suppose our commander is 'almost certain' (subjective probability 'a little below one') that (b) is true; then, is it not right to say that he 'should' cross the 38° parallel? If he is 'almost certain' that (b) is not true (subjective probability 'a little above zero'), he 'should' not cross. One may therefore be tempted to say that there exists a certain critical level for the subjective probability of (b), with the following property: if the subjective probability of (b) is above this level, our commander chooses (I); if it is below, he chooses (II). 'Man is the measure' – if not of all things then, at least, of his own subjective probabilities, as revealed by his action.

A little reflection shows, however, that the commander's action cannot have been determined by his subjective probabilities, unless some – equally subjective – 'values' or 'utilities' had been attached to the outcomes of his actions – to the 'gains', 'losses' and 'stalemates' entered in our table. As a matter of fact, we had already made a statement about the utilities of these outcomes, when we said that gains are preferred to stalemate and stalemate is preferred to losses. If the three outcomes are thus 'completely ordered', we can attach to them 'utility numbers' which would be ordered in a corresponding fashion: for example, 7, 5, 1; or 6, 4, 2; or log6, log4, log2; – in short, any decreasing sequence of three numbers. If any such sequence is used to designate utility numbers, the outcome with a higher number will be preferred to one with a lower number. Yet such ordering of the outcomes is not sufficient to determine choice of action, even if the subjective probabilities of outcomes of a given action are fixed.

Suppose, for example, that two U.N. officers, an American and a South-Korean, agree that the Chinese are as likely as not to counter-attack if we cross 38° parallel. Yet the American may disfavor the crossing, while the South-Korean may advocate it. That is, the American may prefer a stalemate to a 50–50 chance of gains or losses; while the South-Korean (possibly reflecting his government's eagerness to re-unite the country) has an opposite preference. Thus, choice is determined by the complete ordering (the 'order of preferences') of probability distributions of outcomes, not by the complete ordering of the outcomes themselves.

The complete ordering of probability distributions is consistent with (though not necessarily equivalent to) assigning 'utility numbers' to probability distributions of outcomes, as well as to the outcomes themselves, according to the following rule: the utility number attached to a given probability distribution of outcomes equals the average of the utility numbers of the outcomes, weighted with the respective probabilities of those outcomes.[2]

In our example, both the American and the South-Korean may assign the same utility numbers to the best and the worst outcome: say 100 to 'gains', 0 to 'losses'. If they both want to maximize the expected utility, then their assumed disagreement about what to do reveals that, for the American, the utility of a stalemate is larger than 50 – namely, larger than $(\frac{1}{2})(100)+(\frac{1}{2})(0)$ – while for the South-Korean it is less than 50. One can, in fact, imagine an experiment in which a commander has to make (hypothetical) decisions, being faced not only with the choice 'a stalemate or a 50–50 chance of gains or losses', but also with choices such as 'a stalemate or a 60–40 chance of gains or losses', 'a stalemate or a 70–30 chance of gains or losses', etc. Suppose one would thus find a break-even point: for example, suppose that the commander has decided to cross the parallel if he felt that the chance of gains is larger than or equal to 65%; and not to cross if he felt the chance of gains is smaller than 65%. Then we can say that, for him, stalemate is equivalent to a 65–35 chance of gains or losses. Consequently, on a scale of utilities in which 100 and 0 are, respectively, assigned to gains and losses, the utility of stalemate (for that commander) will be 65, because (100) (65%) + (0) (35%) = 65. Thus, if we fix the '0' and '100' points in any arbitrary way (this is similar to the '0' and '212' points of the Fahrenheit scale, or the '0' and '100' of the centigrade scale of temperature), and if we assume that the man is 'doing what he should do' and that he 'should' maximize expected utility, then his actual responses to given probabilities of outcomes of his actions can be interpreted as revealing the utility numbers attached to each of those outcomes.[3]

Conversely, if the utilities attached by the decision-make to alternative outcomes are known, it is possible to infer from his decisions the subjective probabilities that he attaches to alternative outcomes – provided that he 'is doing what he should do' and that he 'should' always maximize expected utility.

It is historically interesting that Thomas Bayes, one of the founders of the theory of probability, used just this kind of inference in order to define probability: In his posthumous essay (famous for another reason) we read[4]

The probability of any event is the ratio between the value at which an expectation depending on the happening of the event ought to be computed, and the value of the thing expected upon its happening (Definition 5); and
'If a person has an expectation depending on the happening of an event, the probability of the event is to the probability of its failure as his loss if it fails to his gain if it happens' (Proposition 2).

Note Bayes' phrase 'ought to be computed'. His definition is a norm of behavior. To your gain (a_1 dollars, say) that is contingent upon an uncertain event, there 'ought to' correspond in your mind a smaller but sure gain (a dollars, say) such that you are indifferent between gaining a_1 upon the happening of the uncertain event, or gaining a with certainty. Hence, there is (or rather ought to be) in your mind also a ratio of these two numbers, $a/a_1 = p_1$, say. It is called by Bayes, probability of the event; while he calls a the 'expectation'. Suppose further that, if the event fails to happen, you neither gain nor lose. Then clearly $a = a_1 \cdot p_1 + 0 \cdot (1 - p_1)$ is the average of gain and loss, weighted with their respective probabilities. You 'ought to compute' this weighted average before making a choice. Of two uncertain gains choose the one with the higher value of expection.

In Bayes' second quoted statement the person must have chosen to conclude a fair bet – that is, the expection value $p_1 a_1 + p_2 a_2 = 0$, where the loss (taken as a positive number) equals to $-a_2$ and has probability $p_2(=1-p_1)$. Hence $p_1/p_2 = -a_2/a_1$.

No problem of ascertaining utility arises for Bayes because his gains and losses are money amounts. We can reformulate his definition of probability as the following normative statement (which we shall call 'Bayes' norm'):

Let the possible decisions be numbered $1, \ldots, n$; let the possible states of the world be numbered $1, \ldots, m$. Denote by a_{ij} the gain that the person will obtain if he takes the jth decision, and the world is in its ith state. Then, if the person behaves 'as he should', there exists a set of m non-negative numbers p_i which add up to unity

$$\sum_{i=1}^{m} p_i = 1$$

and have the following property: one decision (say the jth) is not preferred to another (say the kth) when and only when

$$\sum_{i=1}^{m} p_i a_{ij} \leqslant \sum_{i=1}^{m} p_i a_{ik} \quad (j, k = 1, \ldots, n) \tag{1.1}$$

A number p_i is called the (subjective) probability of the ith state of the world; the two sums in (1.1) are called expected gains associated with, respectively, the jth and the kth decision.

As an example (with $m=n=2$), the possible gains of a man who has decided between buying and not buying stocks are tabulated (See Table I.2.)

If the subject decides according to the norm thus postulated, then there must exist subjective probabilities p_1, $p_2(=1-p_1)$, with the following property: $p_1a_{11}+p_2a_{21} \leqslant p_1a_{12}+p_2a_{22}$ if the subject does not prefer buying to not buying; and such that $p_1a_{11}+p_{21}a_{21} \geqslant p_1a_{12}+p_2a_{22}$ if he does not prefer not buying to buying. Consequently, if he is indifferent between buying and not buying, both these relations are true so that

$$p_1a_{11} + p_2a_{21} = p_1a_{12} + p_2a_{22}$$

$$\frac{p_1}{p_2} = \frac{a_{22} - a_{21}}{a_{11} - a_{12}}, \quad \text{where} \quad p_1 + p_2 = 1. \tag{1.2}$$

(Note that if we had put, for simplicity, $a_{12}=a_{22}=0$, we would obtain Bayes' 'Proposition 2'). Thus by confronting the subject with varying quadruplets of prospective gains one can estimate the subjective probabilities he assigns to the stocks' rise or fall, respectively. For example if (1.2) is satisfied for $a_{11}=-100$ dollars, $a_{21}=+300$ dollars, and $a_{12}==a_{22}=0$, then 'the odds are' $p_1:p_2=3:1$, in favor of falling stocks; or $p_1=\frac{3}{4}, p_2=\frac{1}{4}$.

TABLE I.2

States of the world $i=$	Decisions $j=$ 1. Buy	2. Don't buy
1. Stocks will fall	a_{11}	a_{12}
2. Stocks will rise	a_{21}	a_{22}

It is empirically ascertainable whether a subject's behavior is consistent with this norm. If it is, the subjective probabilities themselves are ascertainable. Consider, for example, the following "payoff matrices' – each being simply the Table 1.2, with captions omitted and letters a_{ij} replaced by dollar figures:

TABLE I.3

$$\begin{pmatrix}-100 & 0\\ 300 & 0\end{pmatrix};\quad \begin{pmatrix}-1 & 0\\ 3 & 0\end{pmatrix};\quad \begin{pmatrix}-2 & -1\\ 4 & 1\end{pmatrix};\quad \begin{pmatrix}-1 & 0\\ 2 & 0\end{pmatrix}.$$

Suppose that the subject is indifferent between buying and not buying when the gains are as in the first matrix. This is simply the case already studied; it has revealed subjective odds 3:1 in favor of falling stocks. Now, the norm implies that if he is indifferent between buying and not buying when faced with the first matrix, he should also be indifferent between buying and not buying when faced with the second and third matrices, but should not buy when faced with the fourth matrix of Table I:3: because not only

$$(-100)\left(\tfrac{3}{4}\right)+(300)\left(\tfrac{1}{4}\right)=(0)\left(\tfrac{3}{4}\right)+(0)\left(\tfrac{1}{4}\right)\quad \text{but also}$$
$$(-1)\left(\tfrac{3}{4}\right)+(3)\left(\tfrac{1}{4}\right)=(0)\left(\tfrac{3}{4}\right)+(0)\left(\tfrac{1}{4}\right)\quad \text{and also}$$
$$(-2)\left(\tfrac{3}{4}\right)+(4)\left(\tfrac{1}{4}\right)=(-1)\left(\tfrac{3}{4}\right)+(1)\left(\tfrac{1}{4}\right);\quad \text{while}$$
$$(-1)\left(\tfrac{3}{4}\right)+(2)\left(\tfrac{1}{4}\right)<(0)\left(\tfrac{3}{4}\right)+(0)\left(\tfrac{1}{4}\right).$$

Such empirical tests of consistency of a man's behavior with some given norm have been occasionally described as meaningless; with the consequence drawn that the (approximate) measurement of subjective probabilities has no meaning. The argument is as follows. Suppose the subject is indifferent between buying and not buying when faced with the first matrix of Table I.3, and also when faced with the fourth matrix. This need not imply that his behavior is inconsistent with Bayes' norm. The subject may have merely changed, during the time required by the experiments, his subjective odds, from 3:1 to 2:1 [since $(-1)(\frac{2}{3})+(2)(\frac{1}{3})=0$]. Suppose, on the other hand, that the subject, when faced with different payoff matrices, almost always makes the same choices as he would make if he maintained unchanged subjective odds and obeyed the Bayes' norm. Yet the subject may have behaved in contradiction with Bayes' norm; he may have changed his opinion about the odds, from experiment to experiment, in exactly such a fashion that the contradiction was masked.

This objection makes it necessary to reformulate every behavior norm by requiring that it should be 'approximately' valid during a specified period of time. But what is meant by 'approximate', and how to determine the time interval over which the norm is valid? This will depend on the use that has to be made of the norm in practice. The next two lectures give several illustrations of how the merely 'approximate' description of human behavior is used for prediction and policy.

What we called the Bayes' norm is quite innocent of the concept of utility. Herein lies its limitation. Most decisions do not result in monetary gains and losses. The military gain, or loss, in our Korean example (Table I.1) is not expressible, either as a money amount or as any other single quantity. It is, at best, a combination of quantities (a 'vector'): so and so many guns, prisoners, villages taken. To be sure (and this will help us later), even when the alternative outcomes differ only because of the presence or absence of some 'qualitative' attributes ('to live in the corn-belt', 'to die in New York') one can express them as a combination of quantities, each possibly having only a finite number of values: e.g., life or death = 1 or 2; corn-belt or New York or West Coast = 1 or 2 or 3; so that life in the corn-belt = vector (1,1). But this may be inconvenient. For our purposes, it is unnecessary. Our Korean example has shown, in a preliminary way, that we can interpret choices by assigning subjective 'utility numbers' to alternative events, the events themselves not having been expressed either as values of single numerical variables (such as the number of guns or of prisoners) nor as combinations of such values (the number of guns and of prisoners). We have seen that, *given the probabilities* of outcomes, one can infer from manifest decisions to underlying subjective utilities, provided the subject has chosen 'as he ought to'. To formalize this statement, let us replace Bayes' norm by the following one:

Let A be the set of all possible outcomes of the subject's decisions. Let a_{ij} $(i=1,\dots m;\ 1,\dots,n)$ be that element of A which he associates with the ith state of the world and his jth decision. If the probability assigned by the subject to the ith state of the world is

$$p_i (p_i \geqslant 0; \textstyle\sum p_i = 1; i = 1, \dots, m)$$

and if he behaves 'as he should' then there exists a real valued function $u(a_{ij}) = u_{ij}$ such that one decision (say, the jth) is not preferred to another (say, the kth) when and only when

$$(3) \qquad \sum_{i=1}^{m} p_i u_{ij} \leqslant \sum_{i=1}^{m} p_i u_{ik} \quad (j, k = 1, \dots, n).$$

The function $u(\ )$ is called utility function; its value u_{ij} is called the utility of the outcome a_{ij}. The two sums in (3) are called expected utilities associated, respectively, with the jth and the kth decision.

The norm just stated presupposes that probabilities are given to the subject; and his actual decisions reveal his system of utilities.

This is, in a sense, opposite to Bayes' norm because if a subject acts according to Bayes' norm his actual decisions reveal his subjective probabilities; while the utilities are given, and are simply identical with amounts of money. We may call the norm just stated, the 'Daniel Bernoulli norm'.[5] His concept of 'moral expectation' is, in fact, identical with the 'expected utility' of the statement just formulated, at least for the special case when each a_{ij} is a number, viz., the monetary wealth of the subject. More generally, the a_{ij} may denote any kind of situation which the subject expects to be the result of a given decision of his.

To exemplify Bernoulli's norm we may use the captions of Table I.2 but replace monetary gains a_{ij} by utility numbers u_{ij}. We can, similarly, interpret the numbers entered in Table I.3 as utility numbers. Note that, in the case when these numbers measure the utilities associated with the monetary gains, it is the utilities not the dollar amounts that have, for example, in the first column of the first matrix, the ratio 1:3. If the person knows (or thinks he knows) the odds to be 3:1 in favor of stocks falling, he will be indifferent between buying and not buying if faced with the first three matrices; and will not buy if faced with the fourth.

If the probability estimates of the subject are known, and if he behaves according to the 'D. Bernoulli norm', it is possible to ascertain the utility numbers he assigns to various events, although only (as with centigrades and Fahrenheit degrees) up to two arbitrary constants. For example, suppose the subject is indifferent between buying and not buying stock when faced with the payoff matrix in dollars, given on the left part of the Table I.4.

TABLE I.4

Payoff in dollars		Payoff in utilities	
$a_{11} = -100$	$a_{12} = 50$	$u_{11} = u(-100) = 0$	$u_{12} = u(50) = ?$
$a_{21} = 200$	$a_{22} = 50$	$u_{21} = u(200) = 1$	$u_{21} = u(50) = ?$

Suppose (as before) that the odds are 3:1 in favor of the first row (falling stock prices). On the right side of Table I.4, we have fixed arbitrarily the zero and unity of the utility scale: 0 = utility of $-\$100$; 1 = utility of \$200. What is, on this scale, the utility of \$50? From the subject's indifference between the two decisions (represented, respectively, by the first and second column) we conclude, using D. Bernoulli's norm: $(0)\ (\frac{3}{4}) + {}$ $+ (1)\ (\frac{1}{4}) = u\ (50) = 0.25$. Thus, by varying the odds on which the subject is supposed to base his decision, and finding dollar payoff matrices such that the subject is indifferent between to decisions, one obtains the subject's utility scale for various outcomes of his decisions having arbitrarily fixed two points on this scale. This has been essentially the procedure of Mosteller and Nogee, already mentioned. The experimental difficulty includes, in particular, the ascertaining that the subject has 'learned' the odds that he is told are prevailing. Moreover, analogous to the discussion we had on the occasion of the Bayes' norm one has to meet the objection that the person may change his behavior parameters (his utility numbers, in the present case) during the experiment.

In the example just used, the outcomes a_{ij} were dollar amounts; it was shown that the utility number corresponding to any given dollar gain or loss – and thus the 'utility function of money gains' – can be ascertained from the actual choices of a subject assumed to obey a certain norm. Instead, the a_{ij} might equally well have been, not dollar gains or losses, nor the values of any other single variable (number of prisoners taken), but vectors of quantities, or 'qualitative' outcomes. Our example illustrates, incidentally, that Bayes' norm is not serviceable, not only because it has to deal with outcomes that are values of a single variable only, but also because it disagrees with the experience that people who can be expected to behave 'as they should' may have non-linear utility functions of money: the gain of $50 is half-way between −$100 and +$200; yet the choice has proved consistent with the utility of $50 being not half-way but one-quarter of the distance between −$100 and +$200. It seems that Bayes overlooked the reasons which had led his predecessors (Daniel Bernoulli, Cramer) to insist on the difference between 'physical wealth' and 'moral wealth': the latter not being, in general, proportional to the former. Present day economists call the latter, 'utility' (of a given monetary wealth or, more generally and precisely, of a given combination of goods in one's present and future possession). Even for the directors of a corporate firm, who decide on the basis of monetary profits and losses and not of ultimate 'pleasures and pains', it is not true that a dollar has the same weight in the decision regardless of the dollars already earned. A loss leading to bankruptcy subtracts more from the utility than a profit of equal size adds to it – the utility function is non-linear. For an attacker bent on destruction, the utility is not a linear function of the physical damage inflicted upon the enemy; rather, destruction beyond a certain point is useless to the attacker. And so on.

The D. Bernoulli norm, formulated in its essence around 1730, was accepted by modern economists like Alfred Marshall. But the assumption that a person computes and compares expected utilities associated with his alternative decisions may appear as complicated and artificial (not more or less, though, than does the computation of expected monetary gains which se med so evident to Bayes as to make him base on it his definition of probability!) In our days, von Neumann and Morgenstern, the authors of the *Theory of Games*, improved on their predecessors by providing a set of postulates, equivalent to, but in some sense simpler more appealing than the postulate of maximizing expected utility. More recent writers have tried to propose postulates that are still more 'transparent'.[6]

It is a remarkable psychological fact that a proposition may be equivalent to a set of intuitively appealing propositions and yet be not itself intuitively appealing. There would be otherwise no need for mathematical textbooks! This is a human limitation. For God, of course, the simplest axioms and the most difficult theorems are equally obvious, and their roles interchangeable. Let us, then, look at behavior postulates that are logically equivalent to but 'psychologically' simpler than the Bernoulli norm.

Let A, B, C,... denote probability distributions of outcomes; (in a special case a 'distribution' may assign probability 1 to one event, and 0 to all others; it is, in this case, identical with that single event). Denote by ABp the following probability distribution: 'probability p that the distribution is A; probability 1-p that the distribution is B'. Let $A \leqslant B$ mean 'A is not preferred to (or 'not better than') B'. '$A = B$' will be written instead of '$A \leqslant B$ and $B \leqslant A$' and will mean 'the subject is indifferent between A and B'. '$A < B$' will be written instead of '$A \leqslant B$ and not $B \leqslant A$' and will mean 'A is worse than B'. Then the subject 'should' obey the following rules:

I. The A, B, C,... are 'completely ordered' by the relation $\leqslant$; that is,
   (1) $A \leqslant B$ or $B \leqslant A$ ('comparability');
   (2) if $A \leqslant B$ and $B \leqslant C$ then $A \leqslant C$ ('transivity').

II. If $A = B$ then $CAp = CBp$.

III. If $A < B$ and $B < C$ then there exists a unique p such that $B = ACp$.

Rule I needs no explanation. A verbal comment on Rule II can be provided as follows. If A is not preferred to B and B is not preferred to C, I am indifferent as between the two. I am now offered two lotteries – one promising either C or A, with odds $p:(1-p)$, and the other promising either C or B, with the same odds. Thus the same outcome, C, with probability p, will occur on both lotteries; and if C does not occur then the first lottery will give me A, while the second will give me B. But I am indifferent between A and B. Hence, there is no reason for me to prefer one lottery to another.

Rule III asserts, in a rather strong form, the 'continuity' of the preference relation. Actually a milder formulation of Rule III, and also of Rule II would suffice to obtain the needed result, viz., the 'D. Bernoulli norm'. Our stronger formulation gives an easier, though more superficial, insight into the matter, although, even so, I shall have merely to hint at the proof. Note first that our rules permit us to 'calibrate' a utility scale as one does a thermometer. Choose three prospects A, B, C such that I am not indifferent between any two of them. Then, by Rule I, they can be ordered in a unique fashion. Suppose this order is: B is preferred to C, and C to A. On a horizontal straight line, plot them in the order (from left to right): A, C, B (Figure I.5). Call a number $u(A)$ the utility of A; this will be also the utility of all prospects A', A'', which, for me, are neither better nor worse than A. Similarly call $u(B)$ the utility of B and its equivalents. What number $u(C)$ shall we then have to assign to the utility of C and of its equivalents? By Rule III there exists a unique probability p such that, to me, C is equivalent to BAp. Call $u(C)$ the number equal to $pu(B)+(1-p)$ $u(A)$. In particular if we arbitrarily fix $u(A)=0$ and $u(B)=1$ then $u(C)$ is simply equal to p. We can now place C on our scale (Figure I.5), making the distance AB to represent one utility unit, and the distance AC to represent p utility units $(0<p<1)$. By Rule II, the number p will also measure the utility of all lotteries such as $A'Bp$, $AB'p$, $A'B'p$, where A' is equivalent to A and B' is equivalent to B. We can thus 'calibrate' the utility scale for all prospects which are not better than B and not worse than A: they will be expressed by appropriate numbers ranging from 0 to 1. If a prospect D is worse than A, then A lies on our scale between D and B. Suppose the odds (those required by the Rule III) which make A equivalent to a lottery promising B or D are q: $(1-q)$; that is, I am indifferent between A and BDq. Then call the utility of D, $u(D)$, a number such that $u(B)\cdot q+u(D)$ $(1-q)=u(A)$. With $u(A)=0$ and $u(B)=1$ this makes $u(D)=-q/(1-q)$.

Outcomes:	D	A	C	B	E
Utilities:	$-q/(1-q)$	0	p	1	$1/r$

$$\overline{AC}:\ \overline{CB} = p:(1-p);\ u(C) = u(B)\cdot p+u(A)\cdot(1-p)$$

$$\overline{BA}:\ \overline{AC} = q:(1-q);\ u(A) = u(B)\cdot q+u(D)\cdot(1-q)$$

$$\overline{AB}:\ \overline{BE} = r:(1-r);\ u(B) = u(E)\cdot r+u(A)\cdot(1-r)$$

Fig. I.5

By an analogous procedure utility numbers are assigned to prospects – such as E in our figure – that are better than B. We have thus calibrated the utilities of all possible prospects. If we now assign the numbers 0 and 1 to the utilities not of A and B, but of some other pair of (non-equivalent) prospects, the origin and the unit of measurement of utilities is changed (just like we can measure the altitude of a mountain from the sea level as well as from a lake level, in yards as well as in feet). But in any case, the Bernoulli norm will follow. For, to take up first the case when a prospect involves only two alternative outcomes, we have seen (see Figure I.5) that the utility of such a prospect equals the sum of the utilities of the outcomes, multiplied by respective probabilities; i.e., the utility of a prospect equals its 'expected utility'. And since higher utilities are preferred to smaller ones, a prospect will not be preferred to another one unless its expected utility is higher. To extend this to the case of prospects involving more than two alternative outcomes is a matter of easy algebra. We shall skip it.

Our Figure I.5 could be also used to explain the approach of Bayes, if we reverse the problem and consider the outcomes as represented by given distances from the zero-point, measured in money units: $A=0$ dollars, $B=1$ dollar. Then Bayes defines the probability of, say, C, by the ratio of the distances $\overline{AC}:\overline{AB}$. This 'calibrates' probabilities.

We can say that in the Bayes norm the utilities were assumed objectively given (viz., identical with money amounts), and the probabilities were derived as parameters of the subject's behavior, as his 'degrees of belief'. Contrariwise, the Bernoulli norm assumes probabilities to be objectively given and derives subjective utilities. We had criticized Bayes' norm for its identifying the outcomes of decisions with the values of a single variable (such as the money gain) observable without reference to the subject. But a similar criticism applies to the Bernoulli norm. The probabilities on which the subject bases his action need not be identical with some objective properties of chance devices (cards, dice) which the experimenter uses. This was observed by the English mathematician and logician, F. P. Ramsey. He shows that manifest decisions can be thought of as revealing *both* the subject's probabilities *and* utilities. We can call 'Ramsey's norm' the following statement:

Let A be the set of all possible outcomes of the subject's decisions. Let a_{ij}

($i=1,\ldots,m; j=1,\ldots,n$) be that element of A which he associates with the ith state of the world and with his jth decision. If the subject behaves 'as he should', then there exists a unique set of numbers $p_i(p_i \geqslant 0; \sum p_i = 1; i=1,\ldots,m)$ and a real valued function $u(a_{ij}) = u_{ij}$ such that one decision (say, the jth) is not preferred to another (say, the kth) when and only when

$$\sum_{i=1}^{m} p_i u_{ij} \leqslant \sum_{i=1}^{m} p_i u_{ik} (j, k = 1, \ldots, n). \tag{3}$$

The numbers p_i are called subjective probabilities (or degrees of belief). The function $u(a_{ij})$ is called utility function; its value u_{ij} is called the utility of the outcome a_{ij}. The two sums in (3) are called expected utilities associated, respectively, with the jth and the kth decision.

A set of behavior rules, equivalent to Ramsey's norm but 'psychologically' more appealing was proposed by Ramsey himself and, in our days, by De Finetti and, especially, by Savage.[7] It would be difficult to convey their proofs in this lecture. But it is possible to indicate that subjective probabilities can be defined on the basis of observable decisions of a subject, even if one rejects the identification (practised by Bayes) between utilities and money gains; and to indicate how this definition of probability is related to the norm requiring maximization of expected utility. Consider the matrix in Table I.6 of outcomes a_{ij}, with $m=n=2$. Suppose I am indifferent between the two decisions. Then Ramsey will define the degrees

TABLE I.6

States of the world (i)	Decisions (j)	
	1	2
1	α	β
2	β	α

of belief in (or the subjective probability of) each of the two states of the world as $p_1 = p_2 = \frac{1}{2}$. For example, suppose an urn contains white and red balls and I am given the choice between the following two options: (1) if I draw white, I die; if red, I live; (2) if I draw red, I die; if white, I live. If I am indifferent between the two options (but not between life and death) I have equal degrees of belief (defined as $\frac{1}{2}$) that the ball drawn will be white or red. We postulate that the subject has consistent degree of belief. That is, he will remain indifferent between any two options represented by the matrix of Table I.6, regardless of what meaning is given to the outcomes α and β. Having thus defined subjective probability$=\frac{1}{2}$ (but not yet any other probabilities) enables Ramsey to define a scale of measurable utilities, as follows. An outcome γ is said to be 'half-way' between α and β if the subject is indifferent between γ and the prospect of having α or β with subjective odds $\frac{1}{2}:\frac{1}{2}$. It is again postulated that the subject is consistent, in the sense that γ will remain 'half-way' between α and β regardless of the particular pair of the states of the world to which the subjective probabilities $\frac{1}{2}$, $\frac{1}{2}$ are attached. Now Ramsey can define the utility of α as zero, the utility of γ as 1, the utility of β as 2, and (with the help of some further axioms on order and continuity) he can construct the scale of utilities. This brings him to the same point at which Bayes had made the start, except that Bayes' money amounts are replaced by utility numbers. Like Bayes, Ramsey can now calibrate probabilities: these are ratios between certain differences between utilities – as on our Figure I.5. The norm that prospects with higher expected utilities should be preferred to those with lower ones follows immediately.

It is worth noting that the logic of connecting between 'measurable', (and not merely 'completely ordered') utilities as required by the Bernoulli and the Ramsey norm has been patterned, to a large extent, after Hilbert's 'Foundations of Geometry'[8] in which the relation was established between points ordered along a straight line and the real numbers measuring distances. In a more general sense, too, discussion of behavior norms is similar to that of foundations of geometry. Various geometries – various internally consistetn sets of axions and theorems – are possible. So are various sets of behavior rules. Such consistent systems do not assert anything about empirical reality – e.g., about physical or psychological phenomena. Yet they do help to order these phenomena, by comparing facts with ideals. The normative discussion of behavior shares this feature with mathematics and logics. In addition, it shares with logic another feature: certain modes of thinking *and* acting may be 'preferable' to others. For example, it is preferable, when one is told that all men are mortals, not to conclude that all mortals are men; and it is preferable, choosing *A* in preference to *B*, and *B* in preference to *C*, not to choose *C* in preference to *A*. We are warned against 'bad logic' as well as against 'inconsistent behavior' (the latter is even called sometimes 'illogical behavior'). The warning is of a pragmatic nature: bad logicians won't survive. In the last lecture, we shall return to this practical aspect of normative social science, and of probabilities in social science.

The approach of Ramsey and of D. Bernoulli is more congenial to social scientists than that of Bayes because Bayes confined himself to outcomes which are money gains. But still more important, the common feature of the approach of both Ramsey and Bayes, is particularly congenial to social scientists. It permits us to deal with 'probabilities of single events'. While the XVIII century Continentals, in Paris or Petersburg, indulged in dice and cards, and watched the frequencies of repeated events, the English seem to have thought more of horses and fighting cocks and wrestlers. The betting books of Oxford colleges are full of guesses such as 'Napoleon is dead' (dated November 1812) accompanied by the betting ratios – whether in guineas or in bottles of port. This is right after the social scientist's taste! He is often unable to observe repeated events.

But, then the following question arises: if I happen to be able to observe repeated events, how shall I use those observations in computing my 'degrees of belief', which are my guide in decision-making? Shall I, for example, equate my degree of belief in drawing a white ball from an urn, to the relative frequency of such drawings in the past, at least as an approximation? In short: *is there any relation between subjective probabilities and the statistical method*? Is there any sense in the statement: 'The chances that I shall survive the operation are the same as getting a royal flush'? (These questions are important for our future discussion because in the two remaining lectures, statistical methods will be applied to human and social phenomena and to policy decisions.)

These questions were, in essence, answered in the affirmative by Bayes himself, and again, in our time, by Ramsey. To justify the affirmative answer, one first shows that the 'law of large numbers', properly interpreted, does follow from the properties of subjective probabilities. To do this, it will be convenient to use the concepts of 'conditional probabilities' and of 'independence'. We shall define them as we proceed. (These concepts will also prove useful in Lectures 2 and 3.)

Let $\bar{W}$ be the negation of the state of the world W, and let $\bar{V}$ be the negation of the state of the world V; and suppose that the subject is indifferent between the following options:

$$\left.\begin{array}{l}\alpha \text{ if } \bar{W}\\ \beta \text{ if } W\end{array}\right\} \text{ and } \left\{\begin{array}{l}\alpha \text{ if } \bar{W}\\ \beta' \text{ if } W \text{ and } V\\ \beta'' \text{ if } W \text{ and } \bar{V}\end{array}\right.$$

For example: let α=death, β=survival; β'=early arrival; β''=late arrival; $\bar{W}$=plane has engine trouble; V=plane is fast. Then the option on the left hand is: to die if the plane has engine trouble; to survive if it has not. The option on the right hand is: to die if the plane has engine trouble; to survive and arrive early if the plane has no engine trouble and is a fast one; to survive and arrive late if the plane has no engine trouble and is a slow one.[9] Our assumption is, then, that I am indifferent between the option on the left hand and the option on the right hand. That is, by Ramsey's postulate, the expected utility of the left-hand option is equal to that of the right-hand option. But the expected utility of the left-hand option is clearly

$$u(\alpha)\, p(\bar{W}) + u(\beta)\, p(W),$$

where $u(\alpha)$, $u(\beta)$ are the utility numbers attached to the outcomes α and β, respectively, and $p(\bar{W})$ and $p(W)$ are the probabilities of the alternative states of the world $\bar{W}$ and W respectively. In a similar notation, the expected utility of the right-hand option is

$$u(\alpha)\, p(\bar{W}) + u(\beta')\, p(W \text{ and } V) + u(\beta'')\, p(W \text{ and } \bar{V}).$$

Hence the indifference between the two options implies the equality of the two expressions we have written. This equality implies – since the term containing $u(\alpha)$ cancels out –

$$(1.3) \qquad u(\beta)\, p(W) = u(\beta')\, p(W \text{ and } V) + u(\beta'')\, p(W \text{ and } \bar{V}).$$

Let us now give the two quantities

$$\frac{p(W \text{ and } V)}{p(W)} \quad \text{and} \quad \frac{p(W \text{ and } \bar{V})}{p(W)},$$

the names 'conditional probability of V given W' and 'conditional probability of $\bar{V}$ given W'; and denote these two quantities, respectively, by

$$p(V \mid W) \quad \text{and} \quad p(\bar{V} \mid W).$$

Then our last equation becomes – dividing by $p(W)$ –

$$(1.4) \qquad u(\beta) = u(\beta') \cdot p(V \mid W) + u(\beta'') \cdot p(\bar{V} \mid W).$$

Now define 'independence' as follows. Suppose the state x_2 is 'irrelevant' to the state x_1 in the sense that the conditional probability of x_1 given x_2 is the same as the probability of x_1:

$$p(x_1 | x_2) = p(x_1).$$

By the definition of conditional probability this means

$$(1.5) \qquad \frac{p(x_1 \text{ and } x_2)}{p(x_2)} = p(x_1),$$

$$p(x_1 \text{ and } x_2) = p(x_1) \cdot p(x_2).$$

Thus the 'irrelevance' of x_2 for x_1 is equivalent to the relation (1.3), which will define 'independence' between x_1 and x_2. Since (1.3) is symmetrical in x_1 and x_2 the following are equivalent: independence between x_1 and x_2; irrelevance of x_2 for x_1; and irrelevance of x, for x_{21}. One can extend the concept of independence to, say, N events and define it by

$$(1.6) \qquad p(x_1 \text{ and } x_2 \text{ and } x_3 \ldots \text{ and } x_N) = p(x_1)\, p(x_2)\, p(x_3) \ldots p(x_N).$$

Thus if one tosses coins, one can compute the probability that the independent events $x_1, \ldots, x_N$ will be all 'heads'; or that the first two are heads and the rest tails; or that some other preassigned proportion of tosses be heads. These computations are a matter of arithmetic. As the result, one finds (one version of) the law of large numbers: if the 'probability of heads' equals p then the 'probability that the proportion of heads in a long sequence of independent throws will converge to p' equals 1. Remember that the probabilities in question (the numbers p and 1 in our last sentence) are subjective degrees of belief, defined as guides in choosing between actions.[10]

We shall now sketch out the proof that any 'preconceived' (or 'a priori') degrees of belief 'should' be modified in the light of experience, in a certain well-defined way, which is fundamentally the one at the basis of sampling statistics. (Note the 'should'! We are talking of norms!).

Suppose that my degree of belief in drawing a black ball from an urn, on condition that the world is in state W, is π. This quantity is also called the 'likelihood of the state W on the basis of an observed drawing of a black ball'. If the urn contains only black and red balls, then clearly the likelihood of W on the basis of an observed drawing of a red ball is $1-\pi$. Similarly, let us denote by $\bar{\pi}$ and $1-\bar{\pi}$, respectively, the likelihoods of the alternative state, $\bar{W}$, on the basis of an observed drawing of a black or of a red ball. Let x_i be the ith independent observation, and let '$x_i=b$' and '$x_i=r$' mean that this observation is the drawing of a black or a red ball, respectively. We can then rewrite our definitions as follows:

$$\pi = p(x_i = b \mid W)\,; \quad 1 - \pi = p(x_i = r \mid W)$$
$$\bar{\pi} = p(x_i = b \mid \bar{W})\,; \quad 1 - \bar{\pi} = p(x_i = r \mid \bar{W})\,.$$

Consider in particular, the first observation, x_1, and write the degree of belief that the world is in the state W *and* that the first drawing will be 'black', thus:

$$p(W\,;\ \text{and}\ x_1 = b)\,.$$

On the other hand, denote separately the degrees of belief that the world is in state W (regardless of observations) and that the first drawing is black, by

$$p^0(W)\ \text{and}\ p(x_1 = b)\,,$$

respectively. If we now recall our definition of conditional probabilities, we have

$$p(W;\ \text{and}\ x_1 = b) = p(x_1 = b \mid W) \cdot p^0(W)$$

and also

$$p(W;\ \text{and}\ x_1 = b) = p(W \mid x_1 = b) \cdot p(x_1 = b)\,.$$

The quantities $p^{\circ}(W)$ and $p(W \mid x_1 = b)$ are called, respectively, the *a priori* and the *a posteriori* degree of belief in W; while $p(x_1 = b \mid W)$ is, as we recall, the likelihood π. Comparing the last two equations, we obtain

$$p(W \mid x_1 = b) \cdot p(x_1 = b) = \pi \cdot p^0(W)\,.$$

And similarly (replacing W by $\bar{W}$ and therefore π by $\bar{\pi}$)

$$p(\bar{W} \mid x_1 = b) \cdot p(x_1 = b) = \bar{\pi} \cdot p^0(\bar{W})\,.$$

Dividing the last equation into the preceding one, one obtains a simple form of the celebrated 'Bayes Theorem':

$$(1.7)\qquad \frac{p(W \mid x_1 = b)}{p(\bar{W} \mid x_1 = b)} = \frac{p_0^0(W)\cdot\pi}{p\ (\bar{W})\cdot\bar{\pi}}$$

In words: the *a posteriori* degree of belief in a certain state of the world, given a certain observation, is proportional to the product of the *a priori* degree of belief in that state of the world *times* the likelihood of that state of the world given the observation. In this way, the observation leads to modifying the *a priori* degree of belief. The likelihoods, π and $\bar{\pi}$, operate as 'correction factors'. If the observation x_1 were 'red' instead of 'black', the correction factors would be $1-\pi$ and $1-\bar{\pi}$, respectively.

Suppose now the process is repeated: we take N independent observations $x_1, x_2, \ldots, x_N$, each time using the previously corrected degree of belief, correcting it further in the light of the new observation. Suppose we drew a black ball n times, (and therefore a red ball $N-n$ times). Applying Bayes Theorem,

$$(1.8)\qquad \frac{p(\bar{W} \mid x_1, \ldots, x_N)}{p(W \mid x_1, \ldots, x_N)} = \frac{p^0(\bar{W})\cdot\bar{\pi}^n(1-\bar{\pi})^{N-n}}{p^0(W)\cdot\pi^n(1-\pi)^{N-n}}.$$

But, by the law of large numbers, as stated above, if the true state of the world is W, then the degree of belief is 1 that the proportion of black drawings, n/N will converge to π. Therefore, the number of black drawings, n, will converge to $\pi\ N$; and the ratio between the *a posteriori* degrees of belief into $\bar{W}$ and W, as given in our last equation, will approach

$$\frac{p^0(\bar{W})}{p^0(W)}\cdot\left(\frac{\bar{\pi}^\pi(1-\bar{\pi})^{1-\pi}}{\pi^\pi(1-\pi)^{1-\pi}}\right)^N.$$

We see that as the number N of observations increases, the role of the *a priori* degrees of belief into the two alternative states of the world, $p^0(\bar{W})$ and $p^0(W)$, diminishes, overshadowed by the results of observations. Furthermore simple calculus shows that the expression

$$\bar{\pi}^\pi(1-\bar{\pi})^{1-\pi},$$

considered as a function of a variable $\bar{\pi}$, has its maximum when $\bar{\pi}=\pi$. Hence, in (1.8), the quantity that is raised to the Nth power, is a ratio of a smaller positive number to a larger one; and its Nth power approaches 0 as N increases. Therefore, of the two *a posteriori* degrees of belief that form the fraction on the left side of (1.8), and that must add up to 1, the numerator converges to 0 and the denominator to 1. That is, the degree of belief that will be assigned to the true state of the world (W) will approach 1. Hence, the investigator who will repeatedly apply Bayes Theorem and choose his decisions on the basis of degrees of belief thus computed will in effect believe that he would obtain a better result than if he would not do so. Perhaps this is what writers on probability mean when they use the expression 'practically certain' or 'certain for all practical purposes',[11] – an expression we shall also have the opportunity for using in the next two sections.

II. PROBABILITIES AND DESCRIPTIVE SOCIAL SCIENCE

We shall concern ourselves now with the uncertainties encountered by the social scientist when he tries to predict the behavior of people. Such prediction is rarely exact. It is usually 'probabilistic' or statistical, even when the sample used is very large and even when the prediction is made, not about individuals, but about large aggregates of people. After discussing the probabilistic character of descriptive social science, I shall give examples illustrating an important methodological problem that has recently occupied statisticians as well as social scientists: that of identifiability of structural characteristics. This will throw some light on the following more general fact: whether statistical data can yield the desired prediction depends not only on the size of the sample and on the goodness of statistical formulae, but also on the nature and validity of the assumptions which the investigator had to make before collecting them. These assumptions (sometimes called 'a model') are, of course, based on formerly acquired knowledge. In the case of a social scientist, this is often the knowledge of 'plausible' or of 'meaningful' relations.

A. *Norms Versus Habits*

We discussed in the first lecture some norms 'recommended' to decision makers who face uncertainty. Those norms or behavior postulates were similar to the rules of logic or geometry. It was not asserted that such norms were fully obeyed by all or even a sizable proportion of men or women, in our own or any other civilization, just as logicians and mathematicians do not assert that all or the majority of their countrymen or of members of any other society are immune to errors of logic or arithmetic.

It is merely recommended that those errors be avoided. Recommended norms and actual habits are not the same thing.

As a matter of empirical psychology it may be interesting to find in what manner a given individual deviates from such norms: how often is he apt to fall victim to a particular sophism, or to have trouble with his sums, or – nearer to our field – to be inconsistent in his preferences. As a matter of social science in general, we may be interested in the ethical and social conditions which affect the frequency of deviations from norms of reasonable thinking, counting and choosing. This knowledge of conditions affecting people's behavior is, first, a matter of scientific curiosity. But is has also its practical side. If we know what makes people more or less illogical or mathematically inept or poor decision makers, we may also find how best to enable them to learn the 'recommended' type of behavior – how, for example, they can get the habit of 'stopping to think'. The normative and the descriptive analysis complete each other.

In the previous section, we did not specify the source of the uncertainty that faces the decision maker. It may be uncertainty about nature. It may be uncertainty about the actions of other men. In our initial example, the U.N. commander had to puzzle out whether his Chinese adversary is or is not 'aggressive' (in the well defined sense of producing certain observable results under specified circumstances). This is uncertainty about people. If our commander estimates (or acts as if he had estimated) that the odds for the Chinese command having 'aggressive' designs are such and such, he has done a bit of descriptive social science. It may happen that, in my best judgment, my adversary behaves as he 'should' behave according to the norms of reasonableness which I recommend to myself. Any application of the Theory of Games (in its present form) is based on the assumption that this symmetry of behavior norms is an actual fact. However, this need not always be the case, nor need it be a useful approximation to reality. It may be more useful to actually study my adversary, as I would study weather or soil or any other uncertain natural phenomenon – provided such study of other people's behavior is feasible and not too costly. A commander – or, for that matter, a diplomat, or a labor union representative – will combine the theory of games ('What would I reasonably do if I were in the other fellow's position?') with as good an intelligence system as his resources can afford, whether by sending spies or by employing anthropologists. And, of course, what was said for a problem arising in fighting an opponent is also true for problems arising in forming an alliance, in building and operating within a social organization – in short in making decisions whose outcome will depend on actions of my fellow men about whom my knowledge is uncertain.

B. *Prediction*

Uncertain knowledge is not ignorance. Nineteenth-century social scientists were fascinated by 'iron laws of nature', when they took eighteenth-century physics for their ideal. It was fashionable, a hundred years ago, to speak of the iron law of demand and supply or (with Karl Marx) to claim predictability for society's future. We have learned today – possibly reflecting some trends in physical sciences – to be quite happy when we can make a prediction only with some (specified) probability. For the 'reasonable' man of our last lecture, a decision maker who weighs utilities with probabilities and maximizes the weighted sum, this kind of knowledge is certainly not useless! At the same time, such knowledge is usually the best that we can ever hope to have, in the field of social sciences, where uncertainties of our physical environment are topped by the diversity and capriciousness of human nature.

Briefly, empirical social science consist of statements about probability distributions. As a trivial but useful example, suppose a social statistician is hired to find what makes people smoke much or little or not at all. Or he wants to find what makes people communists. Let x denote the number of cigarettes smoked by a certain man on a certain day (x may be 0, 1, 2,… a many-valued variable); or let x denote a certain man's being or not being a communist (here $x=0$ or 1: a two-valued variable). What is the probability that x will have a certain value? The tendency to believe in smoking, or in communism, will depend on certain individual characteristics among which one will expect to find the age, sex, education, occupation of the subject; but also his income, the characteristics of his parents and siblings… but possibly also his past income and occupation… but then also his whole past history and that of his ancestors, and, in fact, his whole genetic and cultural endowment. This is a long list of factors. Call them $z^{(1)}, z^{(2)}, \ldots, z^{(N)}$, with N very large. We could make the desired prediction with certainty, for a subject whose $z^{(1)}, \ldots, z^{(N)}$ are known, if we also knew which combinations of the values of those variables make $x=0$, which combinations make $x=1$, etc. That is, the social scientist can predict from $z^{(1)}, \ldots, z^{(N)}$ if there exists a function

$$x = \phi(z^{(1)}, \ldots, z^{(N)}) \tag{2.1}$$

(say) and if he has been able to find this function on the basis of his previous observations on $x, z^{(1)}, \ldots, z^{(N)}$ for each of a sufficient number and variety of persons. However, a complete list of factors that may influence the man's smoking habits or his political beliefs is hopelessly long! The social scientist picks out a smaller number of factors – say $z^{(1)}, \ldots, z^{(n)}$ – and replaces the assumption (2.1) of an 'exact' relationship by a 'probabilistic' assumption, as follows: The variable x is a random variable (also called a chance variable or a stochastic variable); and the probability with which it takes any given value is a function of the variables $z^{(1)}, \ldots, z^{(n)}$ only. In other words, there exists a 'conditional probability of x, given $z^{(1)}, \ldots, z^{(n)}$',

$$\text{(2.2)} \qquad \pi(x \mid z^{(1)}, \ldots, z^{(n)}),$$

say. With the assumption thus changed, the predictor's task is to find, not the function ϕ in (2.1) but the function π in (2.2), from the values of $x, z^{(1)}, \ldots, z^{(n)}$ that he had observed on a sufficient number and variety of individuals. He can then state, for some new individual, with given $z^{(1)}, \ldots, z^{(n)}$ but an unknown x, the probability distribution of x: "the probability that Tom Smith, elevator boy at the State Department, middle-aged and unmarried, is a communist is 0.001%"; "the probability that Mrs. Brown, fashion editor, divorced, smokes 0, 1,..., 30 cigarettes per day is, respectively, 1%, 5%,..., 0%."

A very special, but convenient and familiar, form of this assumption will serve as illustration. One assumes that there exist $n+2$ numbers $\mu, \sigma, \alpha_1, \ldots, \alpha_n$ with the following property: the difference (called 'disturbance')

$$\text{(2.3)} \qquad x - \sum_{i=1}^{n} \alpha_i z^{(i)}$$

is independent of the $z^{(i)}$ and has normal distribution with expectation (mean) μ and standard deviation σ. In this case, the conditional distribution (2.2) of x, given $z^{(1)}, \ldots, z^{(n)}$, is also normal.[12] Its expectation is

$$\mu + \sum_{i=1}^{n} \alpha_i z_i$$

and is called the 'explained part of x'. Its standard deviation, σ, is identical with that of the disturbance (2.3). The numbers α_i can be regarded as 'weights' (not necessarily all positive) attached to the n explanatory variables; each of those variables contributes an additive component $\alpha_i z^{(i)}$ of x. If one could find, on the basis of past observations on the x and the $z^{(i)}$ of a sufficient number and variety of individuals, then, for any new individual, with known $z^{(i)}$ but unknown x, one would be able to make a 'probabilistic' prediction such as, for example: the odds are 19:1 that this man's x lies in the interval

(2.4) $$\mu + \sum \alpha_i z^{(i)} \pm 2\sigma$$

The looks of this interval are familiar enough from textbooks and routines of research workers in social science. I am afraid its understanding is often confused by complications irrelevant from our point of view. One complication is that the constants μ, σ, and the α_i cannot be determined exactly from a finite number of observations. One can only determine their 'estimates'. These are suitably chosen functions of a finite number of observed values of the variables x, $z^{(1)} \ldots, z^{(n)}$. Since these variables are [or at least x is – according to (2.2)] random, the estimates are also random variables (they are 'subject to sampling errors') so that the interval (2.4), computed from those estimates, it itself 'wobbly'. But this is beside the point. We are not interested in sampling theory today. We can assume today that the investigator has collected a very large sample indeed; and that he has used appropriate formulas to compute estimates that are practically certain to approach the estimated constants as the sample increases (such estimates are called 'consistent'). Our point is that, even using an infinite sample and consistent estimates, he will not be able to predict x from a finite number (n) of explanatory variables except in a 'probabilistic' fashion typified by the statement that 'x will fall within the interval (2.4) with probability 0.05'.

Another concept that we wish to disregard here is that of 'errors of observation', a term originating in observatories and physical laboratories There the number N of possible explanatory factors is supposed to be small enough to be manageable; and the fact that the exact, non-probabilistic assumption (2.1) is not satisfied is (or was till the advent of modern statistical physics) blamed upon the frailty of the observer's eye and of his other instruments. In social science, human frailty is shared between the observer and his object. After repeatedly asking a blindfolded man which of two weights is heavier, the psychologist may have to record a frequency distribution of contradictory statements: 'The first weight is heavier', 'It is lighter', or 'No difference'. The psychologist will have to formulate his conclusions and predictions in a probabilistic manner even if he is sure that his own errors of observation (confusing the weights or misunderstanding the subject's responses) are negligible. A 'random disturbance' originating in the observed person not in the observer will always be present. Furthermore, even if it should be possible to design laboratory conditions so as to make both the errors of observation and the random disturbance of the observed phenomenon negligible, this cannot be achieved with data collected outside of laboratory walls – like the data on the smoking or the communist persuasion of persons. The variables, immense in number (N-n), which the investigator of such a problem has decided to leave out of account, are supposed by him to show their joint effect in the random disturbance (2.3). For example, each of the subject's ancestors has contributed something to his make-up, but each only a little: just like each of the innumerable causes that determine an honest card deal contributes a little. Such joint effects of a large number of separately insignificant causes are empirical phenomena that have been idealized in the mathematical concept of a random variable and a probability. An error of observation and a random disturbance, as defined, may both have their origin in those numerous, separately insignificant causes. However, if you prefer to ascribe the randomness of errors and disturbances to the free will of individuals, you may do so. This will not affect the choice of investigation methods.

The selection of the n explanatory variables, and the assumption that the difference (2.3) is independent of z_i and has a normal probability distribution [or, more generally, that x has some probability distribution (2.2) for any fixed value of the n variables selected as explanatory ones] may be false. If it is, it will lead to probabilistic prediction statements that are false, even if they are based on consistent estimates from very large samples. This suggests, of course, that one should test predictions like (2.4) against new facts; and then revise the assumption (2.2) if necessary. For example, one may change the list of explanatory variables or replace the linearity and normality assumptions by other ones. Thus the selection of assumptions need not be entirely based on prescientific knowledge but can be helped by progressive experience.

C. *Aggregation*

Large parts of social science deal, not with single individuals but with averages or aggregates. It has been occasionally remarked that random variations of behavior from one individual to another (or, for the same individual, from one day to another) tend to 'cancel out' when one deals with masses of man. Tseretelli, a political leader of the pre-Communist period of the Russian revolution, even went so far as to say (in predicting the failure of Communists to win the masses!), 'Persons can err, masses never'; and social scientists are apt to quote Boyle's law of gases, which is exact enough, yet can be derived from the random behavior of billions of small particles. Do social scientists fool themselves when they appeal to this analogy, thus trying to reduce the prediction interval to a single point and to evade the inconveniences of probabilistic thinking?

As an example, let me refer to the economists' attempt at explaining the aggregate investment, i.e., the total money outlay on plant and equipment made in a year by all the firms of the country.

This outlay is, of course, the sum of the outlays of individual firms on *their* plant and equipment. One might try to explain the decision of a manager or a management board of an individual firm by those variables that are likely to influence the level of anticipated profits, thus making the expansion of the firm's activities in a given year a promising or a bad proposition. Thus, one would think of explanatory variables like the following: the profits that are already being made at the time of decision; the current demand for the firm's product; the interest rate at which money can be borrowed to expand the firm's plant and machinery; the cost of new machinery and building. Clearly, many other variables will be needed to describe the particular circumstances in which a given firm finds itself, and which will affect the manager's anticipations of the future of his particular market and his decision to build a new wing of the plant or, on the contrary, to sell parts of his machinery for scrap without replacing them by new ones. If the particular circumstances do not vary too strongly from one firm to another, one might be able to explain the annual change in the aggregate plant and equipment of the American industry (so called rate of aggregate investment) as a function of those general variables: the total profits of the past year; the total demand for all products (represented by total national income); the average interest rate, the average cost of machinery and building, etc. To do this, one would be able to utilize the published historical statistics, which gives for each year and even each quarter or month, the aggregate outlays on plant and equipment, the total profits, the interest rate, prices, etc. In this hope, various investigators have looked for a statistical relationship between the aggregate annual investment of the American industry and the several aggregate variables that we have mentioned. In particular, attempts have been made to construct prediction intervals like (2.4), where μ and σ are the mean and standard deviation of the estimate of annual aggregate investment; while the $z^{(i)}$ are the various mentioned explanatory variables, also of aggregative nature: total profits of the preceding year, total national income, average interest rate, etc. However, the standard error σ of the estimate, and hence the prediction interval, proved to be very large; or, what is the same thing, the 'unexplained residual', the 'disturbance' (2.3) – with x interpreted as the annual rate of aggregate investment – has a very large standard deviation. The meaning of the prediction interval being 'very large' is simply this: it is so large as to be useless.

For the social scientists, an interesting possible explanation of the strong random variability of the unexplained residual of some aggregative variables, is the phenomenon variously called 'leadership,' 'imitation', 'contagion', or 'Zeitgeist' or 'fashion'. The random disturbances in the response (e.g., in the decision to expand plant) of any pair of individual members of a human group to a given set of circumstances may be positively correlated, both disturbances being partly determined by unspecified common cause. If this is the case, the response of the corresponding aggregative variable to a given set of circumstances will be subject to more unpredictable random fluctuations than if that correlation were absent.

A mathematical illustration will help. Suppose p variables $v_1, \ldots, v_p$ have a joint normal distribution with a common expectation $Ev_j = 0$ and a common variance $Ev^2 = \sigma^2$. Let them also have a common correlation coefficient for any pair $j \neq k$, $Ev_j v_k / \sigma^2 = \rho > 0$. Thus

$$Ev_j v_k = \begin{cases} \sigma^2 & \text{when } j = k \\ \sigma^2 \rho & \text{otherwise.} \end{cases}$$

What is the distribution of $\bar{v}$, the average of these variables? $\bar{v}$ has normal distribution. Its expectation $=0$. And its variance

$$(2.5) \qquad E(\bar{v})^2 = E\left(\frac{v_1 + \cdots + v_p}{p}\right)^2 = \frac{1}{p^2} E \sum_j \sum_k v_j v_k =$$

$$= \frac{1}{p^2}\left[p\sigma^2 + p(p-1)\sigma^2\rho\right] = \sigma^2\left[\frac{1-\rho}{p}\right] + \rho\sigma^2 .$$

$$E(\bar{v})^2 \to \sigma^2\rho \quad \text{as} \quad p \to \infty .$$

Thus, under our assumptions, the variance of the average tends to zero if and only if the correlation $\rho = 0$. Applying this to our problem of averaging the individual responses (e.g., the investment decisions of a number of firms), we can interpret v_j as follows:

$$(2.6) \qquad v_j = x_j - \sum_{i=1}^{n} \alpha_i z_j^{(i)} - \mu \, (j = 1, \ldots, p)$$

where the α_i and μ have the same meaning as in (2.3), (2.4), and the subscript j indicates the particular firm; its response (investment) x_j is explained by the variables $z^{(1)}, \ldots, z^{(n)}$, except for a random disturbance $\mu + v_j$, which has mean μ and variance σ^2. The variable x_j has then also variance σ^2, the same for all firms. If, for all pairs of firms, the random disturbances are not correlated ($\rho = 0$) then indeed the average of the responses of all firms tends to have zero variance as the number of firms increases. But this is not so if there is, pairwise, a positive correlation between the individual disturbances. In the extreme case, when all firms act in unison ($\rho = 1$), the average has the same variance as any individual response: an obvious result.[13] This mathematical illustration might be made more general – for example we might admit positive correlation coefficients of different sizes for different pairs of firms. But our result suffices, to show how 'fashion' endangers predictability – a warning against the abuse of a misunderstood 'law of averages'. If the decision-makers, however numerous, follow a few leaders, then the personal circumstances, the ulcers or divorce proceedings of the leaders become important factors in predicting the average or aggregate of the decisions.

D. *Identification*

Suppose two random characteristics X_1 and X_2 are being measured on each person of a sample. For example, X_1 may be a person's consumption of cigarettes, and X_2 his consumption of cereals; or X_1 may be the person's answer to the question 'Do you prefer blondes?' and X_2 his answer to the question 'Do you feel comfortable with strangers?' Suppose that a parameter Z is known to exist which varies from person to person but is fixed for each person; and which influences X_1 and X_2 in a 'probabilistic' fashion. That is, the probability that a person's X_1 and X_2 will take a given pair of values (or fall within given intervals) depends on the value of the person's Z. Thus the joint distribution of the numbers of cigarettes and bowls of cereals consumed by a person during a week may depend on the person's income, Z. In the case of the two questions – about blondes and about strangers – Z may stand for some characteristic, such as 'ethnocentricity', of which the answers to the two questions are symptoms.[14] We shall denote the joint probability distributions of X_1, X_2, conditional upon Z, by

$$(2.7) \qquad \pi(X_1, X_2 \mid Z),$$

a function of three variables. It is analogous to (2.2), with the vector $(z^{(1)}, \ldots, z^{(n)})$ replaced by a single Z, and the number x replaced by the vector (X_1, X_2). [In a more general case, both the random variable to the left and the parameter to the right of the bar in (2.7) will be vectors.:]

Suppose one has succeeded in estimating the function π from a sample. This knowledge could then be used in two opposite ways, to answer questions about a person not in the sample:

Question 1: given this person's Z, predict his X's.
Question 2: given his X's, make statements about his Z.

Why either of these applications of our knowledge of the conditional probability function π should ever arise in practice, will belong into our third lecture (on policies). For the time being, we shall regard both questions as legitimate expressions of scientific curiosity.

If the sampled persons had lent themselves to the measurement, not only of their X, but also of their Z, the problem of estimating the function π from the sample, and of subsequently answering Questions 1 or 2 about a person not in the sample, would be a familiar one. For example, the main use of computing a regression equation from a sample is to answer Question 1, in the manner of (2.4); using a sample to answer Question 2 is also a problem well known to statisticians, a discrimination problem.[15]

However, a new twist is introduced by making Z a non-observable (at least not observable on the sampled individuals), a 'latent' characteristic. It is natural to expect that this loss of information must be made up by some additional information if the problem is to remain solvable.

The following simple hypothesis (which is itself a bit of 'additional information') will be used for the case of 'cigarettes and cereals': X_1 and X_2 are proportional to Z, subject to random percentage deviations, denoted by U_1 and U_2, respectively. That is, there exist two constants, Λ_1 and Λ_2 such that

$$X_i = \Lambda_i Z(1 + U_i), \quad (i = 1, 2).$$

Remember that X_1, X_2 have been measured on persons of the sample, but Z has not. (Collectors of family budget data are, in fact, able to ascertain single consumption items but have difficulty in finding the incomes!) It will be convenient to use logarithms. Write $\log Z = z, \log X_i = x_i, \log \Lambda_i = \lambda_i$, $\log(1 + U_i) = u_i \, (i = 1, 2)$. Then

$$(2.8) \qquad x_i = \lambda_i + z + u_i, \quad (i = 1, 2).$$

We shall further assume that random deviations cancel out in a very large sample, in the sense that the expectations of u_1, u_2 vanish:

$$(2.9) \qquad Eu_i = 0 \quad (i = 1, 2);$$

assume also that u_1, u_2 are jointly normally distributed. We shall write $Eu_iu_j = \sigma_{ij} (i, j = 1, 2)$. Our hypothesis involves thus 5 unknown parameters $\lambda_1, \lambda_2, \sigma_{11}, \sigma_{22}, \sigma_{12}$. Can we determine them and use them to make a probabilistic prediction of x_1 and x_2 for any given z?[16]

The answer depends on what information is in our possession *before* we collect the data. The main purpose of the present example is to show how the character of this '*a priori* information' makes the problem determinate or indeterminate. With insufficient *a priori* information, the problem is indeterminate however large the sample.

Assume, for example – in addition to the assumptions already made [(2.8), (2.9) and normality of the distribution of u_1, u_2] – that we know the frequency distribution of z[17]: viz., normal with known mean and variance (ζ and ω, say), and independent of the disturbances u_1 and u_2; hence, $Ezu_1 = 0 = Ezu_2$. As before, we shall neglect sampling errors (by assuming our sample very large), so that the sample averages x_1, x_2 are almost equal to the corresponding expectations; then by (2.8), (2.9), approximately

(2.10) $\bar{x}_i = Ex_i = \lambda_i + \zeta$;

hence

$$\lambda_i = \bar{x}_i - \zeta \quad (i = 1, 2),$$

thus determining the two unknowns λ_1, λ_2[18]. Moreover, the sample moments (sample averages of squares and products) computed from the observed values of x_i in the (very large) sample, serve to determine σ_{11}, σ_{22}, σ_{12}, the parameters of the distribution of u_1, u_2. For, by (2.8), (2.9),

$$x_i - \bar{x}_i = z - \zeta + u_i ;$$

therefore

$$\begin{aligned} E(x_i - \bar{x}_i)(x_k - \bar{x}_k) &= E(z - \zeta)^2 + Eu_iu_k + (z-\zeta)(Eu_i + Eu_k) \\ &= \omega + \sigma_{ik} ; \quad (i, k = 1, 2). \end{aligned}$$

Hence, in a very large sample, approximately

$$\begin{aligned} &\text{sample average of } (x_1 - \bar{x}_1)^2 = \omega + \sigma_{11} \\ (2.11)\quad &\text{sample average of } (x_2 - \bar{x}_2)^2 = \omega + \sigma_{22} \\ &\text{sample average of } (x_1 - \bar{x}_1)(x_2 - \bar{x}_2) = \omega + \sigma_{12}, \end{aligned}$$

where ω and the sample moments are known. The parameters σ_{11}, σ_{22}, σ_{12} thus estimated serve to determine (using the tables for bivariate normal distribution), the probability with which u_1 will fall into some given interval, and u_2 will fall, at the same time, into some given interval.

This would answer our Question 1. As to Question 2, I shall not go into details here. Suffice it to say that, once we know the conditional distribution of x_1, x_2 given z, we can also estimate the parameter z characterizing an individual, from values x_1, x_2 observed (once or in repeated observations) on an individual.

But suppose our *a priori* knowledge is less complete than in the example studied so far. For example, suppose we know the mean (ζ) of z (i.e., the geometric mean of average incomes of the U.S. population) but do not know its variance ω. We see from (2.10), (2.11) that we can then determine λ_1, λ_2 but not σ_{11}, σ_{22}, σ_{12}. Consequently we can predict x_i for a given z only in the sense of providing the conditional expectation of $x_i(=\lambda_i+z)$ but not of stating an interval into which the x_i should fall with preassigned probability. Nor shall we be able to estimate an individual's z from an observation on his x_1, x_2.

Or suppose we have the knowledge of both μ and ω, but have also a larger list of unknowns, because we are convinced that the assumption (2.8) is too special and should be replaced by a more general one:

$$(2.12) \qquad x_i = \lambda_i + \beta_i z + u_i \text{ [19]} \quad (i = 1, 2),$$

with β_1, β_2 unknown. Using this equation, we can again express – similarly to (2.10), (2.11) – the two sample means of x_1 and x_2 and their three sample moments in terms of the 7 unknowns. We shall be 2 equations short. The problem is indeterminate.

Consider, on the other hand, the case when we have fewer unknown constants than we have equations to determine them. Suppose again that we know both ζ and ω and let our hypothesis again be expressed by (2.8), (2.9). But, suppose, in addition, we know from other sources that $\sigma_{12}=0$, i.e., there can be, at any fixed income, no correlation between eating of cereals and smoking. We have then only four constants to determine (λ_1, λ_2, σ_{11}, σ_{22}), yet can derive from the observations the same five equations (2.10), (2.11) as in our first example, in which σ_{12} was unknown. If the hypothesis now used is correct, i.e., if (2.8), (2.9), as well as the assumed frequency distribution of z and the assertion $\sigma_{12}=0$, are all valid, then one of those equations derived from observations is redundant for the purpose of determining unknown parameters. But then it can be used to test the hypothesis. Indeed, the assertion $\sigma_{12}=0$ makes the last of the equations (2.11) into a relation between two known quantities, viz., between the observed cross-moment of x_1 and x_2 and the known variance ω of z. If this relation is not, in fact, satisfied, our hypothesis is wrong: e.g., (2.8) may be false, or z or u_1, u_2 are not distributed normally, or $w \neq$ variance of z, or $\sigma_{12} \neq 0$, etc.[20]

To sum up our examples: We started with a case in which all unknown constants could be determined from an equal number of (independent) equations obtained from observations – all constants were '*identifiable*'. By modifying the assumptions used or the kind of data available we obtained a case in which some of the constants, and another in which all of the constants were (however large the number of observations!) not determinable, '*nonidentifiable*'. Finally, we have had an example of '*over-identification*': observations yielded more (independent) equations than there are unknown constants; if these equations are inconsistent,[21] the hypothesis used must be rejected.

The term identifiability was suggested by T. C. Koopmans and the relevant mathematics were studied by the staff of the Cowles Commission for Research in Economics in considerable detail (see, e.g., the Commission's Monographs No. 10 and 14) because of the importance of the indentification problem in economics.[22] However, the problem seems to be present in other social sciences as well, e.g., in the Lazarfeld theory of latent structures and in Thurstone's factor analysis. In fact, my examples were chosen with the very purpose of providing a link between problems encountered in economics and those more familiar to a sociologist or psychologist, but, alas, less familiar to me. Let me, then, venture again to interpret x_1 and x_2 as answers to two questions asked of a person possessing an unknown degree z of some measurable characteristic. z is a parameter, changing from person to person. It is not a random variable.[23] The variables x_1 and x_2 can each take values 1 (for 'yes') or 0 (for 'no'). Assuming that a very large number of persons have been questioned, we want to determine the conditional joint probability

$$\pi = \pi(x_1, x_2 | z). \tag{2.13}$$

This is the same as (2.2), with $n=1$ and with x interpreted as a vector consisting of two components. Since x_1, x_2 can have only two values each, it is inappropriate to state an assumption about the distribution of a random 'unexplained residual', a continuous quantity such as (2.3), or the u_i in (2.8). Instead, we specify directly the function (2.13) of z, i.e., assume that the respective probabilities of the four possible alternatives [(1) $x_1 = x_2 = 0$; (2) $x_1 = x_2 = 1$; (3) $x_1 = 0, x_2 = 1$; (4) $x_1 = 1, x_2 = 0$] are determined by z in a specified fashion (Lazarfeld's 'trace lines') Suppose, for example, that the function π can be tabulated as follows (each cell corresponding to the probability of one combination of answers)

(2.14)

$x_1 \| x_2$	0	1
0	$\alpha_{00} + \beta_{00} z$	$\alpha_{01} + \beta_{01} z$
1	$\alpha_{10} + \beta_{10} z$	$\alpha_{11} + \beta_{11} z$

(This presupposes of course that z has an upper and a lower limit.) The α's and β's are unknown. Since the four probabilities must add up to 1 for any z, the α's must add to 1, and the β's to 0. We have thus 6 (not 8) unknown constants. Can we determine them from the sample? Call p_{ij} the proportion of people, in a very large sample, whose pair of answers is: $x_1 = i$, $x_2 = j$. Denote by ζ the mean of z in the sample. Then

$$(2.15) \qquad p_{ij} = \alpha_{ij} + \beta_{ij}\,\zeta \quad (i, j = 0, 1).$$

ζ can be chosen as a unit of measurement of the z. The four proportions p_{ij} are all observable, but since they must add up to 1, only three of the four equations (2.15) are independent. This is not enough to determine the 6 unknowns. They are not identifiable.

But suppose we know with certainty the following property of our questionnaire: for any given person, the probability of answering the first question by yes is independent of whether he answers the second question by a yes or a no (though, of course, both probabilities vary from person to person, depending on z). Obviously, not every questionnaire satisfies this condition. This is a case of a 'pure test', in Lazarsfeld's terminology. The probability that a person answers with 'yes' the question 'Is your name John?' depends on how the same person answers the question 'Are you a woman?' If the probability of a person's being a man is 0.5, and the probability of a person's being called John is 0.1 (the average between the probability 0.2 of a man's being called John and the probability 0.0 of a woman's being called John), then the probability of a person's both being a man and being called John is not 0.5×0.1 (as it would be if these two events were independent) but 0.5×0.2.

Or consider two questions that are almost identical in content. Suppose the probability for the first question to be answered affirmatively by any person with z degrees of 'ethnocentricity' is q; the corresponding probability for the second question will then be near q; and the probability that a person with z degrees of ethnocentricity will answer both questions in the affirmative will be, not near q^2 but near q.

It may also be that the degree of dependence between the answers depends itself on z. An extreme ethnocentric may strongly associate dark hair with fast talk (and perhaps dislike both) while a man on the other end of the ethnocentricity scale will not have this ready image in his mind: thus a test may be 'pure' for some persons, not 'pure' for others.

Suppose, however, the investigator is sure to have formulated his questions so that, for a fixed z, the answers are completely independent; he is sure that all traces of possible associations, logical or otherwise, between the questions, have been weeded out. This *a priori* knowledge permits him to specify the function π more narrowly. For example, in the case (2.14) the assumption of independence will be expressed by the condition

$$(2.16) \qquad \frac{\alpha_{00} + \beta_{00} z}{\alpha_{10} + \beta_{10} z} = \frac{\alpha_{01} + \beta_{01} z}{\alpha_{11} + \beta_{11} z}.$$

Multiplying out and transferring all terms to one side, we obtain a quadratic expression in z which must vanish for any z. Hence each of its three terms vanishes, thus providing us with the three missing equations. Our 6 constants have now become identifiable.

In this example, the assumption of independence between answers (in the sense defined) has proved powerful enough to make an otherwise unidentifiable set of unknowns identifiable. The result can be used to estimate the latent characteristic z of a person outside the sample (the discrimination problem mentioned above): e.g., if his answer is 'no' to both questions, the maximum likelihood estimate of his z is obtained by maximizing with respect to z the probability $\pi\ (0, 0|z)$. We therefore put $\alpha_{00} + \beta_{00} z = 1$. One can also estimate an appropriate confidence interval for z. If all the unknown constants α_{00}, β_{00}, etc. had been unidentifiable it would have been impossible to estimate z. We can say that non-identifiability would make the confidence interval for z infinite. It can be conjectured that if z is identifiable both with and without the assumption of independence, the appropriate confidence interval for z is shorter when this assumption is made than when it is not made.

Since the assumption of independence between questions can have such powerful implications, the investigator, in using or designing the questionnaire, will have to be very critical.[24] As in many other cases, the soundness of statistical results will much depend on the soundness of pre-statistical assumptions which prove inaccessible to statistical test.

III. PROBABILITY AND POLICY

In the first lecture we discussed the following rule of conduct: choose that decision which makes the 'moral expectation' (= the mathematical expectation of utility) as large as possible. This presupposes consistency in the decision-maker's system of preferences. A rational policy maker must 'know what he wants'. In addition (at least in the approaches of Bayes and Ramsey), he must 'know what he believes' – his system of subjective probabilites, too, must be consistent. To require these consistencies is on the same plane as to require that the policy maker do not make errors of logic and arithmetic: that he avoid contradictions. Logic is self-control, and this includes logic of decision. In Ramsey's words, one should be able to 'stop to think it out', rather than to act on the temporarily uppermost desire and belief. This is an ideal, a skill which good decision-makers possess in a higher degree than poor ones. A bad decision-maker tosses in bed and decides in a half-dream. A good decision-maker dresses up a payoff matrix (though not necessarily with pen on paper). I suspect this skill is not entirely inborn and can be acquired by training: a fruitful field for applied psychology.

We also found in our first lecture that the rule of maximizing moral expectation leads to the proposition that degrees of belief (which we needed to know in order to compute moral expectations) are, in the limit, equal to relative frequencies obtained from samples. Accordingly, we devoted our second lecture to showing how certain probability distributions that interest a social scientist are obtained from observations. The probability distributions that interest the social scientist must be usable for prediction of the behavior of people. In the concluding part of the second lecture, we found that certain probability distributions needed for such prediction may be inaccessible to estimation, no matter how large the sample. Certain parameters are 'non-identifiable'. Yet these parameters are often just the ones the social scientist is particularly curious about: he feels they constitute his 'theory', as distinct from 'mere description'. He is interested in 'structures', 'latent parameters', and not in mere 'empirical regularities' and must be disappointed whenever he finds that the goal cannot be attained with the available kind of data.

What are those 'latent' properties, those 'theories' behind the manifest data? Why are they interesting? And what makes them so elusive? My tentative answer will be: that 'theories' are sought for the sake of decision-making; and that the difficulty in getting at them is due to the difficulty of performing experiments.

To take up one of the examples of our second lecture: Why is a market research organization not interested in merely estimating from its data the bivariate distribution of the consumption of cigarettes and the consumption of cereals? That would permit them to predict the one from the other. But this is not interesting. Instead, there is lurking a theory that both smoking and the expenditure on cereals depend on the third variable, income, which happen to be difficult to ascertain and is thus 'latent' rather than 'manifest'. We have shown that under certain hypotheses it is possible and under other hypotheses impossible, to obtain from data on cereals and cigarettes consimed by a sample of people, a relationship that will predict cereals consumption from income and that is presumably more 'theoretical', more of a 'structure', than the relationship between the consumption of cereals and that of cigarettes. The relationship involves two kinds of knowledge: the 'prestatistical' hypotheses just mentioned and the numerical parameters estimated from the sample. E.g., the hypothesis may be: cigarettes and cereals are consumed in proportion to incomes, apart from a random percentage deviation for each of the two items, these deviations being distributed normally, with zero correlation. The numerical parameters to be estimated may have been, in this case, the unknown (geometric) mean of the ratios of each of the two expenditure items to the individual's income, and the variances of each of the two deviations. We have seen that if we know the correlation (e.g., zero) between the two deviations, and know the income distribution (though not the individual incomes) in the population from which the sample was taken, the set of parameters is identifiable. But some or all of them become non-identifiable if our *a priori* knowledge is less complete – for example, if we do not have grounds to assume that the average relation between income and smoking or cereal-eating is one of proportionality, or that the two deviations from proportionality are non-correlated (i.e., that a man's smoking beyond his means is compatible with over-eating as well as with under-eating cereals, compared with the average breakfast of his income group). In these cases, knowledge of the 'latent' relation between income and the consumption items becomes inaccessible, with the type of data we have assumed in our example.

Why hanker after this inaccessible knowledge? Why not be content – to continue with our example – with predicting cereal consumption from cigarette consumption or vice versa, which is perfectly possible on the basis of our data? Presumably because the market research organization does not expect the latter kind of prediction to be of much use in future practical situations. It does find it useful to predict consumption from income. Why? Because it visualizes the following situation: given a new market, with customers' income distribution known and different from that of the population previously studied, predict the demand for cereals or cigarettes. If the decision to face new markets would never have to be taken, research about the influence of income (or other such factors) on consumption would be unnecessary: it would suffice to know past consumption.

Similarly, if – in line with the last example of our previous lecture – the manifest data are answers to a questionnaire and the latent parameter deemed to underly those answers is the 'degree of ethnocentricity', the reason why we are interested in measuring the latter is, presumably, its potential usefulness. It is not useful to predict that a 'yes' answer to a certain question entails, with a certain probability, a 'no' answer to another question (with population the same as the sampled one). I presume that what is really wanted is to predict the action of some new individual or group. It is assumed *a priori* that, for example, the discourteous treatment of immigrants by an official is determined by his degree of ethnocentricity which also influences his answers to questionnaires and which (if 'identifiable') is revealed by those answers. One wants to use those answers of the aspirant to an office to predict the behavior of the future official. A convenient way to state the relation between the observable answers to the questionnaire and the virtually observable action of the official is *via* the 'degree of ethnocentricity' which influences both. It is assumed to be 'behind' those observables, just like the genetic make-up of an individual is 'behind' observable data on his and his ancestors' hereditary features, even though genes might never become observable through the strongest ultra microscope. The study both of genotype and of 'ethnocentricities' would not be called for if predictions of the effects of changed genotype and changed ethnocentricity (or their changed distribution within a population), as in problems of animal breeding or the administration of policies towards ethnical minorities, were never to be made.

Permit me to use an example from economics: a severely simplified variant of a 'Keynesian' model designed to discuss fiscal policy as an instrument for maintaining employment and stable prices.

Consider the dollar value of all goods and services produced during a year (not counting those used for repair or renewal of the existing stock).

This dollar amount can be called the (net) national product. It is composed of the dollar amounts – called incomes – paid out, in the course of production, to workers, factory-owners, capital-lenders. Thus net national product is identical with national income. Denote this quantity by y. Consider now another quantity: the dollar value of all goods and services demanded during a year (again not counting repair and renewal). This national demand is composed of three parts: (1) the demand of consumers for food, shelter, etc. – denote it by c; (2) the demand of businessmen for machines and other goods to increase their plants and inventories (a matter I had occasion to mention in the previous lecture) – denote it by b; (3) the demand of the government for the services of its employees and for public buildings, armament goods, etc. – we shall denote it (for reasons that will appear presently) by a Greek letter, ρ (for Roosevelt). In general the national demand $c+b+\rho$ is not identical with the national product (income) y. People who decide about production (and hence about the incomes disbursed) may or may not be able to quickly adjust production to demand. However in our context we need not discuss this adjustment process, its motives and form, except in a footnote later.[25] We shall assume that production is adjusted to demand instantaneously, so that always

(3.1) $$y = c + b + \rho .$$

Of these quantities, only ρ is directly controlled by the policymaker, the government. What determines the rest, namely b and c?

As to b, let us assume that businessmen feel encouraged to expand their plant when the current national income, y, is high; at least they feel so 'on the whole', i.e., apart from some random deviation. To fix the ideas, let us use a linear approximation:

(3.2) $$b = \beta y + v_b, \quad \beta > 0 ;$$

where β is a parameter characterizing businessmen's behavior and v_b is a normally distributed random variable; denote its mean and variance by the Greek letters μ_b and σ_{bb} respectively.

As to c, let us assume that people's consumption depends, apart from a random deviation v_c, only on the amount of income that remains in their hands after payment of taxes, and on nothing else. Using again a linear approximation,

(3.3) $$c = \gamma(y - \tau) + v_c, \quad \gamma > 0;$$

where γ is a parameter descriptive of consumers' behavior and τ denotes the tax collected. The mean and variance of v_c (assumed normal) will be denoted by μ_c and σ_{cc}, respectively. Since the random deviations in the behavior of consumers may or may not be correlated with those in the behavior of businessmen we need also a symbol σ_{bc} to denote their covariance.

Finally, we assume for simplicity that the government determines directly the tax collected, τ (and not, as is actually the case, the tax rates only).

Let us now marshall all our quantities:

> government-controlled: ρ, τ;
> noncontrolled parameters: $\beta, \gamma, \mu_b, \mu_c,$
> $\sigma_{bb}, \sigma_{cc}, \sigma_{bc}$;
> dependent variables: b, c, y;
> random deviations: v_b, v_c.

We have three dependent variables and a system of three equations. We can solve for b, c, y. For example, Equation (3.4) below gives the solution for y. Since the system involves random deviations v_b, v_c, the dependent variables b, c, y are also random: they fluctuate with v_b, v_c. If the deviations v_b, v_c were observable, one could determine, for every pair v_b, v_c, the values that the dependent variables b, c, y would take, provided one knows the parameters ρ, τ, β, γ. Actually v_b, v_c are not observable but their probability distribution is fully determined by the parameters μ_b. μ_c, σ_{bb}, σ_{cc}, σ_{bc}. If one knows these parameters, one can find the probability distribution of b, c, y for any given set of values of the controlled parameters ρ, τ and of β, γ.

We are not concerned here with whether the model is economically sound. It is too crude. We merely use it as an example for our methodological discussion. The model's three equations, together with the probability distribution of the random deviations v_b, v_c, purport to 'explain' the observed distribution of the three dependent variables b, c, y. The model expresses a hypothesis about the behavior of consumers and businessmen, summarized by the non-controlled parameters – the Greek letters excluding ρ and τ. The policy problem is for the government to choose the best values of the controlled parameters ρ, τ, – the values that will maximize the government's 'expected utility', a term defined in our first lecture. If the government were concerned simply with the national income y (a dollar amount, as you remember) it would choose ρ and τ so as to maximize the expected value (the mean) of y – call it μ_y, one of the parameters of the distribution of y. How is the distribution of y determined by ρ and τ? The random variable y is related to ρ, τ in a linear fashion, as is seen by solving our three equations:

$$(3.4) \qquad y = \lambda(\rho - \gamma\tau) + \lambda(v_b + v_c),$$

where $\lambda = 1/(1-\beta-\gamma)$. Since $v_b + v_c$ is distributed normally, so is y. The mean of y is

$$(3.5) \qquad \mu_y = \lambda(\rho - \gamma\tau) + \lambda(\mu_b + \mu_c);$$

this is how μ_y is affffected by the government's choice of public expenditure ρ and tax revenue τ.

Note in passing that the policy-maker might be concerned, not only with a high mean national income but also with a high predictability of national income, as expressed by its variance, σ_{yy}. As the late Senator Arthur Vandenberg said in criticizing the New Deal: 'We don't want to live on a flying trapeze.' It is worthwhile to remark, as an exercise in the logic of these matters, that in our particular model the policy-maker is unable to affect σ_{yy}. The variance of y is not affected by adding to y a constant; it is, by (3.4), simply proportional to the variance of $(v_b + v_c)$ and is equal to

$$(3.6) \qquad \sigma_{yy} = \lambda^2(\sigma_{bb} + \sigma_{cc} + 2\sigma_{bc}).$$

Thus, the knowledge of the last three of the non-controlled parameters of our list above, is irrelevant for policy purposes if the policy goal depends on μ_y and/or σ_{yy}. If our model were nonlinear, the result might be different, and the knowledge of σ_{bb}, σ_{cc}, σ_{bc} important to the policy-maker concerned with high and/or reasonably predictable national income. In any case, this knowledge is necessary if one wants to 'predict', in the sense of our Lecture II, the random variable, income: i.e., if one wants to estimate the distribution of y. This is, in our example, described by μ_y and σ_{yy}, and to know σ_{yy} one has to know σ_{bb}, σ_{cc}, σ_{bc}. But such prediction may be of no concern to a practical policy-maker.

Continuing with a government bent on maximizing the expected value μ_y of national money income, return to our equation (3.5). We shall assume $\lambda > 0$, that is $\beta + \gamma < 1$. This assumption is not based on systematic statistical studies but on a general estimate of plausible behavior of consumers and businessmen and also on the observed 'stability' of a system, a consideration which we cannot discuss here in any detail.[26] If, then, $\lambda > 0$, the expected money incomes μ_y as determined in (3.5) is increased by raising ρ and cutting down τ. If there is an upper limit on government expenditure – say, ρ_{max} – and a lower limit on tax revenue – say, τ_{min} – then money income is highest with $\rho = \rho_{max}$ and $\tau = \tau_{min}$ (possibly zero). No knowledge about the behavior parameters β, γ is necessary to find these optimal values of the government-controlled parameters, except the validity of the assumption $\beta + \gamma - 1 < 0$.

This result is due to the fact that, under our assumptions, – as summarized in (3.5) – the expected money income μ_y changes monotonically (has no turning points) in response to changes in ρ and τ. Therefore y can achieve a maximum only at some boundary values of ρ and τ. If we introduced, for realism's sake, an upper limit on the deficit $\rho - \tau$, the same general result would remain true: no knowledge of the non-controlled parameters would be necessary to determine the policy (ρ, τ) that maximizes expected income (μ_y).

Let us now change our example so as to make it more up-to-date. To think of a government that tries to maximize the expected national income measured in dollars (the money income y) was possible in times of depression when prices were relatively stable, and a rise in money income was about equivalent to a rise in physical production and employment. In present inflationary times one has to think not only of the money income y but also of the price level, call it p. The physical production is $Y = y/p$; and the government is concerned with both Y and p. This is how we modify the previously assumed utility function of the policy maker. We have also to modify the model (3.1), (3.2), (3.3), by adding statements about what determines the dependent variables we have just added to our list, viz., Y and p.

One simple hypothesis is to assume that physical production Y cannot rise above a maximum, η (the 'full employment output'); and that the price level p is constant ($p = \pi$, say), as long as this maximum output is not reached. That is, our two additional dependent variables, Y and p, are determined as follows, in terms of our old dependent variable y and the parameters π and η:

$$(3.9)\qquad \begin{aligned} &Y = y/\pi, p = \pi &&\text{when}\quad y \leqslant \eta\pi \\ &Y = \eta,\quad p = y/\eta &&\text{when}\quad y > \eta\pi\,. \end{aligned}$$

Roughly, the first line corresponds to an unemployment situation and the second line to a full employment situation. In the former, money income y changes because of changes in physical output Y; in the latter, y changes because of changes in price level p. If we retain, in addition, our old Equations (3.1), (3.2), (3.3) and therefore also their implication (3.4) we see from (3.9) that the new dependent variables Y and p are random variables whose distribution depends on the same parameters as does the distribution of y, and, in addition, on the parameters η (maximum output) and π (constant price level during depression).

We can assume that the policy maker regards high physical output as desirable, and a strong rise in prices over their depression level as undesirable – e.g., because of the injustice that such a rise would inflict on certain people. Thus his utility function – $U(Y, p)$, say – is increasing in Y and decreasing in p, with $p \geqslant \pi$. As a simple example, we may have, as his utility

$$(3.10)\qquad u = U(Y, p) = Y - Ap\,,\quad A > 0, p \geqslant \pi\,.$$

The reader will notice that we use italicized capitals to indicate a new class of properties – not the parameters (controlled or non-controlled) of the model but the characteristics of the decisionmaker's valuations, his 'tastes'. In particular, A is the number of units of real income (e.g., billions of dollars with the purchasing power of the year 1940) that he thinks it worthwhile to sacrifice in order to avoid the rise of price level by one point, In assigning any pair of values to the controlled parameters ρ and τ, he will affect the distribution of Y and p, and hence the expected value of u, that is, his 'moral expectation', in the sense of our Lecture 1. Our assumptions (3.9), (3.10) will help as an illustration. Under these assumptions, the utility u is the following function of money income y:

$$(3.11)\qquad u = \begin{cases} \dfrac{y}{\pi} - A\pi & \text{when}\quad y \leqslant \eta\pi \\[2ex] \eta - \dfrac{Ay}{\eta} & \text{when}\quad y \geqslant \eta\pi\,. \end{cases}$$

This function is represented on Figure III.1 by a broken line consisting of two straight line segments: utility u rises with money income till the latter reaches $\eta\ \pi$; then u falls. Each bell-shaped curve (of which only two are drawn) indicates one of the possible normal distribution density functions of y, with a fixed variance [which, by (3.6), does not depend on policies] and a varying mean [which, by (3.5) does depend on ρ and τ]. (The two drawn curves have respective means μ_y'' and μ_y'.) Thus the policy (ρ, τ) determines the position of the bell-shaped curve, i.e., gives the probability that money income y will fall into any given (small) interval. If this probability

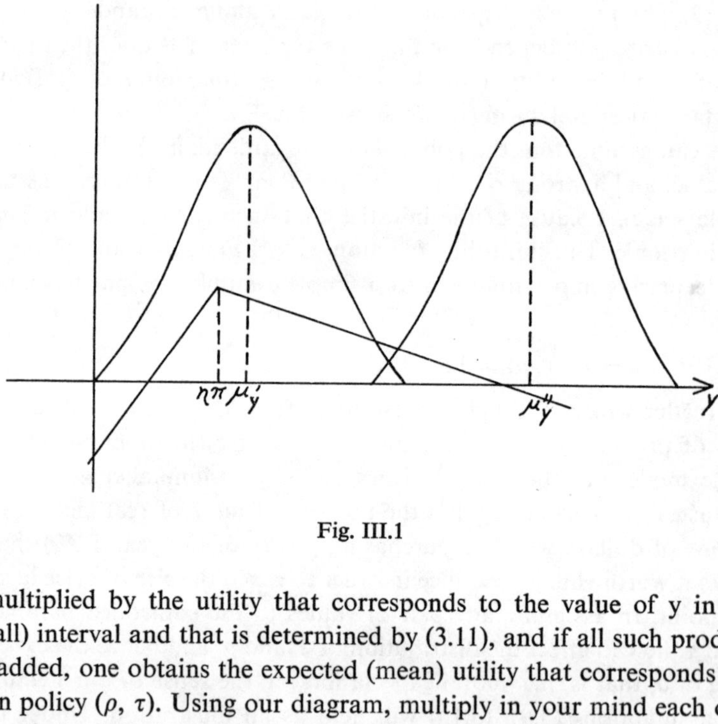

Fig. III.1

is multiplied by the utility that corresponds to the value of y in this (small) interval and that is determined by (3.11), and if all such products are added, one obtains the expected (mean) utility that corresponds to a given policy (ρ, τ). Using our diagram, multiply in your mind each ordinate of the bell-shaped curve by each corresponding ordinate of the broken line, and add all such products. Their sum is the expected utility. Clearly, as the bell-shaped curve moves too far to the right or to the left, the higher utilities (i.e., the ordinates of the broken line taken in the proximity of the full-employment point, $\eta\ \pi$) are multiplied with the lower probabilities (i.e., with the ordinates at the left or right 'tail' of the bell-shaped curve). Hence there exists some intermediate position of the bell-shaped curve – and hence some value of μ_y – that results in the highest expected utility.

To this optimal value of μ_y will correspond, by (3.5), an optimal value of $\rho - \gamma\tau$, given the non-controlled parameters. Hence the knowledge of those parameters (β, γ, μ_b, μ_c) is needed to find those pairs of value of the policy-parameters ρ and τ, that will maximize expected utility, given the 'taste-parameter' A of the policy-maker. Of course, the knowledge of the feasible limits such as $\tau_{\min}$, $\rho_{\max}$ will also have to be used, to sift out the non-feasible combinations of taxes and expenditures. But, unlike in our previous example, this knowledge will not suffice. It becomes necessary to estimate the parameters that characterize the behavior of consumers and businessmen.

We see thus that the need for the knowledge of certain parameters, and therefore for their identifiability (in the sense of Lecture 2), depends, in general, on the whole model in which these parameters occur; and on the utility function of the decisionmaker.

Does not this land us in a rather crass pragmatism? What about theory for its own sake, a theory that is not used to give advice, to choose, to act? A pragmatist will say that theory provides us with solutions which are potentially useful for a large class of decisions. It is welcome because we cannot foresee which particular decisions we shall have to take. Our decisions may or may not be such as to leave certain properties of the system unchanged. Hence, the more we know about its properties the better. If we merely want to know how long it takes to boil an egg, the best is to boil one or two without going into the chemistry of protein molecules. The need for chemistry is due to our want to do other and new things!

The word 'value' is more respectable than 'utility', yet means essentially the same. If the satisfaction of scientific curiosity is recognized by our culture as one of the major values, the search for facts as well as theories is justified even if no predictive uses can be seen for the results. Yet, an additional scrutiny in terms of other social values remains important. Especially in social science there has been a temptation to use statistical tools for laborious rediscovery of the trivial, or the recording of the useless. One should not brush away as 'utilitarian' or 'pragmatic' the reminder that we ought to help in the making of socially important decisions.[27]

NOTES

[1] The lecture was given on 6 December 1950.

[2] Such a weighted average of utilities has been called 'mathematical expectation of utility' or simply 'expected utility'. The founders of the theory of probabilities when speculating about gamblers' choices, called this weighted average the 'moral expectation' (= the mathematical expectation of 'moral' as distinct from physical', or 'monetary' wealth). The term 'military worth' (of a military situation or objective) encountered in military writings is presumably equivalent to 'utility'. It is likely that the often heard term, 'calculated risk' of a military enterprise, if the term has any meaning at all, means the negative of 'expected military worth', in the sense of an average of the utilities of the alternative outcomes of the enterprise, weighted with their respective probabilities.

[3] Actual experiments of this kind were reported by F. Mosteller and P. Nogee in 'An Experimental Measurement of Utility', *Journal of Political Economy*, **59**, (1951) 371–404

[4] 'An Essay towards Solving a Problem in the Doctrine of Chances', *Phil. Trans. Royal Soc. of London* (1763) 370–418. (Facsimile edition by W. Edwards Deming, Washington, D. C., 1940.)

[5] Daniel Bernoulli's 'Specimen theoriae novae de mensura sortis' was published in the 1730–31 volume of transactions of the St. Petersburg Imperial Academy of Sciences, pp. 175–192. A German translation by Alfred Pringsheim, is available: '*Die Grundlage der modernen Wertlehre. Versuch einer neuen Theorie von Glücksfällen*', Leipzig, 1896.

[6] Recent studies by Savage and by Herstein and Milnor (to be published) have simplified or generalized the earlier formulations of von Neumann and Morgenstern, and of J. Marschak.

[7] Frank Plumpton Ramsey 'Truth and Probability' (1926) and 'Further Considerations' (1928) published posthumously in *The Foundations of Mathematics and Other Logical Essays*, London 1931 (republished: The Humanities Press, New York, 1950). De Finetti, Bruno, La Prevision: ses lois logiques, ses sources subjectives', *Annales de l'Institut Henri Poincaré* (1937) 1–68. L. J. Savage, 'Notes on the Foundations of Statistics' (mimeographed), University of Chicago lectures, 1951.

[8] David Hilbert, *Die Grundlagen der Geometrie*, Leipzig 1910.

[9] Note that here and in what follows we are taking a more general view of a 'state of the world' than in our previous examples. A state of the world may now include more than one possibility; and each possibility can, in turn, be subdivided. Thus 'W' is a state of the world, and its subdivision, the alternatives 'W and V' and 'W and $\bar{V}$' are also states of the world.

[10] However the arithmetical operations leading to the statement are independent of this interpretation of it. They are the same as those used by James Bernoulli (Daniel's kin) who possibly did not think of probabilities as subjective.

[11] A rigorous analysis on these lines is contained in an unpublished study by Roy Radner on 'Consistent Decision Functions'.

[12] In our example, this assumption can be used only as an approximation since normal distribution applies to a continuous (and therefore infinite-valued) variable whereas x(cigarettes, communism) is discrete. Such approximations are convenient. For example, in Lloyd Warner's studies, the variable x is social status measured on a 12-point scale on the basis of neighbors' opinions; the $z^{(1)}$, $z^{(2)}$... are, respectively, income, housing conditions (again a discrete variable) etc.; and 'weights' α_i are estimated, as well as μ and σ, by the method of 'multiple regression'. With two-valued variables, this appraisal degenerates into familiar 'tests of dual hypotheses' (chi-squared, analysis of variance).

13 The problem may be posed somewhat differently. Given the joint distribution of the random disturbances v of the responses of individual firms (i.e., given μ, σ and ρ), what is the distribution of the disturbance of the sum (not of the average)? One may, for example, compare the constant ratio σ/μ (the 'coefficient of variation' of v) and the ratio between the following two constants: the standard deviation of the sum of random disturbances and the expectation of this sum. This ratio converges to $(\sigma/\mu)\sqrt{\rho}$. (A more difficult problem is to estimate the coefficient of variation of the sum: it is the expectation of a random ratio, not the ratio of two constants).

14 Cf. Paul Lazarsfeld, 'The Logical and Mathematical Foundations of Latent Structure Analysis', 'The Interpretation of Some Latent Structures', *Measurement and Prediction* **4**, Studies in Psychology of World War II, Princeton University Press, 1950.

15 See, for example, A. M. Mood, *Introduction to the Theory of Statistics*, New York 1950, pp. 299–301. To quote Mood's example, "Anthropologists... make measurements x on skulls, of known age z, then estimate the age z_0 of a skull of unknown age with measurements x'".

16 The random variable $x_1 - z(= u + \lambda_1)$ corresponds thus to the expression (2.3), with $n = 1$ and all the α_i known. It is normally distributed (with mean $\mu = \lambda_1$), jointly with another random variable, $x_2 - z$.

17 For example, although we cannot ascertain the incomes of families who tell us their consumption of cigarettes and cereals, we may know from some other source the distribution of those incomes; e.g., if our sample is large and we have reasons to regard it as representing the whole U.S. population, then the income distribution is known from income tax statistics.

18 Remembering that λ_i, x_i, z stand for the logarithms of Λ_i, X_i, Z, this means that the unknown proportionality factor Λ_i in (2.7), can be estimated as the ratio of the geometric mean of X_i (observed in a large sample) to the (known) geometric mean of Z – a result that is not unexpected, in view of the multiplicative character of the random deviation $(1 + U_i)$.

19 Implying that the consumption item X_i is (apart from random disturbances) proportional, not to the individual's income Z, but to some unknown power of it, Z^{β_i}.

20 If the sample is not very large, the test procedure is more delicate, since the nonfulfillment of equations such as (2.11) may be due to sampling errors. The question asked then is whether the equation is 'significantly' unfulfiled. Further, redundant information (such as $\sigma_{12} = 0$ in our case) may be used, not to test the hypothesis, but to increase the precision of the estimate of the parameters.

21 Rather, '*significantly*' inconsistent, unless the sample is infinite. See previous note.

22 For the history and bibliography of the subject, see Olav Reiersøl and T. C. Koopmans, 'The Identification of Structural Characteristics', *Annals of Mathematical Statistics* **21** (June 1950) 165–181, esp. p. 167; T. C. Koopmans, 'Identification Problems in Economic Model Construction', *Econometrics* **17**, No. 2 (April 1949) 125–144, esp. p. 126; Jerzy Neyman, 'Existence of Consistent Estimates of the Directional Parameter in a Linear Structural Relation between Two Variables', *Annals of Mathematical Statistics* **22** (1951) 497–512.

23 This characterization of z will simplify the exposition that follows presently, and also that of 'policies' to be discussed in lecture III.

24 See also M. A. Girshick, 'Model Construction in the Social Sciences – An Expository Discussion of Measurement and Prediction', *The Public Opinion Quarterly* **14**, No. 4 (Winter 1950–51).

25 See note 26 below.

[26] Suffice it to say that Equation (3.1), stating that production (mesured in dollars), y, is adjusted instantaneously to demand (measured in dollars), $b+c+\rho$, is merely an approximation of some equation that would state how this adjustment proceeds in time. For example, if one thinks that producers are stimulated by the excess of demand over supply one might try to replace (3.1) by the differential equation

$$(3.7) \qquad \mathrm{d}y/\mathrm{d}t = \alpha(b + c + \rho - y),$$

where t is time and α, a positive constant, is a behavior parameter measuring the speed of the producers' reaction to a unit discrepancy between demand and production. Using (3.2), (3.3), the Equation (3.7) becomes

$$(3.8) \qquad \mathrm{d}y/\mathrm{d}t = \alpha[y(\beta + \gamma - 1) + \rho - \gamma\tau + v_b + v_c];$$

if v_b and v_c were constant, (3.8) would imply that y grows exponentially ('explodes') through time if $\beta+\gamma-1>0$, and declines exponentially ('fades out') towards the 'equilibrium value' given in (3.4), if $\beta+\gamma-1<0$. Because of random fluctuations of v_b and v_c, these trends will be distorted somewhat but it remains true that the inequality $\beta+\gamma-1>0$ implies an 'explosive' rise in income (measured in dollars) such as was historically observed only in times of a few exceptional hyper-inflations. At least when one has to decide between small upward or downward variations of ρ and τ, the behavior of consumers and businessmen can be assumed to be such as to preclude explosive hyperinflation, and hence to preclude that $\beta+\gamma>1$, i.e., to preclude λ negative.

[27] See also the author's two papers on 'Statistical Inference from Non-Experimental Observations: An Economic Example' (in: *International Statistical Institute*, 25th Session, 1947. Volume III, Part A, pp. 289–301) and on 'Economic Measurements for Policy and Prediction', *Selected Essays*, 49.

5

NORMS AND HABITS OF DECISION MAKING UNDER CERTAINTY* **

(1955)

> Thinking is as unnatural and arduous an activity for human beings as walking on two legs is for monkeys.
>
> Arnold Toynbee (*Greek historical thought*, preface to 2d edition).
>
> Men must not allow themselves to be swayed by their moods, believing one thing at one moment and another at another.
>
> Bertrand Russell (*Conquest of happiness*)
>
> Industry is discovering that the man who can run one company can run another one making an entirely different product, because the qualities required for most top jobs are virtually identical – the ability ... to make sound decisions quickly and firmly.
>
> *Time*, Oct. 12, 1953. ('The great man hunt: Industry needs more good executives').

I. NORMS, HABITS, TEACHING

We can *prescribe* norms, *describe* habits, and possibly, *teach* habits that approach norms. This applies to norms and habits of thinking as well as to norms and habits of decision making.

The rules of arithmetic, geometry and logic are norms. They may or may not be obeyed in fact when children or abnormal adults or primitive men do their sums, measure plots of land or draw conclusions from premises. As to normal adults in a modern society, they, too, make mistakes in mathematics and are often victims to crude logical fallacies, as many a column of Letters to the Editor will testify. Yet norms can be taught.

When Queen Dido of Carthage acquired land she took advantage of the seller who indiscriminately regarded a plot of land as small whether it was measured by its area (covered by an ox's hide) or by its perimeter (marked by narrow strips made out of the ox's hide). The knowledge that a rectangle's area is length times width, so useful to builders and surveyors, is comparatively recent. The arithmetic of compound interest is a mystery to the Indian peasant at the mercy of the loan shark. Nor is it much better understood, I am afraid, by some Americans who buy refrigerators on installments. According to *Life* magazine, number rackets in the South offer much less favorable odds than they do in the North – presumably because their Southern clientele is less sophisticated in matters of elementary probability calculus. The circular brass basin in King Solomon's temple was said to have a circumference three times as long as its diameter; centuries later Greek youth was taught a much better approximation to π.

Mathematics and logic are normative. But the way in which certain people count, measure and think is the subject of descriptive science – of psychology, I suppose. The methods by which the existing ways of counting, measuring and thinking can be changed and, especially, can be improved (i.e., brought nearer to given norms) is, I suppose, also a problem of psychology – of applied psychology, in this case. In fact, there has been research and teaching on 'How to teach mathematics' – how successful, I don't know.

Similarly, certain formal norms of good decision making have been formulated. They do not, in general, coincide with the habits of decision making among ordinary people in our or any other civilization. These habits can be studied empirically. Moreover, there may be a social need to bring these habits closer to the norms. It is important that at least people whose decisions involve the welfare of many others should fulfill certain norms of consistency, should know, for example, how to 'make up their minds': business administrators, public servants, military leaders. If so, the question of what are and how to change decision habits becomes one of great practical importance.

II. SURE VS. UNCERTAIN PROSPECTS

In general, the outcome of a decision depends not only on the decision itself, but also on the situation which will prevail when the decision becomes effective. Thus to each situation corresponds a set of outcomes, each depending on the decision taken. And to each decision corresponds a set of outcomes, one outcome for each possible situation. We may call this latter set of outcomes, attached to a given decision, a *prospect*. In general, one does not know which situation will prevail in the future. He has to choose among prospects, that is, among sets of outcomes, in the knowledge that each outcome corresponds to some specified situation. This general case is called uncertainty. One can regard the case of certainty as a special case. In this case the future situation is known, so that the decision maker has to choose among prospects each consisting of a single outcome only. These are '*sure prospects*'. Because of its comparative simplicity, it is useful to devote attention to this special case before proceeding to the general one. I shall thus limit the discussion to the norms and habits of decision making under certainty.[1]

We shall give a very rough and tentative sketch of a decision norm. We shall formulate it in such a way as to permit its comparison with habits, for example, with observable actions of a human subject in a laboratory, and not only with his verbal statements about hypothetical decisions. Given the set of alternative outcomes, the *first choice* can be observed as an action, but the second (third, etc.) choice, if stated in the form, 'If I could not obtain x I would try to get y', can be observed only as a verbal statement unless x is actually eliminated from the set of obtainable outcomes, in which case the subject can take y as a *first* choice, an action.

Moreover, since in real life one can never refuse to take a decision (such refusal is itself a decision), we are entitled to formulate the norms so as to exclude incomparability and indifference between any two outcomes.

Finally, since we deal with sure prospects only, we can speak interchangeably of a 'situation' and of a 'set of ourcomes', and identify a decision with the choosing of a single outcome out of a set.

We shall denote outcomes by $x, y, z, \ldots$ and state our norm in two parts:

(1) For any pair (x, y) of outcomes, the following shall be true: If out of a set including x and y the subject chooses x, then, if faced again with this or any other set including x and y, he shall not choose y.

(2) For all triples (x, y, z) of outcomes, the following shall be true: If, out of a set including x and y, the subject chooses x; and if, out of a set including y and z and not x, he chooses y; then, out of a set including x and z, he shall not choose z.

More formally: let X be the set of all outcomes $x, y, z, \ldots$; let X', X'', X''' be subsets of X. Denote by $f(X')$, $f(X'')$, $f(X''')$ the respective *first choices* among the outcomes contained in those subsets. Norm (1) states that if both X' and X'' include x and y and if $f(X')=x$ then $f(X'')\neq y$. Norm (2) states: if X' includes x and y; if X'' includes y and z but not x;

and if X''' includes x and z; then $f(X')=x$ and $f(X'')=y$ imply $f(X''')\neq z$.

In much of the current literature the decision maker is imagined to make choices among two members of a *pair* of outcomes, and a binary relation 'x is not worse than y' is defined that induces an ordering ('complete and weak') on the set of outcomes. It is understood that if x is not worse than y but not conversely, the subject chooses x. But if x is not worse than y and also y is not worse than x, the decision is indeterminate and the subject is said to be indifferent between x and y. However, this cannot be observed by an outsider unless verbal statements and not only actions of the subject are taken as observed facts and are used as data to predict future actual decisions.

The relation between the decision norms (1) and (2) and the properties of the ordering relation 'not worse than' that are usually assumed, explicitly or tacitly, seems to be as follows. Norm (1) is implied by three distinct properties of that ordering relation and by the above exclusion of indifference:

(α) *comparability*: all outcomes are comparable, i.e., for no two outcomes should it be impossible to state that one of them is not worse than the other;

(β) *irrelevance of additional alternatives*: whether x is or is not worse than y is independent of whether z is also available;

(γ) *constancy* of the ordering relation over time: if x is considered not worse than y at one time it should remain so at another.

As to decision norm (2), it is implied by the following property usually assumed about the ordering relation for outcomes:

(δ) *transitivity*: if x is not worse than y, and y is not worse than z, then x is not worse than z.

Norms (1) and (2) can be said to define *consistency of decisions.* In the literature the consistency concept has often been confined to (δ) only; but, no doubt, (γ) and (β) also deserve the name!

If norms (1) and (2) are fulfilled, it is possible to rank all outcomes so as to characterize a given individual by his consistent ranking of outcomes, in the following sense. As before, denote by f the operation of picking a first choice from a given set. Consider a finite set X_0 and let $x_0=f(X_0)$. Denote by $\bar{x}_i$ a set consisting of x_i only; then $X_0-\bar{x}_0$ is a set obtained by eliminating x_0 from X_0. Let $f(X_0 - \bar{x}_0) = x_1$, $f(X_0 - \bar{x}_0 - \bar{x}_1) = x_2$, and, in general,

$$f\left(X_0 - \sum_0^m \bar{x}_i\right) = x_{m+1}, \quad m = 0, 1, \ldots .$$

We obtain a complete and strong ordering: x_0 ranks before x_1, etc. We now state: the ranking $(x_0, x_1, \ldots, x_m, \ldots)$ will prevail for any subset X' of X_0. That is to say, if $x_h, x_i, x_j, \ldots$ are all included in X' and the subscript h is a number smaller than the subscripts of all other elements of X' then $x_h = f(X')$. This follows from our norms (1) and (2).

III. DECISION HABITS

If one investigates empirically whether a subject actually fulfills our decision norm and therefore has a consistent ordering of first choices, one will, I think, almost certainly find that the norm is not fulfilled. This may be blamed on observation errors – e.g., the experimenter's failure to replicate exactly a given set of outcomes or a specified subset of it.

As an alternative explanation, one may suspect with Polonius that "though this is madness it has method." For example, one may find that, for a certain man or even for all members of a group, x is *always* the first choice in (x, y, z) and y is *always* the first choice in (x, y, w), thus breaking norm (1) under well-defined conditions. Or one may find a constant trend over time (due to learning, fatigue, aging, etc.) so that, for example, from a constant set $(x, y, z, \ldots)$ of outcomes, a person *always* makes x his first choice on the first trial, y on the second, z on the third, etc. Thirdly, one may assume that the variation of the subject's ranking order of outcomes is a random variation, satisfying a certain probability distribution that can be estimated from observations. Should this be so, it would be possible to make a statistical prediction of the subject's future decisions in the sense that the scientist will be able to bet specified odds on how the subject will decide in given situations.

In any case, one will try to consider, as a verifiable model of actual decision habits of a person or a group, not the decision norm as stated, but possibly some weakened version of it. It is probably necessary to combine the three escapes just suggested: observation errors, deviations from the norm due to ascertainable causes, and random variations. Let us, for the sake of simplicity, confine ourselves to the third way out, and weaken the 'norms' into 'models of habits' merely by introducing random variations.[2]

In the last paragraph of the preceding section we described the ranking of outcomes by successive elimination of first choices.[3] Now, instead of assuming that this ranking order does not vary, let us assume that it varies according to some probability distribution. If there are altogether n outcomes, $n!$ rankings will be possible. Denote them by r_i, $i=1,\ldots,n!$, and assume that a fixed probability $p_i=p(r_i)$ exists for each of them. Call this model M.

In a somewhat stronger model, one can add another restriction: assume that the set $p_1,\ldots,p_n$ has a unique maximum, say p_m (that is, the ranking order r_m is more probable than all others), and that p_i becomes larger as the number of reversals[4] needed to obtain r_i from r_m become smaller. We may call this assumption M_1, and the resulting model (combination of M and M_1) MM_1.

Another possible restriction is that of transitivity in the following sense. Let R_{xy} be the set of all rankings such that x ranks before y. If we denote by p_{xy} the probability that one of these rankings will be observed, then, by definition, $p_{xy}=\sum_{r\in R_{xy}} p(r)=1-p_{yx}$. Our transitivity requirement for stochastic models (call it M_2) says: for any x, y, z, if $p_{xy}\geqslant\frac{1}{2}$ and $p_{yz}\geqslant\frac{1}{2}$. then $p_{xz}\geqslant\frac{1}{2}$.

Note that, in stochastic models, the concept of indifference becomes independent of the subject's verbal statements, provided the probabilities can be estimated. He is indifferent between x and y if $p_{xy}=\frac{1}{2}=p_{yz}$.

Condition M_2 restricts the class of possible probability distributions of rankings. As an example (due to Christopher Winsten), consider a subject presented with a set of three alternative outcomes x, y, z, and let the probabilities of the six possible rankings be, in an obvious notation,

$$p_{xyz}=p_{zxy}=p_{yzx}=\tfrac{1}{6}+\alpha$$
$$p_{yxz}=p_{zyx}=p_{xzy}=\tfrac{1}{6}-\alpha,$$

where $0<\alpha\leqslant\frac{1}{6}$. Then the probability (denoted by p_{xy}) that, in choices among three outcomes, x is ranked before y is

$$p_{xy}=p_{xyz}+p_{zxy}+p_{xzy}=\tfrac{1}{2}+\alpha>\tfrac{1}{2}.$$

Similarly $p_{yz}=p_{xyz}+p_{yzx}+p_{yxz}=\tfrac{1}{2}+\alpha>\tfrac{1}{2}$.

Yet

$$p_{xz} = p_{xyz} + p_{yxz} + p_{xzy} = \tfrac{1}{2} - \alpha < \tfrac{1}{2}.$$

That is, although x is, more often than not, ranked *before* y; and y *before* z; yet x is, more often than not, ranked *behind* z. We shall have to ask whether there exist probability distributions of rankings that are consistent with M_2. But before doing this, let us stop for some other more or less plausible hypotheses on decision making.

At the end of the preceding section, we stated as a consequence of our 'norm' that the ranking of outcomes obtained by successive elimination of first choices from the sets X_0, $X_0 - \bar{x}_0$, $X_0 - \bar{x}_0 - \bar{x}_1$, etc., shall prevail also in all subsets of X_0. In the current section, we have replaced a unique ranking of outcomes by a probability distribution of such rankings. We can now ask whether the subject who, more often than not, has ranked x before y within the large set X_0 will also, more often than not, rank x before y in each of the subsets of X_0 that contain both x and y. The simplest such subsets are the pairs contained in X_0. It can be asked for each of the $n(n-1)/2$ pairs whether the same ranking of the pair (in the sense of comparative probabilities) is maintained throughout all of the 2^{n-2} sets that contain the pair. Appropriately modified, the same question can be extended from pairs to triples, etc.

A still stronger proposition would be to require that not only should the probabilities of rankings maintain a consistent order when the subject is repeatedly faced with various sets of outcomes; but that the magnitudes of those probabilities should be consistent. That is, let us denote by $p_{xy} | x, y, z$ and by $p_{xy} | x, y$ the probabilities that x be ranked before y when the subject is presented, respectively, with a set of three, and the set of two elements containing x and y. We then require that

$$p_{xy} | x, y = p_{xy} | x, y, z,$$

and not only (as just before), that

$$p_{xy} | x, y \geqslant \tfrac{1}{2} \text{ when and only when } p_{xy} | x, y, z \geqslant \tfrac{1}{2}.$$

We may call these two propositions, M_4 and M_3, respectively.

We now proceed to a very special proposition on the form of the probability distribution of rankings. It is strong enough not only to imply the transitivity condition, M_2, but also to induce a measurement scale on the suitably defined 'utilities' of outcomes.

Consider a set X of n outcomes. It is then asserted that there exists a probability distribution F of n real random variables $U_1,\dots, U_n$ with the following property: if a ranking r places the outcomes in the order x_1^r, $x_2^r,\dots, x_n^r$, then its probability $p(r)$ equals the probability that the inequalities $U_1^r > U_2^r > \cdots > U_n^r$ between correspondingly arranged U_i's are satisfied. Call this assumption M_5.

The following special form of the distribution F is compatible with, and indeed implies, the transitivity condition M_2. Let F be normal with equal variances and equal covariances. Call this assumption M_6. That is, writing $\mu_i = EU_i$ and $\sigma_{ij} = E(U_i - \mu_i)(U_j - \mu_j)$, $i, j = 1,\dots, n$, we assume $\sigma_{ij} = \sigma^2$ for $i = j$, and $\sigma_{ij} = \rho\sigma^2$ for $i \neq j$ (ρ is the correlation coefficient). Let us prove, for the case $n = 3$, that our assumptions imply transitivity, in the sense that if the three outcomes are x_1, x_2, x_3 and if p_{ij} is the probability that p_i is ranked before p_j then the following holds:

$$\text{if } p_{12} > \tfrac{1}{2} \text{ and } p_{23} > \tfrac{1}{2} \text{ then } p_{13} > \tfrac{1}{2}.$$

By M_5 (of which M_6 is a special case), $p_{12} = \text{Prob}\,(U_1 - U_2 > 0)$; and by M_6, $U_1 - U_2$ is distributed normally, with mean $\mu_1 - \mu_2$ and variance $\sigma_{11} + \sigma_{22} - 2\sigma_{12} = 2\sigma^2\,(1-\rho)$. Hence $p_{12} > \frac{1}{2}$ if and only if $\mu_1 - \mu_2 > 0$. Similarly, $p_{23} > \frac{1}{2}$ if and only if $\mu_2 - \mu_3 > 0$. Hence $p_{12} > \frac{1}{2}$ and $p_{23} > \frac{1}{2}$ if and only if $\mu_1 - \mu_3 > 0$, and this is equivalent to $p_{13} > \frac{1}{2}$. We can now restate M_6 as follows. For any (finite) set of outcomes $x_1,\dots, x_n$ there exists a set of real numbers $\mu_1,\dots, \mu_n$, τ such that the probability p_{ij} of ranking x_i before x_j is equal to $G_{ij}(0)$, where G_{ij} is a normal (cumulative) distribution function with mean $\mu_j - \mu_i$ and variance τ^2. [τ^2 is, of course, equal to $2\sigma^2(1-\rho)$, in terms of parameters of the n-variate distribution function F.] Thus, if the sample is large enough to estimate the probability p_{ij} from the frequency with which x_i was observed to be ranked ahead of x_j, then the mean $\mu_j - \mu_i$ can be read from the normal probability table, after fixing arbitrarily the origin (with $\mu_1 = 0$, say) and scale (with $\tau = 1$, say). Also, if the sample is large enough, the hypothesis itself can be disproved from observations: for the number $(n-1)$ of unknown parameters is smaller than the number $n(n-1)/2$ of estimated probabilities, p_{ij}, provided $n > 2$; and if rankings are performed not only on pairs but also on larger sets the difference between the number of knowns and of unknowns is still larger. Usually, the sample will be small, and many of the inconsistencies will be blamed on this smallness!

Assumption M_6 is used in the method of paired comparisons. (Louis Thurstone had originally restricted M_6 still further, by assuming $\rho=0$; F. Mosteller[5] showed this restriction to be unnecessary.) When applied to decisions, the means $\mu_1, \ldots, \mu_n$ have been called utilities because of the property that $\mu_i > \mu_j$ if and only if x_i will, *more often than not*, be ranked ahead of x_j; this property being, of course, weaker than the property assigned to utilities in (non-stochastic) decision norms: the utility of x_i exceeds that of x_j if and only if x_i is *always* ranked ahead of x_j.

The assumption of normality, in M_5 and M_6, is an awkward one in the case – quite usual in economic life – of quantifiable 'goods' (and 'bads'). Suppose x_1 means one meal and x_2 means two meals. Then (unless the cost of throwing a meal away is considerable) we shall expect *with certainty* that the subject will rank x_2 ahead of x_1, with only pathological exceptions. This can be also extended to some outcomes consisting of pairs, or triples, etc., of goods: e.g., if $x_1=1$ meal and 1 theater ticket, $x_2=1$ meal and 2 theater tickets, and $x_3=2$ meals and 2 theater tickets, then the ranking will be, *with certainty*: x_3, x_2, x_1. Yet the assumption of a normal distribution $F(U_1, \ldots, U_n)$ does not admit for any pair x_i, x_j that the probability $p_{ij}=\Pr(U_i-U_j>0)$ be 1 (or 0), unless all choices are non-random. Even a weaker assumption than that of normality is inconsistent with the certainty that more of a good will be chosen in preference to less. Any model that assigns an equal utility difference to all pairs (x_i, x_j), (x_h, x_i), etc., for which the probabilities of ranking p_{ij}, p_{hi} are equal, will lead to an absurd result. For suppose x_1, x_2, x_3 form a sequence of decreasing quantities of a good. Then $p_{12}=p_{23}=p_{13}=1$ and hence $\mu_1-\mu_2=\mu_2-\mu_3=\mu_1-\mu_3$ and therefore $\mu_1=\mu_2=\mu_3=0$, an absurd result.[6]

However, instead of normal distributions, one can use certain distributions in which probabilities are non-zero only for a certain range of values of a variable. In fact, the transitivity condition M_2 is satisfied by any distribution $F(U_1, \ldots, U_n)$ which does not change when the sign of any deviate $(U_i-\mu_i)$ is reversed. If, in addition, F does not change when any two deviates $(U_i-\mu_i)$, $(U_j-\mu_j)$ are interchanged, a scale of utilities can be obtained.

Let me conclude by presenting a model (M_7) that may be used to scale utilities of quantifiable goods. Let a and b be variable *quantities* of two distinct goods, A and B, and let us observe the frequency with which the subject prefers b units of B to a units of A. For a large sample, this frequency will approach a probability to be denoted by $p(b, a)$. As in the method of paired comparisons, let us assume that $p(b, a)$ increases or at least does not decrease, as the difference of utilities of the two outcomes increases:

$$(M_7) \qquad p(b, a) = H[v(b) - u(a)]$$

where H is a monotone non-decreasing function with values between (but possibly excluding) 0 and 1, and $v(b)$ and $u(a)$ are, respectively, the utilities of b units of B and of a units of A. The functions v and u are monotone increasing and are called utility functions. Can we trace them? The observed variables are a, b, and, in a large sample, the probabilities $p(b, a)$. Suppose, then, we have estimated the surface $p(b, a)$. For example, we may have obtained a graph of lines of equal p's in the (a, b)-plane, as on Figure 1.

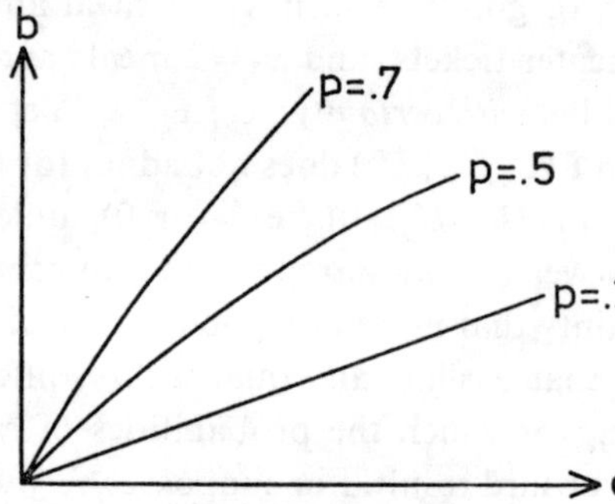

Fig. 1. Hypothetical probabilities of ranking b units of B ahead of a units of A.

The problem is to find a distribution function H such that its inverse should satisfy the condition (implied by M_7):

$$H^{-1}[p(b, a)] = v(b) - u(a) \quad \text{for all} \quad b, a;$$

this implies, for example, that, for any quadruple b, a, b', a',

$$H^{-1}[p(b, a)] - H^{-1}[p(b, a')] = \\ = H^{-1}[p(b', a)] - H^{-1}[p(b', a')].$$

Should such a function H exist, then the utility-differences $v(b) - u(a)$ can be derived for all b, a. And by fixing arbitrarily two values such as $v(b_0)=1$, $u(a_0)=2$, the two utility functions can be found. In practice, the data will, very likely, not admit the existence of a function H which will satisfy exactly the last displayed equation above. But, then, in practice, the sample will not be large enough to get the exact shape of the surface $p(b, a)$. This allows somewhat greater freedom. From the observed frequencies – one frequency for each observed pair b, a – one has to estimate the combined operator H^{-1} $[p(\ )]$, subject to the condition M_7 and consistent with the character of p as a proper fraction, H as a cumulative distribution function, and v and u as monotone increasing functions. While it would be tempting to assume H normal, the considerations given above against M_6 for the case of quantifiable goods warn against this assumption. Rather, ours seems to be a job for nonparametric statisticians.

NOTES

* Research under contract of Cowles Commission with the Office of Naval Research.
** With acknowledgments to Roy Radner and Christopher Winsten, Cowles Commission; T. W. Anderson, Columbia University; Ward Edwards, Johns Hopkins University; Conrad Oort, Fellow of Committee on Behavioral Sciences, University of Chicago.

[1] The paper originally submitted to the Rye conference of 1954 included sections on uncertainty. Some of these have been, in the meantime, reproduced in an article: 'Scaling of Utilities and Probabilities', *Selected Essays*, 3. Rather than republishing the contents of the article and including other sections on uncertainty, the author has now expanded the originally terse and unreadable sections on certainty and hopes to present the rest of the materials on another occasion.

[2] I have learned from Louis N. Thurstone that psychophysical experiments lead naturally to a stochastic interpretation of human responses to stimuli; and Thurstone himself, in his work on consumers' habits, is a pioneer in stochastic interpretation of decisions. Another pioneer was the late Hans Reichenbach, the logician, in an unpublished RAND paper dated August 1949. More recently, stochastic models for decisions under certainty were proposed in experimental studies of Professor Andreas Papandreou and his colleagues at the University of Minnesota (*A Test of a Proposition in the Theory of Choice*), 1954.

Leo Törnqvist (*A Model for Stochastic Decision Making*, Cowles Commission Discussion Paper, Economics 2100, March 1954) and Stephan Vail (*A stochastic model for utilities*, Seminar on the applications of mathematics to the social sciences, University of Michigan, 1953) have proposed appropriate axiomatics, as has done, for a related problem, Karl Menger (Probabilistic Theories of Relations', *Proc. Nat. Acad. Sci.* **37**, (1951), (178–180).

Though not explicitly so, a stochastic model is also in the background of the published experimental studies of F. Mosteller and P. Nogee ('An Experimental Measurement of Utility', *J. Polit. Econ.*, 1952), on decision making under uncertainty. See also p. 76

of Ward Edwards' experimental report ('The Reliability of Probability-Preferences', *Amer. J. Psychol.*, March 1954).

[3] It is probably easier, in performing experiments, to ask the subject to rank all the elements of a set than to ask him for a succession of decisions (i.e., of first choices). I do not insist on the former method, and what follows can equally be applied to both methods. But one should be aware of a smaller predictive value of verbal hypothetical statements compared with actual decision, when observed data are used to predict future actual decisions. Perhaps the second, third, etc., choices should be given smaller weights in statistical computations than is given to the first choice.

[4] See Kendall, M., *The Advanced Theory of Statistics*. Vol. I, p. 391.

[5] Remarks on the method of paired comparisons. I. *Psychometrika*, 1951, 1–9. In practice, Thurstone did not actually maintain the restriction ($\rho = 0$) introduced in his original article: 'A Law of Comparative Judgment', *Psychol. Rev.* (1927) 273–286.

[6] Although I have excluded from this paper the case of uncertainty, the following brief remark is in order. While maintaining the same property of utilities as assigned to the μ_i in the paired comparisons method (viz.: $\mu_1 \geqslant \mu_2$ if and only if $p_{12} \geqslant \frac{1}{2}$), it is possible to obtain another scale of utilities from observations on choices between bets, involving money sums (as in the cited experiments of Mosteller and Nogee) or any other outcomes, possibly all non-quantifiable. The additional proposition used in this case is the 'Bernoulli norm': the utility of a bet is equal to the sum of the utilities of its alternative outcomes, multiplied by respective probabilities (for the justification of this norm, see, for example, my article cited above). In the case of bets, even when the outcomes are not quantifiable goods, normal distribution is ruled out for similar reasons as above. If $\mu_1 > \mu_2$ then of any two bets promising x_1 or x_2, the one attaching greater probability to x_1 will be preferred with certainty. It would be interesting to find whether it is possible to formulate the assumptions of stochastic behavior that would be weak enough to yield a consistent scale of utilities by using bets as well as sure prospects.

6

EXPERIMENTAL TESTS OF A STOCHASTIC DECISION THEORY*

(1959)

Co-author: DONALD DAVIDSON

I. INTRODUCTION

Common experience suggests, and experiment confirms, that a person does not always make the same choice when faced with the same options, even when the circumstances of choice seem in all relevant respects to be the same. However, the bulk of economic theory neglects the existence of such inconsistencies; and the best known theories for decision making, for example, those of von Neumann and Morgenstern [1] or Savage [2], base the existence of a measurable utility upon a pattern of invariant two-place relations, sometimes called 'preference' and 'indifference'. This raises a difficulty for any attempt to use such theories to describe and predict actual behavior.

A number of ways of meeting the difficulty may be mentioned:

(1) It is possible to insist on the normative status of the theory and construe all deviations as evidence of error on the part of the subject.

(2) One may defend the descriptive accuracy of the theory and argue that it has been incorrectly interpreted; for example, by wrongly identifying two options (say winning $1 at time t and winning $1 at time $t+10$ minutes) as the same.

(3) One may interpret every case of inconsistency as a case of indifference: if the subject has chosen a rather than b but soon afterwards chooses b rather than a, this is interpreted as indifference between those two objects; if he chooses a rather than b, b rather than c, and c rather than a, this is interpreted as indifference between those three objects. In empirical application, this approach would probably make indifference all-pervasive.

(4) An alternative approach is to define preference and indifference in terms of probabilities of choice. Mosteller and Nogee, in testing the von Neumann and Morgenstern axioms, considered a subject indifferent between two options when he chose each option half the time [3]; Edwards

[4] has also used this method. In this approach probabilities of choice do not enter the formal axiomatic development.

(5) A fifth strategy, explored in this paper, incorporates probabilities of choice into the axiomatic structure and exploits their properties in scaling utilities.

II. PRIMITIVE AND DEFINED NOTIONS

We now introduce various concepts needed for the subsequent discussion. It should be emphasized that strictness has in many places been sacrificed to perspicuity; we trust that the knowing reader can make the corrections needed for formal accuracy. First we list the primitive notions:

Primitive 1

A set A of *alternatives*.[1] A may include wagers (choices involving risk) as well as sure outcomes. In this and the following section, we shall treat alternatives quite generally. In the section entitled 'Stochastic Theory of Choice Between Subjectively Even-Chance Wagers' we shall use special properties of wagers.

Primitive 2

The *probability* $P(a, b)$ that the subject, forced to choose between a and b, chooses a. We assume, in what follows, for every a and b in A:

(a) $P(a, b) + P(b, a) = 1$.
(b) $P(a, b)$ lies in the open interval $(0, 1)$.

In a fully formalized exposition these assumptions would appear as axioms or theorems; in this paper we shall sometimes leave these assumptions tacit. Under a natural interpretation Primitive 2(a) has empirical content: it implies that, when a subject is asked to choose between a or b, he always chooses a or b. Normally, we are not interested in testing Primitive 2(a); rather, we attempt to make it true by enforcing a choice. Therefore we may want to state our experimental hypothesis as follows: if Primitive 2(a) is true for a given subject, then the other axioms hold; if Primitive 2(a) fails for a subject, we then reject the subject, not the hypothesis. Or we may want to include Primitive 2(a) in the hypothesis and reject the hypothesis for a subject who refuses an offered choice.

For the experiments reported here, the issue is academic. All subjects were docile.

For the case where $a=b$, Primitive 2(*a*) has the consequence $P(a, a)= =\frac{1}{2}$. Formal convenience dictates that we not exclude this case although we give it no empirical meaning.

Before commenting on Primitive 2(b), it will be useful to give some definitions.

DEFINITION 1. a is *absolutely preferred* to b if and only if $P(a, b)=1$. This concept corresponds to the psychologists' 'perfect discrimination'.

DEFINITION 2. a is *stochastically preferred* to b if and only if $\frac{1}{2}< <P(a, b)<1$.

DEFINITION 3. a and b are *stochastically indifferent* if and only if $P(a,b) =\frac{1}{2}$. Since we use the word 'indifferent' in no other sense, we often omit the word 'stochastically'.

DEFINITION 4. c is a *stochastic mid-point* between a and b if and only if $P(a, c)=P(c, b)$.

In situations in which it is natural to apply the theory, it is obvious that cases of absolute preference occur, violating Primitive 2(b). In particular, one would expect that when a and b denote respectively 'receiving m dollars' and 'receiving n dollars' (or, for that matter, m or n units of some commodity), then $m>n$ implies $P(a, b)=1$. More generally, if m_1, n_1 are amounts of some commodity and m_2, n_2 are amounts of a second commodity, and $m_1>n_1$, $m_2 \geqslant n_2$, then the alternative consisting of receiving m_1 and m_2 will be absolutely preferred to the alternative n_1 and n_2. This extends also to bundles consisting of three or more commodities.

In the experimental testing of stochastic theories of choice, various devices may be used to avoid comparisons of alternatives which yield absolute preferences. Papandreou *et al.* [5], using appropriate commodity bundles, avoided cases of the sort just mentioned. The methods used for avoiding comparisons apt to generate absolute preference in the experiments reported here are discussed in what follows.

As long as the assumption stated in Primitive 2(b) remains in force, it is not enough merely to avoid comparing alternatives one of which is absolutely preferred to another; the set A of alternatives to which the theory applies must contain no two such alternatives. Although we have no solution on hand, we shall mention in the next section the possibility of modifying the formal system to eliminate dependence on the assumption in Primitive 2(b).

III. GENERAL STOCHASTIC THEORY OF CHOICE

An important aspect of a general stochastic theory of choice lies in the fact that, without specifically considering wagers, it is possible to obtain forms of measurement stronger than a mere ordering by imposing plausible conditions on probabilities of choice. When conditions of sufficient strength are satisfied, it is possible to interpret a comparison of probabilities as a comparison of differences in subjective value or utility. This idea is captured in a general form by the following definition:

DEFINITION 5. For a given subject, a real-valued function u is called a *utility function* on A (in the sense of Definition 5) if and only if, for every a, b, c, and d in A,

$$P(a, b) \geqslant P(c, d) \quad \text{if and only if} \quad u(a) - u(b) \geqslant u(c) - u(d).$$

The technique of building a subjective scale on the basis of frequency of discriminated differences is common in psychophysics since Fechner [6]; however, the emphasis in psychophysics on relating the subjective (sensation) scale to a physical continuum (which is not assumed in utility measurement) tends to obscure the analogy. Discussion of the relation between psychophysical scaling and utility measurement will be found in Marschak [7] and Luce [8, 9].

There is a much used adage in psychophysics which may be taken as suggesting the principle underlying Definition 5: "Equally often noticed differences are equal [on the sensation scale] unless noticed always or never" (ascribed by Guilford [10] to Fullerton and Cattell). The final phrase of this adage enters a caveat which is clearly as pertinent in utility as in sensation measurement for, in our terms, the caveat concerns the case of absolute preference. Consider the case where $P(6¢, 5¢)=1 =P(\$5000, \$0)$ and hence, by Definition 5, $u(6¢)-u(5¢)=u(\$5000)- -u(\$0)$, which is intuitively absurd. The difficulty created by the existence of absolute preferences is thus clear. The approach to a solution which suggests itself is to add to Definition 5 the caveat "provided neither $P(a, b)$ nor $P(c, d)$ is equal to 0 or 1." This would require modification of the axiomatic conditions needed to prove the existence of a utility function. We have not attempted to carry out this modification, which may well not be trivial.

We now consider what conditions are sufficient for the existence of a utility function (in the sense of Definition 5). Fortunately, in approaching this question, we are able to depend on previous work because any theory which makes essential use of a four-place relation comparing intervals may, with fairly trivial modifications, be reconstrued as a theory in which the atomic sentences are all of the form $P(a, b) \geqslant P(c, d)$, as demanded by Definition 5.[2]

What constitutes sufficient conditions for the existence of a utility function depends, in part, on the nature of the set A. We therefore consider several cases:

Case (*a*). The set A contains a known finite number n of alternatives, $a_1, \ldots, a_n$. In this case, it is always possible, although perhaps tedious, to stipulate conditions on the probabilities $P(a_i, a_j)$ necessary and sufficient for the existence of a utility function. A simple example (for $n=3$) will be treated fully later. In general, it suffices, because of Primitive 2(a), to consider those probabilities $P(a, b)$ that are $\geqslant \frac{1}{2}$; a given complete ordering of these numbers yields, by Definition 5, a sequence of $n(n-1)/2$ inequalities of the form

$$u(a_g) - u(a_h) \geqslant u(a_i) - u(a_k) \geqslant \cdots \geqslant 0$$

involving a set of only n distinct unknowns, viz., the utilities of the n alternatives. Whether these inequalities have a solution can be answered separately for each of the possible $[n(n-1)/2]!$ orderings of the probabilities.

Case (*b*). The set A contains an arbitrary number of alternatives which are equally spaced in utility [such that for every a, b, c, and d in A, if a and b are adjacent in utility[3] and c and d are adjacent, then $P(a, b) = P(c, d)$:. The axioms are an obvious modification of the axioms in Davidson, Suppes, and Siegel [11, p. 31:.

Case (*c*). It will be convenient to give two definitions. The first we owe to Professor Patrick Suppes.

DEFINITION 6. A set A of alternatives is *stochastically continuous* if and only if it meets the following three conditions for every a, b, c, and d in A:

(i) There exists a stochastic mid-point between a and b.

(ii) If $P(c, d) > P(a, b) > \frac{1}{2}$, then there exists a g such that $P(c, g) > > \frac{1}{2}$ and $P(g, d) \geqslant P(a, b)$.

(iii) (Archimedean condition.) If $P(a, b) > \frac{1}{2}$, then for every probability q such that $P(a, b) > q > \frac{1}{2}$, there exists a positive integer n such that $q \geqslant P(a, c_1) = P(c_1, c_2) = \cdots = P(c_n, b) > \frac{1}{2}$.

DEFINITION 7. The *quadruple condition* is satisfied if and only if, for every a, b, c, and d in A, $P(a, b) \geqslant P(c, d)$ implies $P(a, c) \geqslant P(b, d)$.

It follows immediately from Definition 5 that, if a utility function exists on A, then the quadruple condition is satisfied in A. However, we are now in a position to assert more:

THEOREM 1. *If A is stochastically continuous then a utility function exists if and only if the quadruple condition is satisfied.*

A proof of this theorem will not be given here. The general line of demonstration is as follows: Suppes and Winet [12] have given an axiomatization of utility based on a primitive concept which compares utility differences, and they have proved that, if certain axioms on a relation between two pairs of alternatives hold, then utility differences can be defined and, hence, a function analogous to a utility function (in the sense of Definition 5) exists. (See also Alt [13].) Suppes [14] has shown how to express these axioms in terms of relations between probabilities; the new axioms on probabilities (let us call them S) suffice to prove the existence of a utility function in the sense of Definition 5. The three conditions of Definition 6 are trivially equivalent to the continuity axioms of S. Finally, we have been able to prove that all the further axioms of S hold if the quadruple condition is satisfied [and provided, of course, the assumptions specified in Primitives 2(a) and (b) hold]. Hence we know that, if the continuity and quadruple conditions of Definitions 6 and 7 hold, S holds, and there exists a utility function.

Case (*d*) A result similar to Theorem 1 was obtained by Debreu [15] under a different definition of stochastic continuity properties. Debreu has shown that there exists a utility function on A if the following conditions are satisfied:

(i) If a, b, c are in A and $P(b, a) \geqslant q \geqslant P(c, a)$, then there is a d in A such that $P(d, a) = q$.

(ii) The quadruple condition holds for A.

Case (*e*). The set A contains an unknown number (possibly finite) of alternatives. For this case, no axiom system is known, and it has been conjectured by Scott and Suppes [16] that under certain natural restrictions on the form of axioms no axiomatization is possible.

It may be noted that in Cases (b), (c), and (d), the axiom systems adequate to prove the existence of a utility function (in the sense of Definition 5) are adequate to prove also that any such function is unique up to a linear transformation (i.e., the existence of cardinal utilities).

We can submit to direct experimental test a set of the kind described in Case (a) containing a small, known, finite number of alternatives (let us call the set of alternatives under test T). If the quadruple condition is satisfied for every quadruple of alternatives in T, and T is a sample drawn from a larger set A, we may conclude – with a degree of confidence depending among other things on the size of the sample – that the quadruple condition holds for A. If our hypothesis is that a utility function on A exists, then we need further information about A; for example, we may know the (finite) number of its elements, Case (a), or we may hold that A is stochastically continuous, Cases (c) and (d).

In the experiment reported here, one hypothesis is that a utility function exists for the set consisting of all money wagers of a certain sort. If we can assume that A is stochastically continuous in the sense of Cases (c) or (d), e.g., because the money amounts which enters the wagers are, approximately, continuous variables, and if, on the basis of our sample T, we have concluded that the quadruple condition holds for A, then we can conclude, by Theorem 1, that there exists a utility function on A.

Actually, we did not test for the quadruple condition on our sample T. Instead, we tested for certain implications of that condition: if T does not satisfy such an implication, we reject the hypothesis that T satisfies the quadruple condition. Those implications involve triples (not quadruples) of alternatives and will be referred to as stochastic transitivity properties.

Even for relatively small finite sets of alternatives, the existence of a utility function in the sense of Definition 5 implies more than is implied by the quadruple condition alone. This fact suggests a view of the relation between experimental evidence and hypothesis which differs slightly from the one outlined in the preceding paragraphs. For each sample T drawn from A, we may test *all* the conditions necessary and sufficient for the existence of a utility function on T [the general method is given above in the discussion of Case (a)]. We then consider confirmation of the existence of a utility function on T as inductive evidence for the existence of a utility function on A. As will be shown, the condition of strong stochastic transitivity about to be stated gives necessary and sufficient conditions for the existence of a utility function on a set consisting of three alternatives.

CONDITION 1.

(a) *Weak stochastic transitivity* holds in A if and only if, for all a, b, and c in A,

$$\text{if } P(a, b) \geqslant \tfrac{1}{2} \text{ and } P(b, c) \geqslant \tfrac{1}{2}, \text{ then } P(a, c) \geqslant \tfrac{1}{2}.$$

(b) *Strong stochastic transitivity* holds in A if and only if, for all a, b, and c in A,

$$\text{If } P(a, b) \geqslant \tfrac{1}{2} \text{ and } P(b, c) \geqslant \tfrac{1}{2}, \quad \text{then } P(a, c) \geqslant \max[P(a, b), P(b, c)].$$

These terms are due to S. Vail [17]. (We sometimes omit the word 'stochastic'.) Clearly Condition 1(b) implies 1(a), but 1(a) does not imply 1(b); both are implied by the existence of a utility function and are, therefore, necessary conditions for the existence of such a function. Condition 1(b) is equivalent to:

CONDITION 2.

$$\text{If } P(a, b) \leqslant \tfrac{1}{2}, \text{ then } P(a, c) \leqslant P(b, c).$$

Proof: To show that Condition 1(b) implies Condition 2, assume $P(a, b) \geqslant \frac{1}{2}$ and show that, by Condition 1(b), $P(a, c) \geqslant P(b, c)$ for each of the three possible cases:

1. $P(b, c) \geqslant \frac{1}{2}$; then $P(a, c) \geqslant \max[P(a, b), P(b, c)] \geqslant P(b, c)$.
2. $P(b, c) < \frac{1}{2} \leqslant P(a, c)$; then $P(a, c) \geqslant P(b, c)$.

3. $P(b, c) < \frac{1}{2}, P(a, c) < \frac{1}{2}$; then $P(c, a) > \frac{1}{2}$, hence $P(c, b) \geqslant \max[P(c, a), P(a, b)] \geqslant P(c, a), P(a, c) \geqslant P(b, c)$.

It may be left to the reader to prove the converse, i.e., that Condition 2 implies Condition 1 (b).

Consider three fixed alternatives, a_1, a_2, a_3 and label the three relevant probabilities $P(a_1, a_2) = p_1$, $P(a_2, a_3) = p_2$, $P(a_3, a_1) = p_3$. The two

TABLE I

Specimen stimulus cards

For testing transitivity of alternatives

	A	B
ZOJ	− 5¢	+36¢
ZEJ	−21¢	−38¢

	A	B
QUG	+36¢	−54¢
QUJ	−38¢	+22¢

	A	B
WUH	−54¢	− 5¢
XEQ	+22¢	−21¢

For testing transitivity of utility intervals

	A	B
ZOJ	− 6¢	+ 5¢
ZEJ	+24¢	+13¢

	A	B
QUG	+38¢	+31¢
QUJ	+13¢	+24¢

	A	B
WUH	+31¢	+38¢
XEQ	+5¢	− 6¢

kinds of transitivity condition applied to the set consisting of a_1, a_2, a_3 can then be expressed in the following symmetric form:

CONDITION 3

(a) *Weak transitivity*: p_1, p_2, p_3 not all $\geqslant \frac{1}{2}$ or $\leqslant \frac{1}{2}$ unless they are all $= \frac{1}{2}$.

(b) *Strong transitivity*:

$$p_1 \geqslant \tfrac{1}{2} \text{ if and only if } p_2 + p_3 \leqslant 1,$$
$$p_2 \geqslant \tfrac{1}{2} \text{ if and only if } p_3 + p_1 \leqslant 1,$$
$$p_3 \geqslant \tfrac{1}{2} \text{ if and only if } p_1 + p_2 \leqslant 1.$$

In the experiment reported in this paper, we are concerned with triples of alternatives. It is therefore interesting to note that, if the set of alternatives consists of exactly three elements a, b, c, then the condition of strong stochastic transitivity is not only necessary for the existence of a utility function (as mentioned in the foregoing) but also sufficient. For, under strong transitivity, we may assume without loss of generality that $P(a, c) \geqslant P(a, b) \geqslant P(b, c) \geqslant \frac{1}{2}$. The corresponding inequalities between utilities (Definition 5) are: $u(a) - u(c) \geqslant u(a) - u(b) \geqslant u(b) - u(c) \geqslant 0$. These inequalities are satisfied, for example, by the following numbers: $u(a) = 1$, $u(c) = 0$, $u(b) =$ any number between, and including, 0 and 1.

In Table I, the upper three cards show how we tested strong (and weak) transitivity experimentally. The subject made choices between the two columns on a card; the syllables on the left represent events determining the outcome of a wager. On the three cards there are altogether three alternatives (wagers) paired in each of the three possible ways. By testing whether Condition 3(b) holds for a sample consisting of a number of such triples of alternatives, we obtain evidence for or against the hypothesis that a utility function exists on the set of alternatives from which the sample is drawn.

IV. STOCHASTIC THEORY OF CHOICE BETWEEN SUBJECTIVELY EVEN-CHANCE WAGERS

In this section we deal with a special case of the stochastic theory of choice, exploiting some possible properties of choices between wagers of a special sort, namely, those created by chance events with a 'subjective probability of one half'. The theoretical and experimental importance of the nonstochastic theory of choice for such wagers was first pointed out by Ramsey [18]; a formalization of the theory applied to finite sets, and reports of several experimental applications (including one with stochastic aspects) are given in Davidson *et al.* [11].

We assumed in the foregoing section that the set A of alternatives might contain wagers as well as sure outcomes; however, the formal developments made no use of this assumption.

Some additional primitive notions are needed.

Primitive 3
A set X of *states of the world.* The subsets of X are called *events*, denoted by $E, F, \ldots$ and forming a set $\mathscr{E}$.

Primitive 4. If a, b are in A and E is in $\mathscr{E}$, then aEb is the wager which consists in getting a if E happens, and getting b if E does not happen.

Definitions 1 through 4 are applicable to wagers; for example, when $P(aEb, cFd) = \frac{1}{2}$, we say that aEb and cFd are (stochastically) indifferent. We may presume that in certain cases absolute preference occurs. In particular, if a_1, a_2, b_1, b_2 are in A and $P(a_1, b_1) = 1 = P(a_2, b_2)$, then for any event E in $\mathscr{E}$, $P(a_1Ea_2, b_1Eb_2) = 1$.

DEFINITION 8. An event E in $\mathscr{E}$ is an *even-chance event* if and only if, for every a and b in A,

$$P(aEb, bEa) = \tfrac{1}{2}.$$

If E is an even-chance event, we call aEb an *even-chance wager*. It is obvious that the notion of even chance involved in this definition is *subjective*; it makes no appeal to the objective probability of E. The justification for our terminology is simple. Suppose a subject prefers a to b. If he thinks E is more likely to happen than not, he will choose aEb more often than bEa; if he thinks E less likely to happen than not, he will choose aEb less often than bEa. Hence he will choose aEb and bEa equally often if and only if he thinks E is as likely to happen as not, i.e., E has a 'subjectively even chance'.

DEFINITION 9. The subject is said to be *unbiased* if and only if, for any two even-chance events E and F and any a and b in A,

$$P(aEb, aFb) = \tfrac{1}{2}.$$

It is obvious that if this condition is satisfied and there exists a utility function u on A, then for any two even-chance events E and F and any a and b in A,

$$u(aEb) = u(bEa) = u(aFb) = u(bFa).$$

This justifies writing simply ab for aEb where E is any even-chance event;

since we explicitly consider no other events, symbols for chance events need not enter our formalism.

The chief concern of this section may be stated by giving a more restrictive version of Definition 5:

DEFINITION 10. A real-valued function u is an *even-chance wager utility function* (or a *utility function in the sense of Definition* 10) on A if and only if:

(a) u is a utility function on A in the sense of Definition 5;
(b) for every a and b in A and every even-chance event E, $u(aEb) = [u(a)]/2 + [u(b)]/2$.

Definition 10(a) and (b) together express in stochastic form the usual hypothesis that a subject prefers the wager with the higher expected utility (applying this hypothesis to the case of even-chance wagers). Clearly, these conditions imply that $u(aEb)$ has the same value for all even-chance events E in $\mathscr{E}$, and that the subject is unbiased.

Now we wish to state conditions sufficient for the existence of an even-chance wager utility function. To this end we define the following condition:

DEFINITION 11. The *even-chance mid-point* condition holds in A if and only if the subject is unbiased and, for every a and b in A,

$$P(a, ab) = P(ab, b).$$

(Definition 11 says ab is a stochastic mid-point between a and b; see Definition 4.)

We may now state a theorem analogous to Theorem 1:

THEOREM 2. *If A is stochastically continuous, then an even-chance wager utility function on A exists if and only if the quadruple condition (Definition 7) and the even-chance mid-point condition hold in A.*

Proof: Suppose A is stochastically continuous. Then a function u on A such that $P(a, b) \geqslant P(c, d)$ if and only if $u(a) - u(b) \geqslant u(c) - u(d)$ exists if and only if the quadruple condition holds (Theorem 1). Hence the quadruple condition is a necessary condition for the existence of an even-chance wage utility function. And if the quadruple condition is satisfied, then a utility function in the sense of Definition 5 exists; hence:

$$P(a, ab) = P(ab, b) \quad \text{if and only if} \quad u(a) - u(ab) = u(ab) - u(b)$$

that is,

$$u(ab) = \frac{u(a)}{2} + \frac{u(b)}{2}.$$

Therefore the quadruple and even-chance mid-point conditions together are necessary and sufficient for the existence of a utility function in the sense of Definition 10, provided A is stochastically continuous.

An alternative statement of sufficient conditions may now be considered We define:

DEFINITION 12. The *even-chance quadruple condition* holds in A if and only if, for every a, b, c, and d in A,

$$P(a, b) \geqslant P(c, d) \quad \text{if and only if} \quad P(a, bc) \geqslant P(bc, d),$$

and assert:

THEOREM 3. *If A is stochastically continuous then a utility function on A in the sense of Definition 10 exists if and only if the even-chance quadruple condition holds in A.*

Proof. It follows directly from Definition 10 that, if a utility function in the sense of that definition exists, the even-chance quadruple condition holds. We prove the sufficiency of the even-chance quadruple condition by showing that it implies both the even-chance mid-point condition and the quadruple condition, and then applying Theorem 2. By the even-chance quadruple condition we have (replacing b by a, and c and d by b):

1. $P(a, a) = P(b, b)$ if and only if $P(a, ab) = P(ab, b)$.

The right side of (1) (i.e., the even-chance mid-point condition) is true since the left side is true by Primitive 2(a). Using the even-chance quadruple condition again and Primitive 2(a), the following steps lead to the quadruple condition:

2. $P(a, b) \geqslant P(c, d)$ if and only if $P(d, bc) \geqslant P(bc, a)$.
3. $P(d, bc) \geqslant P(bc, a)$ if and only if $P(a, c) \geqslant P(b, d)$.

We may now establish:

THEOREM 4. *If the even-chance quadruple condition holds in A, then for all a, b, c, and d in A,*

$$P(a, b) \geqslant P(c, d) \quad \text{if and only if} \quad P(ad, bc) \geqslant \tfrac{1}{2}.$$

We establish Theorem 4 by noting that, if the even-chance quadruple condition holds, then $P(a, b) \geqslant P(c, d)$ is equivalent to $P(a, bc) \geqslant P(bc, d)$, which in turn is equivalent to $P(ad, bc) \geqslant P(bc, ad)$.

We have seen (in the proof of Theorem 3) that the even-chance quadruple condition implies the quadruple as well as the even-chance midpoint condition. On the other hand, it seems a safe conjecture that these two conditions in conjunction do not imply the even-chance quadruple condition unless the assumption of stochastic continuity is made. With the assumption of stochastic continuity, the implication does hold, as is easily seen from Theorems 2 and 3.

Theorem 4 thus states a strong principle. In interlocks, in effect, the utility scales obtained by comparing differences in utility by two separate methods.

CONDITION 4

(a) *Weak stochastic transitivity for utility intervals* holds in A if and only if, for all a, b, c, d, e, and f in A,

$$\text{if } P(bf, de) \geqslant \tfrac{1}{2} \text{ and } P(ae, cf) \geqslant \tfrac{1}{2}, \text{ then } P(ab, cd) \geqslant \tfrac{1}{2}.$$

(b) *Strong stochastic transitivity for utility intervals* holds in A if and only if, for all a, b, c, d, e, and f in A,

$$P(bf, de) \geqslant \tfrac{1}{2} \text{ if and only if } P(ab, cd) \geqslant P(ae, cf).$$

The analogy between the transitivity conditions for alternatives (Condition 1) and transitivity conditions for intervals (Condition 4) may be brought out as follows. If a utility function in the sense of Definition 10 exists, then Condition 4(a) is equivalent to the statement (holding, identically, for any six numbers):

If

$$[u(b) + u(f)] - [u(d) + u(e)] \geqslant 0$$

and

$$[u(a) + u(e)] - [u(c) + u(f)] \geqslant 0$$

then

$$[u(a)+u(b)]-[u(c)+u(d)]\geqslant 0,$$

and hence to:

CONDITION 5

(a) If $u(b)-u(d)\geqslant u(e)-u(f)$ and $u(e)-u(f)\geqslant u(c)-u(a)$ then $u(b)-u(d)\geqslant u(c)-u(a)$.

Similarly, Condition 4(b) is equivalent to:

(b) $u(b)-u(d)\geqslant u(e)-u(f)$ if and only if $[u(b)-u(d)]-[u(c)-u(a)]\geqslant [u(e)-u(f)]-[u(c)-u(a)]$.

Now let the length of the utility interval $u(b)-u(d)=I$, $u(e)-u(f)==J$, and $u(c)-u(a)=K$. Then Conditions 5(a) and (b) become similar in form to Conditions 1(a) and 2:

CONDITION 6

(a) If $I\geqslant J$ and $J\geqslant K$, then $I\geqslant K$.
(b) $I\geqslant J$ if and only if $I-K\geqslant J-K$.

Thus Conditions 4(a) and (b) may be interpreted as stating conditions on utility intervals analogous to Conditions 1(a) and (b) for alternatives (whether or not these alternatives happen to be wagers). However, it should be emphasized that in testing the transitivity of intervals we must make use of wagers; although we did use wagers in testing the transitivity of alternatives, this is not essential to the theory.

From Conditions 5(a) and (b), it is clear that the transitivity conditions for utility intervals are necessary for the existence of a utility function in the sense of Definition 10.[4] To obtain evidence whether such a function exists for a limited set of outcomes consisting of winning and losing small amounts of money, we tested certain implications of Conditions 4(a) and (b) for sextuples of outcomes which may be regarded as samples from the total set of outcomes. Let us designate six specific money outcomes, a_1, a_2, a_3, a_4, a_5, a_6, arranged in ascending order by monetary value. For reasons given in the next section, we considered the following probabilities only:

$$p_1 = P(a_1a_4, a_2a_3) \qquad p_2 = P(a_6a_3, a_5a_4)$$
$$p_3 = P(a_5a_2, a_6a_1).$$

For these three probabilities the implications of Conditions (4)a and (b) are just:

CONDITION 7

(a) *Weak transitivity of utility intervals:* p_1, p_2, p_3 not all $\geqslant \frac{1}{2}$ or $\leqslant \frac{1}{2}$ unless they are all $= \frac{1}{2}$.

(b) *Strong transitivity of utility intervals*:

$$p_1 \geqslant \tfrac{1}{2} \text{ if and only if } p_2 + p_3 \leqslant 1,$$
$$p_2 \geqslant \tfrac{1}{2} \text{ if and only if } p_3 + p_1 \leqslant 1,$$
$$p_3 \geqslant \tfrac{1}{2} \text{ if and only if } p_1 + p_2 \leqslant 1.$$

It will be noted that Conditions 7(a) and (b) are identical with Conditions 3(a) and (b) where, of course, the three relevant probabilities are differently defined. If a utility function for the six outcomes $a_1, \ldots, a_6$ exists, Conditions 7(a) and (b) will be satisfied; but the converse is not in general true. The existence of a utility function in the sense of Definition 10 implies, even for six outcomes, more than is implied by the transitivity of intervals condition (for example, Theorem 4 is implied by the existence of a utility function but not by the transitivity of intervals condition); and the transitivity of intervals condition alone implies more for six outcomes than is tested by checking the relations given in Conditions 7(a) and (b) and with p_1, p_2, p_3 as defined above.

The second line of specimen cards in Table 1 illustrates the method used in testing Conditions 4(a) and (b). Before the three pairs of wagers on these cards were offered to the subject, it was verified that the chance events underlying the designed money wagers were even-chance events in the sense of Definition 8.[5] This justified the assumption that all wagers on the cards were (for the given subject) even-chance wagers; therefore it could be tentatively assumed that, whenever the subject chose a wager (a column of a card), he could be interpreted as comparing two utility intervals, represented by the rows of the card. On the three cards illustrated, there are three pairs of identical rows: they correspond to the intervals *I*, *J*, and *K* in Conditions 6(a) and (b). (From Conditions 5(a) and (b) it is clear that interchange of rows or of columns in a given card does not matter, nor does the interchange of alternatives in one of the columns.)

V. EXPERIMENTAL DESIGN

The experiment to be described was designed to test the plausibility of the hypothesis that (for given individuals) there exists a utility function in the sense of Definition 10 (or at least, in the sense of Definition 5), defined over a set of alternatives consisting of winning and losing small amounts of money and of even-chance wagers constructed from the basic alternatives. The individuals were 17 students from an elementary logic class at Stanford University. The general hypothesis was tested by testing certain of its consequences: stochastic transitivity (weak and strong) of alternatives as applied to triples of alternatives (interpreted here as wagers), and stochastic transitivity (weak and strong) of utility intervals as applied to sextuples of alternatives.

The obvious way of testing a stochastic theory of choice is to estimate probabilities of choice from frequencies of choice observed when the subject is repeatedly offered the same alternatives. This method, common from psychophysical experiments, has been used with apparent success by a number of workers in decision theory. These workers (who include Mosteller and Nogee, Ward Edwards, and Papandreou) were, of course, aware of the memory effect, and used various techniques in the attempt to cope with it. In a pilot study for the present experiment, we found that, with wagers of the sort we wished to use, the subject almost always made the same choice when offered the same pair of alternatives; thus we would be forced to estimate almost every probability as 0 or 1. The wagers between which the subjects had to choose had the same actuarial value; the wagers could therefore be assumed to be close in subjective utility. Remarks by the subjects led to the suspicion that the cause of the unforeseen consistency was the subject's ability to remember his previous choices (although various masking procedures were attempted such as reversing the order in which the wagers in a pair were offered, and inserting other offers between repetitions of the identical pair of wagers). In psychophysical experiments, memory cannot have this effect since the subject is given no way of identifying the repetition of a stimulus.

To avoid the effect of memory, the same *pair* of wagers was never offered twice to a subject. The method used for testing our hypothesis under this restriction is explained in the next section.

Each subject was asked to make 319 choices; a choice consisted in a

TABLE II

Money amounts (wins and losses) used in constructing stimulus cards

Sequence	*a*	*b*	*c*	*d*	*e*	*f*	*g*
1	−17	−12	−5	+2	+8	+17	+21
2	−20	−16	−11	−4	+3	+10	+15
3	−12	−5	+2	+9	+14	+19	+23
4	−22	−18	−14	−9	−2	+5	+12
5	−14	−8	−4	+5	+13	+20	+26
6	−36	−17	−8	+2	+10	+21	+27
7	−13	−8	−5	−1	+4	+7	+12
8	−35	−28	−22	−15	−8	−2	+6
9	−27	−16	−4	+7	+21	+34	+47
10	−6	+1	+8	+15	+22	+30	+34
11	−39	−25	−9	+6	+23	+40	+56
12	−37	−22	−6	+5	+21	+38	+54
13	−7	−4	−1	+3	+6	+8	+11
14	−14	−9	−6	−2	+3	+6	+11
15	−6	+2	+12	+21	+29	+36	+42
16	−24	−20	−14	−7	+1	+8	+13
17	−31	−17	−5	+8	+21	+33	+46
18	−11	−3	+4	+12	+19	+24	+28
19	−17	−6	+5	+13	+24	+31	+38

verbal response (*A* or *B*) to a stimulus card of the kind illustrated in Table I. In 107 cases selected (with certain limitations to be mentioned later) at random, and unknown in advance to the subject, the response of the subject was followed by playing off the wager selected, and the subject lost or won the appropriate amount of money.

The 319 stimulus cards were designed as follows. Every card displayed four figures (positive or negative) representing a possible outcome consisting of losing or winning the amount of money shown. On the left were two nonsense syllables (*WUH* and *XEQ*; *ZOJ* and *ZEJ*; *QUJ* and *QUG*) which stood for chance events. The events were created by the subject tossing a die with one nonsense syllable on three faces and another nonsense syllable on the other three faces. In an effort to offset recency and memory effects three different dice were used. The two right-hand columns marked *A* and *B*, represent the wagers between which the subject was to choose.

For testing hypotheses concerning the existence of an even-chance wager utility function, it was necessary to ascertain whether the events created by the three dice were even-chance events. In practice, this was tested indirectly by assuming, for any money amounts m and n (in cents):

$$P(mEn, nEm) = \tfrac{1}{2} \quad \text{if and only if} \quad P(mEn, n-1\,E\,m) > \tfrac{1}{2} \quad \text{and} \quad P(mEn, n+1\,E\,m) < \tfrac{1}{2}.$$

Previous experiments had shown that, given this modified interpretation, subjects generally accepted the nonsense-syllable dice as generating even-chance events; therefore we tested each die only a few times with each subject [11, p. 56 and Table I, p. 57]. In all, 12 stimulus cards were used to test the dice; three additional cards were added to this group to familiarize the subject with other sorts of choices.

The remaining cards were intended to test the transitivity of alternatives and of intervals (Conditions 1 and 4). Thirty-eight sequences of seven money amounts were chosen such that the money amounts, in the light of previous experiments [3, 11], would be approximately evenly spaced in utility for most subjects. Table II gives the first 19 sequences; the other 19 sequences were produced from the first by reversing the signs (thus wins become losses and vice versa). This symmetry provides a simple guarantee that the actuarial value of the complete set of wagers is zero; why this is desirable will be explained below. Eight cards were made for each sequence of money amounts, yielding $8 \times 38 = 304$ cards in all. Using the letters at the top of Table II, the eight cards showed the following patterns:

1	2	3	4	5	6	7	8
a b *d c*	*c d* *f e*	*a b* *f e*	*b c* *e d*	*a c* *f d*	*d e* *g b*	*b c* *g f*	*b d* *g e*

It will be observed that the triads 3, 4, 5 and 2, 7, 8 each contain just three alternatives (wagers, represented as columns), and thus may be used to test the transitivity of alternatives. Triads 1, 2, 3 and 4, 6, 7 each compare, in effect, three intervals (represented by rows), and thus may be used to test the transitivity of intervals. Because of this overlap between triples, we have achieved some economy in the number of observations: the total of 304 cards yields 76 triples designed to test the transitivity of alternatives and 76 triples designed to test the transitivity of intervals.

The assignment of one of the three dice to a specific card was random. Because certain wagers (not cards) were repeated once, the column (*A* or *B*) on which a wager appeared was randomized; the row (top or bottom) assigned to an outcome in a wager was also randomized. Finally, the order in which the cards appeared was randomized, except that the 15 cards, used for learning and to test that the dice created even-chance events, preceded all others; and all three cards from a given triple appeared during the same session.

We may now make explicit two rules employed in limiting the offers appearing on the stimulus cards. No sure-thing alternatives were allowed on the ground that these might distort the results should there exist a specific utility or disutility of gambling. The second rule is intended to eliminate cases of absolute preference. In any given triple of cards, there are six distinct outcomes. Let us assign the numbers 1, 2, ..., 6 to the six outcomes in order of monetary value; the number assigned to an outcome denotes its rank. The rule is this: on any given card, the sum of the ranks of the two outcomes in one wager must be equal to the sum of the ranks of the two outcomes in the other wager. Since the outcomes are chosen to be approximately evenly spaced in utility, the rule is designed to insure that two wagers that are compared shall not differ too strongly in expected utility. In application, no two wagers on one card differed by more than $4\frac{1}{2}$ cents in actuarial value. When the transitivity of intervals is tested for six outcomes, the two rules just mentioned limit the pairs of wagers to be compared to exactly three.

Of the 17 subjects 6 were women and 11 were men. Subjects were tested individually. Each subject came to three sessions, spaced a few days apart; two sessions were never on the same day for a given subject, nor more than five days apart. A session lasted between 35 and 55 minutes. Subjects were asked not to discuss the experiment during the testing; none of them had any detailed knowledge of game theory or decision theory.

At the beginning of the first session, a subject was shown the three nonsense-syllable dice and the game he was to play was explained. The subject was given \$2 credit (in chips) and told that this was his stake for the three sessions. At the end of the three sessions, his chips would be redeemed in cash; if he had won, he would receive \$2 plus his winnings; losses would come out of the \$2; greater losses would have to be paid out of his own pocket.

The first stimulus cards have been described; of these, 12 tested whether the subject accepted the dice as creating even-chance events, and three were for learning purposes. In effect, every subject did accept the dice as 'fair'. All of the first 15 cards were played off. After the subject gave his response by choosing wager *A* or *B*, he put the indicated die in a leather cup, shook, and rolled. Depending on the outcome, the experimenter then collected from or paid out to the subject the appropriate number of chips. The rest of the first session consisted in responses to 88 more stimulus cards testing the two sorts of transitivity. Of these, 25 choices were played off; the subject did not, of course, know whether a card would be played until after he had made his choice. The cumulative expected win for a subject who always chose the wager with the higher actuarial value was +44 cents for the 25 cards which were played off. Subjects were urged to take as long as they wished to make a decision.

During the second session the subject was asked to make 112 decisions; of these, 36 were played off. The cumulative expected win for the actuarial chooser was +39 cents.

The last session called for 104 decisions of which 31 with an expected win of +55 cents were played off. During this last session, the experimenter could play off additional wagers to increase the winnings of an unlucky subject.

As mentioned above, the actuarial value of the total of all wagers offered was zero. Since the wagers between which a subject was to choose seldom had exactly the same actuarial value, a consistent 'actuarial chooser' could have expected to win if every choice had been played off. The cards chosen for playing had a small positive actuarial value for the 'random chooser' and a higher actuarial value for the actuarial chooser. The hope was that the average subject with average luck would slowly increase the sum at his disposal; its size would not vary enough to influence choices substantially. It may be doubted whether this hope was entirely realized. In any case, for many subjects the sum at their disposal changed fairly radically during the play, and verbal comments by subjects suggested that this influenced choices. The highest total win (for all three sessions) was $4.87 (including the original $2 stake); the least fortunate subject received a few cents less than $2. However, several subjects had their winnings 'artificially' increased during the last session by the experimenter naming for playoff certain cards on which both wagers had high positive actuarial value; unknown to the subject, it had been decided in advance that no subject would average less than \$1 an hour for his time.

VI. STATISTICAL DECISION RULES

Transitivity Regions. Consider the three related probabilities p_1, p_2, p_3 as defined for the statement of Conditions 3(a) and (b), or as defined for the statement of Conditions 7(a) and (b). Let us denote by $p^i = \langle p_1^i, p_2^i, p_3^i \rangle$ the ith ordered triple of probabilities so defined. p^i is a point in the unit cube U, since each component of p is between 0 and 1.

We now define two subregions of U:

Region W: p^i obeys Condition 3(a) [or 7(a)] (region of weak transitivity).

Region S: p^i obeys Condition 3(b) [or 7(b)] (region of strong transitivity).

Obviously, region S is included in region W. The hypothesis pairs to be tested may be stated:

Hypothesis H_w: For all i, p^i is in W.
Hypothesis H_w^0: There exists an i such that p^i is in $U - W$.
Hypothesis H_s^0: For all i, p^i is in S.
Hypothesis H_0: There exists an i such that p^i is in $U - S$.

Note that each of the hypotheses has two empirical interpretations; one concerns stochastic transitivity of alternatives, the other stochastic transitivity of utility intervals. We need not distinguish between the two interpretations in discussing the method of statistical testing.

Since a given choice was presented to a subject only once, it was impossible to estimate the probability triples p^i from observed frequencies. Corresponding to a given p^i, we made one observation consisting of the three responses of a subject to a triple of related stimulus cards. Suppose, for the sake of simplicity of exposition, that the pairs of wagers on a related triple of stimulus cards are arranged in the order suggested by the definitions of p_1, p_2, p_3 (pp. 141, 148); this has been done for the triples of cards shown in Table I. Then if the subject chooses column A on the first card, there is greater likelihood that $p_1 > \frac{1}{2}$ than that $p_1 < \frac{1}{2}$; if he chooses column A on the third card, there is greater likelihood that $p_3 > \frac{1}{2}$ than that $p_3 < \frac{1}{2}$. An *observation* is an ordered triple of reponses; there are just eight possible observations:

$$O_1 = \langle A, A, A\rangle \quad O_5 = \langle B, A, A\rangle$$
$$O_2 = \langle A, A, B\rangle \quad O_6 = \langle B, A, B\rangle$$
$$O_3 = \langle A, B, A\rangle \quad O_7 = \langle B, B, A\rangle$$
$$O_4 = \langle A, B, B\rangle \quad O_8 = \langle B, B, B\rangle$$

In a nonstochastic theory, observations O_1 and O_8 would be cases of intransitivity. In a stochastic theory, they merely strengthen the evidence in favor of (stochastic) intransitivity. To avoid confusion we call such observations *cyclical* because, e.g., $\langle A, A, A\rangle$ means that a certain wager *a* was chosen in preference to *b*, *b* to *c*, and *c* in preference to *a*, thus forming a cycle.

In its strict formulation, our problem is analogous to the following simpler (one- instead of three-dimensional) problem: "Test the hypothesis that each coin made by a certain coin-making machine has a bias, not necessarily an equally strong one for all coins, in favor of falling heads. You are permitted to take a finite number of coins and to toss each coin just once." Each coin of this example corresponds to a triple of choices from three pairs of our wagers. The parameter space is, respectively, the unit interval (0, 1) or the unit cube U. The interval $(\frac{1}{2}, 1)$ which contains the probability of a biased coin falling heads corresponds to our transitivity region W (or S) which contains all probability triples if the subject satisfies the transitivity condition. Should this formulation be accepted, then, out of the infinite set of potential observations (coins, triples of choices) it would suffice for a single one to be outside of a specified region (the bias interval for coins, the transitivity region for response triples) to rule out the hypothesis in question. But such a fact cannot be ascertained empirically from a finite number of observations. The problem becomes accessible to empirical test if it is reformulated as follows: "A coin-making machine is characterized by an unknown probability distribution of the chance variable p (probability of a coin falling heads); one is permitted to toss coins, each only once, in order to get evidence about the distribution of p." The chance variable p corresponds, in the theory of stochastic choice, to the triple: $\langle p_1, p_2, p_3\rangle$ defined above.

For example, one might test the following hypothesis about the distribution of p: the proportion of coins (or of triples of wagers) whose p falls into a specified region is at least 95 per cent. This approach has been used in a later study, by H. D. Block and J. Marschak [20]; with regions like S, this statistical problem is rather complicated. In the present study, we chose a simpler though more arbitrary approach by adding the following assumption: p is uniformly distributed about an unknown region which is either the whole space of possible p's (the unit cube, in our case) or a specified region (such as W or S). We have thus two pairs of alternative hypotheses:

H_w: p^i is distributed uniformly over W, and $\text{Prob}(p^i \in W) = 1$.
H_0: p^i is distributed uniformly over U, and $\text{Prob}(p^i \in U) = 1$.
H_s: p^i is distributed uniformly over S, and $\text{Prob}(p^i \in S = 1$.
H_0: p^i is distributed uniformly over U, and $\text{Prob}(p^i \in U) = 1$.

It turns out that for testing the statistically reformulated hypotheses, all that matters (the 'sufficient statistic') is the number of cyclical observations. Computations yield the following probabilities of a cyclical observation:

	Probability of a Cyclical Observation
If H_0 is true	$\frac{20}{80}$ or 25.00%
If H_w is true	$\frac{15}{80}$ or 18.75%
If H_s is true	$\frac{11}{80}$ or 13.75%

The reasoning leading to the first figure (25 per cent) is obvious: if p^i is distributed uniformly over the unit cube, each of the eight possible observations $O_1, \ldots, O_8$ is equiprobable. Since two of these are cyclical, the probability that a given observation is cyclical if H_0 is true is $\frac{1}{4}$. The other two figures ($\frac{15}{80}$ and $\frac{11}{80}$) were obtained[6] by integrating over the specified region (W or S, respectively) the expression

$$p_1 p_2 p_3 + (1 - p_1)(1 - p_2)(1 - p_3)$$

(i.e., the probability that O_1 or O_8 will occur), and dividing by the volume of that region.

The *decision rule* used was this (we state if for H_w; that for H_s is analogous). Accept H_w if the number r of cyclical observations is less than c, where c (a number obtainable from tables of binomial distribution) is such that $\text{Prob}(r < c$, when H_0 is true$) = \text{Prob}(r \geqslant c$, when H_w is true$)$. The two probabilities just written are, respectively, that of committing the error of

TABLE III. Decision rules

	Number of Observations	
	$n = 76$ (All Sessions)	$n = 26$ (Session III)
Accept H_w if r is less than:	17	6
Significance level:	24 %	35 %
Accept H_s if r is less than:	15	5
Significance level:	10 %	23 %

TABLE IV

Number of cyclical observations for each subject

	Testing transitivity of alternatives				Testing transitivity of intervals			
Sessions	I	II	III	Total	I	II	III	Total
Number of triples offered	22	28	26	76	22	28	26	76
Expected number under uniform distribution over the region of:	Number of cyclical observations							
Unit cube	5.50	7.00	6.50	19.00	5.50	7.00	6.50	19.00
Weak transitivity	4.13	5.25	4.88	14.25	4.13	5.25	4.88	14.25
Strong transitivity	3.03	3.85	3.58	10.45	3.03	3.85	3.58	10.45
Subject								
A	4	0	0	4	0	0	1	1
B	3	5	2	10	1	6	3	10
C	5	3	3	11	6	5	5	16
D	4	7	0	11	4	5	2	11
E	1	0	0	1	0	3	3	6
F	3	6	0	9	5	10	2	17
G	2	1	2	5	3	0	0	3
H	2	1	1	4	4	2	1	7
I	1	2	1	4	3	3	0	6
J	2	9	5	16	3	3	6	12
K	4	2	2	8	3	5	3	11
L	1	1	0	2	1	1	0	2
M	2	2	1	5	7	5	1	13
N	6	3	7	16	2	0	3	5
O	4	2	1	7	3	2	0	5
P	1	3	3	7	2	1	3	6
Q	7	5	2	14	1	4	2	7
Average no. of cyclical observations	3.06	3.06	1.76	7.88	2.82	3.24	2.06	8.12
Proportion of cyclical observations	13.9%	10.9%	6.8%	10.4%	12.8%	11.6%	7.9%	10.7%

accepting H_w when H_0 is true, and that of committing the error of accepting H_0 when H_w is true. By making them equal, we make the larger of the two error probabilities a minimum. The significance level of test is equal to both of them. If instead of this 'minimax' principle that takes into account both kinds of error, we had followed the custom of merely 'testing the null hypothesis', the decision could have been made, given our number of observations, with a much lower probability of errors of Type I (called 'significance level'). The latter would then have been defined as the probability of rejecting H_0 when it is true. However, the nature of the problem forces us to treat the null hypothesis and its alternative symmetrically.

In the present experiment we made on each subject a total of 76 observations for each hypothesis; 26 observations for each hypothesis were made during the last session. Applying our computations and decision rule to these figures, we obtain Table III.

One obtains, of course, much lower significance levels if one is permitted to regard the responses of all subjects as belonging to the same statistical population, thus increasing the sample size by the factor of 17 (the number of subjects). Using the normal distribution formula, one can compute the decision rules at which the probabilities of errors of both kinds are equal. The rules are, for samples of this magnitude: reject H_w if and only if the proportion of cyclical observations is larger than 21.7 per cent; reject H_s if and only if this proportion is larger than 18.7 per cent (compare these figures with the last line of Table IV). The significance levels are as follows; for Session III, 0.055 for H_w and 0.001 for H_s; for the total of all sessions, 0.003 for H_w and negligible for H_s.

Finally, we observe that, if the proportion of cyclical observations falls very much below the probability indicated above for weak or strong transitivity, we shall presume that the assumption of uniform distribution over the (weak or strong) transitivity region is to be corrected: we shall have to assign lower weights to those points of the region that lie near its boundaries other than the facets of the unit cube.

As another and possibly preferable way of exploiting the information more fully, Herman Chernoff and Roy Radner[7] suggested computing the likelihood ratio for each pair of hypotheses and each possible set of observations. Let $P_0(r, n)$ be the probability that, out of n responses, exactly r are cyclical if H_0 is true. With a corresponding notation for the cases when H_w or H_s are true, we can use the ratios

$$L_w(r, n) = P_w(r, n)/P_0(r, n) \quad \text{and} \quad L_s(r, n) = P_s(r, n)/P_0(r, n)$$

to convey the confidence that one may attach, on the basis of observations, to the hypothesis H_w or H_s, each against the hypothesis H_0. Using the binomial distribution formulas, one derives from the probabilities of cyclical observations ($\frac{20}{80}$ for H_0, $\frac{15}{80}$ for H_w and $\frac{11}{80}$ for H_s), the two likelihood ratios

$$L_w(r, n) = (\tfrac{19}{13})^r \cdot (\tfrac{13}{12})^n \quad \text{and} \quad L_s(r, n) = (\tfrac{11}{23})^r \cdot (\tfrac{23}{20})^n$$

These numbers are tabulated in Table V, for $n=76$ and $n=26$ (with r ranging from 0 to respectively 17 and 7), and can be used to interpret, subject by subject, the results shown in Table IV for the total of observations and for Session III:[8]

TABLE V
Likelihood ratios (approximate)

No. of cyclical responses:	H_ω against H_0		H_8 against H_0	
$r =$	$n=76$	$n=26$	$n=76$	$n=26$
0	430	8.0	40000	38
1	300	5.5	20000	18
2	210	3.8	9300	8.7
3	140	2.7	4500	4.1
4	100	1.8	2100	2.0
5	69	1.3	1000	0.9
6	49	0.9	490	0.5
7	33	0.6	240	0.2
8	23	0.4	110	0.1
9	16		54	
10	11		26	
11	7.6		12	
12	5.3		5.9	
13	3.6		2.8	
14	2.5		1.3	
15	1.7		0.6	
16	1.2		0.3	
17	0.8		0.1	

VII. RESULTS OF EXPERIMENT

Table IV summarizes the main experimental findings. For a large majority of subjects, the number of cyclical responses falls far below the expected frequency under strong transitivity (both of alternatives and of intervals). Under the null hypothesis, one out of four triples could, on the average, be expected to be cyclical; this would result in 38 cyclical responses for the total of 152 triples, or 19 for the 76 triples which tested each of the two varieties of transitivity. The highest total number of cyclical responses for any subject was 28 (subject *J*), while subject *F* had the highest number of cyclical responses (17) for a set of 76 triples. The expected numbers of cyclical responses in 76 triples for H_w and H_s are 14.25 and 10.45 respectively. Two subjects (*J* and *N*) in the case of transitivity of alternatives, and two subjects (*C* and *F*) in the case of the transitivity of intervals, exceeded the number of cyclical responses expected on the assumption that H_w is true. The *average* number of cyclical responses for all subjects on the 76 triples testing transitivity of alternatives is 10.4; the average on the 76 triples testing transitivity of intervals is 10.7. These figures are close to the prediction of 10.45 cyclical responses if strong transitivity holds.

The last line of Table IV should be related to what was said about using the responses of *all* subjects as a sample from the same population (p. 158). On this basis (and under the assumptions of the foregoing section regarding *a priori* distribution), weak as well as strong transitivity, for both alternatives and intervals, should be accepted at a quite low (i.e., strict) significance level.[9]

Table VI applies the decision rules (Table III) to each subject (using the results from all sessions). For all subjects, Hypothesis H_w of weak transitivity had to be accepted with respect both to alternatives and to intervals (though at a very modest, i.e., high, significance level). For all but two subjects, strong transitivity had to be accepted (at a significance level of 10 per cent), but the two subjects were not the same for alternatives and for intervals. The correlation of 0.49 between behavior with respect to alternatives and behavior with respect to intervals is just significant at the 5 per cent level for 17 observation pairs; however, it should not be judged significant at that level if one considers the fact that some of the data were used in two ways as described on p. 151.

An interesting feature of the data displayed in Table IV is the change in

TABLE VI

All sessions (76 triads); distribution of subjects by the number of cyclical observations (correlation coefficient = 0.49)

No. of cyclical observations for alternatives	No. of cyclical observations for intervals 1	2	3	4	5	6	7	8	9	10	11	12	13	14	15	16	17	No. of subjects	
1						*E*												1	Accept strong and weak transitivity
2		*L*																0	
3																			
4	*A*					*I*	*H*											3	
5			*G*										*M*					2	
6																		0	
7					*O*	*P*												2	
8											*K*							1	
0																	*F*	1	
1										*B*								1	
1											*D*					*C*		2	
1																		0	
13																		0	
14							*Q*											1	
15																		0	Accept weak transitivity only
16					*N*							*J*						2	
17																		0	
No. of subjects	1	1	1	0	2	3	2	0	0	1	2	1	1	0	0	1	1		
	Accept strong and weak transitivity													Accept weak transitivity only					

the proportion of cyclical observations from session to session. Although not always evident for individual subjects, when the results for all subjects are averaged there is a systematic decrease in the percentage of cyclical observations from session to session both alternatives and for intervals. During the first session, the over-all proportion of cycles is 13.4 per cent; during the second session, 10.5 per cent; during the third 7.4 per cent.

For the third session, the decision rule indicates that the null hypothesis must be accepted for one subject (*N*) for transitivity of alternatives, and for one subject (*J*) for transitivity of intervals. There is also one subject in each category (subjects *J* and *C* respectively) for whom weak but not strong transitivity must be accepted. In every other case the hypothesis of strong transitivity may be accepted.

During the three sessions, there was an increase in the correlation between performance with respect to alternatives and performance with respect to intervals, as follows:

Session	I	II	III	Total
Correlation	0.00	0.52	0.58	0.49

The change from I to II is significant at the 5 per cent level.

VIII. DISCUSSION

Assuming that a utility function of money unique up to a linear transformation exists for a subject, it is possible to make some rough inferences from the data concerning the shape of the utility curve (a curve which plots utility against the money amount of the basic alternatives). Table VII classifies the responses of each subject to the 304 cards used to test transitivity. On 249 cards the two wagers had different actuarial values; the second and fifth columns in Table VII show in how many cases the subject chose the wager with the higher *actuarial value* ('actuarial responses') and in how many cases the subject chose the wager with the lower actuarial value ('counteractuarial responses'). On every card, one wager involved the highest and lowest of four money amounts, whereas the other wager involved outcomes of intermediate money value; see p. 148. Responses may therefore be classified according as the subjects chose the wager with the greater or the lesser *dispersion* (the dispersion of an even-chance

TABLE VII

Responses for each subject according to actuarial value and dispersion (total number of wagers = 304)

	Pairs of wagers of unequal actuarial value				Pairs of wagers of equal actuarial value		All pairs of wagers	
Subject	Actuarial responses	Counteractuarial responses						
		Dispersion chosen High	Low	Total	Dispersion chosen High	Low	Dispersion chosen High	Low
A	227	10	12	22	11	44	134	170
B	149	75	25	100	41	14	213	91
C	162	54	33	87	37	18	184	120
D	165	75	9	84	43	12	234	70
E	174	45	30	75	29	26	168	135
F	161	73	15	88	41	14	223	81
G	149	79	21	100	43	12	225	79
H	175	65	9	74	46	9	225	79
I	200	36	13	49	34	21	181	123
J	162	50	37	87	27	28	164	140
K	167	54	28	82	34	21	184	120
L	182	15	52	67	18	37	103	201
M	136	49	64	113	28	27	137	167
N	160	53	36	89	37	18	177	127
O	216	12	21	33	12	43	127	177
P	165	23	61	84	18	37	104	200
Q	145	58	46	104	34	21	169	135

wager is the difference in money value between the two outcomes). The second and third columns of figures in Table VII show how often the counteractuarial choices favored high or low dispersion. Fifty-five cards showed wagers of equal actuarial value; these responses are classified to indicate whether the high or the low dispersion wager was chosen. In evaluating the figures in Table VII, it is necessary to know that of the 249 cards with wagers of unequal actuarial value, 124 paired the higher actuarial value with the higher dispersion and 125 paired the higher actuarial value with the lower dispersion.

A subject for whom utility was linear in money and with absolute preferences between all pairs of wagers offered would always choose the wager with the higher actuarial value. There is no subject who did this.

Subjects *A* and *O* come closest with 22 and 33 counteractuarial answers. Both these subjects show some preference for low dispersion when they depart from the actuarial choice.

We may call a subject *conservative* who, when departing from the actuarial answer, more often than not chose the wager with the lower dispersion, for such a subject would, from an insurance point of view, be paying for the privilege of taking the smaller risk. In the same way we may call a subject *venturesome* who, when departing from the actuarial answer, more often than not chose the wager with the higher dispersion. Using this criterion, five subjects were conservative and twelve were venturesome. In the light of previous experimental results with college students [3, 11], the percentage of venturesome subjects is perhaps surprising. Part of the explanation may lie in the fact that the subjects were volunteers and knew, before they volunteered, that the experiment involved some financial risk.

A subject who invariably chose the higher or the lower dispersion would yield no cyclical observations (no pair of wagers showed the same dispersion, since this would lead to absolute preference), whereas the consistent actuarial chooser would be certain to show no more than six cyclical triads of responses (there were six triples of cards where each pair of wagers had the same actuarial value). It is therefore an interesting question to what extent the results obtained were caused by actuarial, conservative, or venturesome strategies (conscious or otherwise) on the part of the subjects. Table VII makes it obvious that no subject consistently followed any of the three policies. Comparison of Tables IV and VII brings out the fact that the four subjects with the largest number of cyclical observations (subjects *C*, *D*, *F*, and *J*) include none of the five subjects with the largest number of counteractuarial responses. On the other hand, subject *L*, with the lowest number (4) of cyclical triples, seems to owe this score in part to a conservative taste for low dispersion wagers, whereas subject *A*, with only five cyclical triples, has the fewest counteractuarial responses.

We may also ask whether the frequency of cyclical observations depends on the size of the differences in the actuarial values of each pair of wagers. One would expect cyclical observations to occur relatively more often in cases where these differences are small and thus provide no guidance, or only a weak one, for the choice between two wagers and

TABLE VIII

Actuarial characteristics of triples offered and the frequency of cyclical observations

	Character of triples offered[a]	Number of observations: Total	Cyclical	Non-cyclical	Percentage of cyclical in total
A	$d = 0$ on all three cards	102	17	85	16.7
B	$0 < d \leqslant \frac{1}{2}¢$ on all three cards	272	59	213	21.7
(A, B)	$0 \leqslant d \leqslant \frac{1}{2}¢$ on all three cards	(374)	(76)	(298)	(20.3)
C	$d \leqslant 1¢$ on all three cards	442	49	393	11.1
D	All other triples	1768	147	1621	8.3
(C, D)	$d > \frac{1}{2}¢$ on at least one of the three cards	(2210)	(196)	(2014)	(9.3)
	Total	2548	272	2312	10.5

Variation of frequency between groups	χ^2	P	Significant?
A against B	1.3	>0.25	No
C against D	3.2	>0.05	Hardly
(A, B) against C	13.7	<0.005	Yes
(A, B) against (C, D)	43	<0.005	Yes

[a] d = difference between actuarial values of the two wagers on a card.

the ranking of three wagers. In Table VIII, four groups – A, B, C, D – of triples are defined, the number of observations (i.e., the number of triples times 17, the number of subjects) is entered for each group, and the frequency of cyclical versus noncyclical observations is given. A finer grouping of triples was precluded by sample size limitations. In fact, the distinction between groups A and B proved to be statistically insignificant (and hence the unexpectedly *lower* percentage of cyclical observations in group A compared with group B is not statistically significant). Significant and interesting results are obtained by comparing group (A, B) (which is the union of A and B and thus consists of all triples with actuarial differences not exceeding $\frac{1}{2}$ cent on any/card) either with group C (actuarial differences not smaller than 1 cent on any card) or with the composite group (C, D) (actuarial difference exceeds $\frac{1}{2}$ cent on at least one card). These comparisons tend to confirm the hypothesis that small actuarial differences favor the occurrence of cyclical choices.

It may be asked whether the decrease in the proportion of cyclical observations from session to session was accompanied by an increase in the proportion of actuarial responses. The following figures show that it was.

	Sessions		
	I	II	III
Number of cards with wagers of different actuarial value	1241	1598	1394
Number of actuarial choices	810	1106	979
Percentage	65.3	69.2	70.2
Number of triples	748	952	884
Number of noncyclical observations	648	845	819
Percentage	86.6	89.5	92.6

The increase in the proportion of actuarial choices was statistically significant ($P<0.05$) from Session I to Session II and definitely not significant ($P>0.50$) from Session II to Session III. On the other hand, the proportion of noncyclical observations increased highly significantly ($P<0.01$) from Session II to Session III, although it did not increase significantly ($P>0.2$) from Session I to Session II. This suggests that, to the extent to which there was an increase in noncyclical observations, it should not be explained by the increase in actuarial choices. However, a more detailed analysis would be necessary to clarify this point.[10]

In the table just given, the proportion of noncyclical observations to the total number of triples of cards is, in each of the three sessions, consistently higher than the proportion of actuarial choices to the total number of cards. A formal test shows the difference between the proportions to be statistically highly significant. Thus, considering all subjects to belong to the same population, the probability that a subject's response to a triad of cards will be noncyclical is higher than the probability that his response to a single card will be actuarial.

Broadly speaking, the present experiment shows that in its context decisions are better explained by certain implications of a stochastic decision theory than by the assumption that choices are made at random. The interest of this result would be impugned if the same data could be as well or better explained by alternative hypotheses. For this reason, we have been considering the plausibility of the claim that, to the extent that subjects avoided cyclical triads of responses (and hence tended to verify the hypotheses under test), this was caused by the more or less consistent employment of actuarial, venturesome, or conservative policies by the subjects. In Table IX we attempt a direct comparison of three alternative theories as predictors of certain observed choices.

Assume that a related triple of cards was always arranged in the 'normal form', shown in Table I, and that the three cards were presented to the subject in order from left to right. If a subject chose one left and one right column for the first two cards, the hypotheses H_w (or H_s) as well as H_0 would predict equal probabilities of choice for each wager on the third card. The interesting cases arise when the left column or the right column is chosen on both the first two cards; then the hypotheses H_w and H_s will give the higher probability of choice to the opposite column on the third card (for example, if column A is chosen on each of the first two cards, column B is more apt to be chosen on the third card if the hypotheses are true).

The first two columns of figures in Table IX show how often the subject chose the more probable wager on the third card for those cases where both of the first two choices were wager A or wager B. The third and fourth columns show how often, for the same cards for which results are given in the first two columns, the subject chose the wager with the higher actuarial value. The total number of predictions is lower because some cards had two wagers with equal actuarial values. The last two columns show, for the same cards again, how often the subject chose in accord with his general tendency to favor low or high dispersion wagers. This tendency was determined from the figures in Table VII, showing how often the counteractuarial responses of the subject favored low or high dispersion.

At the bottom of Table IX, the three theories are compared with respect to the percentage of correct predictions. The expected utility theory is superior to the other two with 81.6 per cent correct predictions; the actuarial theory is slightly better than the dispersion theory with 72.2 per cent correct predictions as compared to 69.0 per cent correct predictions.

TABLE IX

Comparison of expected utility, actuarial, and dispersion theories as predictors

Subject	Expected utility theory		Actuarial theory		Dispersion theory	
	Correct	Incorrect	Correct	Incorrect	Correct	Incorrect
A	84	5	74	5	56	33
B	63	20	39	29	60	23
C	46	27	42	20	44	29
D	86	22	69	24	84	24
E	76	7	56	19	50	33
F	80	26	68	28	74	32
G	86	8	47	33	80	14
H	100	11	74	22	92	19
I	71	10	66	8	50	31
J	49	28	43	25	42	35
K	52	20	43	17	48	25
L	83	4	60	17	64	23
M	57	18	43	25	50	25
N	63	21	53	22	59	25
O	76	12	69	8	57	31
P	70	13	52	24	68	15
Q	70	21	41	35	48	43
Totals	1213	273	939	361	1026	460
Percentage correct	81.6		72.2		69.0	

Each of the differences between these proportions (taken pairwise) is statistically significant ($P<0.01$). It is also worth noting that for every individual subject, the expected utility theory predicted better than the dispersion theory; however, the actuarial theory was very slightly superior to the expected utility theory for two subjects (subjects *C* and *J*).

A remark is called for concerning the marked decrease in the proportion of cyclical observations from session to session. It seems attractive to call this a learning phenomenon. However, what was learned was certainly not connected with specific cards, wagers, money amounts, or triples of cards, for none of these was repeated in two sessions (specific cards and triples were not repeated even in the same session). The evidence indicates that the subjective probability of the chance events was firmly established from the start. We may say that the subject learned transitive behavior or that he learned to maximize expected utility (at least in the sense of our stochastic definitions of these terms). There is also evidence that some subjects learned to make actuarial choices. The matter seems worthy of fuller study, both theoretical and experimental.

IX. SUMMARY

The experiment was designed to test whether certain conditions hold which are necessary for the existence of a utility function over the set of money wagers as well as over the set of money amounts. Seventeen subjects were tested individually in three sessions each. Every choice involved a risk since subjects did not know in advance which choices would be played off, i.e., would result in actually paying (or receiving) money. The main results may be summarized as follows:

(1) For all subjects, the number of intransitive triads of responses (called 'cyclical observations') was, as required by the hypotheses, less than the number expected by chance.

(2) A statistical test, based on responses to nonrepeated choice situations, indicates the acceptance, for all subjects, of the hypotheses of weak stochastic transitivity of alternatives and weak stochastic transitivity of utility intervals.

(3) For 15 subjects in each case, the acceptance of the hypotheses of strong stochastic transitivity of alternatives and of intervals is indicated.

(4) Both in testing the transitivity of alternatives and the transitivity of intervals, there was a systematic decrease in the number of cyclical responses from session to session.

(5) A comparison shows the superior accuracy of a stochastic theory of decision in predicting certain choices as compared to two alternative theories. On the whole, the evidence does not appear to support the claim that the low number of cyclical observations can be wholly explained by simple policies based on the actuarial values of wagers or on the degree of risk (dispersion).

NOTES

* Research undertaken by the Applied Mathematics and Statistics Laboratory, Stanford University, under contract Nonr-225(17), NR 171-034, with the Office of Naval Research, and by the Cowles Commission for Research in Economics under contract Nonr-358(01), NR 047-006, with the Office of Naval Research.

The authors were helped by discussions with G. Debreu, E. Fels, L. Hurwicz, R. Radner, H. Raiffa, R. Summers, R. Savage, and P. Suppes.

1 We use the word 'alternative', as is fairly common in the literature of decision theory, to mean one of two or more things or courses among which a person may choose.

2 The modifications may allow for the special properties of probabilities, and for the fact that $P(a, b) \geqslant P(c, d)$ compares signed intervals whereas the quaternary relations taken as primitive in some theories compare unsigned intervals.

3 Let $P(a, b) \geqslant \frac{1}{2}$; then a and b are said to be adjacent in utility if $P(a, b) \leqslant p(a, c)$ for every c with $P(a, c) \geqslant \frac{1}{2}$.

4 We conjectured that, if the set of alternatives is stochastically continuous, then the conjunction of strong transitivity of alternatives and of strong transitivity of utility intervals is necessary *and sufficient* for the existence of a utility function in the sense of Definition 10. While this paper was in preparation, G. Debreu [19] proved a closely related theorem which seems particularly applicable to wagers in money amounts (or, more generally, in any continuous commodity amounts).

5 A more precise statement of the procedure used will be given in the next section.

6 With the help of Karol Valpreda Walsh and Robert C. Mercer, which we gratefully acknowledge.

7 In an oral communication.

8 Again, if we regard all subjects as belonging to the same statistical population, the likelihood ratios are naturally much higher; they are of the order of many thousands, for both H_w and H_s, even if the proportion of cyclical observations is as high as 15 per cent.

9 The size of the sample used for the *joint* test of transitivity of alternatives *and* of intervals is somewhat reduced by the overlapping between the sets of cards used for these two tests separately (see p. 151); this raises the significance level somewhat.

10 We are grateful to R. Rosett for computations and suggestions.

BIBLIOGRAPHY

[1] von Neumann, J. and Morgenstern, O., *Theory of Games and Economic Behavior*, 2nd ed., Princeton University Press, Princeton, 1947.

[2] Savage, L. J., *Foundations of Statistics*, John Wiley and Sons, New York, 1951. Revised, Dover, 1972.

[3] Mosteller, F. and Nogee, P., 'An Experimental Measurement of Utility', *Journal of Political Economy* **59** (1951) 371–404.

[4] Edwards, Ward, 'Articles on Probability Preferences', *American Journal of Psychology* **66** (1953) 345–364; **67** (1954) 56–67; **67** (1954) 68–95.

[5] Papandreou, Andreas G., with the collaboration of O. H. Sauerlander, Brownlee, O. H., Hurwicz, L., and Franklyn, W., 'A Test of a Stochastic Theory of Choice', *University of California Publications in Economics* **16**, No. 1 (1957) 1–18.

[6] Fechner, Gustav Theodor, *Elemente der Psychophysik*, Leipzig, 1859 and 1889.

[7] Marschak, Jacob, 'Norms and Habits of Decision Making Under Certainty', *Selected Essays*, 5.

[8] Luce, R. Duncan, 'A Probabilistic Theory of Utility', *Econometrica* **26** (1958) 193–224.

[9] Luce, R. Duncan and Raiffa, Howard, *Games and Decisions*, John Wiley and Sons, New York, 1957 (Appendix I, 'A Probabilistic Theory of Utility', pp. 371–384).

[10] Guilford, J. P., *Psychometric Methods*, New York, 1954.
[11] Davidson, Donald, Suppes, Patrick, and Siegel, Sidney, *Decision Making, An Experimental Approach*, Stanford University Press, 1957.
[12] Suppes, P. and Winet, M., 'An Axiomatization of Utility Based on the Notion of Utility Differences', *Management Science* **I** (1955) 259–270.
[13] Alt, Franz, 'Ueber die Messbarkeit des Nutzens', *Zeitschrift fuer National-oekonomie* **7**, No. 2 (1936) 161–169.
[14] Suppes, P., 'A Set of Axioms for Paired Comparisons' (dittoed), Center for Behavioral Sciences, 1956.
[15] Debreu, Gerard, 'Stochastic Choice and Cardinal Utility', *Econometrica* **26** [1958] 440–444.
[16] Scott, Dana and Suppes, P., 'Foundational Aspects of Theories of Measurement', *Journal of Symbolic Logic* **23** (1958).
[17] Vail, Stephan, 'A Stochastic Model for Utilities', Seminar on the Application of Mathematics to the Social Sciences, Ann Arbor, University of Michigan, 1953 (dittoed).
[18] Ramsey, Frank P., *The Foundations of Mathematics and* Other Logical Essays, Routledge and Kegan Paul, London, 1931.
[19] Debreu, Gerard, 'Cardinal Utility for Even-Chance Mixtures of Sure Prospects', *Review of Economic Studies* **26** (1958–1959).
[20] Block, H. D. and Marschak, Jacob, 'Random Orderings and Stochastic Theories of Responses', *Selected Essays*, 7.

7

RANDOM ORDERINGS AND STOCHASTIC THEORIES OF RESPONSES*

(1960)

Co-author: H. D. BLOCK

I. THE PROBLEM

In interpreting human behavior there is a need to substitute 'stochastic consistency of choices' for 'absolute consistency of choices'. The latter is usually assumed in economic theory, but is not well supported by experience. It is, in fact, not assumed in empirical econometrics and psychology.

The stochastic approach brings out the affinity between the phenomenon of choice and the more general psychological phenomenon of response to physical stimuli or, for that matter, to questionnaires, or of the action of 'judges' who compare the performances of individuals.[1]

Let A be the set of all alternatives (or actions) ever to be considered by a given subject. Let F be a subset of A. Let $(a; F)$ denote a 'multiple choice' (also called 'first choice' out of a set), i.e., the following observed fact: When forced to choose one element of F, the subject chose a. In the theory of choice, F is called the feasible set. When F consists of 2, 3,... elements, the multiple choice is called binary, ternary,....

In another language, the set F is associated with a stimulus and consists of all possible responses of the subject to that stimulus; A is then interpreted as the set of all possible responses to all stimuli. In experiments on so-called preferences and attitudes, the stimulus consists in offering a list of alternative menus, alternative political candidates, alternative answers to an item in the questionnaire. This list is then the feasible set F. When a 'judge' makes paired comparisons, the set F is a pair of individuals. In experiments on perceptional discrimination, physical stimuli – sounds, lights, or weights – impinge upon the subject; his response consists in stating that one of those objects is louder, or brighter, or heavier than the other(s). The set F is then the set of the n possible responses (or $n+1$ if 'I don't know' statements are permitted).

Another example of F is the set of all family budgets open to a family with a fixed amount of money, given the prices of goods (see Hotelling [2]). Each element of F is a different way of allocating the money among different goods.

In this paper – subject only to some attempted generalizations in Section VII – we shall call the observed choice, or response, $(a; F)$ the *basic* or *direct observation*. These observations can be counted, and the constraints on (i.e., the relations among) the resulting numbers (which may possibly be only 1's or 0's) we shall call *conditions*. Some of these conditions we shall call *directly testable*. Only those conditions are directly testable which involve the basic observations only. We shall encounter conditions that are not directly testable because they involve certain entities (constructs) that are not directly observable. An important class of these constructs will be called *utilities* (identical with *sensations* in psychophysics, *values* in anthropology, ethics, and older economics). These will be defined in a variety of ways, but will always denote certain real numbers, constant or random, associated with the elements of the set A.

However, to involve basic observations only is a necessary but not a sufficient property of a directly testable condition. For example, if the set A of alternatives is finite but of a size unknown, or too large to be exhausted by experiment, a constraint involving all alternatives simultaneously – such as Condition (o) in Section IV and Condition (P_n) in Section V – cannot be tested.

The purpose of this paper is to study the logical relations between various conditions describing consistency of responses, and in particular the logical relations between certain conditions that are not directly testable and others that are. This will tell whether a given class of observational results would or would not justify the acceptance (or the rejection) of a theory.

Our particular way of defining the class of basic observations and, correspondingly, of the directly testable conditions is to some extent arbitrary. Depending on the range of possible experiments and other observations, it may be preferable to define the class more narrowly, e.g., by including binary choices only. Or we might define this class more broadly. Following the practice of psychologists, we might admit the ranking, by the subject, of three or more objects as an observable fact, although the subject's observed action consists in this case of a verbal statement. (In the case of two objects, ranking and choosing is the same thing.) We might even admit as observable the subject's verbal statements of the relative 'intensity' of his preferences.

Such variations of the domain of testability will be tentatively discussed in Section VII. In the rest of the paper, by using a particular demarcation of the class of directly testable conditions (the one most closely corresponding to the nature of economic observations), we are able to carry out a reasonably complete analysis of the relevant logical relations. The study may thus serve as a start when similar attempts are made under another definition of basic observations.

In particular, our operational approach seems to be unable to handle the following distinction that appears natural on grounds of common sense and may be important for predictions. If out of the pair $F=(a, b)$ of desirable objects a man chooses sometimes a and sometimes b, our introspection tells us that we may ascribe this to either or both of two different 'causes':

1. He may have difficulty in perceiving all the relevant characteristics of the objects, as when a and b are two 10-ton carloads of the same merchandise but the exact quantity (in pounds, net of package) or, for that matter, all the differences in quality cannot be ascertained.
2. Even if he knew exactly the differences in the characteristics of the two objects, he might find them almost equally 'desirable' or containing the promise of equal 'satisfaction', and he will vacillate as a result.

To disentangle the two 'causes' – call them 'perceptibility' and 'desirability' (anticipated 'satisfaction') – may be important if one wants to predict how people will act if perceptibility is kept constant while desirability varies, or vice versa. Economists in particular have mostly considered men's decisions under the assumption of perfect perceptibility, also called perfect information. In the more recent developments of economic decision theory, imperfect information is introduced, but a clear, and probably fruitful, distinction is kept between varying the nature of (so-called) information and varying the satisfaction (the 'payoff') attainable through the choice of action. Economists[2] use the term 'utility' as interchangeable with desirability (satisfaction), and thus independent of perceptibility. Our concept is coarser. All the various definitions of utility given in this paper will be related to the empirical entities, called 'alternatives'. Each of these is identified precisely but combines the two aspects, information and desirability, in some unknown though presumably not-too-changeable fashion. Thus when two carloads are offered again, and, say, the firm's quality-control facilities (or, in a similar example, a housewife's abilities to discriminate between cuts of meat) have not changed, predictions from previous behavior observations can be made. If discrimination is learned, through experience, in some more-or-less-determined manner, the model has to be modified, of course, but we have not attempted to bring in learning.

Stochastic theory introduces the probability $p(a; F)$ of the basic observation $(a; F)$, and it is assumed that inferences about constraints on these probabilities can be made from a finite number of basic observations. These constraints may be described with the help of parameters of certain distributions, and some of these parameters have been called, a century ago, sensations (Fechner [3], see especially pp. 70–103 of the 1889 edition). We shall call them *constant utilities.* Various types of constant utilities have been proposed. They will be studied in Section II. In addition, there emerge naturally the concepts of *random utilities* and *random orderings* to be treated in Section III. Sections IV and V continue the study of directly testable conditions necessary and/or sufficient for the existence of constant and random utilities (and random orderings), respectively. Section VI sums up the main logical relations between the random and the various forms of constant utilities, and includes a very incomplete attempt to relate our various models to the work of other authors. As already mentioned, a generalized experimental situation – the combination of ranking and choosing – will be formulated in Section VII. Section VIII discusses the memory effect and other difficulties of experiments on choice and ranking, difficulties perhaps encountered less in psychophysics proper. We shall postpone the description of Section IX until the end of the present introductory section. Section X deals tentatively with a special statistical problem: how to test statistically our directly testable conditions – i.e., the properties of the probabilities $p(a; F)$ – when (to avoid the memory effect and to avoid assuming that all subjects have identical distribution properties) each set F can be offered only a few times, possibly only once.

Clearly, non-stochastic theory is a special, strong form of stochastic theory. And whenever a theory of choices or responses is being submitted to a statistical test there is, explicitly or not, an underlying model of stochastic behavior of the subject (or possibly of the error-making observer).

We shall conclude this section with a brief examination of the non-stochastic, or absolute, theory of choice. We shall formulate it in terms of our 'basic observations', and not, as usual, in terms of the subject's verbal preference or indifference statements. Define[3] for all a, b in A:

(1.1) '$a > b$' (a preferred to b) means 'never (b; F) if F contains a',
'$a \gtrsim b$' means 'not: $b \succ a$',
'$a \sim b$' (indifference) means '$a \gtrsim b$ and $b \gtrsim a$'.

Thus, if the subject forced to choose between a and b chooses b nine (but not ten) times out of ten, the non-stochastic theory calls him indifferent. We have always $a \gtrsim b$ or $b \gtrsim a$ since the subject is forced to choose. Therefore the relation '$\gtrsim$' is said to induce complete weak ordering on A provided the following condition (testable by basic observations) is satisfied:

(1.2) if $a \gtrsim b$ and $b \gtrsim c$, then $a \gtrsim c$ (transitivity).

If, in addition, the set A is finite, $A = (a_1, \ldots, a_n)$, we can associate with each of its elements a_i an integer r_i, $1 \leqq r_i \leqq n$, called *rank*, such that

(1.3) $r_i \leqq r_j$ if $a_i \gtrsim a_j$.

The vector $r = (r_1, \ldots, r_n)$, which can also be regarded as an integer-valued function on the set of integers $N = (1, \ldots, n)$, is called a ranking on N. If by some arbitrary convention ties are excluded, all r_i's are different integers and r is a permutation. Clearly any strictly decreasing monotone function on the integers $r_1, \ldots, r_n$ induces a real-valued function ω on A which is order-preserving in the sense that

(1.4) $\omega(a_i) \geqq \omega(a_j)$ *if and only if* $a_i \gtrsim a_j$.

The function ω, called the ('*ordinal*') *utility function*, is unique up to increasing monotone transformations.

If the set A of alternatives is not finite, an order-preserving function ω on A need not exist. However, Debreu [5] proved that an order-preserving function exists if A and the ordering relation '$\succsim$' satisfy a certain rather weak condition[4] that may justify the assumption of ordinal utility functions over the space of commodity-bundles.[5]

In the stochastic models that will follow, the (testable) transitivity condition (1.2) and the 'ordinal' utility function ω made possible by it will be suitably generalized. But, in addition, some stronger testable conditions and, correspondingly, more strictly measurable utility functions will arise naturally.

A final remark: The case when the set A includes wagers so that choices are, in general, made under uncertainty, is more general than that of choices among sure alternatives. This case has been often treated, ever since Daniel Bernoulli [8] and, for that matter, Marshall (Note IX, p. 843, [9]), by ordering the wagers according to their 'expected utility'. This leads to a non-stochastic utility that is more strictly measurable than ω: It is unique up to increasing linear transformations. This model, too lends itself to stochastic generalizations, as will be briefly discussed in Section IX.

II. STOCHASTIC CONCEPTS OF CONSTANT UTILITIES

In general, $A=(a, b, \ldots)$ will continue to denote the set of distinct alternatives, and F the feasible subset. For mathematical ease, we shall assume A to be finite, unless otherwise stated, and identify it with $N=(1, \ldots, n)$. A feasible subset will be $M \subseteq N$. The probability that the subject forced to choose an element of M chooses i, denoted previously by $p(i; M)$, can be written more briefly thus: $i(M)$. Clearly

$$(2.1) \qquad i(M) \geqq 0\,; \qquad \sum_{i \in M} i(M) = 1\,.$$

When $M=(i, j, k, \ldots)$, $i(M)=i((i, j, k, \ldots))$ will be written simply $i(i, j, k, \ldots)$. Then $i(M)$ will be called the binary, ternary..., probability when M consists of 2, 3, ..., distinct elements. The binary probability will be sometimes written in still shorter forms: $i(i, j)=ij$, $i \neq j$. It will prove convenient to define $ii=\frac{1}{2}$ so that, using (2.1), always

$$(2.2) \qquad ij + ji = 1\,,$$

whether i and j are distinct or not.

For easier reference, the various *conditions* will be labeled by (more-or less suggestive) letters, thus: (x). *A theorem* is an implication-relation between conditions (the 'hypothesis' and the 'conclusion'); by using arrows several theorems can be combined into one. In addition to the usual signs $\rightarrow$ ('implies') and $\leftrightarrow$ ('implies and is implied by'), we shall also use $\mapsto$ ('implies but is *not* implied by'). When $(x) \mapsto (y)$, (x), is said to be stronger than (y); rejection of (y) forces rejection of (x), but acceptance of (y) is inconclusive. We shall also use the sign $\mapsfrom\!\!\!\mapsto$ for 'does not imply nor is implied by'.

Each of the following three conditions (w), (v), (u), arranged in a sequence of increasing strength, constrains the set of probabilities $i(M)$ by postulating the existence of some real vector of order n (a real-valued function on the set N), called utility vector (utility function), and denoted by w, v, u, respectively. The stronger the constraint, the more strict is the sense in which the utility vector in measurable; that is, the smaller is the group of transformations under which the vector remains indeterminate.

CONDITION (w). *There is a constant real vector* $w=(w_1, \ldots, w_n)$ *such that*

$$(2.3) \qquad w_i \geqq w_j \quad \textit{if and only if} \quad ij \geqq \tfrac{1}{2},$$

where w_i may be called the *weak* utility of i; and w the weak utility function on N.

CONDITION (v). *There is a constant real vector* $v=(v_1, \ldots, v_n)$ *and, associated with it, a distribution function* φ_v, *strictly increasing* [*except when its value is* 0 *or* 1][6], *such that*

$$(2.4) \qquad \varphi_v(v_i - v_j) = ij\,; \qquad \varphi_v(0) = ii = \tfrac{1}{2}.$$

Then v_i may be called a *strong* utility of i; and v, a strong utility function on N.

CONDITION (u). *There is a constant positive vector* $u=(u_1, \ldots, u_n)$ *such that for any* i, j *in* M

$$(2.5) \qquad u_i/u_j = i(M)/j(M), \quad \text{all} \quad M \subseteq N,$$

where u_i may be called the *strict* utility of i; and u the strict utility function on N.

Clearly the weak utility function w is *unique up to an increasing monotone transformation.* It is analogous to the function w of the non-stochastic model (Section 1), with '$a_i \gtrsim a_j$' interpreted as '$ij \geqq \frac{1}{2}$'. We can call the cases $ij > \frac{1}{2}$ and $ij = \frac{1}{2}$, stochastic preference and indifference, respectively. These concepts are implicitly used in experimental work as when, e.g., Mosteller and Nogee [10] define indifference as the case when the subject chooses one of the two offered alternatives half of the time. As in the non-stochastic model, (w) implies a testable

CONDITION (t) (transitivity).

(2.6) *If* $ij \geqq \frac{1}{2}$ *and* $jk \geqq \frac{1}{2}$, *then* $ik \geqq \frac{1}{2}$.

Since always $ij \geqq$ or $\leqq \frac{1}{2}$, transitivity guarantees a (complete weak) ordering on N: the alternative i is ranked above, below, or on the level of j according as $ij >$, $<$, or $= \frac{1}{2}$. Since N is finite we, have (as in Section I):

THEOREM 2.1. $(w) \leftrightarrow (t)$ *provided the set of alternatives is finite.*

If we admit infinite sets of alternatives and redefine the condition (w) accordingly, we have $(w) \rightarrow (t)$. But if we denote by (D) Debreu's Condition (note 4) and replace '$a \gtrsim a'$' and '$ij \geqq \frac{1}{2}$' by '$aa' \geqq \frac{1}{2}$' we can write

THEOREM 2.2. $[(D), t] \mapsto (w) \mapsto (t)$.

Condition (v), the existence of 'strong' utilities, may be made plausible by a physical analogy. Because of random variations in the properties of the air, metals, and so forth, the lowest voltage needed to produce a spark in a given direction is random; assume then that the probability of the occurrence of the spark is the larger, the larger the voltage. Condition (v) has been used in psychophysics (and more recently in the scaling of attitudes) ever since Fechner [3]. It is stated in the psychologists' adage (Guilford, [11]): "*Equally often noticed differences* (on the 'sensation' scale) *are equal* [*unless noticed always or never*]." A similar thought might unify the recent attempts to measure the 'power' of person X over person Y: on the one hand, by the probability that Y obeys X; and on the other hand, by the difference in the payoff (utility) to Y in the case of his obeying, as compared with his disobeying, X.[7]

If (v) is satisfied by some v, φ_v, then clearly for *any increasing linear transform* $v' = \alpha + \beta v$ there exist a $\varphi_{v'}$ satisfying that condition. (If the set of alternatives is continuous, and the distribution φ_v strictly monotone, these are the only admissible transformations.[8]) The scale unit for v may be chosen by setting, for example, the quartile φ_v^{-1} (.25)=1; this or a similarly chosen unit is sometimes called the 'just noticeable difference', we believe. Moreover, because of (2.4), φ_v may be (and, in the continuous case, must be) so chosen that

$$(2.7) \qquad \varphi_v(\zeta) + \varphi_v(-\zeta) = 1$$

for all real ζ. Then φ_v is anti-symmetrical about the point $(0, \frac{1}{2})$; the median and the mean (if it exists) are zero. This is satisfied if φ_v is normal, as assumed by Fechner, whose test of normality was, however, rather crude. Normality of φ_v is also assumed in most textbooks; we do not know whether a formal test of this assumption has been developed. The 'logistic' distribution function $\varphi_v(\zeta)=1/(1+e^{-}\zeta)$ which, as we shall presently see, is required by the next stronger condition (u), also has the property (2.7).

THEOREM 2.3. $(v) \mapsto (w)$.

Proof. Sufficiency. Assume (v) and choose i, j with $v_i \geqq v_j$; then

$$ij = \varphi_v(v_i - v_j) \geqq \varphi_v(0) = \tfrac{1}{2};$$

hence (w) is satisfied, with $w=v$.

No necessity. Let $N=(1, 2, 3)$ and assume $12>13>23>\frac{1}{2}$. Then (w) is satisfied, with $w_1>w_2>w_3$; but no linear function of w will satisfy (v); for, by (v), if $\frac{1}{2}<23$ then $0=v_1-v_1<v_2-v_3$, $v_1-v_2<v_1-v_3$; hence, by (v), $12<13$, which contradicts the assumption.

As to the 'strict' constant utility condition (u), it has been postulated, and developed most fully, by R. D. Luce [15].[9] We shall now give some of his results. Because of (2.1), Condition (u) can be rewritten in the form

$$(2.8) \qquad i(M) = u_i / \sum_{j \in M} u_j, \quad \text{all} \quad M \subseteq N.$$

It follows that the vector u is *unique up to a positive factor* $\lambda = u_i/i(N)$. With N fixed, a convenient normalization is $\lambda = 1 = \sum_{i \in N} i(N)$; $u_i = i(N)$.

Putting $M=(i, j)$, $i(M)=ij$, we see that the probability of a binary choice is related to the ratio u_i/u_j by

$$(2.9) \qquad \psi(u_i/u_j) = ij, \quad \text{where} \quad \psi(x) = \begin{cases} x/(1+x), & x>0, \\ 0, & x \leqq 0. \end{cases}$$

Clearly ψ is a distribution function, for it is increasing, and $\psi(-\infty)=0$, $\psi(\infty)=1$. It is analogous to φ_v of condition (v), with ratios replacing differences, but is restricted to a particular form. Moreover, by putting v_k equal to $\log u_k$, we recover condition (v) itself, with φ_v a 'logistic curve':

$$(2.10) \qquad \varphi_v(\zeta) = 1/(1+e^{-\zeta}).$$

This proves

THEOREM 2.4. $(u) \mapsto (v)$,
for (v) imposes constraints on binary choices only.

We shall now introduce two *directly testable* conditions equivalent to (u). First consider

CONDITION $(p.r)$ (constancy of probability-ratios). $i(M)>0$ *for every* i *in* M; *and for every* i, j *in* N, *the ratio* $i(M)/j(M)$ *is constant over all sets* $M \subseteq N$ *that contain* i *and* j.

Condition $(p.r)$ follows directly from (u); conversely, rewriting $(p.r)$ as

$$(2.11) \qquad i(M)/i(N) = j(M)/j(N) = \sum_{k\in M} k(M) / \sum_{k\in M} k(N),$$

putting $k(N)=u_k$ and using (2.1), we obtain (u). Now consider

CONDITION $(c.p)$ (probability of choice as a conditional probability).

$$(2.12) \qquad 0 < i(M) = i(N) / \sum_{k\in M} k(N) \quad \text{all } i \text{ in } \quad M \subseteq N.$$

The fraction on the right-hand side, is, of course, the conditional probability that the element i of N is chosen *when it is known that the element chosen belongs to the subset M of N*. On the other hand, the quantity on the left-hand side is the probability that the element i of N is chosen *when the subject is forced to make his choice from the subset M of N*. Clearly these two quantities are not identical; $(c.p)$ is a verifiable, empirical proposition which may or may not have intuitive appeal.[10] Condition $(c.p)$ follows directly from (u) written in the form (2.8); on the other hand, on replacing i by j in (2.12) and comparing the two equations, one obtains $(p.r)$ which we have seen to be equivalent to (u). We summarize this and the previous results of this section in the following theorem, placing the directly testable conditions in the lower line:

THEOREM 2.5.

$$\begin{array}{ccccc} (u) & \mapsto & (v) & \mapsto & (w) \\ \updownarrow & & & & \updownarrow \\ (p.r) & \mapsto & (c.p) & \mapsto & (t)\,, \end{array}$$

provided that the Debreu condition is satisfied. (This includes the case of a finite set of alternatives.)

III. RANDOM ORDERINGS AND RANDOM UTILITIES

In the non-stochastic theory briefly reviewed in Section I, the preference statement '$a_i \succ a_j$' assigns probability 1 to a certain class of choices. In the stochastic models of Section II, the corresponding statement '$ij > \frac{1}{2}$' merely sets a lower bound on that probability and is therefore weaker; however, some of those models are weaker than others.

A different way of weakening the non-stochastic theory consists in making the ('ordinal') utility function w a random one; i.e., by defining a probability measure on the space of all real-valued functions on A. In the case of the economic example of Section I, Wald's problem of evaluating the (non-stochastic) utility function w of consumers from their observed choices $(a; F)$ is replaced by the following more general one: Estimate the probability distribution P on the space of random utility functions U, using the probabilities $p(a; F)$ already estimated from the observations $(a; F)$, or using these observations directly. Any random utility function will be regarded as equivalent to any of its increasing monotone transforms.

However, the choice probabilities $p(a; F)$ may or may not be consistent with the existence of a random utility function. That is, the following condition (defining, in fact, that function) may or may not be fulfilled:

CONDITION (U) (existence of random utilities). *There is a random vector $U = (U_1, \ldots, U_n)$ unique up to an increasing monotone transformation and such that, for any i in $M \subseteq N$,*

$$(3.1) \qquad \Pr\{U_i \geqq U_j, \quad \text{all } j \text{ in} \quad M\} = i(M)\,.$$

U_i is called *random utility of i*. Putting $M = (i, j)$,

$$(3.2) \qquad \Pr\{U_i \geqq U_j\} = ij\,.$$

By (2.2), it follows that, for all $i \neq j$,

$$(3.3) \qquad \Pr\{U_i = U_j\} = 0\,;$$

for if $\Pr\{U_i = U_j\} > 0$, then by (3.2) $ij + ji = \Pr\{U_i \geqq U_j\} + \Pr\{U_i \leqq U_j\} = \Pr\{U_i \geqq U_j\} + \Pr\{U_i < U_j\} + \Pr\{U_i = U_j\} > 1$, contradicting (2.2).

When the set of alternatives is finite, we can consider one particular monotone transform of U, the ranking $r = (r_1, \ldots, r_n)$ on the set $N = (1, \ldots, n)$. Because of (3.3), no ties will occur. Hence R, the set of all rankings on N, consists of the $n!$ permutations on N. We shall denote by i_r the element of N that has rank i when the ranking is r; i.e., $r_{i_r} = i$. Using this notation, we write a given ranking $r = (r_1, \ldots, r_n) = 1_r 2_r \ldots n_r$ (without commas and parentheses). Thus, if $n = 3$, the ranking $r = 312$ means that $r_1 = 2$, $r_2 = 3$, $r_3 = 1$, and is therefore identical with $r = (2, 3, 1)$.

Denote by R_{iM} the set of all rankings on N in which i is the first among all elements of $M \subseteq N$:

$$(3.4) \qquad R_{iM} = \{r \mid r_i \leqq r_j, \quad \text{all} \quad j \in M\} \quad i \in M\,.$$

For example, if $N = (1, 2, 3)$, $M = (1, 2)$, $i = 1$, then $R_{iM} = (123, 132, 312)$. Clearly, for every $M \subseteq N$,

$$(3.5) \qquad R_{iM} \textit{ and } R_{jM} \textit{ are disjoint for all } \quad i \neq j \quad \textit{in } M\,;$$

and if we denote by R^M the set of all permutations on M, we have

$$(3.6) \qquad \bigcup_{i \in M} R_{iM} = R^M\,; \qquad \bigcup_{i \in N} R_{iN} = R^N = R\,.$$

The following condition will be presently shown to be equivalent to (U).

CONDITION (P) (existence of a probability distribution of rankings consistent with probabilities $i(M)$). *There are $n!$ numbers $P(r)$ such that*

$$(3.7) \qquad P(r) \geqq 0\,, \qquad \sum_{R_{iM}} P(r) = i(M)\,, \qquad i \in M \subseteq N\,.$$

It follows, using (3.6), (2.1), that $\sum_R P(r) = 1$. We can call $P(r)$ the *probability of the ranking* r.

THEOREM 3.1. $(U) \leftrightarrow (P)$.

Proof. If we assume Condition (U) and define $P(r) = \Pr\{U_{1_r} > U_{2_r} > \cdots > U_{n_r}\}$, we obtain Condition (P). Conversely, assume (P) and define the random vector U thus: For any non-random real vector $s=(s_i, \ldots, s_n)$ let

$$(3.8) \qquad \Pr\{U = -s\} = \begin{cases} P(s), & s \in R, \\ 0, & s \notin R, \end{cases}$$

where R is the set of permutations on N. Then Condition (U) is satisfied.

THEOREM 3.2. *The existence of random utilities U does not imply the existence of weak constant utilities w, let alone the existence of strong or strict utilities, v or u.*

Proof. Let $N=(1, 2, 3)$ and $0<\alpha<\frac{1}{3}$. Let the probabilities of rankings $P(r)$ be

$$P(123) = P(231) = P(312) = \tfrac{1}{6} + \alpha > 0,$$
$$P(321) = P(213) = P(132) = \tfrac{1}{6} - \alpha > 0.$$

(Then $\sum P(r)=1$.) Let the probabilities of choices $i(M)$, $M \subseteq N$, be

$$(3.9) \qquad \begin{aligned} &1(N) = 2(N) = 3(N) = \tfrac{1}{3}, \\ &1(1, 2) = 2(2, 3) = 3(1, 3) = \alpha + \tfrac{1}{2}, \\ &2(1, 2) = 3(2, 3) = 1(1, 3) = -\alpha + \tfrac{1}{2}. \end{aligned}$$

Then $1(N)=P(123)+P(132)$, $1(1, 2)=P(123)+P(132)+P(312)$, etc., and Condition ($P$) – or its equivalent, ($U$) – is satisfied. But Condition (t) is not: $1(1, 2)>\frac{1}{2}$, $2(2, 3)>\frac{1}{2}$, but $1(1, 3)<\frac{1}{2}$. This proves the present theorem, using Theorem 2.5.[11]

We shall show that the following conditions are necessary for (P), and therefore for its equivalent, (U):

CONDITION (e) (effect of enlarging the feasible set). *If* $L \subseteq M \subseteq N$, *then*

$$(3.10) \qquad i(M) \leqq i(L).$$

CONDITION (e_3). *For any three elements* i, j, k *of* N,

$$(3.11) \qquad i(i, j) \geqq i(i, j, k); \textit{ or, equivalently,}$$

$$(3.11') \qquad i(i, j, k) \leqq \min(ij, ik).$$

Clearly (e_3) is a special case of (e); it was exemplified numerically in (3.9), for $n=3$. Applying to (P) the fact that $R_{iM}=\{r \mid r_i \leqq r_j, j \in L\} \cap$

$\cap\{r \mid r_i \leqq r_j, j \in M-L\} \subseteq R_{iL}$, we obtain

THEOREM 3.3. $(P) \rightarrow (e) \mapsto (e_3)$.[12]

THEOREM 3.4. *The existence of random utilities U is not implied by the existence of strong constant utilities v, let alone by the existence of weak constant utilities w.*

Proof. Denote by x, y, z the distinct generic elements of $N=(1, 2, 3)$. There exist three numbers (for example, $v_1=0.2$, $v_2=0.1$, $v_3=0$) such that

$$\begin{aligned}
&0 < v_z - v_y + \tfrac{1}{2} = \beta_{xy} < 1\,,\\
&0 < v_1 - v_2 = \gamma_1 < 1\,,\\
&0 < v_2 - v_3 = \gamma_2 < 1\,,\\
&0 < v_3 - v_1 + 1 = \gamma_3 < 1\,.
\end{aligned}$$

Since $\beta_{xy}+\beta_{zx}=1=\sum_x \gamma_x$, we can put $x(x, y)=\beta_{xy}$, $x(x, y, z)=\gamma_x$. Then Condition (v) is satisfied, with $\varphi_v(\zeta)=\zeta+\frac{1}{2}$. But since $\gamma_3-\beta_{31}=\frac{1}{2}>0$, $3(1,2,3)>3(1,3)$, Condition (e) and therefore also the stronger Condition (P) and its equivalent (U) are contradicted.

In the work of Thurstone [16] the following condition condition seems to be used:

CONDITION ($s.n$) (symmetrical normal). *There is a normal random vector $U=(U_1,\dots, U_n)$ that satisfies Condition (U) and has all variances equal ($\sigma_{ii}=\sigma^2$, say) and all covariances equal ($\sigma_{ij}=\rho\sigma^2$, say).*

Clearly this implies that both (U) and (v) are satisfied: let $v_i=EU_i$ and let φ_v, at all points $\zeta=v_i-v_j$, be normal, with mean zero and variance $2\sigma^2(1-\rho)$. Even the following, weaker condition is sufficient for the conjunction $[(U), (v)]$:

CONDITION (s) (symmetry of adjusted random utilities). *There is a random vector U satisfying Condition (U), and a constant vector $v=$ $=(v_1,\dots, v_n)$ such that $V=U-v$ has a distribution function symmetric in its arguments.*

If U, v satisfy this condition, then any pair of increasing linear transforms $\alpha+\beta U$, $\alpha+\beta v$ (α, β scalars) will satisfy it. Clearly $(s.n)\mapsto(s)$. Moreover,

THEOREM 3.5. $(s.n)\mapsto(s)\mapsto[(U), (v)]$.

Proof. Sufficiency of (s). If (s) is true, so is (U); and $i(i, j) = \Pr\{U_i \geqq U_j\} = \Pr\{V_j - V_i \leqq v_i - v_j\}$ = the value of a distribution function at $v_i - v_j$; because of symmetry, this function is the same for all i, j and can be written as φ_v, satisfying (v).

No sufficiency of $[(U), (v)]$. Let $N = (1, 2, 3)$. Let $v_i = i + 3$, and let V_1, V_2, V_3 be independently distributed with $\Pr\{V_i = 3\} = p_i = 1 - \Pr\{V_i = -3\}$, where $p_1 = 1 - p_3 = p > \frac{1}{2}$, $p_2 = \frac{1}{2}$. If $U = v + V$, then $\Pr\{U_1 > U_3\} = p^2$; $\Pr\{U_1 > U_2\} = p/2 = \Pr\{U_2 > U_3\}$; $\Pr\{U_1 > U_2, U_2 > U_3\} = p^2/2$, etc. Hence U satisfies Condition (U), if $1(1, 2) = 2(2,3) = p/2$; $1(1, 3) = p/2$; $1(1, 2, 3) = p^2/2$, etc. Then Condition (v) is also satisfied, with

$$\varphi_v(v_1 - v_2) = \varphi_v(v_2 - v_3) = \varphi_v(-1) = p/2 > p^2 = \\ = \varphi_v(-2) = \varphi_v(v_1 - v_3).$$

Yet no linear transformation of v or monotone transformation of U can make the distribution of V symmetric, since the p_i are not all equal. If, on the other hand, the set of alternatives is continuous, let V have a joint normal distribution with zero mean and a constant variance τ^2 of differences $V_x - V_y$: $\tau^2 = \sigma_{zz} + \sigma_{yy} - 2\sigma_{xy}$, all x, y, where $\sigma_{11} = \frac{1}{2}$ and (for $x, y \neq 1$) $\sigma_{xz} = 1$, $\sigma_{x1} = 0$, $\sigma_{xy} = \frac{1}{4}$. If $U = V + EU$ satisfies condition (U), then (v) is also satisfied, with $v = EU$ and φ_v normal with zero mean and variance $\tau^2 = \frac{3}{2}$. But no translation can make the distribution function of V symmetric in its arguments.

Mosteller [17] dropped Thurstone's symmetry assumption but maintained normality. We do not know whether tests have been developed for the joint condition $[(U), (v)]$ in general, or for the special case of joint normality with constant variance of differences.

We shall now discuss another condition that is also stronger than the conjunction $[(U), (v)]$ and is of particular interest, being equivalent to Condition (u) of Section II (existence of strict constant utilities). For a given permutation r of the set N define

$$(3.12) \qquad \pi(r) = \prod_{j=1}^{n-1} j_r(j_r, (j+1)_r, \ldots, n_r).$$

For example, $\pi(312) = 3(1, 2, 3) \cdot 1(1, 2)$. Suppose this were the probability of the ranking 312. This would exemplify

CONDITION (π) (probability of ranking as the product of probabilities of successive first choices). *Condition* (P) *is true and, for every ranking* r *of* N, $P(r) = \pi(r)$ *as defined in* (3.12).

Substituting $\pi(r)$ for $P(r)$ in (3.7), we can put Condition (π) into a form involving the 'basic' probabilities (those of 'first choices') only:

$$(3.13) \qquad i(M) = \sum_{r \in R_{iM}} \pi(r), \quad \text{for all } M \text{ and } i \in M.$$

THEOREM 3.6. $(u) \leftrightarrow (\pi)$.

Proof (outline). *Sufficiency of* (u). Define

$$(3.14) \qquad \Omega(r) = \prod_{j=1}^{n-1} u_{j_r} / \sum_{k=j}^{n} u_{k_r}.$$

To prove that (u) implies (π), or (2.8) implies (3.13), is to prove the identity

$$(3.15) \qquad \sum_{r \in R_{iM}} \Omega(r) = u_i / \sum_{h \in M} u_h,$$

for all $i \in M$, all $M \subseteq N$, and any positive numbers $u_1, \ldots, u_n$.[13] Without loss of generality let $M = (1, \ldots, m)$, $m \leqq n$, and, as in (3.6), denote by R^M the set of all permutations of M. Then $r^M = (r_1^M, \ldots, r_m^M) \in R^M$. The set $R = R^N$ is partitioned into m subsets of the form

$$R_{iM}^N = (r^N \mid r_i^N \leq r_j^N; \text{ all } j \in M), \quad i \in M;$$

the set R^N is also partitioned into $m!$ subsets of the form

$$R^N(r^M) = (r^N \mid r_i^N \leqq r_j^N \text{ if } r_i^M \leqq r_j^M; \text{ all } i.j \in M).$$

Similarly, R^M is partitioned into subsets $R^M(r^L)$, $L \subseteq M$. One obtains, by induction on m, first the identities

$$\sum_{r^M \in R^M} \Omega(r^M) = 1, \qquad \sum_{r^M \in R^M(r^L)} \Omega(r^M) = \Omega(r^L),$$

and then (3.15).

Necessity of (u). To show that (3.13) implies (2.8), let $u_i = i(N)$, all $i \in N$. Because of the identity (3.15), all numbers $i(M)$ that satisfy (3.13) also satisfy the system of equations

$$(3.16) \qquad i(M) = \sum_{r \in R_{iM}} u_{1_r} \prod_{j=2}^{n-1} j_r(j_r, \ldots, n_r), \qquad \sum_{i \in M} i(M) = 1.$$

One then proves the uniqueness of this solution: Starting with $M = N$, then taking all sets M with $n-1$ elements, then with $n-2$ elements and so on, one can solve (3.16) for all $i(M)$ and one finds that they are all given by (2.8).

THEOREM 3.7. *If* (u) *is true, then* (P) *and* (U) *hold, with* $P(r)=\pi(r)=\Omega(r)$. This is clearly a corollary to Theorem 3.6, using Theorem 3.1.

Some interest attaches to a condition that, in effect, appears in the work of Luce [15]. In the same way as Condition (u) treats the probabilities of *first* choices, $p(i; M)=i(M)$, this new condition treats the probabilities of *last* choices. We may denote these by $p'(i; M)=i'(M)$ and remark that last choices are not 'basic observations' in our sense. (However, see Section VII on considering the rankings themselves, and hence also the last choices, 'observable'; see also Marschak [20], Section XI.)[14]

CONDITION (u'). *There exists a constant positive vector* $u'=(u'_i, \ldots, u'_n)$ *such that for any* i, j *in* M, $u'_i/u'_j=i'(M)/j'(M)$.

It is possible, however, to prove

THEOREM 3.8. *If* $n>2$, (u') *is inconsistent with* (u) *unless* $i(N)=i'(N)=1/n$ *for all* $i \in N$.

Proof (outline). Define, for each ranking $r=1_r 2_r \ldots n_r$ the inverted ranking $r^*=n_r(n-1)_r \ldots 2_r 1_r$ (hence $r^{**}=r$); and define

$$\Omega'(r) = \prod_{j=1}^{n-1} u'_{j_r} / \sum_{k=j}^{n} u'_{k_r} .$$

By Theorem 3.7. if (u) is true then $P(r)=\Omega(r)$. By the same theorem, if (u') is true then $P(r^*)=\Omega'(r)$, and hence $P(r)=P(r^{**})=\Omega'(r^*)$. Therefore if both (u) and (u') are true,

$$(3.18) \qquad \Omega(r) = \Omega'(r^*) .$$

Define the ranking $s=2_r 1_r 3_r \ldots (n-1)_r n_r$. Since $\sum u_i = 1 = \sum u'_i$ without loss of generality, we have $\Omega(r)/\Omega(s)=(1-u_{2_r})/(1-u_{1_r})$; $\Omega'(r^*)/\Omega'(s^*)=u'_{2_r}/u'_{1_r}$. Since $1_r 2_r$ are arbitrary, we have by (3.18) $u'_i/u'_j=(1-u_i)/(1-u_j)$; and summing on i, we find $u_j=1-(n-1)\,u'_j$. Now define $t=1_r 2_r \ldots (n-2)_r n_r (n-1)_r$; then by (3.18)

$$\Omega(r)/\Omega(t) = u_{(n-1)_r}/u_{n_r} = \Omega'(r^*)/\Omega'(t^*)$$
$$= (1-u'_{(n-1)_r})/(1-u'_{n_r}) ;$$

and in general $u_i/u_j=(1-u_i')/(1-u_j')=[1-(n-1)\,u_i']/[1-(n-1)\,u_j']$; or $(n-2)\,u_i'=(n-2)\,u_i'$. Hence, for $n>2$, we have $u_i'=u_j'$ and $u_i=u_j$; so that $i(N)=i'(N)=1/n$ for all i.

THEOREM 3.9. $(u)\mapsto[(U,v)]\leftarrow\!\dashv(s)$.

Proof. We have $(u)\mapsto(U)$ by Theorems 3.6 and 3.1, since (π) is strictly stronger than (P). Moreover, $(u)\mapsto(v)$, and $(s)\mapsto(U,v)$ by Theorems 2.4 and 3.5. It remains to prove that (U,v) does not imply (u). Consider any normal distribution symmetric in its arguments. Then, by Theorem 3.5, (U) and (v) are both satisfied; and the corresponding φ_v is normal, contrary to the implication (2.10) of (u).

Some of the results of this and the preceding sections are worth summarizing in

THEOREM 3.10.

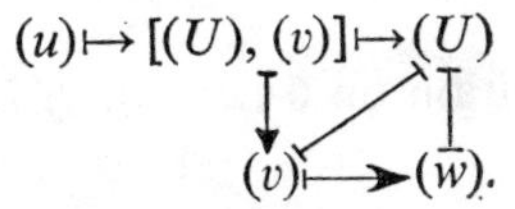

IV. FURTHER DIRECTLY TESTABLE CONDITIONS FOR THE EXISTENCE OF CONSTANT UTILITIES

We shall deal here with 'strong' utilities v only; directly testable conditions for the existence of 'strict' utilities u and 'weak' utilities w were given in Section II. Directly testable conditions for (v) – like those for (w) and unlike those for (u) – can, of course, involve binary choices only.

Unless otherwise stated, the set of alternatives will be assumed finite: $N=(1,\ldots,n)$. It is easy to see that we can rewrite

CONDITION (v). *There is a real vector* $v=(v_1,\ldots,v_n)$ *such that*

$$(4.1) \qquad \text{if} \quad hi\geqq jk \quad \text{then} \quad v_k-v_i\geqq v_j-v_k,$$

provided hi and jk are not both 0 *or* 1.

This implies that $hi\geqq\frac{1}{2}$ if, and only if, $v_k-v_i\geqq 0$. It is seen immediately that (v) implies each of the following conditions:

CONDITION (t) (transitivity). *If* $ij\geqq\frac{1}{2}$ *and* $jk\geqq\frac{1}{2}$, *then* $ik\geqq\frac{1}{2}$.

CONDITION (t_s) (strong transitivity). *If* $ij \geqq \frac{1}{2}$ *and* $jk \geqq \frac{1}{2}$, *then* $ik \geqq \max(ij, jk)$.

CONDITION (t_s^*). *If* $ij \geqq \frac{1}{2}$, *then* $ix \geqq jx$, *all* x *in* N.

CONDITION (t_s^{**}). *If there exists* k *such that* $ik \geqq jk$, *then* $ij \geqq \frac{1}{2}$.

CONDITION (6_w) (weak condition on 6-tuples). *If* $i_1 i_2 \geqq j_1 j_2$ *and* $i_2 i_3 \geqq j_2 j_3$, *then* $i_1 i_3 \geqq j_1 j_3$.

CONDITION (m_w) (weak condition on m-tuples). *For any* $m \leqq n$, *if* $i_k i_{k+1} \geqq j_k j_{k+1}$, $h = 1, \ldots, m-1$, then $i_1 i_m \geqq j_1 j_m$.

CONDITION (q) (quadruple condition). *If* $hi \geqq jk$, *then* $hj \geqq ik$.

CONDITION (6_s) (strong condition on 6-tuples). *If* $i_1 i_2 \geqq i_2 j_3$ *and* $i_2 i_3 \geqq j_1 j_2$, *then* $i_1 i_3 \geqq j_1 j_3$.

THEOREM 4.1.
$$\begin{array}{ccccccccccc} (v) & \mapsto & (6_s) & \mapsto & (q) & \mapsto & (6_w) & \mapsto & (t_s) & \mapsto & (t) \\ & & & & & & \updownarrow & & \updownarrow & & \\ & & & & & & (m_w) & & (t_s^*) \leftrightarrow (t_s^{**}). & & \end{array}$$

Proof. Obviously (v) implies all the other conditions, and obviously $(t_s) \to (t)$. To prove $(t_s) \to (t_s^*)$, let $ij \geqq \frac{1}{2}$ and apply (t_s) to three cases: (1) $jx \geqq \frac{1}{2}$; (2) $jx < \frac{1}{2}$, $xi \geqq \frac{1}{2}0$ (3) $jx < \frac{1}{2}$, $xi < \frac{1}{2}$. To prove the converse, let $ij \geqq \frac{1}{2}, jk \geqq \frac{1}{2}$; by (t_s^*) $ix \geqq jx, jy \geqq ky$; put $x = k$, $y = i$. To prove $(t_s^*) \leftrightarrow (t_s^{**})$, apply a contradiction argument, using (2.2). To prove $(6_w) \to (t_s)$, let $ij \geqq \frac{1}{2}, jk \geqq \frac{1}{2}$ and apply (6_w) with $i = i_1, j = i_2 = j_2, k = i_3$; and (1) $j_1 = j, j_3 = k$; (2) $j_1 = i, j_3 = j$. Condition (m_w) implies, and is itself obtained by successive application of (6_w). To prove $(q) \to (6_w)$ is straightforward. To prove $(6)_s \to (q)$, let $hi \geqq jk$, $i_1 = h$, $j_1 = i_2 = i$, $i_3 = j_2 = j$, $j_3 = k$.

The absence of implications is proved by counterexamples:[15] (t) does not imply (t_s) since, with $n = 3$ and $12 > 13 > \frac{1}{2}$ and $23 > \frac{1}{2}$, (t) but not (t_s) is satisfied. To prove that (t_s) does not imply (6_w), let $n = 4$ and $\frac{1}{2} < 43 < 32 < 21 < 31 < 42 < 41$. To prove that (6_w) does not imply (q), let $n = 4$, and $\frac{1}{2} < 32 < 43 < 21 < 31 < 42 < 41$. To prove that (q) does not imply (6_s), let $n = 5$ and $\frac{1}{2} < 21 < 54 < 32 < 43 < 53 < 31 < 42 < 41 < 52 < 51$. To prove that (6_s) does not imply (v), a counterexample (with $n = 9$) was constructed, but must be omitted here.

All the conditions given so far are necessary but not sufficient for the existence of v. With the exception of (m_w), they all involve binary choices among elements of subsets of fixed size m; $m=3$ in (t) and (t_s); $m=4$ in (q); $m=6$ in (6_w) and (6_s). The exception (m_w) is only apparent as (m_w) is equivalent to (6_w). Therefore all those conditions can be applied even when the size of N (the number n of all alternatives) is unknown. The following two conditions can be applied only if the size of N is known.

CONDITION (m_s) (strong condition on m-tuples). *For any* $m \leqq n$, $i_1 i_m \geqq j_1 j_m$, *if* $i_k i_{1+k} \geqq j_{r_k} j_{1+r_k}$, $k=1,\ldots,m-1$, *where* $r=(r_1,\ldots,r_{m-1})$ *is any permutation of the set* $(1,\ldots,m-1)$.

CONDITION (o) (ordering of the probabilities of binary choices). *Arrange all the* $ij \geqq \frac{1}{2}$ *in a sequence of* $n(n-1)/2$ *inequalities (involving only n distinct alternatives)*: $i_1 i_2 \geqq i_3 i_4 \geqq \cdots \geqq \frac{1}{2}$; *then the corresponding system of* $n(n-1)/2$ *inequalities in n distinct real numbers*

$$v_{i_1} - v_{i_2} \geqq v_{i_3} - v_{i_4} \geqq \cdots \geqq 0$$

must have a solution.

The following needs no proof.

THEOREM 4.2. $(v) \leftrightarrow (o) \rightarrow (m_s) \mapsto (6_s)$.

We have not investigated whether (m_s) implies (o).

Thus, for a finite set N of alternatives we have the condition (o) [perhaps also (m_s)?] sufficient and necessary for the existence of a strong utility vector v, and testable if N has known size. For finite N of unknown size our testable conditions are necessary only.

A summary of the main results of this section, assuming the set of alternatives finite, is given by

THEOREM 4.3.

$$\begin{array}{ccccccccccc} (v) & & & & & & & & (w) & & \\ \updownarrow & & & & & & & & \updownarrow & & \\ (o) & \rightarrow & (m_s) & \mapsto & (q) & \mapsto & (6_w) & \mapsto & (t_s) & \mapsto & (t). \end{array}$$

If the set of alternatives is ascribed some continuity properties (to be defined presently), some of the necessary testable conditions become also sufficient. We give two examples. Suppose one postulates

CONDITION (*s.c*) (stochastic continuity). *For any elements a, b, c of the set A of alternatives such that* $ab<\lambda<ac$, *there is an element d in A with* $ad=\lambda$. Debreu [24] has proved

THEOREM 4.4. $[(s.c), (q)] \mapsto (v)$.
Or one may postulate a stronger

CONDITION (*d.b.p*) (continuous differentiability of binary probabilities). *The set, A, of alternatives is representable by a real interval, and* $p(a, b)=p(a; (a, b))$ *is continuously differentiable with* $\partial p/\partial b<0$, $\partial p/\partial a>0$.
In Block and Marschak [21] proof was given of

THEOREM 4.5. $[(d.b.p), (6_w) \mapsto (v)$.
To show this, one first proves a

LEMMA. *Let* $x, y \in [0, 1]$ *and let* $f(x, y)$ *be continuously differentiable with* $\partial f/\partial y<0$, $\partial f/\partial x>0$. *Then, in order that f admit the representation* $f(x, y)= =h(u(x)-v(y))$, where *h, u, v are monotone increasing functions of one variable, it is necessary and sufficient that there exist functions* $\alpha(x)$, $\beta(y)$ *such that* $(\partial f/\partial x)/(\partial f/\partial y)=\alpha(x)/\beta(y)$.

V. FURTHER DIRECTLY TESTABLE CONDITIONS FOR THE EXISTENCE OF RANDOM ORDERINGS

Directly testable sufficient conditions for (*U*), the existence of random utilities (or, equivalently, for (*P*), the existence of random orderings), were given in Section III. It was shown, for example, that the probabilities $P(r)$ exist if the ratios $i(M)/j(M)$ do not depend on *M*. We have also shown that this condition is not necessary. On the other hand, the directly testable condition (*e*) is necessary: if the $P(r)$ exist, then $i(M) \leqq i(L)$ for any $i \in L \subseteq M \subseteq N$. We shall presently show that this condition is not sufficient. We have not found directly testable conditions that are both sufficient and necessary for the existence of $P(r)$ on *N*. The following partial results may, however, prove useful. They still use finite sets of alternatives only, of known or unknown size. The case of continuous sets has not been explored.

Condition (e_3) defined in Section III (3.11), as a special case of Condition (*e*), can also be conveniently denoted by (P_3), being the first link in a sequence of Conditions (P_m), $m=3, \dots, n$, which we shall state presently. Let us first state

THEOREM 5.1. *If* $n=3$, *then* $(P_3) \leftrightarrow (P)$.

Proof. Sufficiency of (P_3). Denote by x, y, z the generic distinct elements of $N=(1, 2, 3)$, define $Q(zxy)=x(x, y)-x(x, y, z)$, and assume (P_3) or its equivalent, (e_3). Then by (3.11), $Q(zxy) \geqq 0$; and by (2.2), (2.1), the sum of the six numbers $Q(zxy)$ is equal to $3-2=1$; hence (P) is satisfied, with $P(xyz)=Q(xyz)$.

Necessity of (P_3). By Theorem 3.3.

CONDITION (P_4). *For any four distinct elements* w, x, y, z *of* N,

$$w(w, x, y) \geqq w(w, x, y, z); \tag{5.1}$$

$$w(w, x) - w(w, x, y) \geqq w(w, x, z) - w(w, x, y, z). \tag{5.2}$$

THEOREM 5.2. $(P) \rightarrow (P_4) \mapsto (P_3)$.

Proof. Add (5.1) and (5.2) to obtain (P_3) $(=e_3)$ from (P_4). The converse is clearly not true. Moreover, if (P) is true, then

$$w(w, x, y) - w(w, x, y, z) = P(zwxy) + P(zwyx), \tag{5.3}$$

$$w(w, x) - [w(w, x, y) + w(w, x, z)] - w(w, x, y, z) = \\ = P(zywx) + P(yzwx); \tag{5.4}$$

since the expressions on the right-hand side are non-negative, (P_4) is satisfied. The converse is not true, since (P) may involve subsets with more than four elements.

THEOREM 5.3. *If* $n=4$, $(P_4) \leftrightarrow (P)$.

Proof. Sufficiency of (P_4). If x, y, z, w are generic distinct elements of $N=(1, 2, 3, 4)$, then (5.3), (5.4) is a system of 24 equations in as many unknowns, $P(r)$, non-negative and adding up to 1; the knowns being the $x(M)$, $M \subseteq N$. Each permutation r occurs exactly once in the set (5.3) and exactly once in the set (5.4). Thus the system breaks into six sets of four equations; each set involves exactly four permutations r (none of which appears in the other five sets) and is of the form

$$
\begin{aligned}
(5.5)\qquad \alpha &= P(r^{(1)}) + P(r^{(2)}),\\
\beta &= P(r^{(2)}) + P(r^{(3)}),\\
\gamma &= P(r^{(3)}) + P(r^{(4)}),\\
\delta &= P(r^{(4)}) + P(r^{(1)}),
\end{aligned}
$$

where the known α, β, γ, δ are non-negative. They obey the restriction $\alpha+\gamma=\beta+\delta$, so that the four equations are linearly dependent. A non-negative solution for the four $P(r)$ is obtained by putting $0=P(r^{(4)})$ or $0=P(r^{(2)})$ according as $\beta>\gamma$ or not. One then verifies (P) for all $x(M)$ and obtains $\sum_R P(r)=1$.

Necessity of (P_4). By Theorem 5.2.

THEOREM 5.4. *When* $n=4$, $(P_4)\mapsto(e)$.

Proof. Sufficiency. By Theorems 5.3 and 3.3.

No necessity. (P_4) implies

$$(5.6)\quad w(w, x) - w(w, x, y) \geqq w(w, x, z) - w(w, x, y, z) \geqq 0\,;$$

when $n=4$, (e) is the pair of inequalities

$$(5.7)\qquad w(w, x) - w(w, x, y) \geqq 0\,,$$

$$(5.8)\qquad w(w, x, z) - w(w, y, z) \geqq 0\,,$$

which are implied by, but do not imply, (5.6).

Conditions (P_4) and (P_3) are special cases of

CONDITION (P_m). *Let* $y, z, x_1, \dots, x_{m-2}$ *denote* m *generic distinct elements of a set* M *consisting of* m *elements,* $3\leqq m\leqq n$. *Then for any* h, $3\leqq h\leqq m$,

$$
\begin{aligned}
(5.9)\qquad S_h = {} & y(y, z) - [y(y, z, x_1) + y(y, z, x_2) + \cdots +\\
& + y(y, z, x_{h-2})] + [y(y, z, x_1, x_2) + y(y, z, x_1, x_3) +\\
& + \cdots + y(y, z, x_{h-3}, x_{h-2})] \dots \pm y(y, z, x_1, \dots, x_{h-2}) \geqq 0\,.
\end{aligned}
$$

THEOREM 5.5. $(P)\to(P_n)$, *with*

$$(5.10)\qquad S_m = \sum_r P(1_r 2_r \dots (m-2)_r\, yz)\,,\quad m = 3, \dots, n\,;$$

the sum being taken over all permutations r *of the m-element-set* M *which end in* yz.

Proof. Assume (P) and count the number of times, with sign, that any particular permutation is included in S_m. A term of the type $...y...z...$, where $k \geqq 1$ elements besides z follow y, has the coefficient

$$(5.11) \quad 1 - \binom{k}{1} + \binom{k}{2} - ... + \binom{k}{k} = (1-1)^k = 0\,.$$

and so the only remaining terms will be as specified on the right-hand side of (5.10).

We have seen that, in addition, $(P_n) \rightarrow (P)$ for $n \leqq 4$. We do not know whether this is true for $n > 4$. And we note that (P_n) is not testable if n is unknown.

An interesting condition involving binary choices only was formulated independently by several authors (perhaps first by Guilbaud [25]):

CONDITION (c_3) (a condition on cycles of 3 elements).[16] *For any three distinct elements i, j, k of N,*

$$(5.12) \quad 1 \leqq ij + jk + ki \leqq 2\,.$$

THEOREM 5.6. $(e_3) \mapsto (c_3)$.

Proof. Sufficiency. Let $M = (i, j, k) \subseteq N$. By (e_3), $ij \geqq i(M)$, $jk \geqq j(M)$, $ki \geqq k(M)$; add; apply (2.1), (2.2).

No necessity. Use the example of Theorem 3.4, where $ij + jk + ki = \frac{3}{2}$, so that the binary probabilities obey (c_3); but one of the ternary probabilities contradicts (e_3). We shall now prove

THEOREM 5.7. *Condition (c_3) is sufficient and necessary for the binary probabilities to be consistent with Condition (e_3).*

Proof. Sufficiency. Denote by x, y, z the generic distinct elements of $M = (i, j, k) \subseteq N$. We have to show that if the six binary probabilities xy satisfy (c_3), then there exist three numbers γ_z that have the properties required by (e_3) of the ternary probabilities, viz., $\sum_z \gamma_z = 1$, $0 \leqq \gamma_z \leqq$ $\leqq \min(xy, xz)$ for all x. Clearly such numbers exist if

$$(5.13) \quad s = \min(ij, jk) + \min(ji, jk) + \min(ki,)\, kj \geqq 1\,.$$

Let ij be minimal, and hence, by (2.2), ji maximal, among the six xy. If $kj < ki$, then, by (2.2), $s = ij + 1 \geqq 1$; if $kj \geqq ki$, then (c_3) implies $s \geqq 1$.

Hence, (c_3) guarantees the existence of the desired numbers γ_z (in general not unique).

Necessity. By Theorem 5.6.

Theorem 5.7 may be of importance if binary probabilities are the only observable ones (see Section VII). For the same reason, the following theorems, 5.8 and 5.9, will be of interest. We shall first state the relations between (e_3), (c_3), and the two transitivity conditions (t_s) and (t) of Section IV:

THEOREM 5.8. $(t_s) \vdash\!\!\dashv (e_3)$

$\downarrow \quad \searrow\!\!\swarrow \quad \downarrow$

$(t) \vdash\!\!\dashv (c_3)$.

Proof. $(t_s) \mapsto (t)$, $(e_3) \mapsto (c_3)$ by Theorems 4.1, 5.6. To show that (t_s) implies (c_3) assume, for some i, j, k in N, $ij+jk+ki<1$, contradicting (c_3); then $ij+jk<1$, and by (2.2) $ij<kj$; so that, if (t_s) [and therefore, by 4.1, (t_s^{**})] holds, then $ik<\frac{1}{2}$, $ki>\frac{1}{2}$, and by symmetry $ij>\frac{1}{2}$, $jk>\frac{1}{2}$, hence $ij+jk+ki>\frac{3}{2}$, contradicting the assumption. To show that (c_3) does not imply (t), let alone (t_s), consider $N=(i, j, k)$, and make $ij=jk=ki=0.4$, thus satisfying (c_3) but not (t). On the other hand, the case $N=(i, j, k)$, $ij=jk=0.1$, $kj=0.6$ shows that (t) does not imply (c_3). Finally, to see that $(t_s) \vdash\!\dashv (e_3)$ and $(t) \vdash\!\dashv (e_3)$, note that (t_s) and (t) constrain only binary probabilities while (e_3) constrains ternary as well as binary ones, and its constraint on the latter is identical with (c_3), which was just shown not to imply (t_s) or (t).

The following condition on binary probabilities, due to Georgescu-Roegen [22], generalizes (c_3):

CONDITION (c_m). *For any* $x_1, \ldots, x_m$ *in* N,

$$(5.14) \qquad 1 \leqq x_1x_2 + x_2x_3 + \cdots + x_{m-1}x_m + x_mx_1 \leqq m-1\,.$$

A proposition stronger than (c_m) and – as will be proved presently – equivalent to (c_3) is

CONDITION (c^*). (c_m) *holds for all* $m \leqq n$.

THEOREM 5.9. $(c_3) \leftrightarrow (c^*) \mapsto (c_m)$.

Proof. We have only to prove that (c_3) implies (c^*) and is not implied by (c_m), $m>3$. First show that the conjunction $[(c_3), (c_{m-1})] \to (c_m)$: by (c_{m-1}),

$$(5.15) \qquad 1 \leqq x_1 x_2 + x_2 x_3 + \cdots + x_{m-1} x_1 \leqq m-2\,;$$

and, by (c_3)

$$1 \leqq x_{m-1} x_m + x_m x_1 + x_1 x_{m-1} \leqq 2\,,$$

or, by (2.2)

$$(5.16) \qquad 0 \leqq x_{m-1} x_m + x_m x_1 - x_{m-1} x_1 \leqq 1\,;$$

adding (5.15) and (5.16), we obtain (c_m); now put $m=4, 5, \ldots$. To prove that (c_m) does not imply (c_3) let $m=n=4$; if the matrix $[x_i x_j]$ is

$$\begin{bmatrix} 0.5 & 0.8 & 0.2 & 0.5 \\ 0.2 & 0.5 & 0.8 & 0.6 \\ 0.8 & 0.2 & 0.5 & 0.6 \\ 0.5 & 0.4 & 0.4 & 0.5 \end{bmatrix},$$

then (c_4) is satisfied, but (c_3) is not, for $x_1 x_2 + x_2 x_3 + x_3 x_1 = 2.4 > 2$.

The main results of this section can be summarized in

THEOREM 5.10. *If $n \geqq m > 3$, then*

$$\begin{array}{ccccccccccc} (P) & \to & (P_n) & \mapsto & (P_m) & \mapsto & (e_3) & \leftrightarrow & (P_3) & & \\ \downarrow & & & & & & \downarrow & & & & \\ (e) & \mapsto & (c_m) & \leftarrow & (c^*) & \leftrightarrow & (c_3) & \leftarrow & (t_s) & \mapsto & (t)\,; \end{array}$$

if $n=3$ or 4, then $(P) \mapsto (P_n)$.

VI. A SURVEY

Theorem 3.10 summarized the relations between conditions postulating the existence of random orderings, and of constant utilities of various degrees of strength. It is also useful to summarize the relations between Conditions (U), (u), (v), and (w) and some of the testable conditions, mainly from Sections IV and V:

THEOREM 6.1. *For A finite,*

$$\begin{array}{ccccccccccccc} (c.p) & \leftrightarrow & (u) & \mapsto & (v) & \mapsto & (q) & \mapsto & (t_s) & \mapsto & (t) & \leftrightarrow & (w) \\ \updownarrow & & \downarrow & \nearrow & & \searrow & & \swarrow & \downarrow & \nearrow & & & \\ (\pi) & \mapsto & (U) & \mapsto & & & (e) & \mapsto & (c_3). & & & & \end{array}$$

The following attempt to relate our various conditions to the hypotheses stated by earlier authors is very incomplete. Not only could we not do justice to the work of many psychologists; we have also failed to study thoroughly some of the statisticians' work.

In Section II, the ideas of R. D. Luce, imposing a very strong constraint on the probabilities of multiple choices of any order, were identified with Condition (*u*); it can also be found in an early unpublished paper of Törnqvist [26]; and was stated orally (but taken back as unrealistic) by Debreu. R. A. Bradley and M. E. Terry [27] and L. R. Ford [28] applied this condition to binary choices only; in this form it is studied by J. Marschak [20] in some detail. A weaker constraint on the probabilities of binary choices is that of Fechner [3], identified with Condition (*v*). This condition, the still weaker Condition (*w*), and an intermediate case [the 'strong transitivity', (t_s)], was also studied by C. Coombs [29]; H. Gulliksen [30]; the late S. Valavanis-Vail [31], to whom we owe the important Condition (t_s); W. Edwards [32]; A. G. Papandreou *et al.* [33]; K. May [34]; J. M. Davis [35]; and D. Davidson (in collaboration with one of the present authors) [36].

In Section III, we identified an idea of Thurstone's with our Condition (*s.n*) (somewhat weakened in the subsequent work of Mosteller): a special form of combining the model (*v*) of strong constant utilities with the model (*U*) of random orderings. Conditions which can be identified with (*U*) were studied by G. Th. Gilbaud [25], N. Georgescu-Roegen ([22], [37]), D. Rosenblatt [38], R. D. Luce [15], J. Marschak [39], and others.

M. G. Kendall [40], G. L. Mallows [41], I. R. Savage [42], E. L. Lehmann [43], H. D. Brunk [44] and other statisticians (we owe these references to Lehmann) have studied rank-order statistics, 'ranking models', and paired comparisons, starting with problems of statistical inference. For example, given a sample of binary choices, estimate the 'underlying' (constant) ranking (perhaps a vector-parameter of the distribution of our *U*?); or test the hypothesis that a certain parameter is higher with one than with another of a pair of parent populations. To our regret, we have not had the opportunity to do the important job of stating the relations (if any) between our network of conditions and the stochastic models that may underlie the work of these authors. We shall briefly deal with statistical inference in Section X.

VII. VARYING THE DOMAIN OF TESTABILITY

As remarked in Section I, the definition of the class of basic observations, and therefore also of the class of testable conditions, depends on the range of possible experiments and other observations. Moreover, Condition (*o*) of Section IV exemplifies the case of a constraint that involves all elements of the set of alternatives simultaneously; if this set is finite and of unknown size, such a condition is not testable, whatever the definition of the basic observation.

In this paper, the basic observations have been defined as $(a; F)$, the actual *choice* of a single element a out of a feasible subset F of alternatives. It was suspected that the subject's verbal statements about how he *ranks* the elements of a given subset of three or more alternatives were less reliable, for the characterization and prediction of actual behavior, than his actual choices. But this suspecion may have been unnecessary. Psychologists do ask their subjects to rank three or more objects, according to the subject's intensity of perception, or his preferences, etc. They also ask 'judges' to rank individuals according to some characteristics. Presumably some consistency is assumed to prevail among all the rankings of any offered subsets of alternatives, and also between these rankings and the actual choices from any offered subset. In a stochastic model involving a finite set of alternatives $N=(1, 2, 3, 4)$, this would mean that, for example, a subject who, *at a given time*, ranks N in the order 1234, *would*, if asked to rank the subset (2, 3, 4), produce the ranking 234; and if asked to choose from the subset (2, 3, 4), *would* choose 2. The experimenter's faith in such consistency may be increased if the subject is told that the verbal statement about ranking will commit his actual choice when he is later presented with a pair of alternatives (a procedure suggested in a non-stochastic context by W. A. Wallis as quoted by L. J. Savage [45]), or, for that matter, with any subset of alternatives.[17] With the rankings (on the set N of all alternatives) admitted as basic observations, our condition (P) can be reformulated as a testable one, with $P(r)$ indicating the probability of an *observable* ranking r; that is, P is a distribution about which inferences can be made from experiments on rankings.

TESTABLE CONDITION (P). *The numbers* $P(r)$ *have the property* (3.7).

Since ranking experiments can be made on any subset $K \subseteq N$, we may, denoting by $P(r^K)$ the probability of a ranking r^K of K, generalize (P) into the following

TESTABLE CONDITION (P^K). *The numbers* $P(r^K)$ *have the property* (3.7) *with* K *replacing* N, *and with* $M \subseteq K \subseteq N$.

Note that when the subset K consists of two elements, the choosing from the subset and its ranking are the same thing. But the observation of ranking within triples and larger subsets does provide additional testable constraints not covered in the previous sections.

Testability is extended still further if the following procedure is permitted. The subject is given a set $M \subseteq N$, where M consists of m objects, and is told to select l of them ($l \leqq m$) and to rank these l objects. The ranking is denoted by $r^{L,M} = (r_{a_1} \ldots r_{a_l})$ where $L = \{a_1, \ldots, a_l\}$. The condition $(P_{l,m})$ is said to hold if there exist $n!$ non-negative numbers $P(r^{N,N}) = P(r)$ whose sum is unity such that, for each set M having at least l, but not more than m elements, and each subset L of M with l elements

$$(7.1) \qquad P(r^{L,M}) = \sum P(r),$$

the summation being over all rankings r such that $r_i \leqq r_j$ if either (1) $i \in L$ and $j \in M - L$, or (2) $i \in L$, $j \in L$, and $r_i^{L,M} \leqq r_j^{L,M}$.
Note: with $l = 1$, $(P_{1,n})$ *becomes the condition* (P) *of Section* 3, since (7.1) then becomes

$$i(M) = \sum_{r \mid r_i \leqq r_j,\, j \in M} P(r).$$

Thus $(P) \leftrightarrow (P_{1,n})$.

Clearly: $(P_{l,m}) \mapsto (P_{l,m-1})$, $(l < m)$; $(P_{m-1,m}) \leftrightarrow (P_{m,m})$. Moreover:

1. If $L = (i)$, then $P(r^{L,M}) = i(M)$.
2. If $L = (i)$, $M = (i, j)$, then $P(r^{L,M}) = P(ij)$.
3. If $L = (i, j)$, $M = (i, j)$, then $P(r^{L,M}) = P(ij)$.
4. If $L = N$ or $N - 1$, then $P(r^{L,N}) = P(r) = P(1_r 2_r \ldots n_r)$.

So far, we have discussed the possibility of extending the domain of testable conditions beyond the definition given in Section I. On the other hand, the observational possibilities may be such as to make even that definition too wide.

For example, they may be such as to make binary but not ternary, etc. choices observable. As remarked orally by H. Simon, to replace the experiment – in which the subject names the heaviest of two objects placed in his two hands – by a similar experiment with three objects (taken in successive pairs, or weighed on three fingers, etc.) may change experimental conditions so drastically as to invite inconsistencies. On the other hand, no such inconsistencies need be expected in experiments where the subject tells which of the two, or three, or possibly four lights is brighter. In the economics of the actual market, binary choices are often not observable where ternary or higher ones are; for example, a speculator will (1) buy, (2) sell, or (3) do neither of these.

When the testability domain is extended, some sufficient existence conditions become irrelevant. As a simple example let N consist of three elements and first assume that both binary and ternary choices are observable but rankings are not. Theorem 5.1 gives a necessary and sufficient condition for the existence of probabilities of rankings as defined in Condition (P) of Section III. But it does not say that these probabilities will be equal to the numbers $P(r)$ of the Testable Condition (P) of the present section, numbers about which inferences could be made if rankings were observable.

On the other hand, suppose that only binary choices among the three alternatives in N are observable, but neither ternary choice nor rankings are. Then Condition (c_3) ($1 \leqq xy+yz+zx \leqq 2$) becomes important; for, by Theorem 5.7, this condition is sufficient for the existence of the three ternary choice probabilities $i(x, y, z)$ and of the six probabilities of rankings $P(r)$; and nothing stronger can be stated with the observations at hand.

VIII. THE BOUNDARY CASE: PERFECT DISCRIMINATION OR PREFERENCE

The case when the binary probability $p(a; F)$, with $F=(a, b)$, takes the boundary values 1 or 0 is called, in psychology of perceptions, perfect (as distinct from imperfect) discrimination. In the language of the theory of choice there is then perfect (as distinct from imperfect, or stochastic) preference. The term can be extended to the case when the feasible set F contains any number of elements.

To take account of the boundary case, special provisos are needed to make conditions such as (t_s), (v), (u) consistent with empirical observations. To take the weakest of those conditions, (t_s) or its equivalent

(t_s^{**}): if there exists an element k of the set N of alternatives, such that $ik=jk$, then $ij=\frac{1}{2}$. Now, if three bodies i, j, k weigh, respectively, 1000, 10, and 6 grams, and xy is the probability that the subject says that x is heavier than y, then the observations will very likely show $ij=ik$; but they will very unlikely show $jk=\frac{1}{2}$. The conditions (t) and (w), both weaker than (t_s), are not endangered by this fact. But the stronger conditions (v) and (u) are. Without the proviso about boundary cases, made in Section II and again in Section IV, Condition (v) would imply, in our case of three bodies, $v_j=v_k$ for each of the lighter ones, because of the existence of the very heavy body i. Similarly, in Condition (u) all the (strict) utilities u_i had to be assumed positive to prevent any of the probabilities $i(M)$ from being 0 or 1.

Perfect discrimination is circumvented experimentally by presenting to the subject, at each trial, objects not too strongly differing from each other in the relevant physical dimension; and by keeping the subject uninformed of the physical dimension – for example, through blindfolding.

This approach is not sufficient, for experiments on choice, to the extent to which these are intended to reveal 'desirabilities,' with 'perceptibility' kept more or less constant (see Section 1). Ideally, one would like to give the subject all the physical information, making the choice dependent only on his 'desires'. Suppose, then, that two alternatives differ from each other, however slightly, with respect to a single characteristic which is easily identified by the subject and is completely ordered with respect to the subject's choices. He will then presumably show perfect preference. Thus, in particular, when a and b are quantities of an economic 'good' and a exceeds b, he will prefer a with probability 1, even if the difference in quantities is very small. (In fact, this may be regarded as the definition of a 'homogeneous' economic good.) Also, if a and b are two vectors of quantities of the same m goods, $a=(a_1,\ldots, a_m)$, $b=(b_1,\ldots, b_m)$, and if a dominates b, i.e., if $a_i \geqq b_i$ for all i and $a_j > b_j$ for some j, then a will be perfectly preferred to b. The same is true if the vectors a and b are interpreted as two money wagers, (where a_i and b_i are, respectively, the monetary gains awarded when event E_i happens) and a dominates b. On the other hand, if a and b are two vectors neither of which dominates the other, stochastic instead of perfect preference may occur. Accordingly, the pairs of commodity-bundles used in the experiments by Papandreou and others [33] and the pairs of wagers used in the experiments of Davidson and

Marschak [36] were such as to exclude domination.

The vacillation of the chooser between the alternatives has thus been ascribed by Simon [46] and by Quandt [47] to the presence, in each alternative, of several relevant characteristics that themselves are completely ordered, but to which the subject pays attention only one at a time. In general, we need not assume that every alternative is so reduced (albeit 'unconsciously') to a bundle of characteristics, each of them an ordered one, so that the businessman decomposes, as it were, the job-applicant into his 'personality factors', or considers a prospective plant site as a vector of numerical attributes. Yet in some important cases such vectorial representation is indeed manifest. This gives rise to disturbing discontinuities in applying our stochastic models. For example, denote by $a=(a_1, a_2)$, $b=(b_1, b_2)$, and $b'=(b'_1, b'_2)$, three pairs of 'homogeneous commodities' – apples and oranges, not factories and vice-presidents; let ε_1 and ε_2 be two small positive numbers, and let $b_1=b'_1=a_1+\varepsilon_1$, $b_2=a_2$, $b'_2=a_2-\varepsilon_2$. Then, very likely, the binary probability ba is 1; while $b'a$ may be quite close to $\frac{1}{2}$; this big jump in probabilities would result from a very small physical change in the alternatives offered.

For such reasons, the psychophysicist's proviso that the 'differences' should not be 'noticed always or never' is doubly important in designing and interpreting experiments on economic choices,[18] if one wants such experiments to throw light on desirabilities, as separated from the perceptibility aspect of the choice phenomenon.

IX. REMARKS ON CHOICE UNDER UNCERTAINTY

As visualized at the end of Section I, we shall now outline possible stochastic reformulations of the theory of choice under uncertainty, weakening in particular the 'expected utility' condition.

A wager associates each alternative (in the sense defined previously) $i=1,\ldots, n$ with an event. Denote by $q=(q_1,\ldots, q_n)$ any wager in which the event giving rise to alternative i has probability q_i (possibly zero). In its non-stochastic form, the expected utility condition says that there is a constant vector $\bar{\omega}=(\bar{\omega}_1,\ldots, \bar{\omega}_n)$, unique up to an increasing linear transformation, and such that

$$(9.1) \qquad \sum\bar{\omega}_i q_i \geqq \sum\bar{\omega}_i q'_i \quad \text{if and only if} \quad q \gtrsim q',$$

where $\gtrsim$ means 'preferred or indifferent'. Since the observer cannot be sure that two subjects behave as if they ascribed the same probability to any given event, not only the 'utility-numbers' $\bar{\omega}_i$ but also the probabilities q_i have to be interpreted in a subjective sense, thus: For a given subject, there exist a vector $\bar{\omega}$ and, associated with each wager, a vector q such that (9.1) is satisfied.

It has been shown[19] that this condition is implied by other conditions (called 'axioms') that apparently appeal more immediately to what our intuition recommends as rational, or consistent. As we remarked at the beginning, consistency in an absolute sense is likely to be rejected by experience.[20] But it can be replaced by more general conditions, of stochastic consistency; these imply, or are implied by, or both, statistically testable hypotheses. In particular, each of the Conditions (w), (v), (u), (U) of our Sections II and III can be combined with the expected utility principle to yield a stronger condition to be denoted by ($\bar{\omega}$), ($\bar{v}$), ($\bar{u}$), ($\bar{U}$), respectively. In formulating these conditions, we shall denote by Q the set of all wagers (i.e., the set of all vectors q of order n, with $\sum q_i = 1$, $q_i \geqq 0$, all i); the feasible set of wagers will be denoted by $F \subseteq Q$; the probabilities of choices will be denoted as before, e.g., $q(F) = p(q; F)$; $qq' = p(q; (q, q'))$.

CONDITION ($\bar{w}$). *There is a constant vector* $\bar{w} = (\bar{w}, \ldots, \bar{w}_n)$ *such that*

$$(9.2) \qquad \sum \bar{w}_i q_i \geqq \sum \bar{w}_i q'_i, \quad \text{if} \quad qq' \geqq \tfrac{1}{2}.$$

CONDITION ($\bar{v}$). *There is a constant vector* $\bar{v} = (\bar{v}_i, \ldots, \bar{v}_n)$ *and, associated with it, a distribution function* $\varphi_{\bar{v}}$, *strictly increasing except at its values* 1 *and* 0, *such that*

$$(9.3) \qquad \varphi_{\bar{v}}(\sum \bar{v}_i q_i - \sum \bar{v}_i q'_i) = qq'.$$

CONDITION ($\bar{u}$). *There is a constant positive vector* $\bar{u} = (\bar{u}_1, \ldots, \bar{u}_n)$ *such that, for every* $F \subseteq Q$ *and every* q, q' *in* F,

$$(9.4) \qquad \frac{\sum q_i \bar{u}_i}{\sum q'_i \bar{u}_i} = \frac{q(F)}{q'(F)}.$$

CONDITION ($\bar{U}$). *There is a random vector* $\bar{U} = (\bar{U}_1, \ldots, \bar{U}_n)$ *such that for every* $F \subseteq Q$ *and every* q *in* F,

$$(9.5) \qquad q(F) = \Pr\{\textstyle\sum (q_i - q_i')\, \bar{U}_i \geqq 0 ; \quad all \quad q' \text{ in } F\}.$$

Clearly $\bar{w}$ and $\bar{U}$ (unlike w and U) are unique up to an increasing linear transformation. So is $\bar{v}$ (by virtue of the continuity of the set Q; see note 8). And $\bar{u}$ is unique up to a positive multiplier (as is u).

The directly testable conditions of the previous sections – e.g., Conditions (t), (t_s), (q), etc. – can be appropriately reformulated, and some new ones added. A case most easily accessible to observations is that of even-chance wagers: i.e., the case when the subjective probabilities are $\frac{1}{2}$ for each of a pair of alternatives. Let iEj be the wager promising i if event E happens, and j otherwise; then the subjective probability of E (and therefore also each of the subjective probabilities q_i and q_j) is said to be equal to $\frac{1}{2}$ if the subject is indifferent between iEj and jEi. Or, using the stochastic interpretation and denoting by $(iEj \cdot jEi)$ the probability of choosing the first out of that pair of wagers, $q_i = q_j = \frac{1}{2}$ if $(iEj \cdot jEi) = \frac{1}{2}$. In principle this property is operationally ascertainable.[21] Consider an even-chance wager, with $q_1 = q_2 = \frac{1}{2}$, and another, $q_3' = q_4' = \frac{1}{2}$; the expressions $\sum q_i \bar{v}_i$ and $\sum q_i' \bar{v}_i$ in Condition ($\bar{v}$) become, respectively, $(\bar{v}_1 + \bar{v}_2)/2$ and $(\bar{v}_3 + \bar{v}_4)/2$; and so with similar expressions in ($\bar{u}$), ($\bar{w}$) and ($\bar{U}$). We can denote the even-chance wager aEb simply by $\overline{ab}$ (hence $\overline{aa} = a$), and the probability of choice between two such wagers by $(\overline{ab} \cdot \overline{cd})$. Then Condition ($\bar{v}$) can be rewritten – analogous to relation (4.1) and with the proviso that the considered probabilities of choice are not 1 or 0 – thus:

$$(9.6) \qquad \begin{array}{l} if \;\; (\overline{a_1 a_2} \cdot \overline{b_1 b_2}) \geqq (\overline{b_3 b_4} \cdot \overline{a_3 a_4}), \\ then \;\; v_{a_1} + v_{a_2} + v_{a_3} + v_{a_4} \geqq v_{b_1} + v_{b_2} + v_{b_3} + v_{v_4}. \end{array}$$

This clearly implies the following *directly testable* set of conditions:

CONDITION (8_E) (8-tuple condition on even-chance wagers). *If* $(\overline{a_1 a_2} \cdot \overline{b_1 b_2}) \geqq (\overline{b_3 b_4} \cdot \overline{a_3 a_4})$, *then* $(\overline{a_{r_1} a_{r_2}} \cdot \overline{b_{s_1} b_{s_2}}) \geqq (\overline{b_{s_3} b_{s_4}} \cdot \overline{a_{r_3} a_{r_4}})$, *where* (r_1, r_2, r_3, r_4) *and* (s_1, s_2, s_3, s_4) *are arbitrary permutations of* (1, 2, 3, 4).

THEOREM 9.1. $(\bar{v}) \to (8_E)$.

It can be shown that the set (8_E) of conditions is not only necessary but also sufficient for (9.6) provided the stochastic continuity condition (*s.c*) of Section 4 is satisfied with respect to the considered set of even-chance wagers.

If some of the eight alternatives in Condition (8_E) are made identical, weaker directly testable conditions arise, involving a smaller number of distinct alternatives, and necessary for Condition ($\bar{v}$). In certain conjunctions, and assuming stochastic continuity, they are also sufficient for ($\bar{v}$), over the considered set of even-chance wagers. They were studied by Davidson and Marschak [36]; Debreu's paper [54], though dealing with even-chance wagers in a non-stochastic context, is also relevant.

X. TESTING STOCHASTIC CONSTRAINTS WHEN REPLICATIONS ARE FEW[22]

All the considered conditions have been constraints on probabilities of certain responses of the subject to varying external conditions. More precisely, these probabilities have been in the form $p(a; F)$ although in Section VII more general forms were briefly discussed. These probabilities define the coordinates of the parameter space, and each directly testable condition ('hypothesis') defines a certain region of this space. The test consists in deciding, on the basis of observations, whether the parameter point – the set of probabilities $p(a; F)$ for all F – falls into that region.

A trial is easily replicated if the same feasible set F – the same set of stimuli – can be presented to a random sample of subjects *provided* it is reasonable to assume that each member of the parent population is characterized by the same relevant probability distribution of responses. This assumption has been made, in effect (with respect to choices of foods, birthday gifts, etc.) by Jones, Peryam, and Thurstone [55], Thurstone and Jones [56], and Gulliksen [57].

If this assumption of identical distributions is not justified, the hypothesis must be tested separately for each subject to find the proportion of the observed subjects that fail to satisfy certain strong conditions – such as (q) (see Section IV) and therefore (v); the proportion of subjects failing to satisfy weaker conditions – such as (t) and therefore (w); and so forth. One can thus estimate the frequency distribution of the various 'degrees of stochastic consistency' among the parent population, even though the probabilities ($a; F$) are not the same for two persons with the same degree of consistency. Two persons may both obey (w) and both fail to satisfy (v), even though one of them tends to vegetarianism more than the other. In psychophysics, two persons may obey the Fechnerian condition (v)

and yet have different functions φ_v, e.g., have different quartiles or 'just noticeable' differences (see Section II). A frequency distribution of degrees of (stochastic) consistency, in a given culture, is a useful thing to know. One may be interested in training people towards greater consistency, because of its importance for decision-making and leadership. This is not the same thing as inculcating identical tastes.

The number of replications, *for the same subject*, of the same set F of stimuli is limited by the fact that, in the course of successive replications, the subject's characteristic probabilities $p(a; F)$ for a given F may change. Inasmuch as this may be due to fatigue, psychophysicists do not seem to have found it necessary to curtail replications too much; they regard relative frequencies with which given responses a are elicited by a fixed F (e.g., a fixed pair of sounds) as workable estimates of the probabilities $p(a; F)$.

True, in psychophysical experiments the subject must be prevented from identifying the stimuli and remembering them. For example, he must be blindfolded. If he were asked to choose the heavier of two objects (or the string producing the higher pitch) but were not blindfolded, the visual stimulus, added to that of the weight (or sound), might help him to identify and remember the objects and thus possibly influence him when the same object is presented again.

For a similar reason, successive replications may lack independence when subjects have to respond to verbal stimuli, as in questionnaires on attitudes or on voting preferences. Students of attitudes try therefore to repeat a question in a different form, preferably after a lapse of a little time. The same lack of serial independence is likely to occur in the case of choices between verbally stated economic alternatives such as commodities and wagers. It might not be true of 'blindfolded' choices between wines. But, as pointed out in Section I, the economic theorist wants to separate preferences from difficulties of perception; his ideal is to observe the decisions of people while giving them as complete information as possible.

Accordingly, experimenters on choices have used only a small number of repetitions of the same pair of alternatives (Papandreou *et al.* [33]) or have avoided such repetitions altogether (Davidson and Marschak [36]). This creates special problems in devising statistical tests of significance, and at any rate makes such tests relatively weak. To bring out the logical nature of the problem, we shall concentrate on the mathematically easiest (though empirically weakest) case when each set F is presented once only; and we shall limit ourselves to the simplest of our hypotheses, the weak stochastic transitivity condition (t).

During the course of experiment the subject is asked to choose one from each of the sets (a, b), (b, c), (a, c). Denote by p_a, p_b, p_c the binary probabilities ab, bc, ca. Then $p=(p_a, p_b, p_c)$ is a point in $[0, 1]^3$. Assume that the subject has a certain probability distribution $\mathscr{P}$ of choosing points in $[0, 1]^3$; the random choice of triples (a, b, c) leads to a random choice from $[0, 1]^3$ with the distribution $\mathscr{P}$ on it. Let $q_i=p_i-\frac{1}{2}$, $i=a, b, c$. The region of $[0, 1]^3$ where condition (t) is *not* satisfied (call it T) is characterized by the fact that all three q_i are $\geqq 0$ or $\leqq 0$ and are not all $=0$. That is, apart from a set of measure 0, all three q_i have the same sign. It is desired to estimate $\mathscr{P}(T)=\Theta$.

It may be useful to think of an analogous one-dimensional problem. A coin-making machine is characterized by an unknown probability distribution of the chance variable p (probability of a coin falling heads). One is permitted to toss coins, *each only a few times* (*perhaps only once*), in order to get evidence about the distribution of p; for example, one wants to test the hypothesis that the proportion of coins with $p>\frac{1}{2}$ (i.e., biased in favor of heads) is not more than a preassigned number. The region '$p>\frac{1}{2}$' clearly corresponds to our region T, and can be so denoted; the preassigned number is an upper bound Θ' on $\mathscr{P}(T)=\Theta$. Now, an infinite number of coins of which exactly 10% are biased for heads, would, if each is tossed once, show more than 5% (and not more than 55%) heads; hence, if out of a very large number of coins tossed, exactly $\bar{Z}=5\%$ have fallen heads, all we can say is that the proportion of coins biased for heads is less than $\Theta'=10\%=2\bar{Z}$. Thus, *regardless of the number of coins* we are able to toss (each once), we cannot in general make statements involving a pre-assigned upper bound Θ' on the proportion of coins belonging to a given region. If Θ' had been 15%, then we could assert $\Theta<\Theta'$, but if Θ' had been 7%, then we could not assert $\Theta<\Theta'$. Thus, if we want to be sure that we can make an assertion, we can choose Θ' only after the tossings have been observed; if we are willing to accept the possibility of making no assertion, we can preassign Θ'. Similarly, in testing the stochastic transitivity condition (t), we shall be able to post-assign but not always to pre-assign an upper bound Θ' on Θ; and this regardless of the number of triples (a, b, c) we can present – each once – to the subject. The situation there is further complicated by the fact that we have only a finite sample and we introduce other parameters t^0, t' to analyze the confidence level.

Furthermore, if each coin could be tossed twice, we would still be unable to guarantee an assertion with a pre-assigned upper bound to Θ, but the ratio $\Theta'/\bar{Z}$ of the post-assigned bound to the observed proportion of heads would become smaller. And a similar statement can be made about the consequences of duplicating the presentation of each triple (a, b, c) to the subject.

We shall now develop a test of Condition (t). Let

$$(10.1) \quad f(p) = p_a p_b p_c + (1 - p_a)(1 - p_b)(1 - p_c) = \\ = \tfrac{1}{4} + q_a q_b + q_b q_c + q_c q_a,$$

where $q_i = p_i - \frac{1}{2}$. If $p \in T$ then $f(p) \geqq \frac{1}{4}$. If $p \notin T$ then $f(p) \leqq \frac{1}{2}$, for if $q_a = -\alpha$, $q_b = \beta$, $q_c = \gamma$ (α, β, γ non-negative), $f(p) = \frac{1}{4} + \beta\gamma - \alpha(\beta + \gamma) \leqq \leqq \frac{1}{4} + \beta\gamma \leqq \frac{1}{2}$, and the other possibilities are covered by symmetry. Define three random variables X_a, X_b, X_c: $X_a = 1$ if a is chosen from (a, b) and $X_a = 0$ otherwise; $X_b = 1$ if b is chosen from (b, c) and $X_b = 0$ otherwise; $X_c = 1$ if c is chosen from (a, c) and $X_c = 0$ otherwise. Define

$$(10.2) \quad Z = X_a X_b X_c + (1 - X_a)(1 - X_b)(1 - X_c).$$

For a given vector p, $\Pr\{Z = 1\} = f(p)$. Now $\Pr\{Z = 1\} = \Pr\{Z = 1 | p \in T\} \cdot \mathscr{P}(p \in T) + \Pr\{Z = 1 | p \notin T\} \mathscr{P}(p \notin T)$. Hence $\Pr\{Z = 1\} \geqq (\Theta/4) + 0$ and $\Pr\{Z = 1\} \leqq \Theta + \frac{1}{2}(1 - \Theta) = \frac{1}{2} + (\Theta/2)$. Thus Z is a binomial chance variable with mean $\mu = \Pr\{Z = 1\}$ where

$$(10.3) \quad (\Theta/4) \leqq \mu \leqq \tfrac{1}{2} + (\Theta/2).$$

Let $Z_1, \ldots, Z_m$ be independent observations on Z, each based on a different triple (a, b, c). Let $\bar{Z} = \sum_1^m Z_k/m$. Our first test is based on the following considerations:

(1) Let $0 < \Theta' \leqq 1$. If $\Theta \geqq \Theta'$ then $\mu \geqq \Theta'/4$. Let V' be a binomial chance variable with $\Pr\{V' = 1\} = \Theta'/4$. Then $\Pr\{Z_k = 0\} \leqq \Pr\{V' = 0\}$. Let $t' \leqq \Theta'/4$. Then $\Pr\{\bar{Z} \leqq t'\} \leqq \Pr\{\bar{V}' \leqq t'\}$ where $\bar{V}'$ is the mean of m values of V'. If a confidence level α' is specified, one can choose m large enough so that $\Pr\{\bar{V}' \leqq t'\} \leqq \alpha'$. Hence:

$$(10.4') \quad \text{if} \quad \Theta \geqq \Theta', \Pr\{\bar{Z} \leqq t'\} \leqq \alpha'.$$

(2) Similarly, consider Θ^0, with $0 \leqq \Theta^0 < \frac{1}{2}$. If $\Theta \leqq \Theta^0$ then $\mu \leqq \frac{1}{2} + \Theta^0/2$. Let V^0 be a binomial random variable with $\Pr\{V^0 = 1\} = \frac{1}{2} + \Theta^0/2$. Then $\Pr\{Z_k = 1\} \leqq \Pr\{V^0 = 1\}$. Let $t^0 \geqq \frac{1}{2} + \Theta^0/2$. Then $\Pr\{\bar{Z} \geqq t^0\} \leqq \Pr\{\bar{V}^0 \geqq t^0\}$ where $\bar{V}^0$ is the mean of m values of V^0. Again, with a specified confidence level α^0, we can choose large enough m to make $\Pr\{\bar{V}^0 \geqq t^0\} \leqq \alpha^0$. Hence

(10.4⁰) if $\Theta \leqq \Theta^0, \Pr\{\bar{Z} \geqq t^0\} \leqq \alpha^0$.

Summarizing: If $\bar{Z} \geqq t^0$, we assert $\Theta > \Theta^0$; if $\bar{Z} \leqq t'$, we assert $\Theta < \Theta'$; if $t' < \bar{Z} < t^0$, we assert nothing. The consequences of this are shown in the following table of probabilities of occurrence:

Assertion	True state	
	$\Theta \leqq \Theta^0$	$\Theta \geqq \Theta'$
$\Theta > \Theta^0$	$< \alpha^0$	–
$\Theta < \Theta'$	–	$< \alpha'$
Nothing	–	–

where the dashes indicate probabilities that we have not estimated. This procedure protects us against extreme errors of classification, but leaves open the possibility of coming to no decision.

If m is large enough so that the normal approximation to the binomial may be used, then the constants involved in the test are determined by the following equations:

(10.5) $F(s^0) = 1 - \alpha^0, \quad F(s') = 1 - \alpha'$,

where F is the normal distribution function with zero mean and unit variance, and

(10.6′) $s' = (\Theta' - 4t')\sqrt{m}/2\sqrt{\Theta'(1 - \Theta'/4)}$,

(10.6⁰) $s^0 = (2t^0 - 1 - \Theta^0)\sqrt{m}/\sqrt{(1 + \Theta^0)(1 - \Theta^0)}$.

The experimenter may specify the parameters $\Theta^0, \Theta', t^0, t'$ either before or after the experiment. Let us first discuss the case where the choice is made *after* he has the data. Suppose $\bar{Z}$ turns out to be quite high. He is then seeking to make an assertion $\Theta > \Theta^0$. He can do this with confidence level $1 - \alpha^0$ where α^0 is determined from (10.6⁰), provided that $t^0 \leqq \bar{Z}$ and $\Theta^0 \leqq 2t^0 - 1$. He would like Θ^0 to be as high as possible and at the same time $1-\alpha^0$ to be as high as possible. As he takes Θ^0 closer to $2t^0-1$, s^0 tends to zero and α^0 tends to $\frac{1}{2}$, which is not a convincing confidence level. Thus to keep the confidence level $1-\alpha^0$ high he must take Θ^0 much less than $2t^0-1$; on the other hand, the smaller he takes Θ^0, the weaker the impact of his assertion $\Theta > \Theta^0$. Thus it is clear that he should choose t^0 as large as possible, namely $\bar{Z}$. Now if the experimenter wants to work with a fixed confidence level $1-\alpha^0$, he should adjust Θ^0 low enough so that he achieves, by (10.6^0), his desired confidence level. If, on the other hand, there is a fixed 'tolerance level' Θ^0 which the experimenter regards as the significant indicator of inconsistency, then he would use this fixed Θ^0 and again with $t^0 = \bar{Z}$ find his confidence level by (10.6^0). More generally, he can strike what balance he wishes, pushing Θ^0 up while driving $1-\alpha^0$ down, keeping of course $t^0 = \bar{Z}$. If, instead, $\bar{Z}$ is quite low, then he wishes to assert $\Theta < \Theta'$. Here he would like Θ' as small as possible and $1-\alpha'$ as large as possible. Considerations similar to those above, applied now to (10.6′), show that he should choose $t' = \bar{Z}$ and similarly make an arrangement between Θ' and $1-\alpha'$.

It may be, however, that the experimenter is doing many experiments and would like to have a fixed procedure, regardless of the data. He can specify t^0 and Θ^0 in advance, subject to $\Theta^0 \leqq 2t^0-1$, and know that his confidence level is given by (10.6^0). (The larger $2t^0-1-\Theta^0$, the larger the confidence level, but the larger he takes t^0, the more likely he will have nothing to assert, while the smaller he takes Θ^0, the weaker are the assertions he does make; this balance he settles in advance.) Similarly he selects Θ', t' in advance. Now the data from many experiments can be handled by a fixed procedure; if $\bar{Z} \geqq t^0$ or $\bar{Z} \leqq t'$, an assertion is made, while if $t' < \bar{Z} < t^0$, no assertion is made. This procedure will be more convenient, but clearly it involves a loss of one or more of the following: confidence level, strength of assertion, and likelihood of making an assertion, as compared with the method of selecting the parameters after the experiment. However, if the experimenter is testing a large number of individuals in order to select a subset for further testing, he might find it better, as far as the data-processing is concerned, to fix the parameters in advance.

Our second method is to find a confidence interval for Θ. Let $0 < \alpha < 1$ and $0 < \delta < 1$ be given. Then it follows that for m sufficiently large $P(-\delta < \bar{Z} - \mu < \delta) > 1-\alpha$; i.e., $P(\bar{Z} - \mu < \delta$ and $\bar{Z} - \mu > -\delta) > 1-\alpha$, or $P(\bar{Z} < \delta + \mu$ and $\bar{Z} > \mu - \delta) > 1-\alpha$; from (10.3) it follows that $P(\bar{Z} < \delta +$

$+\frac{1}{2}+(\Theta/2)$ and $\bar{Z}>(\Theta/4)-\delta)>1-\alpha$. Thus $P(2\bar{Z}-2\delta-1<\Theta<4\bar{Z}+$ $+4\delta)>1-\alpha$.

While it is true that the length of the confidence interval $(2\bar{Z}-2\delta-1,$ $4\bar{Z}+4\delta)$ is $2\bar{Z}+6\delta+1>1$, it is not centered at $\frac{1}{2}$. Hence, if $\bar{Z}$ is near zero or unity, the effective length of the interval may be quite small; e.g., if $\bar{Z}=0$, the conclusion is $-2\delta-1<\Theta<4\delta$, which has an effective length of only 4δ; while if $\bar{Z}=1$, the conclusion is $1-2\delta<\Theta<4+4\delta$, which has an effective length of 2δ. Since for a prescribed significance level $1-\alpha$ we do not know δ explicitly, we can use the estimate $\delta=k(\alpha)\ \sigma=k(\alpha)\cdot$ $\cdot(pq/m)^{1/2}\leqq k(\alpha)/2(m)^{1/2}$. Thus

$$P\left(2\bar{Z}-\frac{k(\alpha)}{\sqrt{m}}-1<\Theta<4\bar{Z}+\frac{2k(\alpha)}{\sqrt{m}}\right)>1-\alpha.$$

If the normal approximation for the binomial is used, $k(\alpha)$ is determined from the equation

$$(10.7)\qquad F(k(\alpha))=1-\alpha/2,$$

where F is the normal distribution with zero mean and unit variance.

The confidence interval may also be used for making decisions; e.g. let $0<\Theta^*\leqq\Theta^{**}<1$. If the confidence interval is contained in the interval $(0,\ \Theta^*)$, assert that $\Theta\leqq\Theta^*$; if the confidence interval is contained in the interval $(\Theta^{**},\ 1)$ assert that $\Theta\geqq\Theta^{**}$, otherwise assert nothing. In other words, if

$$\bar{Z}<\frac{\Theta^*}{4}-\frac{k(\alpha)}{2\sqrt{m}}.$$

assert that $\Theta\leqq\Theta^*$; if

$$\bar{Z}>\tfrac{1}{2}\left(\Theta^{**}+1+\frac{k(\alpha)}{\sqrt{m}}\right),$$

assert that $\Theta\geqq\Theta^{**}$; otherwise assert nothing. We then get the following table of probabilities.[23]

Assertion	True state		
	$0\leqq\theta<\theta^*$	$\theta^*\leqq\theta\leqq\theta^{**}$	$\theta^{**}<\theta\leqq 1$
$\theta\leqq\theta^*$	–	$<\alpha$	$<\alpha$
$\theta\geqq\theta^{**}$	$<\alpha$	$<\alpha$	–
Nothing	–	–	–

NOTES

* Research carried out mostly under contracts of the Office of Naval Research with the Cowles Foundations for Economics at Yale University and with Columbia University. The paper was completed while Jacob Marschak was Ford Visiting Research Professor at the Graduate School of Industrial Administration, Carnegie Institute of Technology. We owe much to discussions with D. Davidson, G. Debreu, M. DeGroot, L. Hurwicz, and R. D. Luce.

1 While the stochastic approach uses measurable *probabilities*, another approach, also promising to give realism and unity to the understanding of choices and responses, makes use of the measurable *time-delay* of a choice or response. The shorter the delay, the larger is the difference between certain values said to be attached by the subject to two alternative responses. A very long delay reveals a state of (almost) indifference, the 'conflict-situation': Hamlet took a very long time to decide whether to kill his uncle. The logic of this approach and its combination with stochastic theories was treated by Cartwright and Festinger [1].

2 As pointed out by James Tobin in a private communication. *Added in 1974*: Tversky [59, p. 295] regards this distinction as amenable to his experiments on multi-attribute alternatives. See also [60].

3 Preferences thus defined are 'independent of irrelevant alternatives', a principle pointed out by Hotelling's pupil Arrow [4] and much used ever since. A better name for Arrow's principle is 'irrelevance of added alternatives'.

4 The condition is, *A is perfectly separable and is ordered by the relation* '$\succsim$'; *and for every a' in A the sets* $(a \mid a' \succsim a)$ and $(a \mid a \succsim a')$ *are closed.* The condition is trivially fulfilled by every finite set, for it is perfectly separable and all its, subsets are closed. Also, every subset of a finite-dimensional Euclidean space is perfectly separable, and it is reasonable to assume that the sets $(a \mid a' \succsim a)$ and $(a \mid a \succsim a')$ are closed when '$\succsim$' means a consumer's preference over the space of a finite number of commodities.

5 Thus Abraham Wald [6] has suggested a method to evaluate the consumer's ordinal utility function ω from the basic observations $(a; F)$ – purchases made as F varies with incomes and prices – assuming a non-stochastic model and not attempting a statistical estimate. More recently, H. Theil and H. Neudecker [7] gave a stochastic generalization of the same model, specifying, as did Wald, ω to be quadratic in the quantities of the goods consumed.

6 Regarding the proviso in brackets, see Section VIII.

7 These two points of view, the empirical and the game-theoretical, are represented in somewhat modified form by Dahl [12] and by Shapley and Shubik [13], respectively. If one accepts John Harsanyi's proposal to measure the power of X over Y by "how much difference it makes to Y between being X's friend or enemy," this difference between maxmax and maxmin payoffs (see, e.g., Luce and Raiffa [14]) might be related to the probability of Y's decision to be a friend.

8 For, suppose that $\varphi_{v'}(v'(x)-v'(y)) \equiv \varphi_v(v(x)-v(y))$. Then with $\phi = \varphi_{v'}^{-1}\, \varphi_v$ we have (i) $v'(x)-v'(y)=\phi(v(x)-v(y))$, (ii) $v'(y)-v'(z)=\phi(v(y)-v(z))$, and (iii) $v'(x)-v'(z)=\phi(v(x)-v(z))$. Adding (i) and (ii) and using (iii) we find, letting $a=v(x)-v(y)$, $b=v(y)-v(z)$, that $\phi(a+b)=\phi(a)+\phi(b)$. The only solution of this last equation which is not unbounded in every interval is, as is well known, $\phi(a)=\beta a$. Then from (i), with y fixed, we have $v'(x)=\beta v(x)+\alpha$.

9 Occasionally (in his Section 2.D.3, entitled 'A Generalization to Two or More Alternatives') Luce combines Condition (u) with another condition which we shall call (u')

(existence of strict *dis*utilities of *last* choices) and which is not generally consistent with (u): see our Theorem 3.8 below.

10 Luce tries to convey this appeal by an analogy with Arrow's (non-stochastic) principle which we called before the 'irrelevance of added alternatives'.

11 This counterexample is due to C. Winsten. Another interesting proof is due to P. Halmos. Three dice, A, B, C, are loaded so as to turn up with the following probabilities:

Face no.		1	2	3	4	5	6
Die:	A	0	0	.5	5	0	0
	B	0	.6	0	0	0	.4
	C	.4	0	0	0	.6	0

Let a, b, c (independent chance variables) be the number of spots turning up on A, B, C, respectively. Then (P) is satisfied: the probabilities of the six possible rankings of the numbers a, b, c according to magnitude, must be consistent with the probabilities that one of the numbers is the largest in a given pair or triple. But (t) is not satisfied: $\Pr\{a > b\} = .6 > \frac{1}{2}$; $\Pr\{b > c\} = .64 > \frac{1}{2}$; $\Pr\{a > c\} = .4 < \frac{1}{2}$.

12 Whether or not (e) implies (P) will be left open until Section V.

13 Block and Marschak [18] searched for an appropriate urn model, and Debreu [19] found it, thus providing a shorter proof.

14 *Added in 1973*: See now Section 6.3., An 'Impossibility' Theorem, in Luce and Suppes [58].

15 For methods to construct these counterexamples see Block and Marschak [21]. Georgescu-Roegen [22] and Chipman [23] obtained a condition intermediate in strength between (t_s) and (t) by substituting min for max in (t_s). See Marschak ([20]), Section 7.)

16 Since (5.12) can be rewritten $ij + jk \geqslant ik$, this condition has also been called 'triangular'. Its further properties are studied in Marschak [20].

17 On the other hand, the following procedure will not do for our present purposes (it was suggested in an earlier paper of Marschak [39]): to construct the subject's ranking of a set by asking him to make a choice from it; then removing the alternative chosen, and asking him to make a choice from the remaining subset; and so on. In the stochastic case, the subject may shift during the procedure from one ranking to another ranking of the same set. In [39] the case was non-stochastic.

18 The case of absolute preferences is discussed by N. Georgescu-Roegen [22] in the context of the economic theory of demand (for homogeneous commodities). J. S. Chipman [23] drew attention to important anomalies in the case of statistical decisions.

19 This was done by J. von Neumann and O. Morgenstern [48], with q interpreted 'objectively'; their 'axioms' and proof were subsequently simplified by various writers, most concisely by I. N. Herstein and J. Milnor [49]. The 'subjective' interpretation of q was introduced by F. P. Ramsey [50] and made precise by L. J. Savage [45]. See also W. Edwards [32]. R. D. Luce [51] generalized the stochastic theory of choices under uncertainty by introducing random subjective probabilities.

20 See the examples of actual behavior found by M. Allais [52] and discussed also by L. J. Savage ([45], pp. 101–4.)

21 For still greater experimental ease, Davidson and Marschak [36], following the device used by Davidson, Suppes and Siegel [53], and guided by considerations of continuity, assumed that, when the alternatives i, j, i', j' are money amounts, then the

even-chance event E has also the following testable property:

$$(iEj \cdot j'\,Ei) = 1 = (jEi \cdot i'\,Ej),$$

provided $i - i' = j - j' = \varepsilon$, a small positive amount.

22 *Added in 1974:* See now DeGroot [61].

21 Naturally, much stronger tests are obtained if some *a priori* restrictions are admitted. Thus, in the Davidson and Marschak paper [36] two alternative hypotheses were formulated to test a stochastic constraint, viz., the transitivity condition (t) or (t_s): (1) The probability-triples (ac, bc, ca) are distributed uniformly over $[0, 1]^3$; (2) they are distributed over the region defined by Condition (t) or Condition (t_s) uniformly. Mathematical simplicity is about the only serious claim in favor of these restrictions unless one invokes Laplace's 'principle of ignorance'.

BIBLIOGRAPHY

[1] Cartwright, D. and Festinger, L., 'A Quantitative Theory of Decision', *Psychol. Rev.* **50** (1943) 595–621.

[2] Hotelling, H., 'Demand Functions with Limited Budgets', *Econometrica* **3** (1935) 66–78.

[3] Fechner, G. Th., *Elemente der Psychophysik*, Breitkopf & Härtel, Leipzig, 1859.

[4] Arrow, K. J., *Social Choice and Individual Values*, Wiley, New York, 1951.

[5] Debreu, G., 'Representation of a Preference Ordering by a Numerical Function', Chap. 11 in R. M. Thrall, C. H. Coombs and R. L. Davis (eds.), *Decision Processes*, Wiley, New York, 1954.

[6] Wald, A., 'The Approximate Determination of Indifference Surfaces by Means of Engel Curves, *Econometrica* **8** (1940) 144–75.

[7] Theil, H. and Neudecker, H., 'Substitution, Complementarity and the Residual Variation around Engle Curves', *Rev. Econ. Studies* **25** (1957) 114–23.

[8] Bernoulli, D., 'Exposition of a New Theory on the Measurement of Risk' (translated by Dr. Louise Sommer), *Econometrica*, **22** (1954) 23–36.

[9] Marshall, A., *Principles of Economics*, 8th ed. Macmillan, London, 1920.

[10] Mosteller, F. and Nogee, P., 'An Experimental Measurement of Utility', *J. Polit. Econ.* **59** (1951) 371–404.

[11] Guilford, J. P., *Psychometric Methods*, 2d ed., McGraw-Hill, New York, 1954.

[12] Dahl, R. A., 'The Concept of Power', *Behav. Sci.* **2** (1957) 201–15.

[13] Shapley, L. and Shubik, M., 'A Method for Evaluating the Distribution of Power in a Committee System', *Amer. Polit. Sci. Rev.* **48** (1954) 787–92.

[14] Luce, R. D. and Raiffa, H., *Games and Decisions*, Wiley, New York, 1957.

[15] Luce, R. D., *Individual Choice Behavior*, Wiley, New York, 1959.

[16] Thurstone, L. L., 'A Law of Comparative Judgment', *Psychol. Rev.* **34** (1927) 273–86.

[17] Mosteller, F., 'Remarks on the Method of Paired Comparisons', *Psychometrika* **26** (1951) 3–9, 203–6, 207–18.

[18] Block, H. D. and Marschak, J. 'An Identity in Arithmetic', *Bull. Amer. Math. Soc.* **65** (1959) 123–24.

[19] Debreu, G., 'On "An identity in arithmetic"', *Proc. Amer. Math. Soc.* **11** (1960) 220–21.

[20] Marschak, J., 'Binary Choice Constaints on Random Utility Indicators', *Selected Essays*, **8**.

[21] Block, H. D. and Marschak, J., 'Random Orderings', Cowles Foundation Discussion Paper No. 42, Cowles Foundation, New Haven, Conn., 1957 (duplicated).
[22] Georgescu-Roegen, N, 'Threshold in Choice and the Theory of Demand', *Econometrica* **26** (1958) 157–68.
[23] Chipman, J. S. 'Stochastic Choice and Subjective Probability', Technical Report No. 2, School of Business Administration, Univ. of Minn., Minneapolis, Minn., 1958 (duplicated).
[24] Debreu, G., 'Stochastic Choice and Cardinal Utility', *Econometrica* **26** (1958) 440–44.
[25] Guilbaud, G. Th., 'Sur une difficulté de la théorie du risque', *Colloques internationaux du centre national de la recherche scientifique* (*économétrie*) **40** (1953) 19–25.
[26] Törnqvist, L., 'A Model for Stochastic Decision Making', Cowles Commission Discussion Paper, Economics 2100, Cowles Commission, Chicago, 1954 (duplicated).
[27] Bradley, R. A. and Terry, M. E., 'Rank Analysis of Incomplete Block Designs, I. The Method of Paired Comparisons', *Biometrika* **39** (1952) 324–44.
[28] Ford, L. R., 'Solution of a Ranking Problem from Binary Comparisons', *Amer. Math. Month.* **64** (1957) (Aug. suppl.), 28–33.
[29] Coombs, C., On the Use of Inconsistency of Preferences in Psychological Measurement', *J. Exp. Psychol.* **55** (1958) 1–7.
[30] Gulliksen, H., 'Paired Comparisons and the Logic of Measurement', *Psychol. Rev.* **53** (1946) 199–213.
[31] Valavanis-Vail, S., 'A Stochastic Model for Utilities', Seminar on the application of mathematics to social sciences, Univ. Michigan, Ann Arbor, 1957 (duplicated).
[32] Edwards, W., 'Probability Preferences in Gambling', *Amer. J. Psychol.* **66** (1955) 349–64.
[33] Papandreou, A. G. (with the collaboration of O. H. Sauerlender, O. H. Brownlee, L. Hurwicz, W. Franklin), 'A test of a Stochastic Theory of Choice, *Univ. Calif. Publ. in Econ.* **16** (1957) 1–18.
[34] May, K., 'Intransitivity, Utility and the Aggregation of Preference Patterns', *Econometrica* **22** (1954) 1–13.
[35] Davis, J. M., 'The Transitivity of Preferences', *Behav. Sci.* **3** (1958) 26–33.
[36] Davidson, D. and Marschak, J., 'Experimental Tests of Stochastic Decision Theories', *Selected Essays*, 6.
[37] Georgescu-Roegen, N., 'The Pure Theory of Consumer Behavior', *Quart.* J. *Econ.* **50** (1936) 545–93.
[38] Rosenblatt, D., 'On Some Stochastic Process Formulations of Individual Preference and Consumer Behavior (abst.)', *Econometrica* **24** (1956) 347–48.
[39] Marschak, J., 'Norms and Habits of Decision Making under Certainty', *Selected Essays*, 5.
[40] Kendall, M. G., 'Further Contributions to the Theory of Paired Comparisons', *Biometrics* **11** (1955) 43–67.
[41] Mallows, G. L., 'Non-Null Ranking Models, I', *Biometrika* **44** (1957) 114–30.
[42] Savage, I. R., 'Contributions to the Theory of Rank Orders', *Ann. Math. Stat.* **27** (1956) 590–615; **28** (1957) 968–77.
[43] Lehmann, E. L., 'Ordered Families of Distributions', *Ann. Math. Stat.* **26** (1955) 399–419.
[44] Brunk, H. D., 'Mathematical Models for Ranking from Paired Comparisons',

Technical Report No. 11, Air Force Office of Scientific Research, Department of Mathematics, University of Missouri, Columbia, Mo., Nov. 1958 (duplicated).
[45] Savage, L. J., *The Foundations of Statistics*, Wiley, New York, 1954. Revised, Dover, 1972.
[46] Simon, H. A., 'A Behavioral Model of Rational Choice', *Quart. J. Econ.* **69** (1955) 99–118.
[47] Quandt, R. E., 'A Probabilistic Theory of Consumer Behavior', *Quart. J. Econ.* **70** (1956) 507–36.
[48] Neumann, J. von and Morgenstern, O., *Theory of Games and Economic Behavior*, 2d ed. Princeton Univ. Press, Princeton N.J., 1947.
[49] Herstein, I. N. and Milnor, J., 'An Axiomatic Approach to Measurable Utility' *Econometrica* **21** (1953) 291–97.
[50] Ramsey, F. P., *The Foundations of Mathematics and Other Logical Essays*, Kegan Paul, London 1931.
[51] Luce, R. D., 'A Probabilistic Theory of Utility', *Econometrica* **26** (1958) 193–224.
[52] Allais, M., 'Le comportement de l'homme rationnel devant le risque: critique des postulats et axiomes de l'école américaine', *Econometrica* **21** (1953) 503–46.
[53] Davidson, D. and Suppes, P. (in collaboration with S. Siegel), *Decision Making: An Experimental Approach*, Stanford Univ. Press, Stanford, Calif., 1957.
[54] Debreu, G., 'Cardinal Utility for Even-Chance Mixtures of Pairs of Sure Prospects', *Rev. Econ. Studies* **26**(1958/9) 174–77.
[55] Jones, L. V., Peryam, D. R., and Thurstone, L. L., 'Development of a Scale for Measuring Soldiers' Food Preferences', *Food Research* **20** (1955) 512–20.
[56] Thurstone, L. L. and Jones, L., 'The Rational Origin for Measuring Subjective Values', *J. Amer. Stat. Assoc.* **52** (1957) 458–71.
[57] Gulliksen, H., 'Measurement of Subjective Values', *Psychometrika* **21** (1956) 229–44.
[58] Luce, R. D. and Suppes, P., 'Preference, Utility, and Subjective Probability', *Handbook of Mathematical Psychology*, Vol. III, Ch. 19, Wiley, 1965.
[59] Tversky, A., 'Elimination by Aspects: A Theory of Choice', *Psychological Review* **79** (1972) 281–99.
[60] Tversky, A., 'Intransitivity of Preferences', *Psychological Review* **76** (1969) 31–48.
[61] DeGroot, M. H., 'Optimal Allocation of Observations', *Annals of the Institute of Statistical Mathematics*, **18** (1966) 13–28.

8

BINARY-CHOICE CONSTRAINTS AND RANDOM UTILITY INDICATORS*

(1960)

I. THE PROBLEM

This paper contains suggestions for combining various available types of information on economic choice. There are in the main three types.

(i) Controlled experiments on choices from small sets (usually pairs) of alternatives.

(ii) Surveys of consumers' choices from large sets of alternatives, each set being determined by the market prices and by each consumer's monetary resources; similar surveys (*mutatis mutandis*) of producers' choices are also available, especially in the case of farmers.

(iii) Time series of total consumption (or production) of individual commodities, total incomes, and market prices, over a given geographical area.

Various researchers (Marschak [16], and more recently Tobin [19], Wold [22], and Farrell [9]) have tried to combine information on (ii) and (iii). The present paper deals with combining the materials in (i) and (ii), albeit only to the extent of outlining the general problem and of concluding with an example.

Suppose that, given a set of consumers' budgets at varying prices, we want to estimate a function on the commodity space that might be used as a utility indicator (defining a system of 'indifference surfaces') to describe the tastes of the sampled group of people. The desired statistical estimation will usually be preceded by the 'specification' of a class of eligible functions on the commodity space. The continuity and convexity ('diminishing marginal satisfaction') properties postulated in economic theory, partly in connection with its requirement of 'consumer's equilibrium', permit such specification only within very broad limits.

Suppose, however, that, in addition to the consumers' survey data, laboratory data are available that imply that the choices being made by people of a given socio-economic group obey certain constraints. The knowledge of these constraints might provide help in further restricting the set of eligible utility indicators.

It will be realistic to assume that a man's choice from a given set of alternatives is not unique but obeys some probability distribution. This agrees with the approach usual in psychometrics and psychophysics, and may also explain a part of the statistical variations in economic survey data. Accordingly, our approach will be 'stochastic' throughout. We shall study the logical connections between different behavior assumptions made in stochastic theories of decision.

II. BINARY-CHOICE PROBABILITIES

Unless specified to the contrary, all concepts in this paper are associated with a single given person, the 'subject' of experiments. The only experiments considered in this paper – except for cursory remarks on other kinds of experiments, especially in Sections IV, V, and XI – are *binary choices:* the subject is forced to choose one of the pair (x, y) of alternatives. On the other hand, the data resulting from a consumer survey are, of course, *multiple choices* since a consumer's monetary resources permit him, given the prices of goods, to choose from among more than a pair of alternative budgets.

The following notation will be used:

X, the set of *alternatives*, with generic elements $x, y, \ldots,$.

n, the number of elements of X when X is finite; in this case the elements will be identified by integers: $X=(1, \ldots, n)$.

$\boldsymbol{p}$, the class of functions p on $X \times X$ (or, with X finite, the set of matrices $p=[p_{xy}]$) such that

$$(1) \qquad p_{xy} = 1 - p_{yx} \geqq 0 .$$

Hence $p_{xx}=\frac{1}{2}$. When $x \neq y$, the function p_{xy} is called the *probability of a binary choice, viz.*, of the choice of x out of the subset (x, y) of X. A region $\boldsymbol{p}_C \subseteq \boldsymbol{p}$ defines a condition (C) on all p_{xy} and is called a *binary-choice constraint*. It will be convenient to identify such constraints, and other conditions, by symbols in parentheses, thus: (C).

Binary-choice constraints involving no other quantities but the p_{xy} are called *directly testable*: it will be assumed that they can be accepted or rejected, in the sense of statistical inference, on the basis of binary-choice experiments. (However, except in the case of finite X and very large samples permitting the approximation of each p_{xy} by the corresponding observed frequency, difficult statistical problems that cannot be treated here present themselves, but see [1, Section 10].) Constraints on the p_{xy} that are not 'directly testable' involve in particular the existence of the variously defined 'utilities', a theoretical construct. It will be important to find which of the 'directly testable' constraints imply or are implied by the existence of 'utilities' in the various senses of this term.

EXAMPLE. Let $X=(1, 2, 3)$. A function p is completely described by any six numbers p_{xy} obeying (1). The relation $1 \leqq p_{12}+p_{23}+p_{31} \leqq 2$ exemplifies a binary-choice constraint. It is 'directly testable' and is implied by certain 'utility' statements, as will be seen in Section VI.

III. RANDOM UTILITY INDICATOR

A probability measure on the set of real-valued functions on X defines a real-valued random function on X (a random vector if X is finite); its values are random numbers.

DEFINITION. $U^{(2)}$, *a real-valued random function on X, is called a* random utility indicator 'in the binary sense' *if, for every* $x \neq y$,

$$\Pr(U_x^{(2)} \geqq U_y^{(2)}) = p_{xy}. \tag{2}$$

(The idea goes back to Thurstone's 'law of comparative judgment' [18].)

It follows that if F is a random utility indicator in the binary sense, and G is a strictly increasing transform of F (that is, $F_x \geqq F_y$ if and only if $G_x \geqq G_y$, for all x, y), then G is also a random utility indicator in the binary sense.

The following theorem was suggested by M. DeGroot:

THEOREM 1. *If* $U^{(2)}$ *is a random utility indicator in the binary sense, then* $\Pr(U_x^{(2)} = U_y^{(2)}) = 0$ *for every* $x \neq y$.

Proof. Let $x \neq y$ and suppose $\Pr(U_x^{(2)} = U_y^{(2)}) > 0$. Then

$$\begin{aligned} p_{xy} + p_{yx} &= \Pr(U_x^{(2)} \geqq U_y^{(2)}) + \Pr(U_y^{(2)} \geqq U_x^{(2)}) = \\ &= \Pr(U_x^{(2)} > U_y^{(2)}) + \Pr(U_y^{(2)} > U_x^{(2)}) + \\ &\quad + 2\Pr(U_x^{(2)} = U_y^{(2)}) = \end{aligned}$$

$$= \{\Pr(U_x^{(2)} > U_y^{(2)}) + \Pr(U_y^{(2)} > U_x^{(2)}) + \\ + \Pr(U_x^{(2)} = U_y^{(2)})\} + \Pr(U_x^{(2)} = U_y^{(2)}) = \\ = 1 + \Pr(U_x^{(2)} = U_y^{(2)}) > 1,$$

contradicting (1).

EXAMPLES. (i) Let $X=(1, 2, 3)$; then $U^{(2)}$ is a random utility indicator if the six numbers $\Pr(U_x^{(2)})$ are respectively equal to the six numbers p_{xy} which (or some constraints on which) are obtained from observations.

(ii) Let X denote the real m-space with generic point $x=(x_1, \ldots, x_m)$; let $T=(T_1, \ldots, T_m)$ be a random vector such that $0<T_i<1$ $(i=1, \ldots, m)$ and $\sum T_i=1$. Let

$$U_x^{(2)} = \prod_{i=1}^{m} x_i^{T_i} \tag{3}$$

(the 'Cobb-Douglas function' frequently used in economics, with X being the commodity space). If $\Pr(U_x^{(2)} \geqq U_y^{(2)})=p_{xy}$, then $U^{(2)}$ is a random utility indicator 'in the binary sense'. This example will be used again in Section XII.

CONDITION ($U^{(2)}$). The function p is such that $U^{(2)}$ exists.

IV. A REMARK ON MULTIPLE-CHOICE PROBABILITIES

The concepts and the condition just defined can be easily generalized to multiple-choice probabilities. For every $x \in X^*$ and $X^* \subseteq X$, one defines $p_x(X^*)$, obeying

$$p_x(X^*) \geqq 0, \qquad \sum_{x \in X^*} p_x(X^*) = 1. \tag{4}$$

The number $p_x(X^*)$ is interpreted as the probability that the subject, forced to choose from the subset X^*, will choose x. Clearly, p_{xy} is a special case, with $X^*=(x, y)$. The following condition exemplifies an important and plausible constraint that would be directly testable if multiple choices from subsets of various sizes were observable:

$$\text{if} \quad x \in X^{**} \subseteq X^* \subseteq X, \quad \text{then} \quad p_x(X^*) \leqq p_x(X^{**}). \tag{5}$$

In [1], Block and Marschak dealt with multiple-choice probabilities, and had accordingly used the following definition of the random utility indicator, stronger than the one given in Section III:

DEFINITION. *U, a random function on* $\boldsymbol{X}$, *is a* random utility indicator *if, for all* $\boldsymbol{X}^* \subseteq \boldsymbol{X}$,

$$\text{(6)} \qquad \Pr(U_x \geqq U_y, \quad y \in \boldsymbol{X}^*) = p_x(\boldsymbol{X}^*).$$

Correspondingly, Condition ($U^{(2)}$) is replaced by the stronger

CONDITION (U). The set of probabilities $p_x(\boldsymbol{X}^*)$, where $x \in \boldsymbol{X}^*$ and $\boldsymbol{X}^* \subseteq \boldsymbol{X}$ is such that U, in the sense of (6), exists.

Clearly, Condition (U) implies ($U^{(2)}$) and also implies (5).

Some other properties of U will be used later, in Section XI. However, because of experimental difficulties with large subsets of alternatives, it seems worthwhile to devote a special and intensive study to binary-choice probabilities. They cover much of the existing materials on human responses, and many practical situations ('pairwise comparisons'). Moreover, the following needs no proof:

THEOREM 2. *If the* p_{xy} *admit the existence of a function* $U^{(2)}$ *satisfying Condition* ($U^{(2)}$), *then, for every* $x \in \boldsymbol{X}^*$ and $\boldsymbol{X}^* \subseteq \boldsymbol{X}$, *there exists a number* $q_x(\boldsymbol{X}^*) \geqq 0$ *such that, putting* $p_x(\boldsymbol{X}^*) = q_x(\boldsymbol{X}^*)$ *and* $U = U^{(2)}$, *condition* (6) *is satisfied.*

That is, Condition ($U^{(2)}$) guarantees the existence of numbers which, if they were the observed multiple-choice probabilities, would satisfy Condition (U).

Except in Section XI, it will not be assumed in this paper that constraints on non-binary-choice probabilities – such as (5) – can be inferred from observations.

V. PROBABILITY OF RANKING

Similarly, and possibly on still stronger grounds, no reference will be made in this paper to experiments in which the subject is requested, not to make an actual choice but to rank three or more alternatives according to his preferences (with two alternatives, choosing and ranking may be regarded as identical). It will not be assumed that responses obtained in such experiments are in any sense consistent with choices of single alternatives from subsets. To be sure, we shall use the term 'probability of ranking', but not to denote a number that is estimated (or, more generally, whose properties are inferred) from experiments on ranking. Rather, we give the following definition:

DEFINITION. *If* $U^{(2)}$ *is a random utility indicator, then, for any* $x_1, x_2, \ldots, x_m$ *in* X, *the number*

$$(7) \qquad P(x_1 x_2 \ldots x_m) = \Pr(U^{(2)}_{x_1} > U^{(2)}_{x_2} > + > U^{(2)}_{x_m})$$

is called the probability of the ranking (*permutation*) $x_1 x_2 \ldots x_m$. *It follows that* $P(xy) = p_{xy}$.

THEOREM 3. *If* $(U)^{(2)})$ *is satisfied and* $X^* = M = (1, \ldots, m)$ *is a finite subset of* X, *then for any* $i, j \in M$,

$$(8) \qquad p_{ij} = \sum_{r \in R_{ij}} P(r),$$

where R_{ij} *is the set of all rankings* r *on* M *in which* i *precedes* j.

Proof. By (2), (7).

THEOREM 4. $(U^{(2)})$ *is satisfied for* X *finite,* $X = N = (1, \ldots, n)$, *if there is a non-negative function* P *on the set of rankings* r *on* N *such that equation* (8) *holds, provided* R_{ij} *is redefined as the set of all rankings on* N *in which* i *precedes* j.

Proof. Denote by $r = 1_r 2_r \ldots n_r$ the ranking in which the ith place is occupied by i_r. Then, by (7)

$$P(r) = P(1_r 2_r \ldots n_r) = \Pr(U^{(2)}_{1_r} > U^{(2)}_{2_r} > + > U^{2)}_{n_r},$$

and by (8) the condition (2) is satisfied.

VI. A CONDITION FOR EXISTENCE OF A RANDOM UTILITY INDICATOR

CONDITION (Δ) ['triangular']. For all x, y, z in X,

$$(9) \qquad p_{xy} + p_{yz} \geqq p_{xz}.$$

By virtue of (1), this can be rewritten more symmetrically as

$$(9a) \qquad 1 \leqq p_{xy} + p_{yz} + p_{zx} \leqq 2.$$

Define

(10) $\Delta_{xyz} = p_{xy} + p_{yz} + p_{zx} - 1$;

then by (1), $\Delta_{xyz} + \Delta_{zyx} = 1$; and (9a) can be rewritten as

(9b) $0 \leqq \Delta_{xyz} \leqq 1$.

Condition(Δ) was probably first noticed by Guilbaud [13].

THEOREM 5. ($U^{(2)}$) *implies* (Δ). [*And therefore, clearly,* (U) *also implies* (Δ).]

Proof. Denote by x, y, z the generic elements of the subset (1, 2, 3) of X. Then, by the definition (7), the six $P(xyz)$ add up to 1, and each is greater than or equal to 0. If ($U^{(2)}$) is true, then, by Theorem 3,

$$\begin{aligned} p_{12} &= P(132) + P(123) + P(312), \\ p_{23} &= P(123) + P(213) + P(231), \\ p_{31} &= P(312) + P(231) + P(321). \end{aligned} \tag{11}$$

In (11) the sum of the left sides is $\Delta_{123} + 1$; on the right side, the three off-diagonal terms of the symmetric matrix add up to s, say, where $0 \leqq s \leqq 1$; and all nine terms add up to $1 + s$. Hence

$$0 \leqq \Delta_{123} = s = P(123) + P(231) + P(312) \leqq 1,$$

and (9b) is satisfied.

THEOREM 6. *If* $X = (1, 2, 3)$, *then* (Δ) *implies* ($U^{(2)}$).[1]

Proof. Denote by x, y, z the generic elements of X. We shall show that, for any six numbers p_{xy} satisfying (1) and such that $0 \leqq \Delta_{123} = p_{12} + p_{21} + + p_{31} - 1$, one can find six numbers $P(xyz)$, non-negative, adding up to 1, and satisfying (11). We have just seen that if $\sum_{xyz} P(xyz) = 1$, then (11) implies

$$\Delta_{123} = P(123 + P(231) + P(312). \tag{12}$$

Subtracting (12) from each of the equations (11), we obtain

$$\begin{aligned} p_{12} - \Delta_{123} &= P(132) - P(231), \\ p_{23} - \Delta_{123} &= P(213) - P(312), \\ p_{31} - \Delta_{123} &= P(321) - P(123). \end{aligned} \tag{13}$$

Put $0=P(231)$ or $P(132)$ according as $p_{12} \geqq \text{or} \leqq \Delta_{123}$; put $0=P(312)$ or $P(213)$ according as $p_{23} \geqq \text{or} \leqq \Delta_{123}$. Substituting into (13) and (12), one obtains the remaining four $P(xyz)$, non-negative and adding up to 1. Hence, by Theorem 4, $(U^{(2)})$ is satisfied.

AN ALTERNATIVE PROOF OF THEOREM 5. A probability distribution on the set of rankings on $\boldsymbol{X}=(1,\ldots,n)$ is a vector P whose components $P(r^k)$, where $k=1,\ldots,n!$, are non-negative and add up to 1. The set $\boldsymbol{P}$ of all such vectors is convex and has $n!-1$ dimensions and $n!$ vertices. The vertex P_k shall represent the distribution in which $P(r^k)=1$. Suppose $(U^{(2)})$ holds and let $[p_{xy}(P)]$ be the $n \times n$ matrix of binary probabilities generated by P in $\boldsymbol{P}$. Consider the vertex P_k of $\boldsymbol{P}$ and denote by r_x^k the rank assigned to x when the ranking is r^k. Then, for $x \neq y$,

$$p_{xy}(P_k) = \begin{cases} 1 & \text{if} \quad r_x^k < r_y^k, \\ 0 & \text{if} \quad r_x^k > r_y^k. \end{cases}$$

Let x, y, z be all distinct. Since $r_x^k < r_y^k$ and $r_y^k < r_z^k$ imply $r_z^k > r_x^k$, the triple

$$\{p_{xy}(P_k), p_{yz}(P_k), p_{zx}(P_k)\}$$

cannot consist of 1's only or of 0's only. Hence the sum of these three probabilities, for every ranking r^k, is either 1 or 2. Now, every vector P is a convex combination of the unit vectors P_k:

$$P = \sum P_k \cdot P(r^k) \qquad (\sum P(r^k) = 1; P(r^k) \geqq 0; k = 1, \ldots, n!)$$

and

$$p_{xy}(P) = \sum p_{xy}(P_k) \cdot P(r^k).$$

Hence every sum $p_{xy}(P)+p_{yz}(P)+p_{zx}(P)$ is a weighted average of the numbers 1 and 2, so that (Δ) is satisfied.

This proof was obtained after a conversation with Herman Chernoff, who had suggested the following way to prove (or disprove) the converse of Theorem 5.

CONVERSE OF THEOREM 5. Denote by $\boldsymbol{S_P}$ the set of all matrices $[p_{xy}]$ generated by the distributions P in $\boldsymbol{P}$; denote by $\boldsymbol{S_\Delta}$ the set of all matrices $[p_{xy}]$ satisfying (Δ). Each of these sets has $n(n-1)/2$ dimensions and is convex. $\boldsymbol{S_P}$ has $n!$ vertices, each corresponding to precisely one vertex of $\boldsymbol{P}$, and such that for x, y, z distinct, $p_{xy}=1$ or 0, and $p_{xy}+p_{yz}+$ $+p_{zx}=1$ or 2. Hence all vertices of $\boldsymbol{S_P}$ are elements and are, in fact vertices, of $\boldsymbol{S_\Delta}$, and (another way to state Theorem 5) $\boldsymbol{S_\Delta}$ contains $\boldsymbol{S_P}$. If it were possible to prove that all vertices of $\boldsymbol{S_\Delta}$ are vertices of $\boldsymbol{S_P}$, the converse of Theorem 5 would be proved for any n, thus extending Theorem 6. We therefore register (but do not assert to be true!) the following

CONJECTURE 1. *For any finite* $\boldsymbol{X}$, (Δ) *implies* ($U^{(2)}$).[2]

While (Δ) is necessary for ($U^{(2)}$) and therefore for (U), and even if it were true that (Δ) is sufficient for ($U^{(2)}$), it is certainly not sufficient for (U) since (Δ) does not put any constraints on non-binary choices while (U) does [we have seen that (U) implies (5)]. Some sufficient conditions for ($U^{(2)}$) and (U), respectively, will be given in Sections X and XI.

VII. TRANSITIVITY OF STOCHASTIC PREFERENCES

DEFINITION. *Alternative* x *is* stochastically preferred (stochastically indifferent) *to* y *if* $p_{xy}>\frac{1}{2}$ $(p_{xy}=\frac{1}{2})$.

In what follows, the words 'transitivity of stochastic preferences' will be abbreviated to 'transitivity'.

CONDITIONS (t_w) [weak transitivity], (t_m) [mild transitivity], and (t_s) [strong transitivity.[3] If $\min(p_{xy}, p_{yz}) \geqq \frac{1}{2}$, then

$$p_{xz} \geqq \begin{cases} \frac{1}{2} & \text{Condition } (t_w), \\ \min(p_{xy}, p_{yz}) & \text{Condition } (t_m), \\ \max(p_{xy}, p_{yz}) & \text{Condition } (t_s). \end{cases}$$

Equivalently, by (1): if $\max(p_{xy}, p_{yz}) \leqq \frac{1}{2}$, then

$$p_{xz} \leqq \begin{cases} \frac{1}{2} & \text{Condition } (t_w), \\ \max(p_{xy}, p_{yz}) & \text{Condition } (t_m), \\ \min(p_{xy}, p_{yz}) & \text{Condition } (t_s). \end{cases}$$

A more symmetric equivalent form for (t_w) is, by (1),

$$\min(p_{xy}, p_{yz}, p_{zx}) \leqq \tfrac{1}{2} \leqq \max(p_{xy}, p_{yz}, p_{zx}).$$

THEOREM 7. *Condition* (t_s) *is equivalent to the following conditions: if* $p_{xy}\geqq\frac{1}{2}$, *then* $p_{xz}\geqq p_{yz}$, *for all* $z\in\boldsymbol{X}$; *and if* $z\in\boldsymbol{X}$ *and* $p_{xz}\geqq p_{yz}$, *then* $p_{xy}\geqq\frac{1}{2}$.

Proof. See [1], Theorem 4.1.

THEOREM 8. *Condition* (t_s) *is strictly stronger than* (t_m), *and* (t_m) *is strictly stronger than* (t_w).

Proof. Obvious.

THEOREM 9. *Condition* (t_w) *is neither sufficient nor necessary for* (Δ).

Proof. Let $n=3$, and $p_{13}=0.6$. If $p_{12}=p_{23}=0.9$, then (t_w) is satisfied but (Δ) is not. If $p_{12}=p_{23}=0.4$, then (Δ) is satisfied but (t_w) is not.

THEOREM 10. *Condition* (t_m) *is strictly stronger than* (Δ).

Proof. (i) Sufficiency. Consider $(1, 2, 3)\subseteq X$. Using the notation of Section 6, we have to prove that (t_m) implies $0\leqq\Delta_{xyz}\leqq 1$. By (1) we can let $p_{12}\geqq p_{23}\geqq\frac{1}{2}\geqq p_{32}\geqq p_{21}$ without loss of generality; then

$$p_{12}+p_{23}\geqq 1\geqq p_{32}+p_{21}$$

$$p_{12}+p_{23}+p_{31}-1=\Delta_{123}\geqq 0,$$

$$1-\Delta_{123}=p_{21}+p_{32}+p_{13}-1=\Delta_{321}\leqq 1.$$

Now assume (t_m). Then

$$p_{31}\leqq\max(p_{32},p_{21})=p_{32},$$

$$\Delta_{123}\leqq p_{12}+p_{23}+p_{32}-1=p_{12}\leqq 1$$

and

$$p_{13}\geqq\min(p_{12},p_{23})=p_{12},$$

$$\Delta_{321}\geqq p_{21}+p_{32}+p_{12}-1=p_{32}\geqq 0.$$

(ii) No necessity. By Theorems 8, 9.

THEOREM 11. *Condition* (t_m) *is strictly stronger than the conjunction of* (t_w) *and* (Δ).

Proof. (i) Sufficiency. By Theorems 8, 10. (ii) No necessity. Let $X= =(1, 2, 3)$, $p_{12}=.8$. $p_{23}=.7$, and $p_{31}=.4$. Then (t_w) and (Δ) are satisfied. But since $p_{12}>p_{23}>.5$ while $p_{13}=.6<p_{23}$, Condition (t_m) is violated.

Write $\rightarrow$ for 'implies', $\leftrightarrow$ for 'implies and is implied by, $\mapsto$ for 'implies but is not implied by', $\vdash\!\dashv$ for 'does not imply nor is implied by'. Then our results can be summarized in

THEOREM 12.

$$\begin{array}{ccccccc}
(t_s) & \mapsto & (t_m) & \mapsto & (t_w,\Delta) & & \\
 & & & & \downarrow & & \\
(\Delta; n=3) & \mapsto & (U^{(2)}) & \rightarrow & (\Delta) & \vdash\!\dashv & (t_w). \\
 & & \uparrow & & & & \\
 & & (U) & & & &
\end{array}$$

In political science the fact that Condition ($U^{(2)}$) does not imply Condition (t_w) is interpreted as 'intransitivity of the majority rule'. It was pointed out by Kenneth Arrow. We have shown in [1, Theorem 3.2] that even the stronger Condition (U) does not imply (t_w).

VIII. WEAK UTILITY FUNCTION

DEFINITION. *A real-valued function* w *on* X *is called a* weak utility function *if* $w_x \geqq w_y$ when and only when $p_{xy} \geqq \frac{1}{2}$.

CONDITION (w). The function p is such that w exists. It follows that w is unique up to an increasing monotone transformation.

THEOREM 13. $(w) \mapsto (t_w)$.

Proof. (i) Sufficiency. Let $p_{ab} \geqq \frac{1}{2}$, $p_{bc} \geqq \frac{1}{2}$, $a, b, c \in X$. If (w) is true, then $w_a \geqq w_b \geqq w_c$ and $p_{ac} \geqq \frac{1}{2}$. (ii) No necessity, Let X be a real 2-space with generic points $x = (x_1, x_2)$ and assume that $p_{xy} > \frac{1}{2}$ when either $x_1 > y_1$ or $x_1 = y_1$ and $x_2 > y_2$ (lexicographical ordering). Compare Debreu [6].

CONDITION (D). X is perfectly separable (i.e., contains a countable and dense subset); and for every a in X, the sets $(x \mid p_{xa} \geqq \frac{1}{2})$ and $(x \mid p_{xa} \leqq \frac{1}{2})$ are closed. This is adapted from Debreu's paper just cited, which also contains, *mutatis mutandis*, the proof of

THEOREM 14. *If* (D) *is satisfied, then* (w) *and* (t_w) *are equivalent.*

REMARK. Condition (D) is trivially satisfied on X finite. Moreover, every subset of a finite-dimensional real space is perfectly separable; and it is reasonable to assume that Condition (D) is satisfied on a commodity space.

We summarize some of the previous results in

THEOREM 15.

$$\begin{array}{ccccccc} (t_w;\, n \text{ finite}) \mapsto (t_w, D) \mapsto (w) \mapsto & & (t_w) & & & & \\ & & \uparrow & & & & \\ (\Delta;\, n=3) \quad \mapsto \quad U^{(2)} & \rightarrow & (\Delta) & \leftarrow\!\dashv (t_w, \Delta) & \leftarrow\!\dashv (t_m) & \leftarrow\!\dashv (t_s) & \end{array}$$

IX. STRONG UTILITY FUNCTION

DEFINITION. *A real-valued function v on $\boldsymbol{X}$ is called a* strong utility function *if there exists a monotone increasing function ϕ_v such that*

$$(14) \qquad \phi_v(v_x - v_y) = p_{xy};\ \phi_v(0) = \tfrac{1}{2}.$$

CONDITION (v). The function p is such that v exists.

THEOREM 16. *If $\boldsymbol{X}$ is continuous and ϕ_v is strictly monotone, then* (i) *v is unique up to an increasing linear transformation, and* (ii) *for any real number λ*

$$(15) \qquad \phi_v(\lambda) + \phi_v(-\lambda) = 1.$$

Proof. For (i), see [1, Section II]; (ii) is obvious.

Equation (15) implies that ϕ_v is anti-symmetrical about $(0, \tfrac{1}{2})$; the median and the mean (if it exists) are 0.

The strong utility v_x of alternative x corresponds to the 'sensation' produced by a stimulus x, as defined by Fechner [10] in 1859. It also corresponds to the relative position of a gene in the chromosome when inferred from the probability of a 'crossover': this generation of a real line from a set of probabilities was noticed by D. Hilbert.[4]

CONDITION (q) [quadruple condition]. For any x, y, z, t in $\boldsymbol{X}$,

$$(16) \qquad \text{if} \quad p_{xy} \geqq p_{zt}, \quad \textit{then} \quad p_{xz} \geqq p_{yt}.$$

THEOREM 17. *Condition* (v) *implies Condition* (q) [*Proof.* By monotonicity of ϕ_v]; *Condition* (q) *implies Condition* (t_s) [*Proof.* In (16) put $z = t$ and use Theorem 7]; *Condition* (v) *implies Condition* (w) [*Proof.* In (14), put $v = w$].

THEOREM 18. *If $\boldsymbol{X}$ is finite, $\boldsymbol{X} = (1, \ldots, n)$, then* ($q$) *implies* ($v$) *only for* $n \leqq 4$.

Proof. See [1], Proof of Theorem 4. 1.

For $\boldsymbol{X}$ continuous it is useful to consider the following

CONDITION ($s \cdot c$) ['stochastic continuity']. If $p_{xy} < q < p_{xz}$, then there is a t in $\boldsymbol{X}$ such that $p_{xt} = q$. In [7] Debreu has proved

THEOREM 19. *If Condition* ($s \cdot c$) *is satisfied, then* (q) *implies* (v).
If both ($U^{(2)}$) and (v) are satisfied, we can define a random function V_x by

$$(17) \qquad U_x^{(2)} = v_x + V_x, \qquad EV_x = 0,$$

and set up the following three conditions, each stronger than the preceding one:

There exist two functions on X, a real-valued v and a random-valued V, and a distribution function ϕ_v such that

$$p_{xy} = \phi_v(v_x - v_y), \qquad \Pr(V_y - V_x \leqq \lambda) = \phi_v(\lambda),$$

where

CONDITION (V): $\lambda = v_x - v_y$;

CONDITION (V'): $\lambda =$ any real number;

CONDITION (V''): $\Pr(V_x \leqq \alpha,\ V_y \leqq \beta) = \Pr(V_x \leqq \beta,\ V_y \leqq \alpha)$, $\lambda, \alpha, \beta =$ any real numbers.

In Condition (V) the distribution of the differences $V_x - V_y$ is defined only for each pair of alternatives (possibly finite in number); in (V') this distribution is defined for any real argument; in (V''), in addition, the (multivariate) distribution function of V is symmetrical in its arguments. From (17) and Theorem 16 one obtains

THEOREM 20.

$$(V'') \mapsto (V') \mapsto (V) \leftrightarrow (U^{(2)}, v) \quad \textit{if} \quad X \textit{ is finite};$$
$$(V'') \mapsto (V') \leftrightarrow (V) \leftrightarrow (U^{(2)}, v) \quad \textit{if} \quad X \textit{ is continuous}.$$

In the work of Thurstone and his school a condition even stronger than (V'') is used: the distribution function of V is assumed to be normal and symmetric (zero means, equal variances, equal covariances). Actually, a normal distribution of differences ϕ_v (as assumed by Fechner) is consistent also with a normal distribution of V non-symmetrical in its arguments.

For possible application to the commodity space some of our results can be summarized in

THEOREM 21. *If X is continuous and the conditions* (*D*) *and* ($s\cdot c$) *are satisfied, then*

$$\begin{array}{ccccccccccccc} (V'') & \mapsto & (V') & \leftrightarrow & (U^{(2)}, v) & \mapsto & (v) & \leftrightarrow & (q) & \mapsto & (t_s) & \mapsto & (t_w) \\ & & & & \downarrow & & & & & & \downarrow & & \updownarrow \\ & & & & (U^{(2)}) & & \longrightarrow & & & & (\Delta) & \leftarrow & (w). \end{array}$$

X. STRICT UTILITY FUNCTION (IN THE 'BINARY' SENSE)

DEFINITION. *A* positive-valued function $u^{(2)}$ on *X is called a* strict utility function (in the 'binary' sense) *if.*

$$(18) \qquad p_{xy} = \frac{u_x^{(2)}}{u_x^{(2)} + u_y^{(2)}}.$$

Clearly, every positive multiple of a strict utility function is also a strict utility function.

CONDITION ($u^{(2)}$). The function p is such that $u^{(2)}$ exists. Applying (18) one obtains

THEOREM 22. *Condition* ($u^{(2)}$) *is true only if* (i) $0<p_{xy}<1$ *for every* x, y *in* **X**, *and* (ii) *for any subset* $(1, \ldots, m) \subseteq X$ $(m>1)$, *the following equation holds*:

$$(19) \qquad p_{12} \cdot p_{23} \cdots p_{m-1,\, m} \cdot p_{m1} = p_{21} \cdot p_{32} \cdots p_{m,\, m-1} \cdot p_{1m}.$$

Note that (19) is 'directly testable'. Condition ($u^{(2)}$) was formulated by Törnqvist [20], Bradley and Terry [3], and L. R. Ford [11]. It is a weak form of a postulate that has been proposed by Luce [15] and that involves multiple-choice probabilities: see Section XI below.

THEOREM 23. $(u^{(2)}) \mapsto (v)$.

Proof. (i) Necessity. Put $u_y^{(2)} = e^{v_y}$; then by (18) $p_{xy} = \phi_v(v_x - v_y)$, where

$$(20) \qquad \phi_v(\lambda) = \frac{1}{1 + e^{-\lambda}},$$

the 'logistic curve'. (ii) No sufficiency. For *X* continuous, by the above proof of necessity (due to Luce) and by Theorem 16, we see that Condition

$(u^{(2)})$ is not implied by (v), since $(u^{(2)})$ restricts the function ϕ_v to the form (20). For X finite, let

$$(21) \qquad X = (1, 2, 3); \quad p_{12} = .6, \quad p_{23} = .7, \quad p_{13} = .8.$$

Then (v) is satisfied[5] by $v_1 = .3$, $v_2 = .2$, $v_3 = .0$, and $\phi_v(\lambda) = .5 + \lambda$. But (19), and therefore $(u^{(2)})$, is not.

THEOREM 24. *If X is finite, then $(u^{(2)})$ implies $(U^{(2)})$.*

Proof. We shall use an arithmetical identity proved in [1, Theorem 3.6] and [8]:

LEMMA. *Let $N = (1, \ldots, n)$ and denote by $r = (1_r 2_r \ldots n_r)$ the permutation on N in which the* kth *place is occupied by the element k_r; denote by R_{iM} the set of permutations on N in which i precedes all other elements of $M \subseteq N$. Then, for any positive $u_1, \ldots, u_n$,*

$$(22) \qquad \frac{u_i}{\sum_{h \in M} u_h} \equiv \sum_{r \in R_{iM}} \prod_{j=1}^{n} \frac{u_{j_r}}{\sum_{k=j}^{n} u_{k_r}}.$$

To prove Theorem 24 from this Lemma let $X = N$, $M = (i, j)$, $u_x = u_x^{(2)}$; then by (18) the left side of (22) becomes p_{ij}, and the set $R_{iM} = R_{ij}$, as defined in Theorem 3. Since each of the products on the right side is positive and they add up to p_{ij}, we can equate each of them to a probability of ranking in the sense of (7), so that, for any ranking r on N,

$$(23) \qquad P(r) = P(1_r 2_r \ldots n_r) = \frac{u_{1_r}}{u_{1_r} + + + u_{n_r}} \cdot \frac{u_{2_r}}{u_{2_r} + + + u_{n_r}} \cdots \cdots \frac{u_{(n-1)_r}}{u_{(n-1)_r} + u_{n_r}}.$$

Since we interpret each u_i as $u^{(2)}$, then by Theorem 4 $(U^{(2)})$ is satisfied.

If X is continuous, the reasoning just used can be applied to any finite subset of X. Hence the following

CONJECTURE 2. *Theorem* 24 *applies to any X.*

Remark. The proof of Theorem 24 could be much simplified if Conjecture 1 (Section VI) were proved to be true. For it would then suffice to prove that $(u^{(2)})$ implies (Δ). This is indeed the case: for, writing

$u_y^{(2)}/u_x^{(2)}=a$, $u_z^{(2)}/u_y^{(2)}=b$, and $u_x^{(2)}/u_z^{(2)}=c$, we have $abc=1$, and by (10), (18), we obtain

$$(24) \qquad 0<\Delta_{xyz}=\frac{1}{1+a}+\frac{1}{1+b}+\frac{1}{1+c}-1=\frac{1}{1+k}<1,$$

where $k=(1+ab+bc+ca)/(1+a+b+c)>0$, since $a, b, c>0$.

THEOREM 25. *$(U^{(2)})$ does not imply $(u^{(2)})$.*

Proof: Consider again example (21). Since $p_{31}=.2$, it follows that $\Delta_{123}=.5$; hence Condition (Δ) and, by Theorem 6, Condition $(U^{(2)})$ are satisfied. But (19) is not.

Since example (21) was seen to satisfy (v), Theorem 25 can be replaced by the even stronger

THEOREM 26. *The conjunction of $(U^{(2)})$ and (v) does not imply $(u^{(2)})$.*

Some of the results of this and the preceding section can be summarized in

THEOREM 27. *For **X** finite,*

$$\begin{array}{ccccccc} (u^{(2)}) \mapsto [(U^{(2)}),(v)] \mapsto (v) \mapsto (q) \mapsto & (t_s) & \mapsto (t_w) \leftrightarrow (w) \\ \swarrow \qquad\qquad\qquad\qquad & \downarrow & \\ (U^{(2)}) \longrightarrow\longrightarrow\longrightarrow & (\Delta). & \end{array}$$

Remark on the commodity space. If Condition (D) is satisfied on the continuous commodity space and if Conjecture 2 is correct, Theorem 27 applies also to the commodity space; if, in addition, $(s\cdot c)$ is satisfied, then $(v)\leftrightarrow(q)$.

XI. SOME RESULTS ON MULTIPLE-CHOICE PROBABILITIES

In Section IV, the Condition (U) was stated. Clearly, (U) implies $(U^{(2)})$. Similarly, $(u^{(2)})$ can be replaced by the following stronger

CONDITION (u). There exists a positive-valued function u on $\boldsymbol{X}$ such that for any finite subset $\boldsymbol{M}=(x_1,\ldots,x_m)\subseteq\boldsymbol{X}$, the multiple-choice probability

$$(25) \qquad p_{x_i}(M)=\frac{u_i}{\sum_{j\in M} u_j}.$$

The function u may be called a *strict utility function in the multiple-choice sense.*

As was proved in [1], (u) implies that the probability of each ranking in the multiple-choice sense, defined as

$$P(r) = \Pr(U_{1_r} > U_{2_r} > \cdots > U_{n_r}), \quad \text{with} \sum_{R_{iM}} P(r) = p_i(M),$$

exists and is precisely the expression on the right side of (23). For example, if $X=(1, 2, 3)$, then

$$(26) \qquad P(xyz) = \frac{u_x}{u_x + u_y + u_z} \cdot \frac{u_y}{u_y + u_z} = p_x(X) \cdot p_y(y, z),$$

by (25). Thus (u) implies (and, as shown in [1], is equivalent to) the proposition that the probability of a given ranking of a finite set of alternatives is the product of probabilities of multiple choices made successively, from the set itself, then from the subset remaining after eliminating the first choice, then from the subset remaining after eliminating the second choice, etc. Applying the Lemma of Section X we obtain, using (25),

THEOREM 28. *(u)→(U) when* X *is finite.*

This result is discussed in more detail in [1]. We can prove the even stronger

THEOREM 29. *(u)↦[(U), (v)] when* X *is finite.*

Proof. (i) Necessity. By Theorems 28 and 23, remembering that (u) of course implies ($u^{(2)}$). (ii) No sufficiency. Note that for $X=(1, 2, 3)$, condition (u) implies, by (19) and (26) respectively,

$$(27) \qquad p_{12} \cdot p_{23} \cdot p_{31} = p_{13} \cdot p_{32} \cdot p_{21},$$

and

$$(28) \qquad P(123) \cdot P(231) \cdot P(312) = P(213) \cdot P(132) \cdot P(321).$$

Moreover, (U) implies $p_{xy} = P(xyz) + P(xzy) + P(zxy)$ and $p_x(X) = P(xyz) + P(xzy)$. It is easy to construct examples satisfying (v) and (U) but not (27) or (28). For example, use (21), which we have seen satisfies (v) and which contradicts (27); and put, in addition, the following values: for the probabilities of ranking, $P(123)=P(132)=.3$, $P(231)=P(213)=.2$, $P(312)=P(321)=0$; for the ternary probabilities, $p_1(X)=.6$, $p_2(X)=.4$, and $p_3(X)=0$. The foregoing results, together with some obtained in the previous section, can be summarized in

THEOREM 30.

$$\begin{array}{ccccc} (u) & \mapsto & [(U),(v)] & \mapsto & (U) \\ \downarrow & & \downarrow & & \downarrow \\ (u^{(2)}) & \mapsto & [(U^{(2)},(v)] & \mapsto & (U^{(2)}) \\ & & \downarrow & & \downarrow \\ & & (v) & \mapsto & (\Delta) \end{array}$$

Luce [15] proposed a condition still stronger than (u), being a conjunction of (u) and the following

CONDITION (u'). Denote by $p'_x(X^*)$ the probability that x is the *last* choice out of the subset $X^* \subseteq X$. There exists a real-valued function u' on X such that for any finite subset $M=(x_i, \ldots, x_m) \subseteq X$, the probability

$$p'_{x_i}(M) = \frac{u'_i}{\sum_{j \in M} u'_j}.$$

The function u' may be called a *strict disutility function*. However, apart from trivial cases, the functions u and u' cannot both exist:

THEOREM 31. *Conditions (u) and (u') can both hold only if all first choices are equally probable and all last choices are equally probable, or if X has only two elements.*

Proof. If $n \geqq 3$, let $M \subseteq X$ consist of three elements, to be denoted generically by x, y, z. Assume both Conditions (u) and (u'). Without loss of generality, let $u_x+u_y+u_z=1=u'_x+u'_y+u'_z$, so that $p_x(M)=u_x$, $p'_x(M)=u'_x$, for all x in M. Then

$$u_x \cdot \frac{u'_z}{1-u'_x} = u'_z \cdot \frac{u_x}{1-u_z}, \quad \text{all} \quad x, z \text{ in } M,$$

since both the left and the right side express the probability of the same event, viz., of x being the first, and z the last choice. Hence $u'_x=u_z$, $p'_x(M)=p_z(M)$ for any pair x, z of the arbitrary three-elements subset M. Interchanging variables x, y, z, and applying (u), (u'),

$$p'_x(X)p_y(=X) = p'_y(X) = p_x(X), \quad \text{all} \quad x, y \text{ in } X.$$

This proves the Theorem for $n \geqq 3$. When $n=2$, the same reasoning yields trivially the identity $p_x(x, y)=p'_y(x, y)$. For a more detailed proof see [1, Theorem 3.8].

It has been pointed out by Luce (in private correspondence) that while in experiments on choices the probabilities of last choices may or may not be accessible to observations, they definitely are in experiments on perceptions: the subject's decision as to which is the loudest of three sounds is as observable as his decision as to which sound is the softest. If one accepts (u), symmetry requires one to accept (u') also. But, as we have shown, these two conditions are mutually inconsistent.

Therefore, we must limit ourselves to the weaker Condition ($u^{(2)}$). It involves binary choices only, so that, when identifying the loudest sound, the subject identifies also the softest. That is, if the subset $\boldsymbol{X}^*$ consists of two elements, then Conditions ($u^{(2)}$), (u), and (u') are identical. A strict utility function in this limited sense – $u^{(2)}$ rather than u – is compatible with the existence of the corresponding strict disutility function and of a random utility indicator $U^{(2)}$ involving binary choices only. *Added in* 1973: See now Luce and Suppes [23], especially p. 358.

XII. BINARY-CHOICE CONSTRAINTS AND THE FORM OF THE RANDOM UTILITY INDICATOR

Consider Example (ii) of Section III, and let $m=2$, $0<T_1=A<1$, and $T_2=1-A$. Then

(29) $$U_x^{(2)} = x_1^A x_2^{1-A};$$

the function $U^{(2)}$ is monotone increasing in x in the sense that if $x=(x_1, x_2)$, $y=(y_1, y_2)$, $x_1 \geqq y_1$, and $x_2 > y_2$, then $U_x^{(2)} > U_y^{(2)}$ is a random function depending on the random parameter A.[6] If $U^{(2)}$ is a utility indicator in the 'binary' sense of (2), then $p_{xy}=\Pr(U_x^{(2)} \geqq U_y^{(2)}=\Pr(y_1^A y_2^{1-A} \leqq \leqq x_A^1 x_2^{1-A})$. Let $y_1 > x_1$ and $y_2 < x_2$ (so that x does not dominate y, and conversely). Then $\log(y_1/x_1)>0$, $\log(x_2/y_2)>0$, and

$$p_{xy} = \Pr\left(\frac{A}{1-A} \leqq \frac{\log(x_2/y_2)}{\log(y_1/x_1)}\right) = F(\mu_{xy}),$$

where $\mu_{xy}=\log(x_2/y_2)/\log(y_1/x_1)$ and F is a monotone non-decreasing function depending on the distribution of A. We shall now show that the form (29) of the random utility indicator is not consistent with some binary-choice constraints:

THEOREM 32. *If the random utility indicator has the form* (29), *then the strong transitivity condition* (t_s) *is, in general, not satisfied.*

Proof. Consider three points x, y, z with $z_1 > y_1 > x_1$ and $z_2 < y_2 < x_2$. Then

$$p_{xy} = F(\mu_{xy}), \qquad \mu_{xy} = (\log x_2 - \log y_2(/(\log y_1 - \log x_1),$$
$$p_{yz} = F(\mu_{yz}), \qquad \mu_{yz} = (\log y_2 - \log z_2)/(\log z_1 - \log y_1),$$
$$p_{xz} = F(\mu_{xz}), \qquad \mu_{xz} = (\log x_2 - \log z_2)/(\log z_1 - \log x_1),$$
$$\mu_{xz} = \frac{\mu_{xy}(\log y_1 - \log x_1) + \mu_{yz}(\log z_1 - \log y_1)}{(\log y_1 - \log x_1) + (\log z_1 - \log y_1)},$$

a convex combination of μ_{xy} and μ_{yz}. Hence min $(\mu_{xy}, \mu_{yz}) \leqq \mu_{xz} \leqq$ max (μ_{xy}, μ_{yz}); and since F is non-decreasing, min $(p_{xy}, p_{yz}) \leqq p_{xz} \leqq \max(p_{xy}, p_{yz})$. This is consistent with the Weak and the Mild Transitivity Conditions, (t_w) and (t_m) of Section VII, but not with the Strong Transitivity Condition (t_s). All three conditions are directly testable.

Thus (29) is in general inconsistent with the existence of strict or strong utility functions, since those imply strong transitivity (Theorems 17 and 27).

Consider now another random form of the 'Cobb-Douglas function':

(30) $$U_x^{(2)} = x_1^\alpha x_2^{1-\alpha} + V_x,$$

where α is a constant, $0 < \alpha < 1$, and V is a random function on X. If $U^{(2)}$ is a random utility indicator, then

$$p_{xy} = \Pr(U_x^{(2)} \geqq U_y^{(2)}) = \Pr(V_y - V_z \leqq x_1^\alpha x_2^{1-\alpha} - y_1^\alpha y_2^{1-\alpha}).$$

Suppose we have found V such that $\Pr(V_y - V_x \leqq \lambda) = \phi(\lambda)$ for any real λ, with ϕ being a distribution function independent of x, y. Then Condition (V') of Section IX is satisfied, and

(31) $$U_x^{(2)} - V_x = v_x = x_1^\alpha x_2^{1-\alpha}$$

is a strong utility function consistent with the assumed random utility indicator.[7]

If we could accept the still stronger condition (V''), i.e., let the (infinite-dimensional) distribution of V be symmetrical in its arguments $(x, y, \ldots)$, we would have to search for such distributions. However, the symmetry assumption is hardly realistic: for example, in the case of normality it implies that deviations from the average budget composition have not only the same variances everywhere but also the same correlations for any two points of the X-plane, however close or remote in relation to each other.

The examples used in this section have the purpose merely of illustrating the problem: to find a class of random utility indicators consistent with a given set of binary-choice constraints.

NOTES

* Dedicated to Ragnar Frisch, an old and esteemed friend, on the occasion of his sixty-fifth birthday.

The paper was completed during a year's visit at the Carnegie Institute of Technology, The research was carried out partly under a contract of the Office of Naval Research with the Cowles Foundation for Research in Economics at Yale University, Task NR047-006. Previous collaboration with H. D. Block and discussions with Herman Chernoff, Gerard Debreu, Morris DeGroot, Tjalling Koopmans, and R. Duncan Luce were most helpful.

1 See also [1], Theorems 5.7, 5.1.

2 I am told by Professor T. Motzkin that he has proved the conjecture for $n \leqq 5$. Because of applications to the commodity space or to the space of wagers, the continuous case (as in Theorems 19 and 14) would deserve study.

3 Conditions (t_w) and (t_s) were formulated by S. Valavanis-Vail [21] and originated in his work with C. Coombs. Condition (t_m) was formulated by N. Georgescu-Roegen [12] and by John Chipman [4]. Experimental tests of stochastic transitivity conditions were undertaken by Papandreou *et al.* [17] and by Davidson and Marschak [5].

4 In a paper [14] pointed out to me by Hans Rademacher.

5 It is noteworthy that for $n = 3$, Condition (t_s) is not only necessary but also sufficient for (v). This follows from Theorems 17 and 18.

6 Maximizing $U_x^{(2)}$ with respect to x, subject to the constancy of income $x_1 + x_2$, we see that A is the (random) proportion spent on the 1th commodity. Hence the observed frequency distribution of this proportion should help to estimate the distribution of A – assuming that members of the sampled population were characterized by the same random function $U^{(2)}$. (But we shall not pursue this matter here.)

7 One may want to use indifference lines to picture some relevant aspect of a given random utility indicator, and in particular, its mean. In the case just discussed, described by (30) and (31), we may choose V to have 0 expectation; then $EU_x^{(2)} = v_x$. Accordingly, an indifference line through x consists of all points y, with $v_y = v_x$ and $p_{yx} = \phi_v(0) = \frac{1}{2}$ as in (14); it is then the common boundary of the two sets used in Condition (D), Section VIII. On the other hand, if the random utility indicator is described by (29), equation $EU_y^{(2)} = EU_x^{(2)}$, or possibly $E \log U_y^{(2)} = E \log U_x^{(2)}$, gives quite a different representation.

BIBLIOGRAPHY

[1] Block, H. D. and Marschak, J., 'Random Orderings and Stochastic Theories of Responses', *Selected Essays*, 7.

[2] Block, H. D. and Marschak, J., 'An Identity in Arithmetic', *Bulletin of the American Mathematical Society* **65** (1959), 123–24.

[3] Bradley, R. A. and Terry, M. E., 'Rank Analysis of Incomplete Block Designs. I. The Method of Paired Comparisons', *Biometrika* **39** (1952), 324–44.

[4] Chipman, J. S., 'Stochastic Choice and Subjective Probability' (abstract), *Econometrica* **26** (1958), 613.

[5] Davidson, D. and Marschak, J., 'Experimental Tests of Stochastic Decision Theories', *Selected Essays*, 6.

[6] Debreu, G., 'Representation of a Preference Ordering by a Numerical Function', in R. M. Thrall, C. Coombs, and R. L. Davis (eds.), *Decision Processes*, John Wiley and Sons, New York, 1954, pp. 159–66.

[7] Debreu, G., 'Stochastic Choice and Cardinal Utility', *Econometrica* **26** (1958), 440–44.

[8] Debreu, G., 'On An Identity in Arithmetic', *Proceedings of the American Mathematical Society* **11** (1960) 220–21.

[9] Farrell, M. J., 'The Demand for Motor-Cars in the United States'. *Journal of the Royal Statistical Society, A* **117** (1954), 171–93.

[10] Fechner, G. Th., *Elemente der Psychophysik*, 1859 (see especially pp. 70–103 of the 1889 edition).

[11] Ford, L. R., 'Solution of a Ranking Problem from Binary Comparisons', *American Mathematical Monthly* **64** (1957), No. 8 (supplement), 28–33.

[12] Georgescu-Roegen, N., 'Threshold in Choice and the Theory of Demand', *Econometrica* **26** (1958, 157–68.

[13] Guilbaud, G., 'Sur une difficulté de la théorie du risque', *Colloques Internationaux du Centre National de la Recherche Scientifique* (*Econométrie*) **40** (1953), 19–25.

[14] Hilbert, D., 'Naturerkenntis und Logik', *Gesammelte Abhandlungen* **3** (1935), esp. pp. 379–80.

[15] Luce, R. D., *Individual Choice Behavior*, John Wiley and Sons, New York, 1959.

[16] Marschak, J., 'Money Illusion and Demand Analysis', *Selected Essays*, 46.

[17] Papandreou, A. G. (with the collaboration of O. H. Sauerlender, O. H. Brownlee, L. Hurwicz, W. Franklin), 'A Test of a Stochastic Theory of Choice', *University of California Publications in Economics* **16** (1957), 1–18.

[18] Thurstone, L. L., 'A Law of Comparative Judgment', *Psychological Review* **34** (1927), 273–86.

[19] Tobin, J., 'A Statistical Demand Function for Food in the U.S.A.', *Journal of the Royal Statistical Society A* **113** (1951), 113–49.

[20] Törnqvist, L., 'A Model for Stochastic Decision Making', *Cowles Commission Discussion Paper*, Economics 2100, 1954 (duplicated).

[21] Valavanis-Vail, S., 'A Stochastic Model for Utilities', seminar on the application of mathematics to social sciences, University of Michigan, 1957 (duplicated).

[22] Wold, H. (with L. Jureen), *Demand Analysis*, John Wiley and Sons, New York, 1953.

[23] Luce, R. D. and Suppes, P., 'Preference, Utility, and Subjective Probability', *Handbook of Mathematical Psychology*, Vol. III, Ch. 19, Wiley, 1965.

9

ACTUAL VERSUS CONSISTENT DECISION BEHAVIOR*

(1964)

I. PURPOSE

Like any other specialist in decision-making, the manager expects science to answer two questions:

(1) What is the manager's optimal (effective, efficient) behavior, in the face of a given task? That is, how should *he* impinge upon Nature (including humans) to achieve, on the average, results that are best from his point of view? (*Normative science*: engineering, operations research, medicine and other 'know-how' sciences).

(2.) How does Nature (including humans) behave? (*Descriptive science*: physics, psychology, biology).

Normative science develops methods that use the findings of descriptive science to predict results from actions, and thus choose optimal actions.

One particular subject of descriptive sciences of behavior is the study of the *limitations of men's capacities* for finding optimal decisions; or, more generally, the study of the *cost of decision-making*, in a society with a given supply of, and demand for, decision-making skills. The normative science of management must take these limitations and costs as described by behavioral science into account, and seek optimum results of decisions *feasible* under limited decision capacity, and *net* of decision cost. Also, descriptive behavioral science may help to determine optimal strategies for training decision-makers.

The 'humans' in the two questions above are the manager's customers, competitors, coworkers, etc., including himself. Three particular (and not exhaustive) classes of managerial action are:

(1) to assign decisions to men in an optimal way;

(2) to remedy the failure of some men (including himself) to optimize their actions; and

(3) to exploit the failure of other men to optimize *their* actions.

Each class calls for contributions of descriptive behavioral science. In particular, Class 1 calls for measurement of relevant variables (dimensions of decision-making capacity, e.g., speed, memory, and size and frequency of deviations from optimum under varying conditions such as cultural background, business experience, and stress.

Class 2 calls for the study of the behavior of *successful* optimizers. The study (by simulation or otherwise) of traditional, possibly outdated decision routines and habits of average managers is of smaller practical value. Besides the study of successful decision techniques, Class 2 calls also for the study of processes of learning and training.

By contrast, Class 3 calls for the study of average and below-average types of decision-makers: installment buyers who fail to compute the true interest rates, or housewives fascinated by 'economy-size' packages.

In the next section some general hypotheses of decision behavior will be stated. They are, at least in part, mutually exclusive: if actual behavior confirms one hypothesis it may contradict another one.

Finally, the concluding section will contain suggestions of possible experiments to test the hypotheses. Few of these experiments have been carried out on a convincing scale. Tentative explorations performed by the author over a number of years on his own graduate students, or by these students on their wives or friends, do supply some preliminary evidence which deserves to be tested in a more rigorous way. It would be worthwhile to peform such experiments on mature executives (in business or in public agencies) rather than on students.

II. GENERAL HYPOTHESES

The following general hypotheses, or some of their implications, will be considered.

A. *Hypothesis 1. 'Rational' or 'Consistent' Behavior*

The subject's actions (choices) are consistent with a constant system of numerical utilities (attached by him to the possible outcomes of his actions, and characterizing his 'tastes') and of numerical subjective probabilities (attached by him to events that he does not control and characterizing his 'beliefs'). These numbers, constant over some reasonably long period of time, have the following property: out of any set of feasible actions, the subject always chooses one with the highest average of utilities of outcomes, weighted by the subjective probabilities of events. This average is called 'mathematical expectation of utility' or simply 'expected utility'. This 'expected utility principle' follows, by ordinary rules of logic, from much simpler, basic postulates. These I shall state presently. Later, I shall illustrate them, as well as some of their logical implications, by appropriate experiments. Note, however, that a person whose behavior conforms with these postulates in simple experimental situations may or may not, when faced with more complex situations, obey the logical implications of these postulates, such as the expected utility principle. For it may be a stiff requirement for a man to be logical! This was, in fact, proved by some of the experiments.

An action is defined by the different outcomes it yields when different, specified events occur. In this sense, 'not to act' (e.g., 'not to invest', i.e., to keep cash) is also an action. Thus, any subject is forced to decide between actions; but he can find himself indifferent. In what follows, the case of indifference is sometimes omitted to simplify presentation. In this and several other respects our presentation, sufficiently precise for its purpose, is not precise enough for complete logical analysis. This will be found in Savage (1954). Roughly, our Postulate I is his P1; our Postulate 2 is his P3; and out Postulate 3 is his P2 and P4. An elementary exposition will be found in Marschak and Radner (1963). Most of the logical work deriving the expected utility principle from some basic postulates was done by F. Ramsey in the 1920's, B. de Finetti in the 1930's, J. Von Neumann and O. Morgenstern in the 1940's, and L. J. Savage in the 1950's.

1. *Postulate of consistent preferences between actions.* If the subject prefers action *A* to *B*, and *B* to *C*, he prefers *A* to *C*. It follows that outcomes of actions are also ranked consistently, since a given outcome (e.g., a 'job') can be identified with an action (viz., 'choosing the job') that yields this outcome with certainty whatever the external events. Choice under certainty is a special case of choice under uncertainty. In fact, Postulate 1 suffices for the economic theory of certainty; but to tackle economics of uncertainty, it is to be supplemented by Postulates 2 and 3 which follow.

2. *Admissibility postulate.* Suppose two actions, *A* and *B*, would result in

the same outcomes if certain events would occur; and that otherwise *A* results in an outcome that is preferable to *B*'s outcome. Then *A* itself is preferable to *B*. (Laws that threaten the death penalty for desertion from the battlefield utilize, in effect, this postulate!)

3. *Postulate of independence of tastes and beliefs*. If the subject's choice among actions reveals that, in his view, one event is more probable than another, then, in the absence of new information, his subsequent choices must be consistent with this view, regardless of the outcomes. One should neither think wishfully nor be subject to persecution mania!

The experiments that follow below tend to confirm that the basic postulates are actually obeyed when and only when stress is absent (e.g., memory is not overloaded, ample time is provided, etc.) and, above all, when and only when the structure of the problem is very simple and is laid bare, by the use of lucid syntax, tabular presentation, etc.

Thus, Roger Crane, a member of a nationally known accounting firm, reports the use of 'Payoff Tables' in his attempt to make the discussions at Corporation Board meetings more orderly and fruitful, and even to apply the expected utility principle. Uncontrolled events (e.g. the future possible states of the market) head the columns of the table; the available actions (whether to merge with firm *A*, *B*, *C*, or not at all) head the rows of the table; and the outcome of a given action and a given event is entered in the appropriate cell of the table.

Under stress, or if the problem is complex, or has not been prestructured ('predigested') for the subject' use, the 'rational' hypothesis seems to be rarely satisfied; it is not good descriptive psychology. Other hypotheses present themselves.

B. *Hypothesis 2. Learning Theory*

As trials are repeated, the subject approaches asymptotically a stable behavior (which is, in general, not the rational one). In particular, his decision may depend on the success or failure (possibly measured from some 'aspiration level') of his previous decision; and the degree of this dependence – the 'reinforcement parameter' – determines the speed of learning characterizing a given subject (Bush and Mosteller, 1955; Estes, 1950).

C. *Hypothesis 3. Stochastic Decision Theory*

The subject's choices are described by probability distributions which can be construed as weak (i.e., generalized) forms of rational behavior (Becker *et al.*, 1963; Block and Marschak, 1960; Luce, 1959; Marschak, 1960; and Restle, 1961). For example, a very weak postulate of stochastic behavior is this: "If the subject is more likely to prefer, than not to prefer, *A* to *B*; and is more likely to prefer, than not to prefer, *B* to *C*; then he is more likely to prefer, than not to prefer, *A* to *C*." On the other hand, a very strong postulate of stochastic behavior ('Luce's Axiom') is this: "If, when presented with the triple (*A*, *B*, *C*) the subject chooses *A* or *B* or *C* with relative frequencies in proportion $p_A : p_B : p_C$; then, if presented with the pair (*A*, *B*), he will choose *A* or *B* with relative frequencies in proportion $p_A : p_B$." This leads to a new definition of utilities (viz., numbers proportionate to $p_A, p_B, p_C \ldots$).[1] A stochastic behavior postulate of intermediate strength has been used by the late L. L. Thurstone and his followers who, in essence, equate utility with 'subjective sensation', taken from Fechner's psychophysics (1859). Still another postulate (also weaker than Luce's Axiom) assumes that the subject's ranking of all considered alternative actions varies according to some probability scheme.

D. *Hypothesis 4*

This is a combination of Hypotheses 2 and 3 (Estes, 1960; Luce, 1959; Suppes and Atkinson, 1960, Ch. 11).

E. *Hypothesis 5. Application of Gestalt Theory*

The subject has *sudden insight* into the rational structure of a decision problem ('Aha!').

F. *Hypothesis 5. Effect of Training*

The subject's insight can be brought about or accelerated by appropriate training strategies.

III. EXPERIMENTS

A. *Experiments 1. Consistent Ranking of Actions*

Experiment 1a. Complex objects such as 'a patent', 'a labor contract', 'plant', etc., each described in detail, each fraught with uncertainties, and none having a market price, are presented in pairs, without cost to chooser (or with cost counted in), in the following order:

$$\begin{aligned}&\text{the } (A, B)\text{-pairs: } (A_1, B_1); (A_2, B_2); \ldots; (A_m, B_m);\\&\text{the } (B, C)\text{-pairs: } (B_1, C_1); (B_2, C_2); \ldots; (B_m, C_m);\\&\text{the } (C, A)\text{-pairs: } (C_1, A_1); (C_2, A_2); \ldots; (C_m, A_m).\end{aligned}$$

The subject is not consistent if he prefers A_i to B_i, and B_i to C_i, yet also prefers C_i to A_i, for some i.

Experiment 1b. If for a given number (m) of trials (A_i, B_i, C_i), the subject has behaved consistently in Experiment 1a, he is now made to choose from a set such as (A_1 B_1, C_2). He is not consistent if he prefers A_1 when presented with the pair (A_1, B_1), yet prefers B_1 when presented with the triplet (A_1, B_1, C_2). We invariably laugh at the story of the man who chose steak from a menu containing steak and fish; but changed his choice to fish when told that chicken was also available! (The story is Luce's; its principle was first stated by Arrow.)

Experiment 1c. Finally, the subject is asked to rank all $3m$ alternatives. The ranking is tested against his preferences as exhibited in Experiment 1a.

Preliminary evidence. Experiments on my own students suggest that they satisfied the Postulate of Consistent Preference if, in Experiment 1a, m, the number of triads used, was small; e.g., $m=5$. Inconsistencics arose more often in Experiments 1b and 1c. However, the objects considered were those appropriate for the experience of (married) graduate students, rather than businessmen: jobs, trips, apartments, house furnishings, investment information, medical care, etc.

In other experiments, on students of logic and mathematics at Stanford University, the weak stochastic hypothesis mentioned above under Hypothesis 3 was satisfied by almost all subjects; but not the Fechnerian hypothesis. The objects considered were small monetary wagers (see Davidson and Marschak, 1959).

B. *Experiments 2. Admissibility Principle*

Experiment 2a. "You may get a job in a foreign country or an equally good one at home. If a revolution in a foreign country occurs you lose the job; but it can't happen here. Your choice?"

Experiment 2b. "Write down, but don't tell me, the *cash value* (v) of your property to you: that is, the smallest acceptable price. Then name your asking price (a); after this, I (your broker) shall draw at random a number (b) as the buying price. If b exceeds a you'll get b. Otherwise you will keep your property. Now name your asking price."

Experiments performed in my class on my students, and by them on their friends or wives, tend to suggest the following evidence:

In Experiment 2a the foreign job is rejected, in accordance with the admissibility principle. But in Experiment 2*b* the admissibility principle is applied only if the experimenter "untwists" the problem by presenting and explaining a formula, a table, or a diagram, for example: Suppose the value of the property to you is $v=25$. It is arranged that if $b>a$ you receive b; if $b \leqq a$, you keep v. Hence the payoff will depend on a (which you control) and b (which you don't control) in the following way:

	b: 10	20	30	40
a:	Outcomes, when $v=25$			
15	25	20	30	40
25	25	25	30	40
35	25	25	25	40

Clearly the only admissible action is to name an asking price a equal to 25, i.e., to the value of the property to you (v). If you ask more or less than 25, you lose (compared with the admissible action) whenever b happens to fall between a and v, and you fare equally well otherwise. Honesty is (in this case at least) the best policy! Instead, most subjects named an asking price in excess of the value of the property to them. Perhaps they assumed, albeit unconsciously, that some bargaining will ensue, although this was explicitly excluded under the conditions given in the experiment.

(Later the experiment was modified to free it from associations with the real estate market. Here v equaled the money amount entered on a check or I.O.U. signed by the experimenter and picked up by the subject at random from an urn filled with such checks, each with a different value. In this modified situation the admissibility postulate was transgressed less frequently.)

C. *Experiment 3. Independence of Tastes and Beliefs*

Consider the following events, not controlled by you:

X: Democrats win in 1964
$\bar{X}$: they do not win
Y: next card drawn is a spade
$\bar{Y}$: it is not.

We consider now 6 actions (bets) A, B, C, A', B', C', and tabulate their outcomes (gains and losses) which depend on the events, as follows:

Events: Actions:	X	$\bar{X}$		$\bar{X}$	X		Y	$\bar{Y}$
A:	\$100	\$ 0	B:	\$100	\$ 0	C:	\$100	\$ 0
A':	\$ 50	\$ −50	B':	\$ 50	\$ −50	C':	\$ 50	\$ −50

If you prefer A to B (i.e. bet on the Democratic candidate rather than on his rival); and B to C (i.e. bet on the non-Democratic candidate rather than on spades); then we usually say that you think X is more probable than $\bar{X}$, and that $\bar{X}$ is more probable than Y. This is the common English use of the subjective probability concept. The experiment consists in finding whether a subject retains this ranking of the three probabilities also when the stakes are changed: on bets A', B', C', instead of gaining \$100 or nothing, he now will gain or lose \$50. If his beliefs and tastes are independent, this change of outcomes should not affect his ranking of events according to their probabilities: X should, as before, appear to him more probable than $\bar{X}$, and $\bar{X}$ more probable than Y, and this should be reflected in his choice of action. Hence he should prefer A' to B', and B' to C'.

When the conditions are presented in tabulated form as above, few subjects show inconsistency. But would they remain consistent if the job of structuring had been left to them?

Experiment 3 verifies, or refutes, the independence of tastes and beliefs. We have seen that if such independence prevails, a probability ranking of events will express the subject's beliefs. Moreover, if Postulates 1, 2, and 3 are verified, and, in addition, the subject follows rules of logic, then it can be shown that his beliefs can be expressed by assigning to the events not only probability ranks, but actual numbers which we can call (subjective) probabilities because they have the same mathematical properties as those established in the classical theory of probabilities. In particular, if two events X and Y are mutually exclusive the subjective probability assigned to the event 'X or Y' is the sum of the probability of X and of that of Y (the 'additivity law'). The logical grounds for the existence of such numerical subjective probabilities can be roughly illustrated in the context of the following experiments.

D. *Experiment 4. Numerical Subjective Probabilities*

Denote by '*D.J.*' the 'Dow-Jones stock price average at this year's end', and by x some positive number. Consider two actions (bets) A and B such that:

> if you choose A you will get \$100 if *D.J.* exceeds x, and you will get \$0 otherwise;
> if you choose B you will get \$0 if *D.J.* exceeds x, and you will get \$100 otherwise.

By definition, if your beliefs and tastes are independent, your preference ranking as between the two actions will remain the same if the pair of outcomes (\$100, \$0) is replaced by some other pair (O_1, O_2) such that O_1 is better than O_2. Your choice as between A and B will indicate whether you consider the event '*D.J.* exceeds x' more or less probable than its negation. Therefore, if we adopt the useful convention that the probabilities of an event and of its negation add up to 1, we shall say that the subjective probability of the event '*D.J.* exceeds x' is larger than $\frac{1}{2}$ if you prefer A to B; smaller than $\frac{1}{2}$ if you prefer B to A; and equal to $\frac{1}{2}$ if you are indifferent between A and B. Hence, by adjusting the variable x upward and downward we can find a value of x such that your subjective probability of the event '*D.J.* exceeds x' is equal to $\frac{1}{2}$.

We can find in a similar way two numbers y_1 and y_2 such that you will be *indifferent* between three following bets C, D, E:

> If you choose C you will get \$100 if *D.J.* is less than y_1, and \$0 otherwise;
> if you choose D you will get \$100 if *D.J.* is y_1 or more, but less than y_2, and \$0 otherwise;
> if you choose E you will get \$100 if *D.J.* is y_2 or more, and \$0 otherwise.

Or, in tabular form:

	I	II	III
	0	y_1	y_2
C	$100	$ 0	$ 0
D	$ 0	$100	$ 0
E	$ 0	$ 0	$100

Your indifference between *C*, *D*, *E* will indicate that you deem the three mutually exclusive events (the three intervals I, II, III on the *D.J.* scale) to be equally probable. In other words, their subjective probabilities are $\frac{1}{3}, \frac{1}{3}, \frac{1}{3}$ – *provided* your (the subject's) tastes and beliefs are independent. This can be tested by finding whether you are also indifferent between the following three bets (with the same meaning of y_1, y_2):

	I	II	III
	0	y_1	y_2
C'	$100	$ 0	$100
D'	$ 0	$100	$100
E'	$100	$100	$ 0

(your indifference between *C* and *D* revealed that, for you, events I and II are equally probable; this belief should not be changed if the outcome of either action in case of event III is changed from $0 to $100; hence you should be indifferent between *C'* and *D'*; and similarly between *D'* and *E'*) On the other hand, any of the actions *C'* *D'*, *E'* is better than any of the actions *C*, *D*, *E*, by the admissibility principle. Accordingly, having assigned probabilities $\frac{1}{3}$ to each of the events I, II, III, we may assign probabilities $\frac{2}{3}$ to the events 'I or II', 'II or III', 'I or III', thus at the same time satisfying the additivity law for probabilities. And if we call $100, $0, 'success' and 'failure' respectively we see that you prefer that action which has a higher subjective probability of success. Again, this agrees with usual English.

Using three mutually exclusive and exhaustive events, we have defined subjective probabilities $\frac{1}{3}$ and $\frac{2}{3}$ as revealed by a consistent subject's preferences between actions. This reasoning can be extended to any number – 4, 5,..., *n* of events, and leads to the definition of any subjective probability expressed by a rational fraction m/n; and, in fact, as expressed by any number (whether rational or irrational) between 0 and 1. If each of two actions A_1 and A_2 can yield either 'success' or 'failure', and if A_1 is preferred (or indifferent) to A_2, then the probability of success, p_1, of A_1 is larger than (or equal to) the probability of success, p_2, of A_2, as viewed by the subject.

Let us agree to assign utility $=0$ to failure (and to an action that always leads to failure). Then the utility of success (and of an action that always leads to success) must be larger; let it be $=1$. By the admissibility principle, any action that yields possibly success, and possibly failure, is better than sure failure and worse than sure success. Therefore its utility must be assigned a number between 0 and 1. In particular, to a lottery (action, bet, venture) A_i that succeeds with probability p_i, we may assign the utility p_i: this will agree with our previous statement that A_i is preferred to (hence is utility is larger than that of) A_2 if $p_1 > p_2$. Now note that *such an assignment of utilities agrees with the expected utility principle*; for indeed

$$p_i \cdot 1 + (1 - p_i) \cdot 0 = p_i .$$

Consider now a "mixed" lottery. It yields a ticket of A_1 with subjective probability π_1, a ticket of A_2 with subjective probability π_2, etc. Since the ordinary probability laws are obeyed, such a mixed lottery will yield success with subjective probability $p_1\pi_2 + p_2\pi_2 + \cdots$. And since we have agreed to equate a lottery's utility with its chance of success we see that the utility of the mixed lottery is the weighted average of the utilities of the component lotteries that are its outcomes. Again, *this agrees with the expected utility principle.*

As a further step, extend this reasoning to *any* outcomes that are not better than the 'success' and not worse than the 'failure' defined so far. The consistent man will be indifferent between such an outcome and some lottery which has probability p_i (say) of success; hence this outcome's utility can be set equal to p_i. And an action which yields, with respective probabilities $\pi_1, \pi_2, \ldots$, objects whose utilities are $p_1, p_2, \ldots$, will be equivalent, in that man's view, to the mixed lottery whose utility we have seen to be $p_1\pi_1 + p_2\pi_2 + \cdots$. *This agrees again with the expected utility principle.*

A complete and rigorous proof that the expected utility principle follows from the three basic postulates by ordinary rules of logic is more lengthy and cannot be given here. Indeed this logical process, though elementary, does not seem to correspond to the behavior of an untrained, unprepared, or inexperienced 'average' man of our culture. This is illustrated by the following experiment.

E. *Experiment 5. Existence of a Utility Function*

Consider the following four lottery tickets:

Lottery ticket	If Heads, you get:	If Tails, you get:	Cash equivalent?
A	$100	$0	$*a*
B	$100	*A*	$*b*
C	$0	*A*	$*c*
D	*B*	*C*	$*d*

We either assume that the subjective probabilities of Heads and Tails are equal (i.e., that the subject is indifferent between betting something on Heads or betting the same thing on Tails) or we test this assumption by actual trials. (This was done by Davidson and Suppes [1957] who painted one nonsense syllable on three sides of a die and another nonsense syllable on the three remaining sides, and tested whether the subject who chose to bet on the first nonsense syllable changed the choice when the rewards on that bet were lowered very slightly.) Under Hypothesis 1, the hypothesis of consistent behavior, the subject assigning a winning chance $\frac{1}{2}$ to A should also assign:

a winning chance $(\frac{1}{2})\cdot(1) + (\frac{1}{2})\cdot(\frac{1}{2}) = \frac{3}{4}$ to B;
a winning chance $(\frac{1}{2})\cdot(0) + (\frac{1}{2})\cdot(\frac{1}{2}) = \frac{1}{4}$ to C; and therefore
a winning chance $(\frac{1}{2})\cdot(\frac{3}{4}) + (\frac{1}{2})(\frac{1}{4}) = \frac{1}{2}$ to D. Consequently he should declare $b > d = a > c$.

Moreover, if he is consistent and 'averts risk' – so that, for him, money has 'decreasing marginal utility' – he would name $a<50$, $b<(100+a)/2$, $c<a/2$. The three cash amounts a, b, c permit us to estimate three non trivial points on the curve representing his utility function of money gains and monetary wagers $u(g)$, *provided his consistency has been confirmed* by his naming $d=a$. For we are free to fix two points arbitrarily (as when 'calibrating' a thermometer scale): say, $u(\$100)=1$, $u(\$0)=0$. Then, $u(a)=u(A)=(1+0)/2=.5$; $u(b)=u(B)=(1+.5)/2=.75$; $u(c)=u(C)=$ $=(0+.5)/2=.25$.

In experiments with students they usually failed to name $d=a$, unless they stated values $a=d=50$, $b=75$, $c=25$. In this case we suspect that they have parrot-like followed the rule (which they have heard somewhere) of computing actuarial values, and did not name their genuine subjective cash equivalent. To check this, and educate them for later experiments, we have asked them whether they are really indifferent between 'gain \$100, lose \$100 on the toss of a coin' and 'gain a dime, lose a dime on the toss of a coin', thus dispelling the learned myth of actuarial values.

Experiment 5 can be generalized to the case when the subjective odds are not necessarily 1:1, and indeed are unknown to the experimeter (Becker *et al.*, 1963; the point was also made by Jacques Drèze). Instead of 'Heads–Tails', we may use the events: 'The next student to speak to me in this classroom will be less (not less) than 25 years old' (if the experiment is performed in a graduate classroom). Note that the choices (B) and (C) may imply a second, and choice (D) even a third trial. Now, a consistent man will behave as if he assigned to the alternative events some probabilities, p and q, say, with $p+q=1$. Moreover, if as before (without loss of generality) the utility scale is calibrated so that $u(\$100)=1$, $u(\$0)=0$, then a consistent man will behave as if he assigned to the four lottery tickets of the experiment the following utilities:

$$\begin{aligned} u(A) &= p\cdot u(\$100) + q\cdot u(\$0) = p \\ u(B) &= p\cdot u(\$100) + q\cdot u(A) = p + qp \\ u(C) &= p\cdot u(\$0) + qu(A) = 0 + qp \\ u(D) &= p(p + qp) + q(qp) = p, \end{aligned}$$

since $p+q=1$. And since $p\geqslant 0$, $q\geqslant 0$, we obtain the following ranking of utilities: $u(B)\geqslant u(A)=u(D)\geqslant u(C)$; accordingly the consistent man should name cash-equivalents of the four lotteries, ordered thus: $b\geqslant a=d\geqslant c$. If neither event is judged impossible by the consistent man, i.e., if $p>0$, $q>0$, the ranking is exactly the same as before, viz. $b>a=d>c$.

Gordon Becker collected evidence that in some cases the subject's cash-equivalents do gradually approach a consistent pattern as the experiment is continued (a lottery E is formed: D if Heads, \$100 if Tails; etc.). It is not clear whether such subjects 'learn' in the sense of Hypothesis 2 or have a sudden insight ('Aha!)') as in Hypothesis 5. To decide this, appropriate significance tests need to be developed.

NOTES

* Based on studies carried out at the Western Management Science Institute, University of California at Los Angeles, partially supported by the Office of Naval Research, Task 047-041 and by the Ford Foundation.

1 Think of the opinion-polled housewife in the *New Yorker* cartoon (November 14, 1959): "I'd say I'm about 42 percent for Nixon, 39 per cent for Rockefeller, 19 per cent undecided!"

BIBLIOGRAPHY

Becker, G. M., DeGroot, M. H., and Marschak, J., 'Stochastic Models of Choice Behavior', *Selected Essays*, 10.

Becker, G. M., DeGroot, M. H., and Marschak, J., 'Measuring Utility by a Single-response Sequential Choice', *Selected Essays*, 15.

Block, H. D. and Marschak, J., 'Random Orderings and Stochastic Theories of Response', *Selected Essays*, 7.

Bush, R. R. and Mosteller, C. F., *Stochastic Models for Learning*, Wiley, New York, 1955.

Crane, R. R. and Wanthal, A. E., 'An Approach to the Problem of Growth by Company Acquisition', Paper read at the Orientation Seminar Appraising Corporation Mergers and Acquisitions, American Management Association (Mimeo).

Davidson, D. and Marschak, J., 'Experimental Tests of a Stochastic Decision Theory', *Selected Essays*, 6.

Davidson, D. and Suppes, P., *Decision Making: an Experimental Approach*, Stanford Univ. Press, Stanford, Calif., 1957.

Estes, W. K., 'Toward a Statistical Theory of Learning', *Psychol. Rev.* **57** (1950) 94–107

Estes, W. K., 'A Random Walk Model for Choice Behavior' in K. Arrow *et al.* (eds.), *Mathematical Methods in the Social Sciences*, Stanford Univ. Press Stanford, Calif., 1960.

Fechner, G. T., *Elemente der Psychophysik*. Breitkopf & Haertel, Leipzig, 1859.

Luce, R. D., *Individual Choice Behavior*, Wiley, New York, 1959.

Marschak, J., Binary Choice Constraints on Random Utility Indicators', *Selected Essays*, 8.

Marschak, J. and Radner, R., *Economic Theory of Teams*, Ch. I, Working Paper No. 67, Center for Research in Management Science, Univ. of California, Berkeley, 1963 (Mimeo). *Added in 1974*: Now in book form, Yale University Press, 1972.

Restle, F., *Psychology of Judgment and Choice: a Theoretical Essay*, Wiley, New York, 1961.

Savage, L. J., *Foundations of Statistics*, Wiley, New York, 1954.

Suppes, P. and Atkinson, R. C., *Markov Learning Models for Multiperson Interactions*, Stanford Univ. Press, Stanford, Calif., 1960.

10

STOCHASTIC MODELS OF CHOICE BEHAVIOR*

(1963)

Co-authors: G. M. Becker and M. H. DeGroot

I. INTRODUCTION

Let S denote a finite set of n objects, or rewards, which can be thought of as being numbered serially, 1, 2,..., n. An *offered set* is a nonempty subset of S. We will be concerned with experiments in which a subject chooses a reward from each of several offered sets. The word 'rewards' is used here to describe the objects in S in order to convey the notion that the subject will choose the reward that he prefers from any offered set. Thus, if the subject knows he will receive the reward that he chooses, presumably he will choose the reward that he would most like to possess.

From these considerations it would seem plausible to postulate the existence of an ordering (by preference) of the n objects in S such that from any offered set the subject will choose that object which ranks highest in the ordering. The existence of an ordering of this type implies that the subject's choices from various offered sets will be consistent in a very strong sense. For example, if a subject chooses object x from the offered set $\{x, y\}$ containing the two objects x and y, and if he chooses y from $\{y, z\}$, then he must choose x from $\{x, z\}$. Furthermore, if he is presented with the offered set $\{x, y\}$ at two different times under similar conditions, then his choice should be the same at both times.

It is not difficult to envisage situations in which the subject's choices would be consistent in the sense just described. If, for example, the objects in S were different amounts of money, presumably the subject would always choose the largest amount present in any offered set. On the other hand, simple experiments reveal that if S comprises different commodity bundles, or different lottery tickets whereby the subject receives a random amount of money according to some probability distribution, or indeed any objects for which there is no 'natural' simple ordering, then the subject's choices will very often not be consistent.[1] In order to account for these inconsistencies it is convenient to introduce what is called a stochastic model.

A *stochastic model* is a specification, for each offered set M and each object $x \in M$, of the probability that the subject will choose x from M. This probability is denoted by $x(M)$. Clearly, under any stochastic model it must be true that $0 \leqslant x(M) \leqslant 1$ and $\sum_{x \in M} x(M) = 1$ for all x and all M.

II. RANDOM UTILITY MODELS

A large class of stochastic models, called the random utility models, can be derived from the following considerations.

Each object $x \in S$, no matter how simple it might appear, has many attributes. For each $x \in S$, let Ω_x denote the set of all attributes of x. To simplify the following discussion it is assumed that each set Ω_x is finite. When making a choice from among the objects in S a subject does not necessarily consider all of the attributes of all of the objects. Rather, he may consider for each $x \in S$ some subset A_x of its attributes that happens to come to mind and seems to be particularly relevant at the time that he must make a choice. Thus, for each object, we can think of the subset of attributes that the subject considers at a given time as being randomly chosen according to some probabilistic law. Let $Pr\{A_x; x \in S\}$ denote the probability that the subject considers the subset A_x, $x \in S$. Finally, for each $x \in S$, there is a number $U_x(A_x)$ associated with each subset A_x of attributes. This number can be thought of as the utility of x with respect to the given subset A_x. The subject, when choosing from S, considers a subset A_x of attributes for each $x \in S$ that is determined by the probability distribution $Pr\{A_x; x \in S\}$ and chooses that object x from S for which $U_x(A_x)$ is largest.

When choosing from an offered set M, other than S, the subject chooses that object $x \in M$ for which $U_x(A_x)$ is largest among all objects in M. In making this statement we are, in effect, assuming that the subsets of attributes that the subject considers are always determined by the probability distribution $Pr\{A_x; x \in S\}$ regardless of the offered set from which the subject is choosing. A more elaborate theory in which the probability distribution of subsets of attributes depends on the offered set could be given, but it does not seem worthwhile to do so at this stage of development. Since the subsets of attributes that the subject considers are randomly chosen, it follows that the utilities U_x, $x \in S$, constitute a random vector. Furthermore, if the subject considers a certain subset of attributes of one of the objects in S, then it is likely that he will consider subsets of similar attributes of the other objects. In other words, it is not necessarily true that $Pr\{A_x; x \in M\}$ and $\prod_{x \in M} Pr\{A_x\}$ are always equal. Thus, the random utilities U_x, $x \in S$, need not be independent random variables.

To clarify these notions consider the following simple example (see also Quandt, 1956). A person is trying to decide which of three suits of clothes, x, y, and z, to wear on a certain occasion. When making this decision he might: (1) consider the style of a suit of primary importance and the material secondary; (2) consider the material of primary importance and the style secondary; or (3) consider style and material of equal importance. Let us say that the occurrence of (1) means that the person considers the subsets A_x, A_y, and A_z of attributes of x, y, and z; the occurrence of (2) means that he considers the subsets B_x, B_y, and B_z; and the occurrence of (3) means that he considers C_x, C_y, and C_z.

Suppose that $Pr\{A_x, A_y, A_z\} = \frac{3}{8}$, $Pr\{B_x, B_y, B_z\} = \frac{1}{8}$, and $Pr\{C_x, C_y, C_z\} = \frac{4}{8}$. These are the probabilities of occurrence of (1), (2), and (3).

Suppose also that $U_x(A_x) > U_y(A_y) > U_z(A_z)$, $U_z(B_z) > U_y(B_y) > U_x(B_x)$, and $U_y(C_y) > U_x(C_x) > U_z(C_z)$. Then, x is preferred when (1) occurs; z is preferred when (2) occurs; and y is preferred when (3) occurs.

It follows that when the subject chooses from the set S containing all three suits, the probabilities of choice are $x(S) = \frac{3}{8}$, $y(S) = \frac{4}{8}$, and $z(S) = \frac{1}{8}$. If suit z is being cleaned at the time of decision so that the choice is restricted to the set M containing only x and y, then $x(M) = \frac{3}{8}$ and $y(M) = \frac{5}{8}$.

The following formal definition was given by Block and Marschak (1960). (The term 'random utility indicator' is used in Marschak [1960].) A stochastic model is said to be a *random utility model* if there exists a random vector $(U_1, \ldots, U_n)$ such that, for all offered sets M and all $x \in M$,

$$(1) \qquad x(M) = Pr\{U_x \geqslant U_y \quad \text{for all} \quad y \in M\}.$$

It is an easy consequence of this definition and is proved in Block and Marschak (1960) that under any random utility model

$$(2) \qquad Pr\{U_x = U_y\} = 0 \quad \text{for all} \quad x \neq y.$$

In effect, this means that every time the subject makes a choice from an offered set it is possible for him to strictly order the objects by their utilities, although this ordering is random and may change for the next choice the subject makes. The possibility that two objects have equal utility could be admitted at the expense of a more complicated definition instead of Equation (1). This will not be done here.

III. LUCE OR STRICT UTILITY MODELS

We now define a special class of stochastic models originally introduced by Luce (1959). A stochastic model will be called a *Luce or strict utility model*[2] if there exist positive constants $u_1, \ldots, u_n$ such that

$$x(M) = \frac{u_x}{\sum_{y \in M} u_y}, \tag{3}$$

for all offered sets M and all $x \in M$. It is easily seen that this is equivalent to the requirement that $x(S) > 0$ for all $x \in S$ and

$$x(M) = \frac{x(S)}{\sum_{y \in M} y(S)}, \tag{4}$$

for all M and all $x \in M$. The following theorem is stated and proved in Block and Marschak (1960).

THEOREM I. Every Luce model is a random utility model.

The meaning of this theorem is that if the probabilities $x(M)$ are given by Equation (3) for some set of positive numbers $u_1, \ldots, u_n$, then there exists a random vector $(U_1, \ldots, U_n)$ with an appropriate multivariate distribution such that the probabilities $x(M)$ are also given by Equation (1). Thus, the Luce models form a subclass of the random utility models.

We will now give two characterizations of this subclass, but before doing so it is convenient to introduce some notation. For a given random utility model and any two offered sets $L \subset M$, let $E(L, M)$ denote the event that there exists an object $x \in L$ such that $U_x \geqslant U_y$ for all $y \in M$. Thus, $E(L, M)$ is the event that the object with largest utility among all the objects in M belongs to the subset L. When $x \in M$, and L contains only the object x, we write $E(x, M)$ instead of $E(L, M)$. If $x \in L \subset M$ then $E(x, M) \subset E(L, M)$, $E(x, M) \subset E(x, L)$ and $Pr\{E(L, M\} = \sum_{y \in L} y(M)$.

THEOREM II. A random utility model is a Luce model if and only if $x(S) > 0$ for all $x \in S$ and

$$(5) \qquad x(M) = Pr\{E(x, S) \mid E(M, S)\}$$

for all M and all $x \in M$.

Proof. If $x(S) > 0$ for all $x \in S$ then

$$(6) \qquad Pr\{E(x, S) \mid E(M, S)\} = \frac{Pr\{E(x, S) \cap E(M, S)\}}{Pr\{E(M, S)\}} = \\ = \frac{Pr\{E(x, S)\}}{Pr\{E(M, S)\}} = \frac{x(S)}{\sum_{y \in M} y(S)}.$$

Hence, if $x(S) > 0$ for all $x \in S$ and Equation (5) holds, then

$$(7) \qquad x(M) = x(S) / \sum_{y \in M} y(S),$$

and these are the defining properties of a Luce model.

Conversely, if the random utility model is a Luce model, then by definition, $x(S) > 0$ for all $x \in S$ and Equation (7) holds. Consequently, so do Equations (6) and (5).

THEOREM III. A random utility model is a Luce model if and only if $x(S) > 0$ for all $x \in S$ and, for every offered set M,

$$(8) \qquad Pr\{E(x, S) \mid E(x, M)\} = k_M, \quad \text{a constant, for all} \quad x \in M.$$

Proof. If $x(S) > 0$ for all $x \in S$ then

$$(9) \qquad x(S) = Pr\{E(x, S)\} = Pr\{E(x, S) \cap E(x, M)\} \\ = P\{E(x, S) \mid E(x, M)\} \, Pr\{E(x, M)\} \\ = P\{E(x, S) \mid E(x, M)\} \, x(M),$$

for all M and all $x \in M$.

Hence, if $x(S) > 0$ for all $x \in S$ and Equation (8) holds, then

$$(10) \qquad x(S) = k_M x(M)$$

and

$$(11) \qquad \sum_{x \in M} x(S) = k_M \sum_{x \in M} x(M) = k_M.$$

Thus

$$(12)\qquad x(M)=\frac{x(S)}{k_M}=\frac{x(S)}{\sum_{y\in M} y(S)}$$

and the model is a Luce model.

Conversely, if the random utility model is a Luce model, then by definition, $x(S)>0$ for all $x\in S$ and Equation (7) holds. Hence, from Equation (9),

$$(13)\qquad Pr\{E(x,S)\mid E(x,M)\}=\frac{x(S)}{x(M)}=\sum_{y\in M} y(S),$$

which is constant for all $x\in M$. This concludes the proof.

IV. FECHNER OR STRONG UTILITY MODELS

In many experiments each of the offered sets from which a subject must choose contains exactly two of the objects in S. An experiment of this type is called a *binary experiment* and an offered set containing exactly two objects is called a *binary offered set*. Binary experiments have been discussed in detail by Marschak (1960). In such experiments the specification of the probabilities $x(M)$ for offered sets M containing more than two objects is irrelevant, since no pertinent experimental data can be obtained. A specification of the probabilities $x(M)$ for all binary offered sets M is called a *binary model.*

Clearly every stochastic model can be thought of as a binary stochastic model simply by considering only those probabilities $x(M)$ that refer to binary M. Thus, all random utility models and, in particular, all Luce models are binary stochastic models when the defining Equations (1) and (3) are restricted to binary M. These restricted models will be called *binary random utility models* and *binary Luce models.* A binary model is called a *strong utility or Fechner model* if there exist constants $v_1,\ldots,v_n$ and a nondecreasing real-valued function $\Phi(r)$ defined for all real numbers r, such that for every binary offered set $M=\{x,y\}$,

$$(14)\qquad x(M)=\Phi(v_x-v_y).$$

Since (14) restricts the values of $\Phi(r)$ at only a finite number of values of

r and since $x(M)+y(M)=1$, it is easily seen that $\Phi(r)$ can be chosen to be a continuous, non-decreasing function such that

$$(15)\qquad \lim_{r\to-\infty} \Phi(r)=0, \qquad \lim_{r\to\infty} \Phi(r)=1, \quad \text{and} \quad \Phi(r)+\Phi(-r)= \\ =1 \quad \text{for all} \quad r.$$

The following derivation of the Fechner models, in the same spirit as the derivation given for the random utility models, is sometimes helpful. The function $\Phi(r)$ can be thought of as the distribution function of a continuous random variable ε, with a symmetric distribution around the value 0. For each object $x\in S$, the number v_x represents, in some appropriate sense, the utility, or value, of x to the subject. Thus, when presented with a choice from $\{x, y\}$, the subject would ideally want to choose x if $v_x-v_y>0$ and y if $v_x-v_y<0$. However, because of some inherent limitations in the choice-making process (e.g., not being able to consider all attributes of both x and y) the subject cannot calculate v_x-v_y exactly, but rather can calculate only $v_x-v_y+\varepsilon$, where ε is the random variable just defined. He then chooses x if $v_x-v_y+\varepsilon>0$ and y otherwise. This leads to Equation (14).

We now mention some relations between the Fechner, binary Luce, and binary random utility models.

THEOREM IV. Every binary Luce model is a binary random utility model, but not conversely.

THEOREM V. Every binary Luce model is a Fechner model, but not conversely.

Calling a Luce model strict and a Fechner model strong is justified by Theorem V, the word ‘strict’ conveying the greater restriction. Correspondingly, the constants $u_1,\ldots, u_n$ are called strict utilities, and the constants $v_1,\ldots, v_n$ are called strong utilities, both distinct from the random utilities $U_1,\ldots, U_n$ which are random variables, not constants.

Proofs are given in Block and Marschak (1960). (Indeed, Theorem V is proved by choosing $\Phi(r)$ as in Equation (17) below.) It is also shown there that not every binary random utility model is a Fechner model, but it is not known whether every Fechner model is a binary random utility model. However, the following theorem shows that at least a large class of Fechner models are also binary random utility models.

THEOREM VI. Every Fechner model such that $\Phi(r)$ is the distribution function of the difference of two independent and identically distributed random variables is a binary random utility model.

Proof. Define the random vector $(U_1,..., U_n)$ by

$$U_i = v_i + \varepsilon_i, i = 1,..., n$$

where $\varepsilon_1,..., \varepsilon_n$ are independent and identically distributed random variables such that $\Phi(r)$ is the distribution function of $\varepsilon_i - \varepsilon_j$ for all $i \neq j$, and $v_1,..., v_n$ are the constants appearing in the Fechner model. Then, for any $M = \{x, y\}$,

$$\begin{aligned} (16) \qquad x(M) &= Pr\{U_x \geqslant U_y\} = Pr\{v_x + \varepsilon_x \geqslant v_y + \varepsilon_y\} = \\ &= Pr\{\varepsilon_y - \varepsilon_x \leqslant v_x - v_y\} = \Phi(v_x - v_y). \end{aligned}$$

It follows from this theorem that, for example, any Fechner model in which $\Phi(r)$ is a normal distribution function is also a binary random utility model.

V. STATISTICAL ANALYSIS OF EXPERIMENTAL DATA

Consider an experiment in which a subject makes choices from several offered sets. It is assumed throughout this paper that the subject's choices in such an experiment are independent. That is, it is assumed that for any finite collection $M_1,..., M_k$ of the offered sets presented in the experiment, the probability that the subject will choose object x_i from M_i, $i = 1,..., k$, is $\prod_{i=1}^{k} x_i(M_i)$. This assumption excludes the possibility that the subject undergoes some learning process in the course of the experiment whereby his choice from an offered set depends on the previously offered sets from which he has already chosen and on his choices from those offered sets. The reason for making the assumption of independence of choices is that it yields an explicit, simple probabilistic model for a wide variety of situations. However, in order that the assumption be satisfied in an experiment, it is very often essential that the subject does not make a choice from any particular offered set more than a few times. Indeed, if some offered set is to be presented to the subject more than once during the experiment it is important that sufficient precautions are taken to insure that when the subject is presented with the offered set for the second time he has forgotten his earlier choice.

In general, the purpose of performing an experiment and observing the subject's choices is to gain information about the probabilities $x(M)$, which are typically not completely known to the experimenter (or to the subject). The questions about the probabilities $x(M)$ that the experimenter wants to answer can very often be classified either as questions of testing some hypotheses about the stochastic model or as questions of estimating some parameters appearing in the stochastic model. To the authors' knowledge, the only relevant statistical methods that have thus far appeared in the literature are concerned with Fechner models for binary experiments.

Consider a Fechner model in which the function $\Phi(r)$ is the logistic function

$$\Phi(r) = \frac{1}{1 + e^{-r}}. \tag{17}$$

(Fechner models in which $\Phi(r)$ is of the form of Equation (17) are also binary Luce models. We will return to this relationship below.) Berkson (1955, 1957) has used this function in problems of bioassay. His approach can be slightly generalized as follows. Suppose that on each of a sequence of trials one observes either a success or a failure. Suppose that the probability p of observing a success on a given trial is

$$p = \frac{1}{1 + Exp\left\{-\sum_{i=1}^{n} c_i v_i\right\}}, \tag{18}$$

where $v_1, \ldots, v_n$ are unknown parameters and $c_1, \ldots, c_n$ are known constants whose values are fixed by the experimenter on each trial. The problem is to estimate the parameters $v_1, \ldots, v_n$ from observations made at several sets of constants $c_1, \ldots, c_n$. Berkson has derived the maximum likelihood and other estimates of $v_1, \ldots, v_n$ and Cox (1958) has suggested some further techniques. Their methods obviously apply to experiments on binary choices by regarding the presentation of the offered set $\{x, y\}$ as the assignment of the values $c_x = 1$, $c_y = -1$, $c_i = 0$ for $i \neq x$, $i \neq y$, and regarding the choice of x from $\{x, y\}$ as the observation of a success. However, the known properties of their estimates are large sample properties, and no evaluation has been made when none of the sets of constants $c_1, \ldots, c_n$ are repeated in the experiment.

If, in a Fechner model, $\Phi(r)$ is given by Equation (17), then it is readily verified that the model is also a binary Luce model, with the relation between the constants $u_1,\ldots, u_n$ of the Luce model and the constants $v_1,\ldots, v_n$ of the Fechner model given by

$$(19) \qquad u_i = e^{v_i}, \quad i = 1,\ldots, n.$$

Maximum likelihood estimation of the parameters $u_1,\ldots, u_n$ has been discussed by Abelson and Bradley (1954), Bradley (1954a, 1955), Bradley and Terry (1952), and Ford (1957) in the context of paired comparisons, but again this is a large sample technique. The maximum likelihood estimates of $u_1,\ldots, u_n$ and of $v_1,\ldots, v_n$ are related by Equation (19), just as the parameters are, but the work dealing with the logistic function and that dealing with paired comparisons seem to have developed independently of each other.

Brunk (1960) has presented a technique for computing the maximum likelihood estimates of the parameters $v_1,\ldots, v_n$ in a Fechner model when the function $\Phi(r)$ belongs to an exponential family of distribution functions.

Bradley (1954b) has derived a test of goodness-of-fit for testing whether a binary stochastic model is a binary Luce model, but the distribution of his test statistic is known only when each binary offered set is presented many times.

To summarize, no statistical techniques have as yet been given for other than binary experiments, and for binary experiments the existing techniques depend on repetitions of the offered sets. Such repetitions should not be essential since if S contains n objects there are $2^n - n - 1$ distinct offered sets containing at least two objects, and $\binom{n}{2}$ distinct binary offered sets. Hence, if the stochastic model is known except for the values of n parameters, then even though no offered set is presented to the subject more than once during the experiment, the number of choices that the subject makes will still be much larger than the number of unknown parameters when n is not too small. In this situation one would still expect to be able to find good estimates of the parameters, but as yet no general techniques are known.

VI. WAGERS

In many situations, each of the objects in an offered set from which a subject must choose contains some degree of uncertainty, in the sense that even after having chosen one of the objects from the offered set, the actual reward that the subject will receive is a random variable. In such situations, by choosing an object from an offered set, the subject is in fact choosing a probability distribution for the reward that he will receive. The offered set is simply some set of possible (or available) probability distributions. We now make this notation precise.

As before, let S denote a finite set of n rewards numbered $1, 2, \ldots, n$. Let $E_1, \ldots, E_t$ denote a finite class of mutually exclusive and exhaustive events. (For example, in simple experiments the events $E_1, \ldots, E_t$ might be the various possible outcomes when a card is drawn from a deck of some specified composition.) For convenience we assume that each of the events $E_1, \ldots, E_t$ has positive probability. A *wager* $\mathbf{w} = (w_1, \ldots, w_t)$ is a vector such that each component w_i, $i = 1, \ldots, t$, is one of the integers $1, 2, \ldots, n$. In other words, a wager associates with each of the events E_i a reward w_i in S. An *offered set* is a nonempty, finite subset of the set of all wagers.

The interpretation is as follows. A subject must choose one of the wagers from a given offered set. If he chooses the wager $\mathbf{w} = (w_1, \ldots, w_t)$ then he receives one of the rewards $w_1, \ldots, w_t$ depending on which of the events $E_1, \ldots, E_t$ occurs. Thus, the subject's preferences among the rewards in S will lead to preferences among the wagers in the offered set.

For any wager $\mathbf{w}$, let $p_i(\mathbf{w})$ be the probability of receiving reward i, $i = 1, \ldots, n$. Thus, $p_i(\mathbf{w})$ is the total probability of those events E_j for which $w_j = i$. Let $\mathbf{p}(\mathbf{w})$ denote the vector $(p_1(\mathbf{w}), \ldots, p_n(\mathbf{w}))$, and consider two wagers $\mathbf{w}$ and $\mathbf{w}'$ such that $\mathbf{p}(\mathbf{w}) = \mathbf{p}(\mathbf{w}')$. Since the probabilities of receiving the various rewards are identical for both of the wagers $\mathbf{w}$ and $\mathbf{w}'$, it seems reasonable to assume that a subject would be indifferent when making a choice between them. In order for this assumption to be reasonable it is essential that the occurrence of any of the events $E_1, \ldots, E_t$ does not affect the worth of any of the rewards to the subject. In other words, it is essential that the only features of the events $E_1, \ldots, E_t$ that are relevant to the subject's choice are the probabilities of the events. For this reason it is convenient to think of the events $E_1, \ldots, E_t$ as outcomes of some gambling device such as a deck of cards or a pair of dice.

We make full use of this argument by assuming that if $\mathbf{p}(\mathbf{w}) = \mathbf{p}(\mathbf{w}')$ then the wagers $\mathbf{w}$ and $\mathbf{w}'$ are interchangeable in the sense that we can replace one of them by the other in any offered set without changing the chances of any of the wagers in the offered set being chosen. Indeed, the stochastic models for wagers to be presented in the next section depend on the wagers in an offered set only through the vectors $\mathbf{p}(\mathbf{w})$.

Consider now the situation in which the n rewards in the set S are n different amounts of money. Suppose that reward i is the amount a_i, $i = 1, \ldots, n$, and suppose that the rewards have been numbered so that $a_1 < a_2 < \cdots < a_n$. It seems reasonable to assume that any subject, when asked to choose from among different amounts of money, will always choose the largest amount.

Let $\mathbf{w} = (w_1, \ldots, w_t)$ and $\mathbf{w}' = (w'_1, \ldots, w'_t)$ be two wagers such that $w_i \geqslant w'_i$, $i = 1, \ldots, t$, and $w_i > w'_i$ for at least one value of i. We then say that $\mathbf{w}$ *dominates* $\mathbf{w}'$. It follows that a subject will never choose the wager $\mathbf{w}'$ if the wager $\mathbf{w}$ is also available in the offered set. This is so because no matter which event E_i occurs, the subject will receive at least as much money from $\mathbf{w}$ as from $\mathbf{w}'$, and might receive more from $\mathbf{w}$.

It is convenient to make the following definition. The wager $\mathbf{w}$ is said to be *absolutely preferred* to the wager $\mathbf{w}'$ if, for every offered set M containing both $\mathbf{w}$ and $\mathbf{w}'$, $\mathbf{w}'(M) = 0$. Thus, if $\mathbf{w}$ dominates $\mathbf{w}'$ then w is *absolutely* preferred to w'.

Suppose then that

(20) $$w_i \geqslant w'_i, \; i = 1, \ldots, t.$$

Since, regardless of which event occurs, the reward received from $\mathbf{w}$ is at least as large as the reward received from $\mathbf{w}'$, it follows that for any amount of money a, the probability of receiving at least a is at least as large for $\mathbf{w}$ as it is for $\mathbf{w}'$. Thus,

(21) $$\sum_{j=x}^{n} p_j(\mathbf{w}) \geqslant \sum_{j=x}^{n} p_j(\mathbf{w}'), \; x = 1, \ldots, n,$$

and if inequality holds in (20) for at least one value of i, then inequality holds in (21) for at least one value of x.

Furthermore, it can be shown that if (21) holds for some pairs of wagers

$\mathbf{w}$ and $\mathbf{w}'$ with inequality for some value of x then there exist wagers $\mathbf{w}''$ and $\mathbf{w}'''$ such that $\mathbf{p}(\mathbf{w}'')=\mathbf{p}(\mathbf{w})$, $\mathbf{p}(\mathbf{w}''')=\mathbf{p}(\mathbf{w}')$, and $w_i'' \geqslant w_i'''$, $i=1,\ldots,t$, with inequality for some value of i. Thus, $\mathbf{w}''$ dominates $\mathbf{w}'''$ and, hence, $\mathbf{w}''$ is absolutely preferred to $\mathbf{w}'''$. Since, $\mathbf{w}$ and $\mathbf{w}''$ are interchangeable and $\mathbf{w}'$ and $\mathbf{w}'''$ are also interchangeable, it follows that $\mathbf{w}$ is absolutely preferred to $\mathbf{w}'$. Hence, we conclude that if $\mathbf{w}$ and $\mathbf{w}'$ satisfy (21) with inequality for some value of x, then $\mathbf{w}$ is absolutely preferred to $\mathbf{w}'$.

All of this can be illustrated with an example. Suppose that the ten events, $E_1,\ldots, E_{10}$, are equally probable, and consider the wagers $\mathbf{w}^1$, $\mathbf{w}^2$, and $\mathbf{w}^3$ associating rewards (integers representing amounts of money) with outcomes as follows:

	E_1	E_2	E_3	E_4	E_5	E_6	E_7	E_8	E_9	E_{10}
$\mathbf{w}^1$:	3	1	4	2	2	5	3	4	4	2
$\mathbf{w}^2$:	4	2	4	3	2	5	3	4	5	2
$\mathbf{w}^3$:	2	4	2	4	5	1	4	3	2	3

It is immediately seen that for every event the reward from $\mathbf{w}^2$ is at least as large as the reward from $\mathbf{w}^1$. Hence, $\mathbf{w}^2$ dominates $\mathbf{w}^1$ and is absolutely preferred to $\mathbf{w}^1$. Since the rewards from $\mathbf{w}^2$ are simply a permutation of the rewards from $\mathbf{w}^1$ (and all E_i are equally probably), $\mathbf{w}^3$ and $\mathbf{w}^1$ are interchangeable, and hence $\mathbf{w}^2$ is also absolutely preferred to $\mathbf{w}^3$. In an actual experiment a subject might easily note that $\mathbf{w}^2$ dominates $\mathbf{w}^1$ and would never choose $\mathbf{w}^1$. However, since $\mathbf{w}^3$ yields larger rewards than $\mathbf{w}^2$ for some events, a subject might at times choose $\mathbf{w}^3$ in preference to $\mathbf{w}^2$. If, as is done in the stochastic models that will now be presented, a wager $\mathbf{w}$ is characterized simply by the vector $\mathbf{p}(\mathbf{w})$, it must be reasonable to assume that such violations of interchangeability do not occur. This assumption is very often reasonable when dealing, for example, with fewer than ten events, or when the subject has ample time to consider his choice.

VII. STOCHASTIC MODELS FOR WAGERS

As discussed in the preceding section, we now represent a wager as an n-dimensional vector $\mathbf{p}=(p_1,\ldots,p_n)$ such that $p_i\geqslant 0$, $i=1,\ldots,n$, and $\sum_{i=1}^{n} p_i=1$. The interpretation is that if a subject chooses the wager $p=(p_1,\ldots,p_n)$ from some offered set then he receives reward i with probability p_i, $i=1,\ldots,n$. (An offered set is accordingly to be thought of as a finite set of vectors of the above form.)

For reasons similar to those given in the Introduction (and which are no doubt even more compelling when dealing with wagers), it is again convenient to introduce a stochastic model for subjects' choices.

A *stochastic model for wagers* is a specification, for every offered set M and every wager $\mathbf{p}\in M$, of the probability that $\mathbf{p}$ will be chosen from M. This probability is denoted by $\mathbf{p}(M)$. Clearly, under any stochastic model for wagers it must be true that $0\leqslant\mathbf{p}(M)\leqslant 1$ and $\sum_{\mathbf{p}\in M}\mathbf{p}(M)=1$.

The celebrated von Neumann-Morgenstern (1947) concept of utility provides a very special type of model for a subject's choices. A model for wagers is said to be a *von Neumann-Morgenstern* model if there exist constants $t_1,\ldots,t_n$ with the property that, for any offered set M and any wager $\mathbf{p}\in M$, $\mathbf{p}(M)=0$ whenever there exists $\mathbf{q}\in M$ with

$$\sum_{i=1}^{n} q_i t_i > \sum_{i=1}^{n} p_i t_i .$$

The constant t_i is called the *utility of reward* i, $i=1,\ldots,n$, and $\sum_{i=1}^{n} p_i t_i$ is called the *utility of the wager*, $\mathbf{p}$. Thus, the von Neumann-Morgenstern model says that the utility of a wager is the expected utility of the reward received from the wager, and the subject always chooses, from any offered set, a wager of maximum utility.

Except for those offered sets in which more than one wager has maximum utility (in this case nothing has been said about the subject's choice from among them), the above model is nonstochastic in the sense that it exactly specifies the subject's choices. Consequently, it is desirable to develop models that admit more randomness in these choices. The stochastic models for wagers that will now be presented attempt to combine the stochastic models given in the earlier sections of this paper with the von Neumann-Morgenstern concept of the utility of a wager.

A stochastic model for wagers is said to be a *random utility model for wagers* if there exists a random vector $(U_1,\ldots,U_n)$ such that, for any offered set M and every $\mathbf{p}\in M$,

$$\text{(22)} \qquad \mathbf{p}(M) = Pr\left\{\sum_{i=1}^{n} p_i U_i \geqslant \sum_{i=1}^{n} q_i U_i \quad \text{for all} \quad \mathbf{q}\in M\right\}.$$

A wager $\mathbf{p}$ such that $p_i=1$ for some value of i is said to be a *sure thing*:

in this case the subject is certain of the reward that he will receive from this wager. Clearly, if the only wagers that appear in the offered sets presented to the subject are sure things, then these models[3] reduce to the random utility models presented in the section on Random Utility Models. Analogous to (2), it follows from Equation (22) that

$$(23) \qquad Pr\left\{\sum_{i=1}^{n} p_i U_i = \sum_{i=1}^{n} q_i U_i\right\} = 0 \quad \text{for all} \quad \mathbf{p} \neq \mathbf{q}.$$

A stochastic model for wagers is said to be a *Luce model for wagers* if there exist constants $u_1, \ldots, u_n$ and a positive, strictly increasing function $h(r)$ defined for all real numbers r, such that

$$(24) \qquad \mathbf{p}(M) = \frac{h\left(\sum_{i=1}^{n} p_i u_i\right)}{\sum_{q \in M} h\left(\sum_{i=1}^{n} q_i u_i\right)}$$

for all M and every $\mathbf{p} \in M$. Again, if the only wagers appearing in an experiment are sure things, then these models reduce to the Luce models presented earlier, with u_i as defined there equal to $h(u_i)$ as defined here, $i = 1, \ldots, n$.

An offered set containing exactly two wagers is a *binary offered set.* An experiment in which the only offered sets presented to the subject are binary is a *binary experiment*. A stochastic model for wagers that specifies the probabilities $\mathbf{p}(M)$ only for binary M is a *binary stochastic model for wagers*. The *binary random utility models for wagers* and *binary Luce models for wagers* are obtained by restricting the definitions of Equations (22) and (24) to binary M.

A binary stochastic model for wagers is said to be a *Fechner model for wagers* if there exist constants $v_1, \ldots, v_n$, a strictly increasing function $k(r)$, and a nondecreasing function $\Phi(r)$, defined for all real numbers r, such that for every binary $M = \{\mathbf{p}, \mathbf{q}\}$,

$$(25) \qquad \mathbf{p}(M) = \Phi\left(k\left(\sum_{i=1}^{n} p_i v_i\right) - k\left(\sum_{i=1}^{n} q_i v_i\right)\right).$$

Clearly, $\Phi(r)$ can be chosen so that

$$(26) \qquad \Phi(r) + \Phi(-r) = 1$$

for all r. Again, if the only wagers considered are sure things, then the Fechner models for wagers reduce to the Fechner models defined earlier, with v_i as defined there equal to $k(v_i)$ as defined here, $i=1,\ldots,n$.

VIII. RELATIONSHIPS AMONG THE MODELS

In the section on Fechner Models we discussed various inclusion relations between the stochastic models. Not surprisingly, some of these relations no longer hold between the corresponding stochastic models for wagers. Indeed, the class of Luce models for wagers is not contained in the class of random utility models for wagers. This is seen by considering four wagers

(27) $\mathbf{p}^j = (p_1^j, \ldots, p_n^j), j = 1, 2, 3, 4,$

such that

(28) $p_i^1 - p_i^2 = p_i^3 - p_i^4, i = 1, \ldots, n.$

It follows from (22) that under any random utility model for wagers,

(29) $$\begin{aligned}\mathbf{p}^1(\{\mathbf{p}^1, \mathbf{p}^2\}) &= Pr\left\{\sum_{i=1}^n p_i^1 U_i \geqslant \sum_{i=1}^n p_i^2 U_i\right\} = \\ &= Pr\left\{\sum_{i=1}^n (p_i^1 - p_i^2)\, U_i \geqslant 0\right\} = \\ &= Pr\left\{\sum_{i=1}^n (p_i^3 - p_i^4)\, U_i \geqslant 0\right\} = \\ &= \mathbf{p}^3(\{\mathbf{p}^3, \mathbf{p}^4\}).\end{aligned}$$

Clearly, this equality need not hold under a Luce model for wagers. Furthermore, since the only offered sets used in this demonstration were binary, we can conclude that the class of binary Luce models for wagers is not contained in the class of binary random utility models for wagers.

THEOREM VII. Every binary Luce model for wagers is a Fechner model for wagers.

Proof. Consider a binary Luce model for wagers defined by constants $u_i, \ldots, u_n$ and the function $h(r)$. A Fechner model for wagers is characterized by the constants $v_i, \ldots, v_n$ and the functions $k(r)$ and $\Phi(r)$. It is readily checked that if these are defined by

$$(30)\qquad \begin{aligned} v_i &= u_i,\ i = 1, \ldots, n, \\ k(r) &= \log h(r), \\ \Phi(r) &= \frac{1}{1 + e^{-r}}, \end{aligned}$$

then the two models yield the same values for all $\mathbf{p}(M)$.

It follows from Theorem VII and the comments preceding it that the class of Fechner models for wagers is not contained in the class of binary random utility models for wagers. Finally, it can be easily checked that no inclusion relationships in the reverse direction hold.

IX. ABSOLUTE PREFERENCES AND STOCHASTIC MODELS

Let us now return to the situation discussed under Wagers, where the set S of rewards comprise different amounts of money. Reward i is the amount a_i, $i=1, \ldots, n$; and

$$a_1 < a_2 < \cdots < a_n.$$

It was argued there that if the wagers $\mathbf{p}=(p_1, \ldots, p_n)$ and $\mathbf{q}=(q_1, \ldots, q_n)$ satisfy the relations

$$(31)\qquad \sum_{j=x}^{n} p_j \geqslant \sum_{j=x}^{n} q_j,\ x = 1, \ldots, n,$$

with inequality for at least one value of x, then $\mathbf{p}$ is absolutely preferred to $\mathbf{q}$. That is, the probability that $\mathbf{q}$ will be chosen from an offered set that also contains $\mathbf{p}$ is 0.

However, it is important to recognize that no provision has been made for this property in the Luce and Fechner models for wagers as presented above. Indeed, in the Luce model for wagers as given by Equation (24) it is readily seen that, since $h(r)>0$ for all values of r, every wager in any offered set has positive probability of being chosen. In the Fechner model for wagers as given by Equation (25), it is quite possible for two wagers $\mathbf{p}$ and $\mathbf{q}$ to satisfy Equation (31) and still have a very small difference,

$$k\left(\sum_{i=1}^{n} p_i v_i\right) - k\left(\sum_{i=1}^{n} q_i v_i\right).$$

Thus, in conducting an experiment relating to these models, special treatment is required for offered sets containing a pair of wagers satisfying (31).

Finally, we point out that the concept of absolute preference between wagers can be naturally injected into the random utility models for wagers. In fact, the statement that a subject always prefers a larger amount of money to a smaller amount is precisely the statement that the distribution of the random vector $(U_1, \ldots, U_n)$ satisfies the condition.

$$(32) \qquad Pr\{U_1 < U_2 < \cdots < U_n\} = 1\,.$$

It then follows easily that if **p** and **q** are two wagers such that (31) holds, then

$$(33) \qquad Pr\left\{\sum_{i=1}^{n} p_i U_i \geqslant \sum_{i=1}^{n} q_i U_i\right\} = 1\,,$$

and, hence, **p** is absolutely preferred to **q**.

X. SOME PROPERTIES OF THE MODELS

In this section we will derive a few special properties of the stochastic models for wagers that were presented earlier. These properties make it possible to test certain hypotheses about the models on the basis of observations of the subject's choices from a limited number of offered sets.

Consider a Luce model for wagers, defined by the constants $u_1, \ldots, u_n$ and the function $h(r)$, and suppose that $h(r) = r$ for all real numbers r. Then, for any offered set M and any wager $\mathbf{p} \in M$,

$$(34) \qquad \mathbf{p}(M) = \frac{\sum_{i=1}^{n} p_i u_i}{\sum_{q \in M} \sum_{i=1}^{n} q_i u_i}\,,$$

where the constants $u_1, \ldots, u_n$ are necessarily positive.

Let M^* be an offered set containing the $m+1$ wagers

$$(35) \qquad \mathbf{p}^j = (p_1^j, \ldots, p_n^j),\ j = 1, \ldots, m+1\,,$$

and suppose that

$$(36) \qquad p_i^{m+1} = \frac{1}{m} \sum_{j=1}^{m} p_i^j,\ i = 1, \ldots, n\,;$$

that is, the wager p^{m+1} is the average of the other m wagers in M^*. It then follows from (34) and (36) that

$$\text{(37)} \qquad \mathbf{p}^{m+1}(M^*) = \frac{\sum_{i=1}^{n} p_i^{m+1} u_i}{\sum_{j=1}^{m} \sum_{i=1}^{n} p_i^j u_i + \sum_{i=1}^{n} p_i^{m+1} u_i} = \frac{\frac{1}{m} \sum_{i=1}^{n} \sum_{j=1}^{m} p_i^j u_i}{\sum_{j=1}^{m} \sum_{i=1}^{n} p_i^j u_i + \frac{1}{m} \sum_{i=1}^{n} \sum_{j=1}^{m} p_i^j u_i} = \frac{1}{m+1}.$$

Thus, $\mathbf{p}^{m+1}(M^*) = 1/(m+1)$ regardless of the values of $u_1, \ldots, u_n$. This provides an obvious test of the model (34) as follows. If a subject is presented with several distinct offered sets, each having the form of M^* (i.e., each containing an 'average wager'), then under this model the distribution of the number of times the subject chooses the average wager is binomial with parameter $1/(m+1)$.

Furthermore, if in a Luce model for wagers the function $h(r)$ is convex, then it can be shown that $\mathbf{p}^{m+1}(M^*) \leqslant 1/(m+1)$ for all values of $u_1, \ldots, u_n$. If $h(r)$ is concave then $\mathbf{p}^{m+1}(M^*) \geqslant 1/(m+1)$ for all values of $u_1, \ldots, u_n$. These remarks indicate that the usual 1-tailed or 2-tailed test of the hypothesis that $\mathbf{p}^{m+1}(M^*) = 1/(m+1)$ would be appropriate for testing the linearity of h.

We now consider the same probability $\mathbf{p}^{m+1}(M^*)$ under a random utility model for wagers. From Equation (22),

$$\text{(38)} \qquad \mathbf{p}^{m+1}(M^*) = Pr\left\{\sum_{i=1}^{n} p_i^{m+1} U_i \geqslant \sum_{i=1}^{n} p_i^j U_i \text{ for } j = 1, \ldots, m\right\}.$$

But

$$\text{(39)} \qquad \sum_{i=1}^{n} p_i^{m+1} U_i = \frac{1}{m} \sum_{i=1}^{n} \sum_{j=1}^{m} p_i^j U_i = \frac{1}{m} \sum_{j=1}^{m} \left(\sum_{i=1}^{n} p_i^j U_i\right);$$

that is, $\sum_{i=1}^{n} p_i^{m+1} U_i$ is the average of the m quantities $\sum_{i=1}^{n} p_i^j U_i$, $j = 1, \ldots, m$. Hence,

(40) $$\sum_{i=1}^{n} p_i^{m+1} U_i \leqslant \max_{j=1,\ldots,m} \sum_{i=1}^{n} p_i^j U_i,$$

and equality holds if and only if the quantities $\sum_{i=1}^{n} p_j^i U_i, j=1,\ldots, m$, are all equal. But it follows from (23) that

(41) $$Pr\left\{\sum_{i=1}^{n} p_i^1 U_i = \ldots = \sum_{i=1}^{n} p_i^m U_i\right\} = 0.$$

Hence,

(42) $$Pr\left\{\sum_{i=1}^{n} p_i^{m+1} U_i < \max_{j=1,\ldots,m} \sum_{i=1}^{n} p_i^j U_i\right\} = 1$$

and, from (38),

(43) $$p^{m+1}(M^*) = 0.$$

Equation (43) provides a test of the random utility models[4] for wagers: if the 'average wager' is ever chosen from an offered set of the form M^* the stochastic model cannot belong to this class.

The results of an experiment testing both the Luce and the random utility model for wagers will be published in a separate paper. Consider now a Fechner model for wagers defined by the constants $v_1, \ldots, v_n$ and the functions $k(r)$ and $\Phi(r)$. Then for every binary offered set $M = \{\mathbf{p}, \mathbf{q}\}$,

(44) $$\mathbf{p}(M) = \Phi\left[k\left(\sum_{i=1}^{n} p_i v_i\right) - k\left(\sum_{i=1}^{n} q_i v_i\right)\right].$$

Suppose that the n rewards in S are different amounts of money, numbered in order of increasing amount. It is then reasonable to assume that in the Fechner model for wagers, $v_1 < v_2 < \cdots < v_n$. Consider c binary offered sets $M^j = \{\mathbf{p}^j, \mathbf{q}^j\}$, $j=1,\ldots, c$, where the wagers $\mathbf{p}^j = (p_1^j, \ldots, p_n^j)$ and $\mathbf{q}^j = (q_1^j, \ldots, q_n^j)$, $j=1,\ldots, c$ have been chosen so that

(45) $$p_j^i - q_j^i = d_i, j = 1, \ldots, c;\ i = 1, \ldots, n,$$

and

(46) $$\sum_{l=x}^{n} q_l^j \geqslant \sum_{l=x}^{n} q_l^{j'}, x = 1, \ldots, n,$$

whenever $j > j'$.

As examples of such wagers, suppose that $n=3$ and define

$$(47) \quad \begin{array}{ll} \mathbf{p}^1 = (.8, 0, .2), & \mathbf{p}^2 = (.7, 0, .3), \\ \mathbf{p}^3 = (.6, .1, .3), & \mathbf{p}^4 = (.4, .2, .4), \\ \mathbf{q}^1 = (.7, .3, 0), & \mathbf{p}^2 = (.6, .3, .1), \\ \mathbf{q}^3 = (.5, .4, .1), & \mathbf{q}^4 = (.3, .5, .2). \end{array}$$

The binary offered sets $M^j = \{\mathbf{p}^j, \mathbf{q}^j\}, j=1, 2, 3, 4$, satisfy (45) and (46), and it should be clear from (47) how this list could be made arbitrarily long.

It follows from (44) and (45) that

$$(48) \quad \mathbf{p}^j(M^j) = \Phi\left[k\left(\sum_{i=1}^{n} q_i^j v_i + \sum_{i=1}^{n} d_i v_i\right) - k\left(\sum_{i=1}^{n} q_i^j v_i\right)\right],$$

and from (46) that

$$(49) \quad \sum_{i=1}^{n} q_i^1 v_i < \sum_{i=1}^{n} q_i^2 v_i < \cdots < \sum_{i=1}^{n} q_i^c v_i .$$

Hence, if $k(r)$ is a convex function of r, then either $\mathbf{p}^1(M^1) \leqslant \cdots \leqslant \mathbf{p}^c(M^c)$ or $\mathbf{p}^1(M^1) \geqslant \cdots \geqslant \mathbf{p}^c(M^c)$, depending on whether $\sum_{i=1}^n d_i v_i \geqslant 0$ or $\sum_{i=1}^n d_i v_i \leqslant 0$. A similar statement can be made if $k(r)$ is concave. In particular, if $k(r)$ is linear, then $\mathbf{p}^1(M^1) = \cdots = \mathbf{p}^c(M^c)$. These equalities would also hold if $\sum_{i=1}^n d_i v_i = 0$, but since the experimenter typically has at least a rough idea of the magnitudes of $v_1, \ldots, v_n$, he can choose $d_1, \ldots, d_n$ so that the chance that $\sum_{i=1}^n d_i v_i = 0$ is negligible.

We can then test the hypothesis that $k(r)$ is linear against the alternative that it is strictly convex or concave as follows.

Record the subject's choices from the offered sets $M^1, \ldots, M^c$ as a sequence of *p*s and *q*s. Then conditionally on the observed number of *p*s and *q*s in the sequence, all sequences with these numbers are equally likely if $k(r)$ is linear, whereas there is a greater chance that the *ps* will be grouped at one end and the *qs* at the other if $k(r)$ is strictly convex or concave. Thus, the usual runs test would be appropriate. If $k(r)$ is linear, the number of runs of *p*s and *q*s in the sequence has the distribution that results when all sequences are equally likely; if $k(r)$ is strictly convex or concave, we would expect to observe fewer runs.

Finally, it is easily seen from Equations (22) and (45) that under any binary random utility model for wagers,

$$\mathbf{p}^j(M^j) = Pr\left\{\sum_{i=1}^{n} d_i U_i \geqslant 0\right\}, j = 1, \ldots, c. \tag{50}$$

Hence, $\mathbf{p}^1(M^1) = \cdots = \mathbf{p}^c(M^c)$, and rejection of this hypothesis implies rejection of the binary random utility models for wagers.

XI. THE SIGN TEST

The following situation arises quite often in analyzing experiments of the type we are considering in this paper. Let $(R_1, T_1), \ldots, (R_m, T_m)$ be m independent pairs of random variables. (This does not assume that R_j and T_j are independent.) Suppose that each of the random variables R_j, T_j, $j = 1, \ldots, m$, takes only the values 0 and 1, and let

$$\begin{aligned} &Pr\{R_j = 1, T_j = 1\} = \pi_{11}^j, \\ &Pr\{R_j = 1, T_j = 0\} = \pi_{10}^j, \\ &Pr\{R_j = 0, T_j = 1\} = \pi_{10}^j, \\ &Pr\{R_j = 0, T_j = 0\} = \pi_{00}^j, j = 1, \ldots, m. \end{aligned} \tag{51}$$

Define $D_j = R_j - T_j$, $j = 1, \ldots, m$. Then

$$\begin{aligned} &Pr\{D_j = 1\} = \pi_{10}^j, \\ &Pr\{D_j = 0\} = \pi_{11}^j + \pi_{00}^j, \\ &Pr\{D_j = -1\} = \pi_{01}^j, j = 1, \ldots, m. \end{aligned} \tag{52}$$

Suppose that we are interested in testing the hypothesis

$$H_0 : \pi_{10}^j = \pi_{01}^j, j = 1, \ldots, m, \tag{53}$$

against one of the hypotheses

$$\begin{aligned} &H_1 : \pi_{10}^j > \pi_{01}^j, j = 1, \ldots, m, \\ &H_2 : \pi_{10}^j < \pi_{01}^j, j = 1, \ldots, m, \\ &H_3 : \text{Either } H_1 \text{ or } H_2. \end{aligned} \tag{54}$$

It follows from (52) that

$$Pr\{D_j = 1 \mid D_j \neq 0\} = \frac{\pi_{10}^j}{\pi_{10}^j + \pi_{01}^j} \gtreqless \tag{55}$$

$$\gtreqless \tfrac{1}{2} \quad \text{according as} \quad \pi_{10}^j \gtreqless \pi_{01}^j .$$

Let

$$m^* = \sum_{j=1}^{m} |D_j|, \tag{56}$$

$$(56) \qquad D^* = \tfrac{1}{2} \sum_{j=1}^{m} D_j(1 + D_j);$$

that is, m^* is the number of nonzero observations D_j, and D^* is the number of D_j such that $D_j=1$. It follows from (53) and (55) that if H_0 is true, the conditional distribution of D^*, given the value of m^*, is a binomial distribution with parameter $\frac{1}{2}$, and a 1-tailed or 2-tailed test is appropriate depending on which of the alternative hypotheses H_1, H_2, or H_3 is of interest. Furthermore, if for each conditional value of m^* a test of size α is used, then the over-all test of H_0 has size α.

We now give two examples of the use of this test. The first example is based on a comment of Debreu (1960); the second deals with the problems of predicting subjects' choices. The examples do not deal with wagers explicitly, and so we revert to the term 'objects' to denote the alternatives in an offered set.

Consider m pairs of offered sets, $M_j=\{x_j, y_j\}$ and $M'_j=\{x_j, y_j, y'_j\}$, $j=1,\ldots, m$, where the objects y_j and y'_j are essentially identical (or indistinguishable) in each pair, $j=1,\ldots, m$. There are (at least) two points of view regarding the probabilities $x_j(M_j)$ and $x_j(M'_j)$. One point of view is that since y_j and y'_j are essentially identical objects, adding y'_j to the offered set M_j should not affect the probability that x_j is chosen; that is, $x_j(M_j)=x_j(M'_j), j=1,\ldots, m$. The second point of view – as would be true, for example, under the Luce model – is that adding another object to the offered set M_j should reduce the probability that x_j is chosen; that is, $x_j(M_j)>x_j(M'_j), j=1,\ldots, m$.

Let $R_j=1$ if x_j is chosen from M_j and let $R_j=0$ otherwise; let $T_j=1$ if x_j is chosen from M'_j and let $T_j=0$ otherwise. Then assuming all choices are independent,

$$(57) \qquad \begin{aligned} Pr\{D_j = 1\} &= \pi^j_{10} = [x_j(M_j)]\,[1 - x_j(M'_j)], \\ Pr\{D_j = -1\} &= \pi^j_{01} = [1 - x_j(M_j)]\,[x_j(M'_j)]. \end{aligned}$$

It is readily checked that the hypothesis that $x_j(M_j) = x_j(M'_j), j=1,\ldots, m$, is the hypothesis H_0 of Equation (53), and the hypothesis that $x_j(M_j> >x_j(M'_j), j=1,\ldots, m$, is the hypothesis H_1 of (54).

An experiment testing these two hypotheses will be reported in a separate paper.

As a second example, consider two techniques, A and B, for predicting a subject's choices from offered sets. Suppose that each technique is used to predict the choices from offered sets M_j, $j=1,\dots,m$. Let $T_j=1$ if A predicts the correct choice from M_j and let $R_j=0$ otherwise; let $R_j=1$ if B predicts the correct choice from M_j and let $T_j=0$ otherwise. Suppose that one person claims that $Pr\{R_j=1\}=Pr\{T_j=1\}$, $j=1,\dots,m$, and another claims that $Pr\{R_j=1\}>Pr\{T_j=1\}$, $j=1,\dots,m$. That is, one person claims that both techniques have the same chance of being correct on each offered set and another claims that A has a better chance than B of being correct. Note that R_j and T_j are not necessarily independent, since A and B are predicting the choice from the same offered set. Since

$$(58) \qquad \begin{aligned} Pr\{R_j = 1\} &= \pi^j_{10} + \pi^j_{11}, \\ Pr\{T_j = 1\} &= \pi^j_{01} + \pi^j_{11}, \end{aligned}$$

it is easily seen that the two claims correspond to the hypotheses H_0 and H_1 of (53) and (54).

XII. HETEROGENEOUS POPULATIONS

Very often an experiment on choice behavior is performed not just with one subject but with a random sample of subjects from some population. In this situation the experimenter is typically interested not only in deciding whether the choice behavior of each subject satisfies a certain condition but also in making some inference about the proportion of individuals in the population whose choice behavior satisfies the condition. It is this problem that will now be considered.

Suppose that a random sample of s subjects is selected from some population and the choices of each subject from several offered sets are observed. Denote the probability distribution of the choices of the jth subject by f_j, $j=1,\dots,s$. Suppose that we want to decide for each subject in the sample whether his probability distribution f_j satisfies a certain condition C (written $f_j \in C$) or not ($f_j \in' C$). Assume that for each subject in the sample we perform a test of the hypotheses

$$(59) \qquad \begin{aligned} &H_0 : f_j \in C \\ &H_1 : f_j \in' C, \end{aligned}$$

of size α. That is, for each subject the probability of rejecting H_0 when it is true is at most α.

Let π represent the proportion of individuals in the entire population whose probability distribution f of choices satisfies the hypothesis $f \in C$. Suppose we are also interested in testing the hypotheses

$$(60) \qquad \begin{aligned} &H_0' : \pi \geqslant 1 - \delta \\ &H_1' : \pi < 1 - \delta , \end{aligned}$$

where δ is a fixed (typically small) positive number. Intuitively, if we reject H_0 too many times when testing each individual in the sample, then we will want to reject H_0'. More precisely, let β denote the probability that H_0 will be rejected for a subject drawn at random from the population. Then

$$(61) \qquad \begin{aligned} \beta = &Pr\{\text{Rej. } H_0 | f \in C\} \, Pr\{f \in C\} + \\ &+ Pr\{\text{Rej. } H_0 | f \in' C\} \, Pr\{f \in' C\} \leqslant \\ &\leqslant \alpha\pi + (1 - \pi) = 1 - (1 - \alpha)\,\pi . \end{aligned}$$

If H_0' is true, then $\pi \geqslant 1 - \delta$ and

$$(62) \qquad \beta \leqslant 1 - (1 - \alpha)(1 - \delta) = \alpha + \delta - \alpha\delta .$$

Thus, under H_0' the number of subjects in the sample for whom H_0 is rejected has a binomial distribution with parameter $\beta \leqslant \alpha + \delta - \alpha\delta$. Thus, we can test the hypotheses (60) with the usual 1-tailed test of a binomial parameter.

NOTES

* This paper is one of a series resulting from the co-operation of the three authors at the Western Management Science Institute, University of California at Los Angeles, in 1960-1961. The work was supported in part by the Ford Foundation, the Behavioral Research Service, General Electric Company, and a contract with the Office of Naval Research, Task Number 047-041.

[1] If the objects in S are commodity bundles, lottery tickets, or other objects that can be represented as vectors, then there is a natural partial ordering of the objects, and a subjects choices from among the objects in a simply ordered subset of S would typically be consistent. Thus, if every component of commodity bundle a is larger than the corresponding component of commodity bundle b, then a subject would typically always choose a rather than b. Situations of this type are discussed in the section on Wagers.

[2] Luce admitted the further possibility that $x(M)$ might be 0 or 1, in which case Equation (3) need not hold. The general question that this raises is discussed in the section on Wagers.

[3] It should be noted that in Equation (22) only a single realization of the random vector $(U_1 \ldots, U_n)$ is needed. Under an alternative class of models one might assume that independent realizations of $(U_1, \ldots, U_n)$ are made for each wager in M. When choosing from offered sets containing sure things, these models would not reduce to the

ones presented in the section on Random Utility Models unless the components of $(U_1, \ldots, U_n)$ were independent.

[4] Under the alternative models mentioned in note 3, $\mathbf{p}^{m+1}(M^*)$ need not be 0.

BIBLIOGRAPHY

Abelson, R. M. and Bradley, R. A., 'A 2 × 2 Factorial with Paired Comparisons', *Biometrics* **10** (1954) 487–502.

Berkson, J., 'Maximum Likelihood and Minimum χ^2 Estimates of the Logistic Function', *J. Amer. Statist. Assoc.* **50** (1955) 130–162.

Berkson, J., 'Tables for the Maximum Likelihood Estimate of the Logistic Function', *Biometrics* **13** (1957) 28–34.

Block, H. D. and Marschak, J., 'Random Orderings and Stochastic Theories of Response', *Selected Essays*, 7.

Bradley, R. A., 'Rank Analysis of Incomplete Block Designs. II. Additional Tables for the Method of Paired Comparisons', *Biometrika* **41** (1954) 502–537. (a)

Bradley, R. A., 'Incomplete Block Rank Analysis: on the Appropriateness of the Model for a Method of Paired Comparisons', *Biometrics* **10** (1954) 375–390. (b)

Bradley, R. A., 'Rank Analysis of Incomplete Block Designs. III. Some Large Sample Results on Estimation and Power for a Method of Paired Comparisons', *Biometrika* **42** (1955) 450–470.

Bradley, R. A. and Terry, M. E., 'Rank Analysis of Incomplete Block Designs. I. The Method of Paired Comparisons', *Biometrika* **39** (1952) 324–345.

Brunk, H. D., 'Mathematical Models for Ranking from Paired Comparisons', *J. Amer. Statist. Assoc.* **55** (1960) 503–520.

Cox, D. R., 'The Regression Analysis of Binary Sequences', *J. Royal Statist. Soc., Series B* **20** (1958) 215–242.

Debreu, G., 'Review of R. D. Luce's *Individual Choice Behavior*', *Amer. Econ. Rev.* **50** (1960) 186–188.

Ford, L. R., Jr., 'Solution of a Ranking Problem from Binary Comparisons', *Amer. Math. Monthly* **64** (1957) 8 (suppl.), 28–33.

Luce, R. D., *Individual Choice Behavior*, Wiley, New York, 1959.

Marschak, J., 'Binary-Choice Constraints and Random Utility Indicators', *Selected Essays*, 8.

von Neumann, J. and Morgenstern, O., *Theory of Games and Economic Behavior*', Princeton Univ. Press, Princeton, N.J., 1947.

Quandt, R. E., 'A Probabilistic Theory of Consumer Behavior', *Quart. J. Econ.* **70** (1956) 506–536.

11

ON ADAPTIVE PROGRAMMING*

(1963)

In general, it is non-optimal to estimate, on the basis of past experience and as a basis for present action, an *a posteriori* statistical parameter other than the optimal action itself.

I. PURPOSE OF THIS NOTE

'Adaptive programming' consists in finding the best sequence of rules of action when properties of the relevant probability distribution, to be used in choosing an action, have to be inferred from the effects of previous actions.

This note proposes to drive home a point about 'adaptive programming' which, while obvious, often seems to be misunderstood. It is often stated that, in the case of adaptive programming, each action in the sequence is determined in 'two steps' of data processing: (1) re-estimating the probability-distribution *a posteriori,* and (2) computing the action on the basis of the new estimate.

In this general form, the statement is correct. But it is misunderstood whenever the estimation of the *a posteriori* probability distribution is reduced to estimating some of its parameters (such as the mean) chosen by statistical habit and convenience without reference to the givens of the problem. These givens include, in particular, the transformation function (which relates the state resulting from an action to the state preceding it) and the utility, or criterion, function (the maximand expressed as a function of the final state). To justify the reduction of an *a posteriori* distribution to its mean (say) rather than to some other parameter(s), one would have to assume a very special class of transformation and criterion functions.

One way to make the statement both specific and correct is to say: the optimal action, as a function of the previous states and all other information currently available to the decision maker, is itself a parameter of the probability distribution. It is this parameter that one has to estimate on the basis of current information.

The misunderstanding is particularly glaring when one recalls that the usually recommended theoretical estimators of a parameter are themselves chosen on the basis of their 'optimal properties'. An estimator is recommended because it maximizes a likelihood function, or minimizes the sum of squares of residuals, or the variance of the difference between the estimate and the true value of a parameter, etc. Thus, once having decided, for whatever reason, to represent the *a posteriori* distribution by a certain parameter, the two-steps procedure would first minimize the sum of squares of residuals (for example), to obtain the estimate of the parameter; it would then insert the estimate into the expression for expected utility and then perform a second extremization – viz., that of the expected utility with respect to action. But the decision maker's goal is fully expressed by his utility function! To maximize the latter under the constraint that the sum of squares of residuals also be maximized, will in general depress the utility obtained and thus decrease the efficiency of programming.

I do not believe the pioneering books of Abraham Wald [1] and of Richard Bellman [2], [3] contain the misleading statement. As only few problems in adaptive programming have so far received specific treatment, the statement is mostly heard as a general and somewhat vague prescription. A field in which students have indeed come to grips with the question raised here, and where the misleading statement has been made and contested, and has been, in fact, prevalent in practice, is that of economic policy to be derived, given the utility function, from a system of stochastic simultaneous equations. A rather full analysis of this case was given recently by Walter Fisher in [4], where some earlier literature is also discussed.

This note deals with a particular class of transformation and utility functions. However, the class is broad enough to illustrate the statement that it is not, in general, optimal to reduce the *a posteriori* distribution to a particular parameter, or set of parameters, unless these parameters happen to be the ones called for by the particular transformation and utility functions. Thus, in a particular case (in this note, the case of a quadratic transformation function) one will indeed need to compute and recompute the mean. But this does not apply in general.

To give better insight, the adaptive model will be preceded by a corresponding stochastic model (probability distribution known) and this, in turn, will be preceded by a corresponding deterministic model.

II. GENERAL FORMULATION

Define:

$[x_t]$, $t=0, 1, \ldots, T$: the sequence of *states*.

$[y_t]$, $t=0, 1, \ldots, T-1$: the sequence of *actions*.

In a programming problem, *given* are:

(1) x_0, the *initial state*.

(2) ψ, the *utility function* of the final state's utility $u=\psi(x_T)$.

(3) a *transformation function* g such that

$$x_{t+1} = g(x_t, y_t), \quad t = 0, 1, \ldots, T-1 .$$

To find: the value $[y_t^*]$ of $[y_t]$ such that

(1) for every $t(=0, 1, \ldots, T-1)$, y_t^* depends at most on $(x_0, x_1, \ldots, x_t)$, and

(2) the expectation of utility is maximized. The sequence $[y_t^*]$ is called *optimal program.*

III. ASSUMPTIONS OF THIS NOTE

In general, each x_t and each y_t is a vector or, even more generally, an element of some abstract set. For present purposes, x_t, y_t will be real numbers.

As we are not interested here in the asymptotic properties of long sequences of actions, we shall put $T=2$, to achieve the greatest possible simplicity without loosing the essence. For the same purpose we shall assume that

$$u = x_T = x_2 \; ; \tag{3.1}$$

and that

$$x_{t+1} = g(x_t, y_t) = x_t - f(y_t - x_t - a_t), \quad t = 0, 1 , \tag{3.2}$$

where f is a twice differentiable function satisfying appropriate second-order conditions (these may vary from model to model and will not be stated explicitly) to ensure that a finite maximum of expected utility is achieved when its first derivatives with respect to actions vanish.

The term a_t may be random. If it is, we shall assume that a_0 and a_1 have identical independent distributions.

It will be convenient to define

$$z_t \equiv y_t - x_t\,;$$

then

$$(3.3) \qquad x_{t+1} = x_t - f(z_t - a_t), \qquad y_t = x_t + z_t\,;$$

and we can replace the search for the optimal sequence (y_0^*, y_1^*) by the search for the optimal sequence (z_0^*, z_1^*).

In each of the three models, the quadratic case

$$(3.4) \qquad x_{t+1} = x_t - (z_t - a_t)^2/2$$

will be presented first, to exploit its elementary properties.[1] (Also, in this case, the reader will easily prove that the required second-order conditions are satisfied in each model). This will be followed by the general case (3.3). We shall also briefly contrast the quadratic case with the slightly more general one:

$$(3.5) \qquad x_{t+1} = x_t - h\,[(z_t - a_t)^2/2],$$

where h is a positive-valued function. For example, when $h(r)=e^{-r}$, the quadratic case is replaced by that of a Gaussian one (both occur in practice).

IV. DETERMINISTIC MODEL

To start with the quadratic case (3.4), let $a_t = a$, a known constant. Then

$$(4.1) \qquad x_1 = x_0 - (z_0 - a)^2/2$$

$$(4.2) \qquad u = x_2 = x_1 - (z_1 - a)^2/2\,.$$

Clearly, from (4.2),

$$(4.3) \qquad z_1^* = a\,; \qquad y_1^* = x_1 + a\,;$$

inserting into (4.2)

$$\max_{z_1} u = x_1\,,$$

so that, by (4.1),

$$\max_{z_1} u = x_0 - (z_0 - a)^2/2\,,$$

(4.4) $z_0^* = a\,; \qquad y_0^* = x_0 + a\,.$

The maximum utility is

(4.5) $\max_{z_0 z_1} u = x_0\,.$

Of course we could obtain the same result by simply maximizing u simultaneously with respect to z_0 and z_1, after inserting x_1 from (4.1) into (4.2). But we wanted to exhibit the procedure of 'advancing backward', characteristic of dynamic programming in more complicated cases.

The same optimal actions would be also found in the case (3.5) such as the 'Gaussian' case. But this similarity will break down in the stochastic and deterministic models.

Now, in the more general case of our deterministic model (3.3),

(4.6) $x_1 = x_0 - f(z_0 - a)$

(4.7) $u = x_2 = x_1 - f(z_1 - a)\,.$

Since we have assumed f to fulfill the second order condition for the maximum of u, we obtain z_0^*, z_1^* by differentiation.

Again, we use the 'advancing backward' method, starting with the final action, z_1:

(4.8) $\partial u/\partial z_1 = 0 = -f'(z_1 - a), \quad \text{when} \quad z_1 = z_1^*.$

Denote by f^D a function such that

(4.9) $f'(r - a) = 0 \quad \text{when} \quad r = f^D(a)\,.$

f^D is '*the Transform of f appropriate for the Deterministic model*'. Then, from (4.6), (4.8),

(4.10) $z_1^* = f^D(a)\,; \quad y_1^* = x_1 + f^D(a)\,.$

Inserting into (4.6), then into (4.7)

(4.11) $\max_{z_1} u = x_0 - f(z_0 - a) - f[f^D(a) - a]\,.$

The last term on the right side depends only on a and on the function f (from which f^D is derived). Hence, differentiating (4.11) with respect to z_0:

$$f(z_0^* - a) = 0\,,$$

so that by the definition of f^D in (4.9)

$$(4.12) \qquad z_0^* = f^D(a); \qquad y_0^* = x_0 + f^D(a).$$

The results (4.3), (4.4) of the quadratic case are, of course, recovered, since in that case $f'(r-a)=r-a, f^D(a)=a$.

V. STOCHASTIC MODEL

We shall confine ourselves to the simple case when the successive random disturbances a_0, a_1 have identical and independent distributions. More particularly, assume

$$(5.1) \qquad \Pr(a_t = 1) = \alpha; \qquad \Pr(a_t = 0) = \beta, \quad t = 0, 1,$$

where α is known and $\alpha+\beta=1$. For any function ϕ of (a_0, a_1) we shall denote by $E_{a_t}\,\phi$ its expectation taken over the values of a_t. Hence

$$(5.2) \qquad \begin{aligned} E_{a_1}\phi(a_0, a_1) &= a\phi(a_0, 1) + \beta\phi(a_0, 0) \\ E_{a_0}\phi(a_0, a_1) &= \alpha\phi(1, a_1) + \beta\phi(0, a_1) \end{aligned}$$

$$(5.3) \qquad \begin{aligned} &E_{a_1}E_{a_0}\phi = E_{a_0}E_{a_1}\phi \\ &\quad E_{a_t} = \alpha; \qquad E_{a_t}(a_t - \alpha)^2 = \operatorname{Var} a_t = \alpha\beta, \quad t = 0, 1 \end{aligned}$$

However, we shall omit the subscript under E whenever ambiguity is absent. We want to maximize expected utility defined as

$$(5.4) \qquad U = E_{a_1}E_{a_0}u = E_{a_0}E_{a_1}u.$$

In the quadratic case (3.4)

$$(5.5) \qquad \begin{aligned} x_1 &= x_0 - (z_0 - a_0)^2/2 \\ u &= x_1 - (z_1 - a_1)^2/2 \end{aligned}$$

'Advancing backward' find z_1^* first, noting that

$$\partial u/\partial z_1 = -(z_1 - a_1).$$

Then by (5.4),

$$(5.6) \qquad \partial U/\partial z_1 = E_{a_1}E_{a_0}(\partial u/\partial z_1) = E_{a_1}[-(z_1 - a_1)] = -(z_1 - \alpha) = = 0,$$

when $z_1 = z_1^*$: for we have assumed in Section III that the second order conditions, appropriate to the model considered, are satisfied. Hence

$$(5.7) \qquad z_1^* = \alpha, \qquad y_1^* = x_1 + \alpha.$$

Inserting into (5.6), we obtain, for $z_1 = z_1^*$,

$$u = x_0 - (z_0 - a_0)^2/2 - (\alpha - a_1)^2$$
$$\partial u/\partial z_0 = -(z_0 - a_0)$$
$$\partial U/\partial z_0 = E_{a_0}E_{a_1}(\partial u/\partial z_0) = -(z_0 - \alpha) = 0$$
$$(5.8) \qquad z_0^* = \alpha, \qquad y_0^* = x_0 + \alpha.$$

The results (4.3), (4.4) of the corresponding deterministic model (with $a = 1$) are recovered putting $\alpha = 1$. Note also that the maximum expected utility, in the stochastic case, is, by (5.4)

$$\max U = x_0 - \operatorname{Var} a_t = x_0 - \alpha\beta,$$

to be compared with (4.5). Thus, in the quadratic stochastic case, the loss due to uncertainty is equal to the (known) variance of the random disturbance.

Note also that, in the stochastic model, the solution in the Gaussian case is different from the solution in the quadratic case: (5.6) is replaced by

$$-\partial U/\partial z_1 = \alpha \cdot (z_1 - 1) \cdot e^{-(z_1-1)^2/2} + \beta \cdot z_1 e^{-z_1{}^2/2} = 0.$$

Now to the general case (3.3):

$$(5.9) \qquad u = x_1 - f(z_1 - a_1)$$

$$(5.10) \qquad x_1 = x_0 - f(z_0 - a_0).$$

We want to maximize expected utility U, defined in (5.4). As in (5.6),

$$\partial E_{a_1}(u)/\partial z_1 = E_{a_1}(\partial u/\partial z_1) = -E_{a_1}f'(z_1 - a_1).$$
$$(5.11) \qquad -E_{a_1}(\partial u/\partial z_1) = \alpha f'(z_1 - 1) + \beta f'(z_1).$$

Let f^S be a function such that

$$(5.12) \qquad af'(r-1) + \beta f'(r) = 0 \quad \text{when} \quad r = f^S(\alpha).$$

f^S is '*the Transform of f appropriate for the Stochastic Model*'. Then, since the appropriate second-order condition is assumed fulfilled, we have, by (5.11), (5.12)

$$(5.13) \qquad z_1^* = f^S(\alpha), \qquad y_1^* = x_1 + f^S(\alpha).$$

Inserting into (5.10), we obtain by the same reasoning

$$(5.14) \qquad z_0^* = f^S(\alpha), \qquad y_0^* = x_0 + f^S(\alpha).$$

In the quadratic case, for example, $f^S(\alpha)=\alpha$, yielding (5.7), (5.8). And the results of the general deterministic case (4.6), (4.7), with $a=1$ are also recovered, by putting $\alpha=1$ so that (5.12) becomes (4.9).

VI. ADAPTIVE MODEL

We shall retain the assumptions and notations of the stochastic model, but assume that not α itself but only an *a priori* distribution p^0 of α is known before action y_0 is taken. We shall confine ourselves to the case when this distribution is finite:

$$\text{(6.1)} \qquad \textit{A priori} \quad \Pr(\alpha = \alpha_k) = p_k^0 > 0 \quad \text{if} \quad k = 1, \ldots, K$$
$$= 0 \text{ otherwise}$$

Thus p^0 is positive-valued only on a specified finite subset $(\alpha_1, \ldots, \alpha_K)$ of the interval [0, 1]. We conjecture, however, that our results can be extended to a continuous distribution p^0 defined on the whole unit interval so that the specification of the α_k is unnecessary.

For a given action y_0 the resulting state x_1 has a $1-1$ relation to the value actually taken by the random disturbance a_0:

$$\text{(6.2)} \qquad x_1 = x_1(a_0) = \begin{matrix} x_0 - f(z_0 - 1) \\ x_0 - f(z_0) \end{matrix} \quad \text{according as} \quad a_0 = \begin{matrix} 1, \\ 0 \end{matrix}$$

where, of course, x_0 and f have been known from the beginning; $z_0=y_0-x_0$ characterizes the action already taken (and presumably remembered); and x_1 has been that action's result. The knowledge of a_0 inferred by (6.2) is used to replace the *a priori* distribution

$$p^0 \equiv \{p_k^0\} \equiv (p_1^0, \ldots, p_K^0)$$

by an *a posteriori* distribution depending on a_0 and denoted thus:

$$p^1(a_0) \equiv \{p_k^1(a_0)\} \equiv (p_1^1(a_0), \ldots, p_K^1(a_0)).$$

By Bayes' theorem and (5.1),

$$\text{(6.3)} \qquad \textit{A posteriori} \quad \Pr(\alpha = \alpha_k \mid a_0) \equiv p_k^1(a_0) \quad \begin{matrix} = \alpha_k p_k^0 / \sum \alpha_j p_j^0 \quad \text{if} \quad a_0 = 1; \\ = \beta_k p_k^0 / \sum \beta_j p_j^0 \quad \text{if} \quad a_0 = 0. \end{matrix}$$

Here the summation is over $j=1,\ldots, K$. It will be convenient to denote by E_{p^0} and $E_{p^1(a_0)}$, respectively, the expectations taken when the *a priori* distribution p^0 or the *a posteriori* distribution $p^1(a_0)$ is used. Therefore, for example, because of (5.3),

$$(6.4) \qquad E_{p^1(a_0)}[E_{a_1}(a_1)] = E_{p^1(a_0)}(\alpha) = \sum p_k^1(a_0)\cdot a_k.$$

On the basis of the knowledge of a_0 we shall have to choose y_1 (or, equivalently, z_1) so as to maximize the expected utility given a_0

$$U(a_0) \equiv E_{p^1(a_0)}E_{a_1}[u(a_0)],$$

where, in the quadratic case which we want to handle first,

$$u(a_0) = x_1(a_0) - (z_1 - a_1)^2/2.$$

But $\partial U(a_0)/\partial z_1$ vanishes if and only if $z_1 = z_1^*$ (since the second order conditions are easily shown to be fulfilled). Hence,

$$0 = E_{p^1(a_0)}[E_{a^1}(z_1^* - a_1)] = z_1^* - E_{p^1(a_0)}(a_1);$$

and by (6.4), (6.3)

$$(6.5) \qquad z_1^* = \sum \alpha_k p_k^1(a_0)\begin{cases} = \sum \alpha_k^2 p_k^0 / \sum \alpha_j p_j^0 & \text{if} \quad a_0 = 1; \\ = \sum \alpha_k \beta_k p_k^0 / \sum \beta_j p_j^0 & \text{if} \quad a_0 = 0. \end{cases}$$

Hence the maximum expected utility, given a_0, is

$$(6.6) \qquad U^*(a_0) \equiv \max_{z_1} U(a_0) = E_{p^1(a_0)}[E_{a_1}u^*(a_0)]$$

where by (6.5)

$$u^*(a_0) \equiv x_1(a_0) - [\sum \alpha_k p_1^k(a_0) - a_1]^2/2,$$
$$x_1(a_0) = x_0 - (z_0 - a_0)^2/2,$$

so that

$$(6.7) \qquad \partial u^*(a_0)/\partial z_0 = -(z - a_0) = E_{p^1(a_0)}[E_{a_1}\partial u^*(a_0)/\partial z_0],$$

because a_0, a_1 are independent. We use this result to maximize, with respect to z_0, the *a priori* expectation of utility, written as

$$(6.8) \qquad U^* \equiv E_{p^0}E_{a_0}U^*(a_0) = \sum p_k^0[\alpha_k U^*(1) + \beta_k U^*(0)]$$

(compare (5.2)). Now by (6.6), (6.7)

(6.9) $\partial U^*(a_0)/\partial z_0 = E_{p^1(a_0)}[E_{a_1}\partial u^*(a_0)/\partial z_0] = -(z_0 - a_0)$.

Now since, again, the second order conditions are known to be fulfilled,

$$\partial U^*/\partial z_0 = 0 \quad \text{when} \quad z_0 = z_0^* ;$$

so that by (6.8), (6.9)

(6.10) $$0 = \sum p_k^0 [\alpha_k(z_0^* - 1) + \beta_k z_0^*]$$
$$z_0^* = \sum \alpha_k p_k^0 .$$

It is seen from (6.10), (6.5) that, in the quadratic case, the optimal values z_0^*, z_k^1, do turn out to be the means of the unknown parameter α computed on the basis of the *a priori* distribution p^0 or the *a posteriori* distribution $p^1(a_0)$, respectively. The optimal actions $y_t^* = x_t + z_t^*$, $t = 0, 1$, are chosen on the basis of those means.

Now let us turn to the general case (5.9), (5.10) [but with α unknown]:

$$\partial u/\partial z_1 = -f'(z_1 - a_1),$$

so that

$$\partial U/\partial z_1 = E_{p^1(a_0)}[E_{a_1} f'(z_1 - a_1)],$$

the value of a_0 having been inferred from x_1 as in (6.2). Hence, since the appropriate second order conditions for maximum expected utility have been assumed to be fulfilled by the function f,

$$0 = \sum p_k^1(1) [\alpha_k f'(z_1^* - 1) + \beta_k f'(z_1^*)] \quad \text{if} \quad a_0 = 1$$
$$0 = \sum p_k^1(0) [\alpha_k f'(z_1^* - 1) + \beta_k f'(z_1^*)] \quad \text{if} \quad a_0 = 0 .$$

Denote the solution of each of these two equations by

(6.11) $$z_1^* = f^A(p^1(a_0)) ; \quad a_0 = 1, 0 .$$

The function f^A is, then, the '*Transform of f appropriate to the Adaptive Model*'. Check for the quadratic case: then

$$f'(z_1^* - 1) = z_1^* - 1, \quad f'(z_1^*) = z^* ,$$

and we recover the solution (6.5). To continue with the general case, retaining the definition (6.6), we obtain, instead of (6.7),

$$u^*(a_0) = x_1(a_0) - f[f^A(p^1(a_0)) - a_1]$$
$$x_1(a_0) = x_0 - f(z_0 - a_0),$$

$$\partial u^*(a_0)/\partial z_0 = \partial x_1(a_0)/\partial z_0 = -f'(z_0 - a_0) = \partial U^*(a_0)/\partial z_0,$$

since a_1, a_0 are independent. Moreover

$$\begin{aligned} U^* &\equiv E_{p^0}E_{a_0}U^*(a_0) = \sum p_k^0 [\alpha_k U^*(1) + \beta_k U^*(0)] \\ \partial U^*/\partial z_0 &= \sum p_k^0 \cdot [\alpha_k \cdot \partial U^*(1)/\partial z_0 + \beta_k \cdot \partial U^*(0)/\partial z_0] \\ &= -\sum p_k^0 [\alpha_k f'(z_0 - 1) + \beta_k f'(z_0)] = 0, \end{aligned}$$

when $z_0 = z_0^*$. Hence, by the above definition of f^A,

$$(6.12) \qquad z_0^* = f^A(p^0)$$

We can, in fact, consider z_1^* in (6.11) and z_0^* in (6.12) as the relevant parameters of the *a posteriori* and the *a priori* distributions, respectively: relevant, that is, to the particular problem characterized by the function f. Suppose that, instead of using the transform f^A of f, we would have proceeded as follows: after inferring a_0 from x_1 exactly by (6.2), and constructing the *a posteriori* probability distribution $p^1(a_0)$ of the a_k, compute the mean

$$\sum \alpha_k p_k^1(a_0) = \bar{\alpha}(a_0),$$

say. Insert this into the stochastic *non-adaptive* model of Section V, to replace α in (5.1), (5.13), obtaining

$$f^S(\bar{\alpha}(a_0)) = \bar{z}_1, \quad \text{say}.$$

This would be perhaps a '2-step procedure', in the (misleading) sense described in our introductory section. It is not clear what $\bar{z}_0$ would be. Perhaps it is obtained by inserting $\bar{z}_1$ into the utility expectation U computed on the basis of the *a priori* probability distribution p^0, and then maximizing U with respect to z_0? Or perhaps $\bar{z}_0$ is computed by assuing

$$\alpha = \bar{\alpha}^0(a_0) \equiv \sum \alpha_k p_k^0,$$

and assuming, as was done with z_1, that the model is a non-adaptive one?

Any such solution would be non-optimal except in special cases.

[*Added in* 1973. With adaptive programming implying the knowledge of prior probabilities it is, in fact, formally identical with stochastic programming. (See 'Proposition 1' in Koichi Miyasawa [9].) In terms more general than those of our text, let $a = (a_1, \dots, a_T)$ be a time sequence of random (and not necessarily additive and independent) shocks, with a belonging, for simplicity, to a countable set. In stochastic programming, the probability $p(a)$ is assumed known. In adaptive programming, there exists an unknown distribution of the sequence a, characterized by an unknown parameter α (possibly a vector, or a point in the space of all distributions of a). But a prior distribution $F(\alpha)$ is known and so is the conditional probability $q(a \mid \alpha)$ (say). Then

$$p(a) = \int q(a \mid \alpha) \, \mathrm{d}F(\alpha).$$

Hence the givens, (q, F), of an adaptive problem determine also the given, p, of the stochastic problem. Thus maximizing expected utility of a strategy, given (q, F), is the same as to maximize it, given p. (A strategy is defined as a sequence of decision functions, each associating the information available at a given time with the action to be taken at that time.)]

VII. CONCLUDING REMARK

In pure as distinct from applied research one usually does not know in advance what the applications will be. When estimating a planetary orbit Gauss [6] argued for maximizing what is today called the likelihood function of observations. Under his assumption that observation errors are normally distributed this implied the least squares method. Later, he justified the method differently (see Neyman [7]): by the need to minimize the expected loss due to estimation errors admitting that the loss function quadratic in these errors is merely the simplest of the infinitely many other loss functions that might be considered. Whatever the justification, he could not know what particular use will be made of his estimate. Perhaps it is not too far fetched to suggest that, when making more precise estimates of the position of the moon for the landing of a modern astronaut, one should maximize the now relevant criterion function (which may depend on the date and safety of landing, etc.) simultaneously with respect to the estimate *and* to the structural characteristics of the spaceship.

Some time ago, Sir Ronald Fisher [8] deplored the recent Russian "ideal that research in pure science can and should be geared to technological performance" and the American tendency "to confuse the process appropriate for drawing correct conclusions with those aimed at... saving money." Yet, I do not know whether an all-purpose scientific induction criterion has ever been constructed or even proved to exist. Perhaps we must share Gauss' latter and resigned view that any such criterion is arbitrary, apart from simplicity. Be it as it may. Problems of programming are always applied ones. And even though disagreement may exist as to the precise criterion function that the program has to maximize, we have seen that on formal grounds it will be, in general, inefficient to separate the estimation procedure from the determination of optimal rules of action.

NOTES

* Supported by the Office of Naval Research under task number NR-047-041, by the Electronic Systems Division, Systems Design Laboratory under contract number AF 19(628)-31, and by a grant from the Ford Foundation to Western Management Science Institute.

[1] Analogous results are obtained in a multi-variate quadratic case studied by Joseph and Tou [5].

BIBLIOGRAPHY

[1] Wald, Abraham, *Statistical Decision Functions*, 1950.
[2] Bellman, Richard, *Dynamic Programming*, 1957.
[3] Bellman, Richard, *Adaptive Control Processes*, 1961.
[4] Fisher, Walter D., 'Estimation in the Linear Decision Model', *International Economic Review*, **3**, No. 1 (January 1962), 1–29.
[5] Joseph, Peter D. and Tou, Julius T., 'On Linear Control Theory', *Applications and Industry*, publ. by American Institute of Electrical Engineers, September 1961.
[6] Gauss, Carl Friedrich, *Aus der Theorie der Bewegung der Himmelskoerper* (1809), 2. Buch, 3. Abschnitt, Sec. 176–179. Translation from Latin in selected *Abhandlungen zur Methode der kleinsten Quadrate* (A. Boersch and P. Simon, eds.), Berlin 1887, pp. 99–104.
[7] Neyman, Jerzy, 'Note on an Article by Sir Ronald Fisher', *Journal Royal Stat. Soc.* **B18** (1956), 288–294. Neyman quotes from Gauss' *Theorie der ... Combination der Beobachtungen* (1821), Sec. 6, also included in the *Abhandlungen ...*, (see preceding footnote), pp. 5–6.
[8] Fisher, Sir Ronald, 'Statistical Methods and Scientific Induction', *Journal Royal Stat. Soc.* **B 17** (1955), 69–78.
[9] Miyasawa, Koichi, 'Information Structures in Stochastic Programming Problems', *Management Science* **14** (1968) 5, esp. p. 276.

12

AN EXPERIMENTAL STUDY OF SOME STOCHASTIC MODELS FOR WAGERS*

(1963)

Co-authors: G. M. BECKER and M. H. DEGROOT

In this paper we report the results of an experiment designed to test the appropriateness of certain models for choices among wagers. These models and the test procedure to be used have previously been described in this journal in some detail (Becker *et al.*, 1963), but for convenience we will briefly restate them here. The reader should, however, refer to Becker *et al.* (1963) for precise statements of the basic concepts of rewards, wagers, offered sets, and stochastic models for wagers, and for proofs of theorems.

Two particular models of choice among wagers will be studied here. For easier explanation, we shall briefly recall the two corresponding models of choice among objects that are not necessarily wagers. Let all the objects used in a series of experiments belong to a finite set S of n objects; these can therefore be thought of as numbered from 1 to n. The probability that object i will be chosen from the subset M of S, offered in a given trial, is denoted by $i(M)$.

In the *strict utility (or Luce) model*, this probability $i(M)$ is assumed to be proportional to a positive constant characterizing the object i and called its *strict utility* u_i, fixed for a given person.

In the *random utility model*, on the other hand, the choice of a particular object i from an offered subset M of S is thought to depend on the way in which the person has ranked, at the time of making the choice, all objects in S. Each ranking (permutation of S) is assumed to have a probability, fixed for a given peson. That is, the set $S=(1,\ldots, n)$ of objects is associated with a vector $(U_1,\ldots, U_n)$ of random utilities, whose joint probability distribution is such that, for example, $Pr(U_{i_1} > U_{i_2} > \ldots > U_{in})$ is the probability that the elements $i_1, i_2,\ldots, i_n$ of S are ranked in that order.[1] The object chosen is the one ranked highest. Hence $i(M)=Pr(U_i \geqslant U_j$, all j in $M)$.

In applying these two models to the special case when the choice is among wagers, we exploit the additional hypothesis that such choice depends on the 'expected utility' of the wager, a concept that must be defined in a different way in each of the two models. We shall assume that all of the rewards used in the experiment form a finite set. We shall now denote this set of all rewards used (not the set of all wagers used) by $S=(1,\ldots, n)$. Any wager p can then be represented as an n-dimensional vector $\mathbf{p}=(p_1,\ldots, p_n)$, where p_i is the probability of receiving reward i, for $i=1,\ldots, n$. For any offered set M (i.e., any finite set of wagers) and any wager $\mathbf{p}\in M$, $\mathbf{p}(M)$ is the probability that a subject will choose $\mathbf{p}$ from M.

By u_i and U_i $(i=1,\ldots, n)$ we denote, as before, the strict and the random utility of the reward i. This yields two alternative definitions of expected utility of a wager $\mathbf{p}$ in a stochastic model: viz., the weighted averages $\sum_{i-1} p_i u_i$ and $\sum_{i-1} p_i U_i$.

In the *strict utility* (*or Luce*) *model for wagers*, the probability $\mathbf{p}(M)$ of choosing wager $\mathbf{p}$ from an offered subset M is proportional to that wager's 'strict utility', a quantity that is the greater, the greater $\sum p_i u_i$. In the *random utility model for wagers* the probability $\mathbf{p}(M)$ is equal to the probability that $\mathbf{p}$ is ranked higher than other wagers in M; the wagers being ranked according to their 'random utilities', $\sum p_i U_i$. Let us state this more precisely.

A stochastic model for wagers is said to be a *strict utility* (*or Luce*) *model for wagers* if there exist positive constants $u_1,\ldots, u_n$, and a positive, strictly increasing function h, defined for all real numbers r in some interval containing all the values $u_1,\ldots, u_n$, such that

$$\text{(1)} \qquad \mathbf{p}(M) = \frac{h\left(\sum_{i=1}^{n} p_i u_i\right)}{\sum_{q\in M} h\left(\sum_{i=1}^{n} q_i u_i\right)}$$

for every M and every $\mathbf{p}\in M$.

A model is a *random utility model for wagers* if there exists a random vector $(U_1,\ldots, U_n)$ such that

$$\text{(2)} \qquad \mathbf{p}(M) = Pr\left[\sum_{i=1}^{n} p_i U_i \geqslant \sum_{i=1}^{n} q_i U_i \quad \text{for all} \quad \mathbf{q}\in M\right]$$

for every M and every $\mathbf{p}\in M$.

Let M^* be an offered set containing the $m+1$ distinct wagers

$$\text{(3)} \qquad \mathbf{p}^j = (p_1^j,\ldots, p_n^j), j = 1,\ldots, m+1,$$

where

$$(4) \qquad p_i^{m+1} = \frac{1}{m} \sum_{j=1}^{m} p_i^j, \; i = 1, \ldots, n;$$

that is, $\mathbf{p}^{m+1}$ is the average of the other m wagers in M^*. Let $p = \mathbf{p}^{m+1}$ (M^*). It has been shown (Becker *et al.*, 1963) that under any strict utility model for wagers and any values of $u_1, \ldots, u_n$, $p \leqslant 1/(m+1)$ if h is a convex function and $p \geqslant (1/(m+1)$ if h is a concave function. In particular, $p = 1/(m+1)$ if h is a linear function. Furthermore, it was shown (Becker *et al.*, 1963) that under any random utility model for wagers, $p = 0$.

Suppose that it is possible to observe a subject's choices from each of several distinct offered sets, each having the form of M^* (i.e., each containing one wager that is the average of the others). The above remarks indicate how one might test (1) the hypothesis that the appropriate stochastic model describing the subject's choices is a strict utility model for wagers with a linear function h against a class of alternatives that includes the strict utility models with a strictly convex or concave function h; or (2) the hypothesis that the appropriate stochastic model is a random utility model for wagers.

I. EXPERIMENT

Let (w_i, x_i, y_i, z_i), $i = 1, \ldots, 25$, denote 25 distinct quadruples of monetary rewards, ordered so that for each value of i, $w_i < x_i < y_i < z_i$. From each of the quadruples (w_i, x_i, y_i, z_i), $i = 1 \ldots, 25$, an offered set M_i^* was constructed as follows. Let $\mathbf{A}_i$ be the wager that yields the rewards w_i and z_i, each with probability $\frac{1}{2}$. Let $\mathbf{B}_i$ be the wager that yields the rewards x_i and y_i, each with probability $\frac{1}{2}$. Let $\mathbf{C}_i$ be the wager that yields each of the rewards w_i, x_i, y_i and z_i, with probability $\frac{1}{4}$. Then, for $i = 1, \ldots, 25$, the wager $\mathbf{C}_i$ is the average of the wagers $\mathbf{A}_i$ and $\mathbf{B}_i$, in the sense of the preceding section, and the offered set M_i^* containing the three wagers $\mathbf{A}_i$, $\mathbf{B}_i$, and $\mathbf{C}_i$ is of the same form as the offered set M^* described above (with $m = 2$).

In Table I the actual rewards used in the experiment are shown. Thus, e.g., wager $\mathbf{A}_1$ yields the reward 3 or 89, each with probability $\frac{1}{2}$; $\mathbf{B}_1$ yields the rewards 31 or 65, each with probability $\frac{1}{2}$; and $\mathbf{C}_1$ yields the rewards 3, 31, 65, or 89, each with probability $\frac{1}{4}$.[2]

Subjects were 62 students registered in a course in introductory psychology. Students in the course were required to serve six hours as experi-

TABLE I
Rewards and offered sets in the experiment

i	A_i		B_i	
1	3	89	31	65
2	0	72	17	51
3	1	45	13	37
4	10	62	20	54
5	60	88	72	78
6	20	56	30	54
7	2	44	11	33
8	2	80	17	63
9	22	78	35	63
10	3	87	29	57
11	29	61	41	55
12	4	45	18	42
13	8	50	19	35
14	16	84	18	72
15	6	90	21	73
16	14	88	53	57
17	23	55	39	49
18	21	93	27	73
19	4	62	24	36
20	6	76	12	72
21	2	98	26	80
22	3	71	33	37
23	16	42	24	38
24	2	32	10	28
25	0	36	7	25

mental subjects or else to write a term paper. Each student who participated in our experiment received one hour credit toward fulfilling this requirement.

Each subject received a test booklet containing the 25 offered sets M_i^*, $i=1,\ldots, 25$, as well as 100 other offered sets designed for another purpose, together with instructions.

In 31 of the test booklets, the instructions informed the subject that the rewards represented dollars, and the subjects were encouraged to win as much money as possible. These subjects (the Score group) did not expect to be actually rewarded with the amount they won. The other 31 subjects (the Pay group) were informed that the rewards represented pennies and that they would actually be paid as much as they won from some of the wagers that they chose. The subjects were divided into the two groups at random.

Each reward in a wager was associated with the drawing of a card from a deck containing four cards labelled ZEJ, ZOJ, XEH, and XIH. In each offered set M_i^*, the wagers $\mathbf{A}_i$ $\mathbf{B}_i$, and $\mathbf{C}_i$ (although not identified as such to the subjects) appeared in a random order. Thus, for example, the offered set M_1^* appeared in the printed test booklet as follows:

ZEJ	3	31	3
ZOJ	89	65	31
XEH	3	31	65
XIH	89	65	89

The subject was asked to choose one of the three columns. He would then receive the reward appearing in the row corresponding to the card that would be drawn from the deck.

II. RESULTS AND ANALYSIS

As noted above, the statistic of interest is, for each subject, the number of times that he chose the wager $\mathbf{C}_i$ from the 25 offered sets M_i^*, $i=1, \ldots, 25$. Table 2 gives the distribution of subjects according to the number of times the 'average wager' $\mathbf{C}_i$ was chosen. Thus, for example, nine of the subjects in the Score group chose the wager C_i from exactly seven of the 25 offered sets.

A chi-square test did not reveal any significant difference between the distributions of the Pay and Score groups, and hence we studied only the last column of Table II, which gives the distribution of all subjects participating in the experiment.

One striking result to be noted immediately is that 60 of the 62 subjects chose the 'average wager' $\mathbf{C}_i$ at least once. Thus, the random utility model for wagers must be rejected for these 60 subjects.

Now suppose that the strict utility model for wagers is appropriate for some subject. If h is a linear function, then the distribution of the number N of times the 'average wager' is chosen by the subject is binomial with

TABLE II

Distribution of subjects according to the number of times C_t was chosen from the 25 offered sets

Number of choices of C_t	Pay group	Score group	All subjects
0	2	0	2
1	1	1	2
2	1	3	4
3	0	3	3
4	4	3	7
5	3	2	5
6	1	1	2
7	2	9	11
8	3	4	7
9	2	0	2
10	6	2	8
11	2	0	2
12	1	0	1
13	1	1	2
14	0	0	0
15	1	0	1
16	0	0	0
17	0	1	1
18	0	0	0
19	1	1	2
20 or more	0	0	0
Total	31	31	62

parameter $p=\frac{1}{3}$. Using a 2-tailed test of level of significance $\alpha=.088$ (a natural significance level resulting from the discreteness of the binomial distribution), the hypothesis that h is linear (i.e., that $p=\frac{1}{3}$) should be rejected if $N\leqslant 4$ or $N\geqslant 13$. It is readily found from Table II that performing this test on each of the 62 subjects leads to the rejection of the hypothesis for 24 of the subjects.

Suppose that for a given subject, after rejecting the hypothesis that the stochastic model is a strict utility model with linear h, it was desired to classify the stochastic model determining the subject's choices as either a Luce model with a strictly convex function h or a Luce model with a strictly concave function h. It follows from the remarks made earlier that a reasonable procedure would be to decide that h is strictly convex if $N\leqslant 4$ and that h is strictly concave if $N\geqslant 13$. From Table II it is seen that of the

24 subjects for whom the hypothesis that h is linear is rejected, 18 would be classified as having a strictly convex h and 6 as having a strictly concave h.

If we consider the 62 subjects as forming a random sample from some population, it is possible, by a technique described in Becker *et al.* (1963, p. 55), to obtain a confidence interval for the proportion of the population for whom the Luce model with linear h is not appropriate. The construction of a confidence interval with confidence coefficient .99, based on the observation that this model was rejected for 24 of the 62 subjects in the sample, leads to the statement that for at least 18 per cent of the population the Luce model with linear h is inappropriate.

Thus, in the experiment described above, neither the random utility model for wagers nor the strict utility model for wagers with linear h is adequate for describing the chice behavior of a large proportion of the population under study.

NOTES

* The work described in this paper was sponsored by the Western Management Science Institute, University of California at Los Angeles, under grants from the General Electric Company and its Behavioral Research Service, the Ford Foundation, and a contract with the Office of Naval Research, Nonr 233(75).

[1] It can be proved that $Pr(U_i \geqslant U_j) = 0$ for all $i \neq j$. In this sense, the random utility model excludes ties. See Equation (2), Becker *et al.* (1963), and Block and Marschak (1960).

[2] The expected monetary rewards are larger for A_i than B_i in twelve cases, and smaller in thirteen cases. The standard deviations of monetary rewards are $(z_i - w_i)/2$ and $(y_i - x_i)/2$, for every A_i and B_i, respectively, and the former is larger than the latter. In this sense, A_i is more 'risky' than B_i, for every i, as pointed out by a referee.

BIBLIOGRAPHY

Becker, H. M., DeGroot, M. H., and Marschak, J., 'Stochastic Models of Choice Behavior', 1963, *Selected Essays*, 10.

Block, H. D. and Marschak, J., 'Random Orderings and Stochastic Theories of Response', 1960, *Selected Essays*, 7.

THE PAYOFF-RELEVANT DESCRIPTION OF STATES AND ACTS*

(1963)

Typically, a problem in information economics consists of choosing simultaneously an optimal pair: (1) an information channel producing messages, and (2) a decision rule associating each message with an act. The givens of the problem are: the probability distribution on the states of the world, and the utility yielded by each combination of act and state, taking account of message costs.

Whatever the costs, probabilities, and utilities, a preliminary step consists in formulating a given information problem with just as much detail as neccessary. In particular, two descriptions of possible states and acts, one detailed and one less detailed, may be such as to lead to exactly the same physical outcomes or the same amounts of utility; yet it can be assumed that the more detailed description should be avoided. The situation is similar to that of optimal production programs: the set of possible programs is reduced to an efficient subset on the basis of the sole proposition that 'large inputs are bad, large outputs are good', regardless of a specific objective function on the set of programs.

Accordingly, this Note will deal with the reduction of descriptions of states and acts to relevant ones.[1] Another paper[2] will develop the concepts used in the first paragraph.

I. DESCRIPTIONS OF STATES AND ACTS

Consider the set $\{Z\}$ consisting of all possible partitions $Z=\{z\}$, $Z'=$ $=\{z'\},\ldots$ of a fundamental set of *states*, $X=\{x\}$. Each partition Z is called a set of (mutually exclusive and exhaustive) *state descriptions*.

Similarly, consider the set $\{C\}$ consisting of all partitions $C=\{c\}$, $C'=\{c'\},\ldots$ of a fundamental set of *acts*, $A=\{a\}$. Each partition C is called a set of (mutually exclusive and exhaustive) *act descriptions*.

A binary relation '$\leqslant$' is defined on $\{Z\}$ and, similarly, on $\{C\}$ as follows:

(1) DEFINITION: $Z \leqslant Z'$ (*Z is finer than* Z'; or equivalently, Z' *is coarser than* Z) *if*, for every z in Z, there is a z' in Z' with $z \subseteq z'$.

The relation '$\leqslant$' induces a strict partial ordering on $\{Z\}$ and, similarly on $\{C\}$. Moreover, $\{Z\}$ is a lattice possessing a (unique) finest element, $\{(x)\}$, the finest partition of X, and a (unique) coarsest element (X), the coarsest partition of X. Similarly $\{C\}$ is a lattice, with $\{(a)\}$ and (A) as its (unique) finest and coarsest elements.[3]

II. OUTCOME CONDITION

Define a function from $X \times A$ to the set of *outcomes* $O = \{o_{xa}\}$; that is, to each pair (x, a) there corresponds one element o_{xa} in O. For a given pair Z in $\{Z\}$, C in $\{C\}$, define an *outcome function* from $Z \times C$ to the set of all subsets of O; thus

$$w_{ZC}(z, c) \subseteq O\,; \quad z \text{ in } Z,\, c \text{ in } C\,.$$

To simplify notation we shall consistently denote by $z, z' \ldots$ (possibly with a subscript) an element of $Z, Z', \ldots$, respectively; and similarly for $c, c', \ldots$ and $C, C', \ldots$. This will often permit us to drop the subscripts under w, as its domain $Z \times C$ is indicated unambiguously by the lower case letters in the argument. Moreover, we shall sometimes write x, a instead of $(x), (a)$; and X, A instead of $\{(x)\}, \{(a)\}$ without danger of ambiguity.

A set W of outcome functions w_{ZC}(all Z in $\{Z\}$, all C in $\{C\}$) is called an *outcome condition* if the following consistency requirement is satisfied:

$$(2) \qquad w_{ZC}(z, c) = \bigcup_{x \text{ in } z} \bigcup_{a \text{ in } c} (o_{xa})\,, \quad \text{all } z \text{ in } Z,\, c \text{ in } C\,.$$

III. SUFFICIENTLY FINE DESCRIPTION SETS

DEFINITION: A *pair of sets* (Z, C) *is sufficiently fine* (*s.f.*) *for* W if every value of every outcome function in W consists of a single element of O.

By (2) this means that

$$(3) \qquad w(z, c) = (o_{xa})\,, \quad \text{all } x \text{ in } z,\, a \text{ in } c,\, z \text{ in } Z,\, c \text{ in } C\,.$$

DEFINITION: A set Z is *s.f.* for W if the pair (Z, A) is *s.f.* for W.

By (3) this means that

$$(4.1) \qquad w(z, a) = (o_{xa})\,, \quad \text{all } x \text{ in } z,\, a \text{ in } A,\, z \text{ in } Z\,.$$

Similarly,

DEFINITION: A set C is *s.f.* for W if

(4.2) $\quad w(x, c) = (o_{xa})$, all a in c, x in X, c in C.

This language is justified by

THEOREM I: *If Z (or, respectively, C) is s.f., and $Z' \leqslant Z$ (or, respectively, $C' \leqslant C$) then Z' (C') is s.f.*

Proof. By (1), (2).

We also have

THEOREM II: *(Z, C) is s.f. for W if and only if Z and C are s.f. for W.*

Proof of sufficiency. From (4.1), (4.2) using (2). *Proof of necessity.* In (3) replace c, C, z, Z by a, A, x, X.

IV. EQUIVALENT STATES (ACTS) AND SUFFICIENTLY COARSE DESCRIPTION SETS

DEFINITION: z_1, z_2, in Z are *W-equivalent given C* if

(5.1) $\quad w(z_1, c) = w(z_2, c)$, all c in C.

(It is easily seen that W-equivalence is a genuine equivalence relation.)

DEFINITION: c_1, c_2 in C are *W-equivalent given X if*

(5.2) $\quad w(z, c_1 = w(z, c_2)$, all z in Z.

DEFINITION: A *pair of sets (Z, C) is sufficiently coarse (s.c.) for W* if no distinct elements of Z are W-equivalent given C; and no distinct elements of C are W-equivalent given Z.

That is (using (5.1), (5.2)), for all z_1, z_2 in Z and all c_1, c_2 in C

(6.1) $\quad w(z_1, c) = w(z_2, c)$ for all c in C implies $z_1 = z_2$;

and

(6.2) $\quad w(z, c_1) = w(z, c_2)$ for all z in Z implies $c_1 = c_2$.

DEFINITION: A *set Z is sufficiently coarse for W* if no distinct elements of Z are W-equivalent given A; that is (using (6.1)), for all z_1, z_2 in Z,

$$(7.1) \qquad w(z_1, a) = w(z_2, a), \quad \text{all } a \text{ in } A, \text{implies } z_1 = z_2 .$$

Similarly,

DEFINITION: A *set C is sufficiently coarse for W* if, for all c_1, c_2 in C,

$$(7.2) \qquad w(x, c_1) = w(x, c_2), \text{ all } x \text{ in } X, \text{implies } c_1 = c_2 .$$

This language is justified by

THEOREM III: *If the pair of sets* (*Z*, *C*) *is s.c. for W then Z and C are s.c. for W* (but the converse is not true: see Note below).

Proof. Suppose (Z, C) is s.c. for W. To prove that Z is s.c. let $z_1 \neq z_2$ be two elements of Z. Then by (2), (6.1),

$$\bigcup_{a \text{ in } c_0} \bigcup_{x \text{ in } z_1} (o_{xa}) \neq \bigcup_{a \text{ in } c_0} \bigcup_{x \text{ in } z_0} (o_{xa}) \quad \text{for some } c_0 \text{ in } C ;$$
$$\bigcup_{a \text{ in } c_0} w(z_1, a) \neq \bigcup_{a \text{ in } c_0} w(z_2, a) \quad \text{for some } c_0 \text{ in } C ;$$
$$w(z_1, a_0) \neq w(z_2, a_0) \quad \text{for some } a_0 \text{ in } A ;$$

hence $z_1 \neq z_2$ implies $w(z_1, a_0) \neq w(z_2, a_0)$ for some a_0 in A; and this is equivalent to (7.1). One proves similarly (using (2), (6.2), (7.2)) that C is s.c. for W.

Note. Theorem III is analogous to the necessity part of Theorem II; but, unlike Theorem II, no sufficiency part holds. A counter-example is instructive as an exercise. Let O be the set of integers and consider the following matrix $[o_{xa}]$:

	x_1	x_2	x_3	x_4
a_1	1	2	1	3
a_2	3	4	2	4

Let $c = (a_1, a_2)$, $z_1 = (x_1, x_2)$, $z_2 = (x_3, x_4)$ so that $z_1 \neq z_2$. Then the pair (Z, C) is not sufficiently coarse, for the outcome function $w(z, c)$ is as follows:

$w(z, c)$

	z_1	z_2
c	(1, 2, 3, 4)	(1, 2, 3, 4)

Yet both Z and C are sufficiently coarse, for the outcome functions $w(z, a)$ and $w(x, c)$ are represented by the following two matrices:

$w(z, a)$	z_1	z_2
a_1	(1,2)	(1,3)
a_2	(3,4)	(2,4)

$w(x, c)$	x_1	x_2	x_3	x_4
c	(1,3)	(2.4)	(1,2)	(3,4)

V. UNIQUENESS AND EXISTENCE OF AN OUTCOME-RELEVANT PAIR (Z, C)

DEFINITION: *A pair (Z, C) is called outcome-relevant for W (or, briefly, W-relevant) if (Z, C) is both sufficiently fine and sufficiently coarse for W.*

THEOREM IV: *There is one and only one W-relevant pair.*

Proof of uniqueness. Suppose (Z, C) and (Z', C') are two W-relevant pairs. Then, by Theorems II and III, Z, C, Z', C' are sufficiently fine and sufficiently coarse. We shall show that $Z = Z'$ which means that

(8) $\quad$ for any z in Z, z' in Z', either $z \cap z' = \phi$ or $z = z'$.

Let $z \cap z' \neq \phi$. Then, since Z, Z' are s.f. for W, we have by (4.1),

(9) $\quad w(z, a) = (o_{xa}) = w(z', a), \quad$ all x in $z \cap z'$, all a in A.

Further, suppose x_0 is in z and hence by (4.1), (9),

(10) $\quad (o_{x_0 a}) = w(z, a) = w(z', a), \quad$ all a in A;

it follows that x_0 is in z'. For, let x_0 in z'_0 in Z'; then by (4.1), (10)

$$(o_{x_0 a}) = w(z'_0, a) = w(z', a), \quad \text{all } a \text{ in } A;$$

and, since Z is sufficiently coarse for W, $z'_0 = z_0$ by (7.1). Thus x_0 in z implies x_0 in z'. By symmetry of reasoning, x_0 in z' implies x_0 in z. Hence $z = z'$, proving (8). Hence $Z = Z'$. By similar argument, $C = C'$.

Proof of existence. Let z^W be a class of all x that are w-equivalent, given A. Accordingly, define $Z^W = \{z^W\}$, a partition of X, as follows:

(11.1) $\quad Z^W = \{z^W : x_1, x_2 \text{ in } z^W \quad \text{if and only if} \quad o_{x_1 a} = o_{x_2 a}, \quad \text{all } a \text{ in } A\}$.

Define similarly C^W, a partition of A:

$$(11.2)\quad C^W = \{c^W : a_1, a_2 \text{ in } c^W \quad \text{if and only if} \quad o_{xa_1} = o_{xa_2}, \quad \text{all } x \text{ in } X\}.$$

Clearly Z^W is sufficiently fine, with

$$(12)\quad w(z^W, a) = (o_{xa}), \quad \text{all } a \text{ in } A, \text{ all } z^W \text{ in } Z^W.$$

Similarly with C^W. Hence (Z^W, C^W) is sufficiently fine. Now, to show that (Z^W, C^W) is sufficiently coarse, suppose

$$(13.1)\quad w(z_1^W, c^W) = w(z_2^W, c^W), \quad \text{all } c^W \text{ in } C^W,$$

and suppose

$$(13.2)\quad w(z^W, c_1^W) = w(z^W, c_2^W), \quad \text{all } z^W \text{ in } Z^W;$$

and let x_1 in z_1^W, x_2 in z_2^W; then by (12) and (13.1)

$$(o_{x_1a}) = w(z_1^W, c^W) = w(z_2^W, c^W) = (o_{x_2a}), \quad \text{all } a \text{ in } A.$$

Hence by the definition of z^W in (11.1), z_2^W and z_1^W are identical equivalence sets. Thus (13.1) implies $z_1^W = z_2^W$. Similarly, (13.2) implies $c_1^W = c_2^W$. Hence (Z, C) is sufficiently coarse. Hence (Z^W, C^W) is W-relevant.

COROLLARY: *The only W-relevant pair is* (Z^W, C^W) *defined in* (11.1), ((11.2). *Accordingly,* Z^W *and* C^W *can be called the unique outcome-relevant description sets.*

VI. PAYOFF-RELEVANT DESCRIPTION SETS

A *utility function* $u(.)$ maps O into the set R of real numbers: $u(o)$ is the utility of an outcome o. Hence, with each $Z \times C$ and each outcome condition W is associated a subset of R:

$$u[w_{ZC}(z, c)] \equiv v_{ZC}(z, c) \subseteq R.$$

The function v_{ZC} just defined, a composition of w_{ZC} and u, is called the *payoff function*. A consistent set V of payoff functions is defined analogously to W in (2): V consists of all functions v_{ZC} such that

$$v_{ZC}(z, c) = \bigcup_{x \text{ in } z} \bigcup_{a \text{ in } c} (u(o_{xa})).$$

Again, we can often omit the domain index ZC without ambiguity. The concepts of sufficiently fine and coarse sets or pairs of sets, defined previously for W can be redefined for V in analogous fashion. In addition, $v(z, c)$ being, in general, a subset of real numbers, *a domination* relation between real-valued functions can be exploited: whenever, for a c_0 in C and all z in Z, there exists a c_1 in C such that (1) $v(z, c_0) \neq v(z, c_1)$, and (2) no element of $v(z, c_0)$ is larger than any element of $v(z, c_1)$, we say that c_0 is inadmissible. By eliminating all inadmissible elements from each set C, we obtain a smaller set of act descriptions, and the set $\{C\}$ of all such sets is redefined correspondingly.

A *payoff-relevant pair* (Z^V, C^V) defined analogously to (Z^W, C^W) exists and is unique by the same reasoning as in the proof of Theorem V. We give without proof

THEOREM V: *For any W, v and $u(.)$,*

(1) *if (Z, C) is sufficiently fine for W it is s.f. for V; but not conversely;*
(2) *if (Z, C) is sufficiently coarse for V it is s.c. for W; but not conversely;*
(3) $Z^W \leqslant Z^V$; $C^W \leqslant C^V$.

VII. SUMMARY

The domain $Z \times C$ of a payoff function is the product of a set of state descriptions and a set of act descriptions; the range of a payoff function is the power set of the set of real numbers (utilities). The domain is called payoff-relevant if it is both sufficiently fine (i.e., the payoff function is real valued everywhere) and sufficiently coarse (i.e., the payoff function is not constant for any fixed element of Z or of C). Given a consistent set V of payoff functions, there is one and only one payoff-relevant domain, $Z^V \times C^V$.

This result is derived from a more general one. An outcome function maps $Z \times C$ into the power set of a set O of ('physical') outcomes. An outcome-elevant domain is defined appropriately. Given a consistent set W of outcome functions there is one and only one outcome-relevant domain, $Z^W \times C^W$.

NOTES

* Supported by the Office of Naval Research under task number NR-047-041 and the Western Management Science Institute under its grant from the Ford Foundation.
[1] Thanks are due to J. MacQueen and T. Ferguson who have helped to outline some of the questions, and to Ray Radner and Zivia Wurtele who helped to outline some of the proofs.

[2] J. Marschak [1963].

[3] See Birkhoff [1948], especially p. 2, Example 6; p. 17, Example 4; p. 107, Theorem 8. The relation 'finer than' is closely related to Savage's [1954] relation 'extension of'; the latter is not anti-symmetric and induces a partial *pre*-ordering on X.

BIBLIOGRAPHY

[1] Birkhoff, G., *Lattice Theory* (2nd ed.), American Mathematical Society, New York, (Colloquium Publications, Vol. 25), 1948.
[2] Marschak, J., 'Problems in Information Economics'.(1963), *Selected Essays*, 25.
[3] Savage, L. J., *The Foundations of Statistics*, Wiley and Sons, New York, 1954. Revised, Dover, 1972.

14

PROBABILITIES OF CHOICES AMONG VERY SIMILAR OBJECTS: AN EXPERIMENT TO DECIDE BETWEEN TWO MODELS*

(1963)

Co-authors: G. M. Becker and M. H. DeGroot

The purpose of this paper is to report an experimental investigation of individual choice behavior in certain situations suggested by Debreu (1960) in his review of Luce's book (1959). Let T denote the set of all possible alternatives from among which a subject might be required to choose. For any finite subset S of T (we call S the 'offered set') and any alternative x in S, let $x(S)$ denote the probability that the subject, when choosing among the alternatives in S, will choose x. Thus $x(\{x, y\})$ is the probability that the subject will choose from the pair $\{x, y\}$ the alternative x rather than y. When $x(\{x, y\})=1$, or equivalently $y(\{x, y\})=0$, we say that x is absolutely preferred to y. The Luce model[1] as presented in his book (1959) states that if no element of T is absolutely preferred to another element of T, then every element x of T is associated with a positive number $v(x)$ (which we have called 'strict utility of x') such that, for every offered subset S of T,

$$x(S) = \frac{v(x)}{\sum_{y \in S} v(y)};$$

(that is, the elements of any offered set are chosen with probabilities proportional to their strict utilities).

We will assume throughout this paper that $x(\{x, y\})$ is neither 0 nor 1 for every pair x, y in T. Then it follows from the Luce model that for any alternatives x, y, z in T, $x(\{x, y, z\}) < x(\{x, y\})$. Debreu has criticized this property of the Luce model, contending that if the alternatives y and z are in some sense equivalent, then the addition of z to the set $\{x, y\}$ should not reduce the probability that x will be chosen. Indeed, the Luce model can lead to the result that although a person is more likely to choose coffee than to choose tea from a tray containing one cup of coffee and one cup of tea, he is more likely to choose tea than to choose coffee from a tray containing one cup of coffee and two cups of tea. Specifically, suppose that x is a cup of coffee and y and z are cups of tea. Suppose further that $y(\{y, z\})=\frac{1}{2}$, therefore $v(y):v(z)=1:1$; and that $x(\{x, y\})=\frac{3}{5}$, therefore $v(x):v(y)=3:2$. Then $v(x):v(y):v(z)=3:2:2$ and hence $x(\{x, y, z\})=\frac{3}{7}$. Thus $x(\{x, y\})>\frac{1}{2}$ but $x(\{x, y, z\})<\frac{1}{2}$. Debreu suggests that in a situation of this type $x(\{x, y\})$ and $x(\{x, y, z\})$ should be more nearly equal, if not precisely equal. If Debreu's criticism is valid then the use of the Luce model must be restricted to distinct, dissimilar alternatives. This, of course, raises the delicate question as to when two alternatives should be considered to be dissimilar. In the example given above, if the two cups containing tea were easily distinguishable should they be considered as dissimilar alternatives?

In experiments to be described here, the above problem was investigated in situations where the alternatives from among which a subject must choose were wagers yielding monetary rewards.

Let $E_1, E_2, \ldots, E_t$, $t \geqslant 2$, be mutually exclusive and exhaustive events. A *wager* **W** is a vector $\mathbf{W}=(W_1, \ldots, W_t)$ where each W_i, $i=1, \ldots, t$, is a real number representing an amount of money. The interpretation is that if a subject chooses the wager $\mathbf{W}=(W_1, \ldots, W_t)$ from some offered set, then he will be rewarded with the amount W_i if the event E_i occurs, $i=1, \ldots, t$.

When a set of alternatives is presented to a subject, the alternatives must be presented in some media and in some order. Each wager must also be displayed in some configuration, i.e., the events and rewards must be arranged in some spatial or temporal configuration. A person's reaction to a set of wagers may be influenced by such configurations. For example, if the list of available wagers is sufficiently long, the person may select a wager before examining all of the alternatives on the list. Similarly, if the wagers depend upon a large number of events (i.e., if t is large), the subject may pay attention to only a few of the events and ignore others. In the experiments to be described here, an effort was made to ensure that these influences would be absent.

Suppose that the events $E_1, \ldots, E_t$ are equiprobable (as is the case in the experiments to be described here). We then say that the wagers $\mathbf{W}=(W_1, \ldots, W_t)$ and $\mathbf{W}'=(W_1', \ldots, W_t')$ are *similar* if the rewards $(W_1', \ldots, W_t')$ are simply a permutation of the rewards $(W_1, \ldots, W_t)$. Thus, in particular, if $\mathbf{W}=\mathbf{W}'$ (i.e., $W_i'=W_i$, $i=1, \ldots, t$) then **W** and **W**$'$ are similar;

in this case we say **W** and **W**′ are similar and identical.

If the offered set of wagers from which a subject must choose is presented to him as a printed list it is possible that the list contains duplications. In other words, it is possible that a given wager appears more than once in the list. Accordingly, it is permissible to speak of an offered set containing the three alternatives **W**, **W**′, and **W** repeated again. In fact, offered sets of precisely this form are of interest in the present paper.

Let M be an offered set containing two dissimilar wagers, **A** and **B**, and let M' be an offered set containing the three wagers **A**, **B**, and **C**, where **B** and **C** are similar. In some of the experiments that were carried out, **C** was actually identical with **B**, and in others **B** and **C** were similar but not identical. In either case it is not unreasonable to interpret Debreu's comments as stating that $\mathbf{A}(M)=\mathbf{A}(M')$, whereas under the Luce model, $\mathbf{A}(M)>$ $>\mathbf{A}(M')$. (Recall that $\mathbf{A}(M)$ is the probability that **A** is chosen from M.)

Let $M_j=\{\mathbf{A}_j, \mathbf{B}_j\}$ and $M_j=\{\mathbf{A}_j, \mathbf{B}_j, \mathbf{C}_j\}$, $j=1,\ldots,n$, be n pairs of offered sets, each pair having the same form as the pair M and M' just described. (The wagers $\mathbf{A}_j$, $\mathbf{B}_j$ and $\mathbf{C}_j$ may, however, vary with j.)

It is known (see, e.g., the last two sections of Becker *et al.* [1963a]) that for a given subject, the hypotheses

$$H_0: \mathbf{A}_j(M_j)=\mathbf{A}_j(M'_j), j=1,\ldots,n,$$
$$H_1: \mathbf{A}_j(M_j)>\mathbf{A}_j(M'_j), j=1,\ldots,n,$$

can be tested as follows.

Let n^* denote the number of pairs, M_j and M'_j, such that $\mathbf{A}_j$ is chosen from either M_j or M'_j *but not from both*. Let D^* denote the number of these pairs such that $\mathbf{A}_j$ is chosen from M_j but not from M'_j. Then, for a given value of n^*, the probability distribution of D^* is binomial with parameter $p=\frac{1}{2}$ if H_0 is true, whereas larger values of D^* are more probable if H_1 is true. Thus, the usual 1-tailed test of the hypothesis that the binomial parameter $p=\frac{1}{2}$ is appropriate.

Furthermore, suppose that this test has been carried out, at level of significance α, on each subject in a random sample of N subjects drawn from some population of interest. (α is the probability of rejecting H_0 for a given subject when it is, in fact, true.) Let π denote the proportion of the population for whom H_0 is true, and suppose that it is desired to test the hypothesis $H'_0:\pi\geqslant 1-\delta$, where δ is some given number, $0<\delta<1$. If H'_0 is true, then Y, the number of subjects in the sample of N for whom H_0 was rejected, has a binomial distribution with parameter $p \leqslant \alpha + \delta - \delta\alpha$. Thus, H_0' can be tested by a 1-tailed binomial test based on Y or equivalently, an upper confidence limit for π can be computed from Y.

I. EXPERIMENTAL DESIGN[2]

Let the events E_1, E_2, E_3 and E_4 be the four possible outcomes when one card is drawn from a deck of four cards. Each of the four cards is labeled

TABLE I
Amounts used in the experiment

i	w_i	x_i	y_i	z_i
1	19	9	7	1
2	18	11	9	4
3	36	18	12	4
4	40	26	10	0
5	58	36	22	2
6	52	28	22	8
7	70	35	25	0
8	74	51	27	6
9	68	43	33	12
10	86	66	18	8
11	87	64	32	11
12	98	79	15	0
13	100	75	25	2
14	86	52	48	18
15	91	66	26	11
16	92	74	44	28
17	94	67	51	28
18	96	70	50	34
19	93	76	62	47
20	94	69	67	46
21	96	73	59	46
22	97	81	77	63
23	98	82	76	64
24	93	81	73	71
25	99	95	85	83

with a different nonsense syllable and the deck is shuffled, so it is reasonable to assume that the four events are considered to be equiprobable by each of the subjects.

TABLE II

Experimental data

Subject	Hypothesis pair 1			2			3			4		
	n^*	D^*	Sig. level	n^*	D^*	Sig. level	n^*	D^*	Sig. level	n^*	D^*	Sig. level
1 SB	10	5		14	9		11	7		13	7	
2 PF	8	1		10	2		6	1		7	2	
3 PF	3	2		5	5	.031	5	5	.031	2	2	
4 SB	4	2		8	3		10	5		7	4	
5 SF	2	1		1	1		3	3	.125	2	2	
6 PF	12	6		9	3		7	2		10	5	
7 SC	6	1		5	1		9	3		6	1	
8 PB	0	0		0	0		2	0		3	1	
9 SB	6	3		7	3		6	3		7	4	
10 SB	3	0		1	0		3	1		3	0	
11 SF	11	6		12	5		11	6		8	6	.145
12 PB	13	6		9	5		12	5		13	4	
13 SB	6	4		4	2		4	3		7	6	.008
14 SF	0	0		0	0		0	0		0	0	
15 PF	1	0		1	0		0	0		1	0	
16 PF	12	7		11	8	.113	19	15	.010	18	13	.048
17 PB	5	3		8	6	.145	10	4		7	2	
18 SF	14	6		8	6	.145	13	6		13	3	
19 SF	5	3		4	2		3	1		4	2	
20 SB	13	9	.133	11	10	.006	12	11	.003	10	8	.055
21 PF	10	3		9	4		9	5		8	3	
22 PB	9	5		12	5		11	5		14	8	
23 SB	3	1		3	2		6	4		6	3	
24 PF	11	4		12	7		12	5		11	2	
25 PB	0	0		0	0		0	0		0	0	
26 PB	6	3		9	5		8	3		8	3	
27 SB	8	7	.008	7	6	.062	10	8	.055	11	9	.033
28 SF	5	1		4	1		7	3		6	2	
29 PB	5	1		6	3		8	4		10	4	
30 PF	9	9	.002	5	4		4	3		10	9	.001
31 SF	9	0		8	3		5	2		10	1	
32 SF	10	5		7	4		10	6		10	6	
33 PF	4	0		6	0		8	0		6	0	
34 PB	1	0		0	0		1	0		1	0	
35 SB	0	0		0	0		0	0		0	0	
36 SF	10	5		14	6		9	6		12	8	
37 PB	9	5		6	3		6	3		11	6	
38 SB	11	6		10	5		7	3		11	5	
39 PB	11	1		12	4		12	3		16	3	

TABLE II

Experimental data (*Continued*)

	Hypothesis pair											
	1			2			3			4		
Subject	n^*	D^*	Sig. level	n^*	D^*	Sig. level	n^*	D^*	Sig. level	n^*	D^*	Sig. level
40 PF	8	4		10	5		11	5		9	4	
41 PF	17	5		13	7		18	12	.119	10	4	
42 PB	7	1		9	3		9	5		7	3	
43 PF	8	3		9	3		5	1		4	1	
44 SF	9	5		8	5		11	6		10	5	
45 SB	1	0		1	0		2	1		2	1	
46 SF	1	1		1	1		2	1		2	1	
47 SB	10	4		11	4		9	4		13	7	
48 PB	10	5		8	2		10	7		12	10	.019
49 PB	11	6		8	7	.035	12	20	.019	11	7	
50 PB	10	7		10	9	.011	11	11	.000	9	8	
51 SF	12	6		8	5		9	4		13	5	
52 PB	9	2		13	5		14	5		9	2	
53 SB	12	11	.003	11	9	.033	12	8		11	9	
54 SB	5	3		5	2		4	2		4	3	
55 SF	14	9		13	9	.133	15	11	.059	12	9	.073
56 PF	9	7	.090	13	11	.011	12	10	.019	13	9	.133
57 SF	0	0		0	0		1	0		1	0	
58 SF	8	3		8	5		6	4		10	4	
59 PB	8	4		8	5		5	3		5	2	
60 PF	12	7		13	9	.133	10	8	.055	9	6	
61 PB	5	3		6	4		7	5	—	5	3	
62 PF	5	3		8	2		6	1		7	4	

Note: The symbols P or S, and F or B, following the subject serial number indicate whether the subject belonged to the Pay or Score, and Fore or Back, groups. The significance levels are those for a 1-tailed binomial test. Only values less than .15 are listed.

The sets of wagers from among which the subjects must choose are constructed as follows. For each i, $i=1, 2, \ldots, 25$, let $S_i=\{w_i, x_i, y_i, z_i\}$ be four amounts of money such that $w_i>x_i>y_i>z_i$. Define the wagers $\mathbf{T}_i$, $\mathbf{U}_i$, and $\mathbf{V}_i$ to be $\mathbf{T}_i=(w_i, w_i, z_i, z_i)$, $\mathbf{U}_i=(x_i, x_i, y_i, y_i)$ and $\mathbf{V}_i=(y_i, y_i, x_i, x_i)$. In other words, in the wager $\mathbf{T}_i$ the reward is w_i if the event E_1 occurs, w_i if E_2 occurs, z_i if E_3 occurs, and z_i if E_4 occurs, and similarly for the wagers $\mathbf{U}_i$ and $\mathbf{V}_i$. Finally, define the offered sets L_i, L_i', L_i'', L_i'''

to be $L_i = \{\mathbf{T}_i, \mathbf{U}_i\}$, $L_i' = \{\mathbf{T}_i, \mathbf{U}_i, \mathbf{U}_i\}$, $L_i'' = \{\mathbf{T}_i, \mathbf{U}_i, \mathbf{V}_i\}$, and $L_i''' = \{\mathbf{T}_i, \mathbf{V}_i\}$. Thus L_i and L_i''' are binary sets (pairs), while L_i'' and L_i' are ternary sets (triples).

Thus, from each of the 25 sets S_i of monetary amounts, four different offered sets of wagers were constructed. Accordingly, each subject in the study chose one wager for each of 100 offered sets.

The monetary amounts used in the experiment are shown in Table I. The sets were presented in booklet form, approximately eight offered sets on each page. The order of presentation was essentially random, except that all of the binary offered sets, L_i and L_i''', $i = 1, \ldots, 25$, were presented either before or after the entire group of ternary offered sets L_i' and L_i'', $i = 1, \ldots, 25$. Furthermore, care was taken to try to eliminate the possibility of the relative position of the wagers having an influence on the subjects' choices.

II. SUBJECTS AND EXPERIMENTAL GROUPS

Sixty-two students registered in an introductory psychology course volunteered as subjects for this experiment. Each student received one hour credit toward completion of a course requirement of six hours spent as an experimental subject. Students who did not complete this requirement were required to write a term paper.

Half of the subjects were told that they would be paid whatever they won from some of the wagers that they chose (the Pay group). To these subjects, the amounts appearing in the wagers were described as pennies. The other subjects (the Score group) were told that they would not be paid, but were instructed to win as much money as they could. The payoffs for the Score group were described as dollars. The same wagers were presented to both groups with only the instructions in the first part of the booklet varying. Also, half of the subjects chose from the 50 ternary offered sets first and then chose from the 50 binary offered sets (the Fore group). The other half of the subjects (the Back group) made their choices in the reverse order.

The subjects were randomly assigned to one of the four groups (Pay or Score, Fore or Back) according to the test booklet they received at the beginning of the session. All subjects were tested in a single group session that lasted approximately 45 minutes.

III. RESULTS

Referring to the definitions of the offered sets L_j, L'_j, L''_j and L'''_j, $j=1,\ldots,$ 25, it is seen that there are several possible pairs that could be chosen to play the role of the offered sets M_j and M' in the hypotheses H_0 and H_1 presented earlier. Thus, it would be reasonable to let (1) $M_j=L_j$ and $M'_j=L'_j$, or (2) $M_j=L_j$ and $M'_j=L''_j$, or (3) $M_j=L'''_j$ and $M'_j=L''_j$, or (4) $M_j=L'''_j$ and $M'_j=L'_j$. For any one of these definitions (1), (2), (3), or (4), we could carry out the test of the hypotheses H_0 and H_1 described above. Ideally, of course, it would be best to develop one composite test that would subsume all of these individual pairings, but it did not seem worthwhile to investigate such a test at the present stage of study.

The observed values of n^* and D^* for each of the subjects and each of the above four pairs of hypotheses are given in Table II. A simple tabulation from Table II will give, for any level of significance $\alpha \leqslant .15$, and any one of the four pairs of hypotheses, the number of subjects for whom H_0 would be rejected. This tabulation is given in Table III. Since there did not appear to be any significant difference between the Pay and Score, and Fore and Back groups, only the totals for all subjects are given.

Let us now regard the 62 experimental subjects as a random sample from some population of interest, and let π be the proportion of this

TABLE III

Number of the 62 subjects for whom H_0 is rejected

	Hypothesis pair			
	1	2	3	4
$\alpha = .15$	5	12	11	11
$\alpha = .05$	3	6	6	7

population for whom Debreu's comments are valid; i.e., π is the proportion of the population for whom H_0 is true. As described earlier, it is possible to use any single entry in Table III to obtain an upper confidence limit for π. A simple computation yields the following results, for confidence coefficient .90. The upper confidence limit for π corresponding to the observed result for $\alpha=.05$ and hypothesis pair 4 is .968. All other entries in Table III yield an upper limit 1 for π.

Thus, the observed data provide no reason to doubt that Debreu's comments are valid for most of the population.

NOTES

* The work described in this paper was supported by the Western Management Science Institute, University of California at Los Angeles, under its grant from the Ford Foundation, a grant from the General Electric Company, and a contract with the Office of Naval Research, Task Nonr 233(75). The statistical computations were carried out at the Western Data Processing Center, University of California at Los Angeles.

1 The Luce-Debreu controversy submitted here to an empirical test was briefly considered by the authors of the present article in the section 'The Sign Test' of their theoretical article (Becker *et al.*, 1963a). In that article, the 'Luce model' was also called 'strict utility model'. The notation in the present article follows Luce's book (1959) in some respects, thus slightly differing from the notation in Becker *et al.* (1963a).

2 It was possible to carry out this experiment in the same session with that described in Becker *et al.*, (1963b).

BIBLIOGRAPHY

Becker, G. M., DeGroot, M. H., and Marschak, J., 'Stochastic Models of Choice Behavior', (1963) (a) *Selected Essays*, 10.

Becker, G. M., DeGroot, M. H., and Marschak, J., 'An Experimental Study of Some Stochastic Models for Wagers', (1963) (b) *Selected Essays*, 12.

Debreu, G., 'Review of R. D. Luce, *Individual Choice Behavior*', *Amer. Econ. Rev.* **50** (1960) 186–188.

Luce, R. D., *Individual Choice Behavior*, Wiley, New York, 1959.

15

MEASURING UTILITY BY A SINGLE-RESPONSE SEQUENTIAL METHOD

(1964)

Co-authors: G. M. BECKER and M. H. DEGROOT

The purpose of this paper is to describe a sequential experiment that provides, at each stage in the sequence, an estimate of the utility to the subject of some amount of a commodity (e.g., money), and to present a few experimental results obtained with the method. The procedure is based upon the following well-known 'expected utility hypothesis'. For each person there exist numerical *constants*, called *utilities*, associated with the various possible outcomes of his actions, given the external events not under his control. If, for a given subject, we could know the values of these constants and the ('personal') probabilities he assigns to the various external events we could, according to this model, predict his choice from among any available set of actions. He will choose an action with the highest expected utility; i.e., with the highest average of utilities of outcomes, weighted by the probabilities he assigns to the corresponding events. He will be indifferent between any two actions with equal expected utilities. Note that (by the nature of weighted averages) the comparison between expected utilities does not depend on which two particular outcomes are regarded as having zero-utility and unit-utility.

Other models of choice behavior, called *stochastic models*, do not predict the actual choices of a subject from each given set of available actions but rather they make statements about the *probabilities* that the scientist might assign to the various actions being chosen by the subject. It is assumed that these probabilities do not change during the time period under consideration, thus precluding learning or any systematic change of behavior. Relations between these probabilities of choice and the expected utilities described above are postulated.

One such postulate (associated with the name of Fechner) specifies that, for a given subject, action A has a larger expected utility than action B if and only if, when forced to choose between A and B, the probability that he chooses A is larger than the probability that he chooses B. It follows that if a choice between A and B is made many times under identical conditions, the person will choose the action with the larger expected utility more than half of the time. If he is indifferent he will choose each action 50 per cent of the time.

Mosteller and Nogee (1951), in what was perhaps the first laboratory measurement of utility, based their experiment on the Fechner postulate. They offered a subject choices of the following type: either accept a wager $(a, p, -b)$ in which you will win a dollars with probability p and you will win $-b$ dollars (i.e., lose b dollars) with probability $1-p$, or do not bet at all. They repeated the same offer several times, thereby obtaining the proportion of times that the subject decided to accept the wager. By holding p and b constant and varying a they were able to estimate the amount of money a_0 at which this proportion was 50 per cent. Then by assumption the subject was indifferent between accepting the wager $(a_0, p, -b)$ and not betting at all. Hence, these two actions have equal expected utilities. Therefore, denoting by $u(x)$ the utility of gaining x dollars,

$$u(0) = pu(a_0) + (1-p)\,u(-b).$$

As stated above, one can arbitrarily fix $u(0)=0$ and $u(-b)=-1$. Then

$$u(a_0) = (1-p)/p.$$

By keeping b constant and using the above technique for seven different values of p, Mosteller and Nogee estimated seven points on the subject's 'money-gain utility curve (function)', which represents the relation between money gains and their utilities.

The experiment just described depends heavily on the assumption that the subject's probabilities of choice remain constant throughout the many times that he is choosing from the same available set of actions, and also on the assumption that each of the seven values of p used in the experiment is 'understood' by the subject: i.e., that his personal probability of winning a dollars in a given wager is in fact p.

The procedure to be presented here differs from that of Mosteller and Nogee in several respects. No choice is repeated, but a check on the subject's consistency, or on his learning process, is provided. This is achieved by letting each set of available actions depend on the subject's previous responses in a manner that leads to repeated estimates of the same points on his utility curve. Some of these checks for consistency would be applicable even if the personal probabilities p of the subject were not known to the experimenter. However, the only odds used in our experiment were 1:1 and 3:1, and it did not seem unreasonable to assume that the simple probabilities $\frac{1}{2}$ and (to a lesser extent) $\frac{3}{4}$ were 'understood' by the subject.

I. THE SEQUENTIAL PROCEDURE

Let p be the probability of an event E, and let (y, p, z) be a wager in which one wins the amount y if the event E occurs and one wins the amount z if E does not occur. If a subject is indifferent between accepting the wager (y, p, z) and accepting a certain monetary gain of amount x, we shall call x his cash-equivalent of (y, p, z). Thus, $u(x)=pu(y)+(1-p)\,u(z)$.

Let a and b, with $a<b$, be two convenient amounts of money and fix arbitrarily $u(a)=0$, $u(b)=1$. In the next section we shall describe a method for determining a subject's cash-equivalent of any given wager. For the moment let us assume that we know how to do this. Then, if x_1 is the cash-equivalent of the wager (a, p, b), we have

$$u(x_1) = pu(a) + (1 - p)\,u(b) = 1 - p\,.$$

Similarly, if x_2 is the cash-equivalent of (b, p, a), then

$$u(x_2) = pu(b) + (1 - p)\,u(a) = p\,.$$

The amounts x_1, x_2, a, and b can now be used in later stages of a sequential experiment to form ten new wagers, (a, p, x_1), (x_2, p, b), etc., and the cash-equivalents of each of these wagers can also be determined.

If we define $u^*(y, p, z)=pu(y)+(1-p)\,u(z)$ to be the utility of the wager (y, p, z) then it is easily verified that

$$\begin{aligned}
u^*(x_1, p, a) &= u^*(a, p, x_2) = p(1 - p)\,,\\
u^*(x_2, p, b) &= u^*(b, p, x_1) = 1 - p + p^2\,,\\
u^*(a, p, x_1) &= (1 - p)^2\,,\\
u^*(x_1, p, b) &= 1 - p^2\,,\\
u^*(x_2, p, a) &= p^2\,,\\
u^*(b, p, x_2) &= p(2 - p)\,,\\
u^*(x_1, p, x_2) &= 2p(1 - p)\,,\\
u^*(x_2, p, x_1) &= 1 - 2p + 2p^2\,.
\end{aligned}$$

It is seen from these equations that, regardless of the value of p, the wagers (x_1, p, a) and (a, p, x_2) have the same utility and consequently they also have the same cash-equivalent. Similarly, (x_2, p, b) and (b, p, x_1) have the same cash-equivalent. Thus the determination of a subject's cash-equivalents of the wagers (x_1, p, a) and (a, p, x_2), say, provides a check on whether the subject is behaving in a manner consistent with a well-defined utility functions as specified by the utility model. If p is known, further checks of this kind can be established, as will be seen later.

The same general procedure can be followed throughout the experiment using at each stage a different probability p' selected so that some of the wagers formed with p' will have the same utilities as some of the wagers formed with p.

II. DETERMINING THE CASH-EQUIVALENT OF A WAGER

The following method can be used to determine the cash-equivalent of a wager (y, p, z) for a given subject. The subject is told that he will be rewarded from the wager (y, p, z); i.e., that he will receive the amount y if the event E of probability p occurs and he will receive the amount z otherwise.

The subject is then told that as an alternative to receiving this random reward from the wager he has the privilege of trying to sell the wager for cash. Accordingly, he is asked to state the smallest amount s that he will accept (his *selling price*) in lieu of being rewarded from the wager. The understanding is that if a buyer can be found who is willing to pay an amount $b \geqslant s$ then the subject will receive b. If no buyer can be found who is willing to pay at least s then the subject retains the wager and receives the random reward, either y or z, as specified by the wager.

Let s be the subject's selling price and let e be his cash-equivalent of the wager. Let b be the maximum amount that any buyer is willing to pay. It is assumed that b does not depend on s, but the method of generating b is otherwise irrelevant. If $b \geqslant s$, the subject will receive the amount b. If $b < s$, the subject will receive a random reward as specified by the wager.

We claim that it is to the subject's advantage for his selling price to be precisely his cash-equivalent of the wager; that is, to have $s = e$. This can be seen as follows.

From the definition of e, $u(e) = u^*(y, p, z)$ and, hence, receiving the certain cash amount e is equivalent to the subject to receiving a random reward from the wager. Now suppose $s>e$. If $b<e$ or $b \geqslant s$, the subject's fortune changes just as it would had his selling price been $s=e$. However, if b is such that $e \leqslant b<s$, the subject does not sell the wager and he receives a random reward whose cash-equivalent is e. Had his selling price been $s=e$, then for the same value of b he would have received the amount $b \geqslant e$. Thus, for all possible values of b, the expected utility of the subject's reward is at least as large when his selling price is $s=e$ as it is when $s>e$, and for some values of b it is strictly larger.

To complete the argument, suppose $s<e$. If $b<s$ or $b \geqslant e$, the subject's fortune changes just as it would had his selling price been $s=e$. However, if $s \leqslant b<e$, the subject receives the amount b whereas had his selling price been $s=e$ he would not sell the wager and would receive a random reward with cash-equivalent $e>b$. Thus, again, for all values of b the expected utility of the reward is at least as much when $s=e$ as it is when $s<e$, and for some values of b it is strictly larger. This demonstrates that the subject's optimal selling price is $s=e$. It brings him the highest expected utility.[1]

III. EXPERIMENTAL PROCEDURE

At the ith stage ($i=1, 2, \ldots, 24$) of the sequential experiment, the subject was presented with a wager from which he would receive the amount A_i if a number X_i selected at random from a rotating bingo basket containing balls with the integers 1 through 100 was less than or equal to C_i, and he would receive the amount B_i if X_i was greater than C_i. (In the notation of the preceding sections, this is the wager $(A_i, C_i/100, B_i)$ if we make the assumption that all integers between 1 and 100 have the same probability of being selected.) After each selection the ball was put back into the basket.

Before X_i was selected, the subject named his selling price s_i for the wager. A random integer Y_i was then selected from the basket. If $Y_i \geqslant s_i$, the subject received the amount Y_i. In effect, he had sold the wager for the amount Y_i. If $Y_i \leqslant s_i$, the subject did not sell the wager, X_i was observed, and the subject received either A_i or B_i, according as $X_i \leqslant C_i$ or $X_i > C_i$.

The amounts A_i, B_i, C_i used at each of the 24 stages of the sequential experiment are shown in Table I together with the utilities of the wagers under the arbitrary assignment of the two values $u(0)=0$ and $u(100)=1$.

TABLE I

Experimental design

Stage, i	A_i	B_i	C_i	s_i	$u(s_i)$
1	0	100	50	s_1	1/2
2	0	100	75	s_2	1/4
3	0	100	25	s_3	3/4
4	s_1	100	50	s_4	3/4
5	0	s_1	50	s_5	1/4
6	s_2	s_3	75	s_6	3/8
7	s_2	s_3	25	s_7	5/8
8	100	s_3	25	s_8	13/16
9	s_5	100	50	s_9	5/8
10	s_5	s_1	50	s_{10}	3/8
11	0	s_3	25	s_{11}	9/16
12	s_2	100	75	s_{12}	7/16
13	s_4	100	50	s_{13}	7/8
14	s_7	s_8	75	s_{14}	43/64
15	s_5	s_4	50	s_{15}	1/2
16	s_9	100	50	s_{16}	13/16
17	s_6	s_7	75	s_{17}	7/16
18	s_9	s_{13}	50	s_{18}	3/4
19	s_{11}	s_8	75	s_{19}	5/8
20	0	s_{13}	50	s_{20}	7/16
21	s_1	s_4	50	s_{21}	5/8
22	s_{11}	s_8	25	s_{22}	3/4
23	0	s_4	50	s_{23}	3/8
24	s_{11}	100	75	s_{24}	43/64

It should be noted that several of the 24 wagers have the same utility; e.g., $u(s_3)=u(s_4)=u(s_{18})=u(s_{22})=\frac{3}{4}$.

Moreover, even if the subject does not feel that all integers have the same probability of being selected, it is still true that

$$u(s_3) = u(s_{22}),$$
$$u(s_7) = u(s_{19}),$$
$$u(s_9) = u(s_{21}),$$
$$u(s_{10}) = u(s_{23}).$$

To see why this is so, we will prove, for example, that $u(s_3)=u(s_{22})$.

Let p be the probability that the number selected at random will be at most 25. Then it is seen from Table I that $u(s_{22})=u^*(s_{11}, p, s_8)= =pu(s_{11})+(1-p)\,u(s_8)$. But it is also seen from Table I that $u(s_{11})=$

$=u^*(0, p, s_3)=(1-p)\ u(s_3)$ and $u(s_8)=u^*(100, p, s_3)=p+(1-p)\ u(s_3)$. Furthermore, $u(s_3)=u^*(0, p, 100)=1-p$. Thus, $u(s_{22})=p(1-p)\ u(s_3)+$ $+p(1-p)+(1-p)^2\ u(s_3)=1-p=u(s_3)$.

The selling price s_i at a given stage is sometimes used as one of the rewards in the wagers presented at later stages. It should be noted that the subject can increase the utility of wagers presented at later stages by naming a higher selling price for wagers presented at earlier stages. In order to prevent the subject from recognizing that he had such control, his earlier selling prices were not used until several stages later.

In order to avoid changing the total capital of the subject during the sequence, the subject was not paid on any trial during the experiment and in fact was told that he would be paid on only one of the 24 trials. This trial was determined by drawing a number between 1 and 24 at random at the end of the session.

IV. INSTRUCTIONS

The subjects were instructed as follows:

Stage 1 only. "In this game we will draw a number between 1 and 100. If the number is equal to or less than 50, you will win nothing. If the number is greater than 50 you will win 100 cents. How much are you willing to accept instead of playing the game? After you tell me how much you are willing to take for the game, I will draw a number between 1 and 100. If the number I draw is equal to or greater than the price you asked, I will pay you whatever number I drew and you will not play the game. If the number I draw is less than the price you ask, you will play the game and win nothing if the next number I draw is equal to or less than 50, or you will win 100 cents if that number is greater than 50.

Do you have any questions?

What is the lowest amount you are willing to take for the game?"

Stages 2 through 24. "This time you will win the amount A_i if the number is equal to or less than C_i or you will win B_i if the number is larger than C_i.

Do you have any questions?

What is your lowest price for the game?

Subjects. Two male students were obtained through the Yale Student Placement Office to serve as subjects in an economic experiment being conducted at the Cowles Foundation for Economic Research, Yale

University. Subject 1 was an undergraduate in the Department of Psychology. Subject 2 was a graduate theology student. Each subject was guaranteed $1.25 per session (i.e., for his responses to the full sequence of 24 stages) and each subject participated in three sessions. In addition the subject received a bonus each session consisting of his winnings at one of the stages in the sequence. As already described, the subject was not told which stage would be used to determine his bonus until the end of the session.

V. RESULTS

Since each subject participated in three sessions the data provide an opportunity for the study of the change in the subjects' behavior as they grew familiar with the task.

Their selling prices for the wagers at each stage of each session, and the actuarial value of each wager (i.e., the expected monetary reward $(C_i/100)$ $A_i+(1-C_i/100)\,B_i$) are shown in Table II. (Note that the selling prices named by Subject 1 were always multiples of 5 cents. Although such rounding violates the assumption of a strictly monotonic utility function, the effects of the violation are negligible here.)

As discussed earlier, $u(s_3)=u(s_{22})$, $u(s_7)=u(s_{19})$, $u(s_9)=u(s_{21})$, and $u(s_{10})=u(s_{23})$, regardless of the value of p used in computing the utilities of the wagers. Thus, if the subjects' behavior is consistent with the expect, ed utility model their selling prices should be such that $s_3=s_{22}$, $s_7=s_{19}$, $s_9=s_{21}$, and $s_{10}=s_{23}$. The observed differences $s_{22}-s_3$, etc., are shown in Table III. Since most of these differences are nonzero the data are not consistent with an expected utility model.

It should also be noted, however, that the differences in prices decrease, on the average, from session to session, indicating that behavior does become, in some sense, more consistent with an expected utility model as the subject becomes more familiar with the task. Thus, despite the fact that the model does not precisely fit the behavior of the subjects, there is some indication that it approximates such behavior and that the model becomes more appropriate as the subject becomes more familiar with the experiment.

Now let us again assume that the values $\frac{1}{2}$, $\frac{1}{4}$, and $\frac{3}{4}$ are in fact the subjects' personal probabilities of the relevant events (i.e., we assume that, for the subjects, all integers are equally probable of being selected). The

TABLE II

Selling prices of the wagers

Stage	Subject 1			Subject 2		
	Session 1	Session 2	Session 3	Session 1	Session 2	Session 3
1	65 (50)	45 (50)	50 (50)	60 (50)	80 (50)	65 (50)
2	40 (25)	25 (25)	25 (25)	50 (25)	55 (25)	45 (25)
3	80 (75)	80 (75)	75 (75)	80 (75)	90 (75)	75 (75)
4	70 (83)	65 (73)	65 (75)	100 (80)	92 (90)	80 (83)
5	30 (33)	25 (23)	30 (25)	24 (30)	65 (40)	54 (33)
6	40 (50)	25 (39)	50 (38)	65 (58)	75 (64)	79 (53)
7	60 (70)	65 (66)	60 (63)	75 (73)	80 (81)	65 (68)
8	75 (85)	90 (85)	75 (81)	95 (85)	98 (83)	87 (81)
9	45 (65)	40 (63)	40 (65)	75 (62)	80 (83)	75 (73)
10	40 (48)	30 (35)	40 (40)	40 (42)	70 (73)	55 (55)
11	60 (60)	65 (60)	50 (56)	75 (60)	80 (68)	60 (56)
12	50 (55)	40 (44)	50 (44)	80 (63)	75 (66)	70 (59)
13	65 (85)	65 (83)	75 (83)	100 (100)	99 (96)	95 (90)
14	65 (64)	75 (71)	60 (64)	90 (80)	95 (85)	82 (71)
15	40 (50)	40 (45)	50 (48)	60 (62)	78 (79)	70 (63)
16	55 (73)	60 (70)	65 (73)	90 (88)	95 (90)	90 (88)
17	45 (45)	45 (35)	55 (53)	75 (70)	79 (76)	70 (76)
18	50 (55)	55 (53)	60 (60)	95 (88)	98 (90)	93 (85)
19	65 (64)	70 (71)	60 (56)	85 (80)	95 (85)	75 (67)
20	25 (33)	45 (33)	50 (38)	50 (50)	60 (50)	63 (48)
21	65 (68)	55 (55)	60 (58)	75 (80)	89 (86)	78 (73)
22	65 (71)	80 (84)	70 (69)	90 (90)	97 (94)	82 (80)
23	25 (35)	45 (33)	45 (33)	50 (50)	55 (46)	55 (40)
24	65 (70)	65 (74)	60 (63)	90 (81)	98 (91)	80 (70)

Note: The figures given in parentheses are the actuarial values of the wagers.

TABLE III

Differences in selling prices of wagers of equal utility

	Subject 1			Subject 2		
	Session 1	Session 2	Session 3	Session 1	Session 2	Session 3
$s_{22} - s_3$	−15	0	−5	10	7	7
$s_{19} - s_7$	5	5	0	10	15	10
$s_{21} - s_9$	20	15	15	0	9	3
$s_{23} - s_{10}$	−15	15	5	10	−15	0

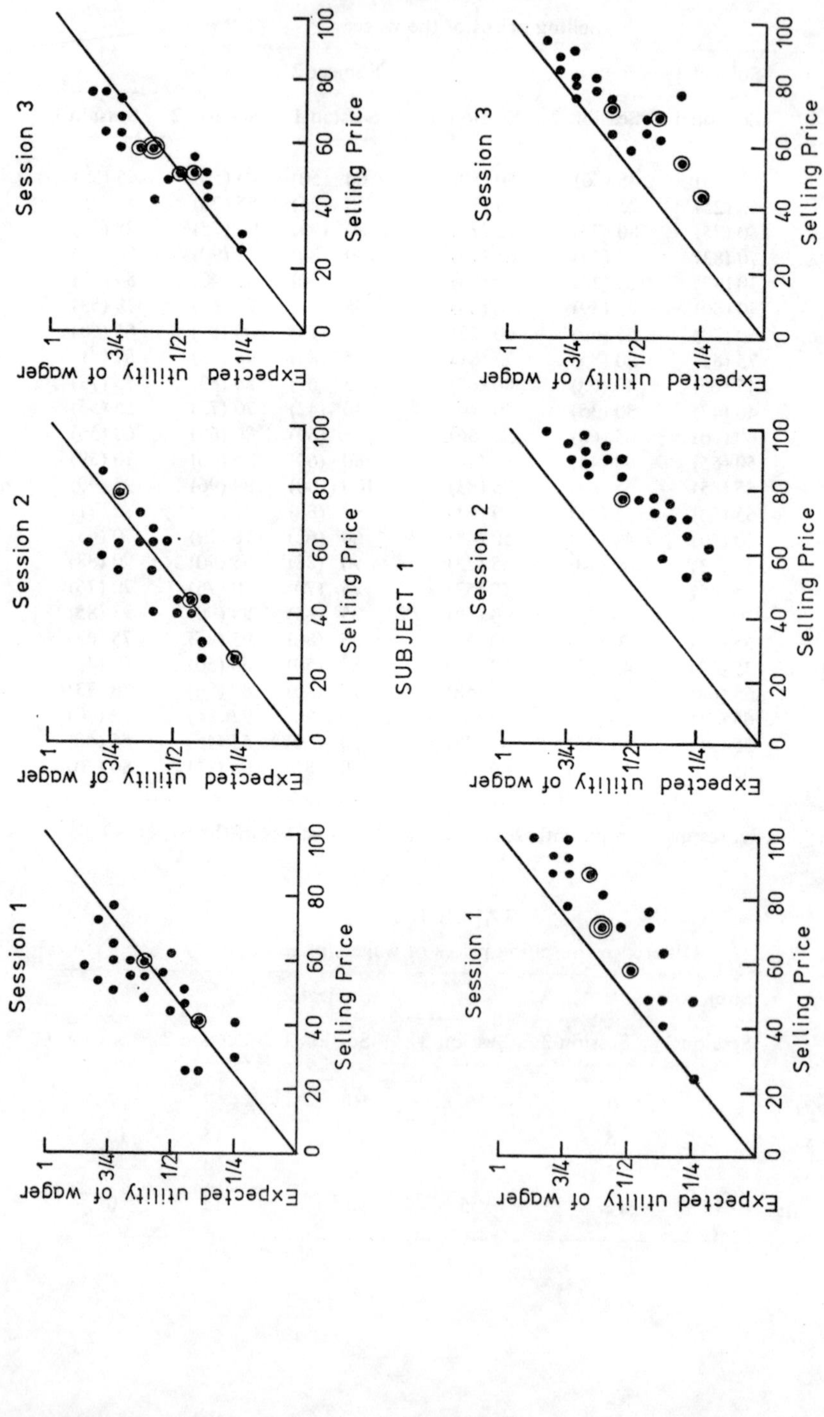

Fig. 1. Scatter Diagram of Subjects' Selling Prices Plotted against the Utilities of the Wagers. A circled dot indicates two coincident points. A twice-circled dot indicates three coincident points.

utilities of the wagers used in the experiment are given in Table I and, since the optimal selling price of a wager is its cash-equivalent, the selling prices named by a subject provide estimates of the amounts of money having these utilities. Thus, a scatter diagram of the selling prices named by a subject plotted against the utilities of the wagers should provide some suggestion of the subject's utility curve. These diagrams are given in Figure 1.

When viewing these diagrams it should be kept in mind that at each stage the utility of the wager was fixed and the selling price was the observed variable. Hence, the horizontal spread of points with the same utility is indicative of the inconsistency of the subjects' responses. In attempting to fit utility curves to these points, either 'by eye' or by some more refined method, the horizontal distances should perhaps be given primary consideration. Nevertheless, this discussion is not intended to minimize the relevance of the vertical spread of the utilities of wagers with the same selling price.

Because of the sequential nature of the experiment there is a dependence among the observations that makes a precise statistical analysis along traditional lines impractical. Accordingly, we content ourselves here with giving just a few general comments.

For both subjects, the horizontal spread of the points obtained in Session 3 at the fixed utility levels is relatively small. Thus, there is a trend toward the adoption of response patterns consistent with a set of constant utilities.

For a given wager, the larger the selling price named by a subject, the more willing he is to take risks. The selling prices named by Subject 1 were, in general, largest in Session 3. The linear (or actuarial) utility curve provides a not unreasonable fit to the observed points for this subject, although he is slightly more willing to take risks with small amounts and less willing with large amounts.

The observed points for Subject 2 in Session 3 lie below the linear utility curve, indicating the subject's willingness to take risks. For each subject, it is felt, a reasonable estimate of his utility curve can be sketched.

VI. CONCLUSIONS

An attempt has been made to measure the utility of money. Estimates of the amounts of money having been given, preselected utilities were obtained in a sequential procedure. At each stage of the procedure the subject stated the lowest price he would accept in lieu of a wager in his possession. It was shown that under the utility model this selling price will be the subject's cash-equivalent of the wager.

The inconsistency of the response of two subjects led to the rejection of the model. However, as the subjects became more familiar with the task their experience appeared to lead to more consistent behavior and less deviation from the results specified by the utility model. Thus, despite the rejection of the model in the strict sense, it is felt that it does, at least, approximate the observed behavior.

It is also our feeling that the procedure used here might provide useful data for the study of specific stochastic models of choice behavior, such as those given by Becker *et al.* (1963), and that it might be possible to use this procedure, alone or in combination with others, to estimate both personal probabilities and utilities of an experienced subject.

NOTE

[1] *Added in 1973.* Whether subjects do actually choose the optimal selling price was discussed by Marschak (1964) ('Experiment 2b') and (1968, p. 388). Further applications were suggested by Savage (1971), especially pp. 785–786.

BIBLIOGRAPHY

Becker, G. M., DeGroot, M. H., and Marschak, J., 'Stochastic Models of Choice Behavior' (1963), *Selected Essays*, 10.

Mosteller, F. and Nogee, P., 'An Experimental Measurement of Utility', *J. Polit. Econ.* **59** (1951) 371–404.

Added in 1973:

Marschak, J., 'Actual versus Consistent Decision Behavior' (1964), *Selected Essays*, 9.

Marschak, J., 'Decision Making: Economic Aspects' (1968), *Selected Essays*, 16.

Savage, L. J., 'Elicitation of Personal Probabilities and Expectations', *J. Amer. Statist. Assn.* **66** (1971) 783–801.

16

DECISION MAKING: ECONOMIC ASPECTS

(1968)

The distinction between prescriptive and descriptive theories of decision is similar to that between logic – a system of formally consistent rules of thought – and the psychology of thinking. A logical rule prescribes, for example, that if you believe all *X* to be *Y*, you should also believe that all non-*Y* are non-*X*, but not that all *Y* are *X*; and if you believe, in addition, that all *Y* are *Z*, you should believe all *X* to be *Z* (a logical rule known as transitivity of inclusion). Here, *X*, *Y*, and *Z* are objects or propositions. Such prescriptive rules do not state that all people of a given culture, social position, age, and so forth, always comply with them. If, for example, the links in a chain of reasoning are numerous, the rule of transitivity will probably be broken, at least by children or by unschooled or impatient people.

Descriptions, and consequently predictions, of 'illogical' behavior, as indeed of all human behavior, are presumably a task for psychologists or anthropologists. Such predictions are obviously important to practicing lawyers, politicians, salesmen, organizers, teachers, and others who work with people, just as predictions of the behavior of metals and animals are important to engineers and dairy farmers. These practitioners are well advised to know the frequencies of the various types of illogical behavior of their clients, adversaries, or students. But they are also well advised to avoid logical errors in their own behavior, as when they apply their knowledge of men (and of all nature, for that matter) to win lawsuits or elections or to be successful in organizing or teaching. For example, their propositions *X*, *Y*, and *Z* may be about another's madness, yet should obey the rule of transitivity of inclusion. Moreover, if you want to train future lawyers, statesmen, or businessmen, you are well advised to learn, from your own or other people's experiences, the techniques needed to make your pupil not only knowledgeable about other men's logical frailties but also strong in his own thinking and able to solve the brain twisters his future will offer. These pedagogical techniques are, of course, objects of descriptive study.

To illustrate the prescriptive-descriptive distinction in the domain of decisions, let us consider one of the rules proposed by prescriptive decision theory. We choose the rule called transitivity of preferences (other proposed rules will be discussed below) because of its special similarity with transitivity of inclusion. If you prefer *a* to *b* and *b* to *c*, you should prefer *a* to *c*. Here, *a*, *b*, and *c* are, in general, your actions with uncertain outcomes, although in the special case of 'sure actions', the outcome, e.g., gaining or losing an object, is unique, in which case preferring action *a* is, in effect, the same as preferring the outcome of action *a*. If an individual disobeys the transitivity rule and prefers *a* to *b*, *b* to *c*, and *c* to *a*, we would say that he does not know what he wants. Surely we would advise or train a practitioner to develop the ability for concentrated deliberation, weighing advantages and disadvantages in some appropriate way. This should result in a consistent ranking, from the most to the least preferable, with ties (i.e., indifference between some alternatives) not excluded, of alternative actions from which the decision maker may be forced to choose.

The statement that "given a set of feasible alternatives the 'reasonable' (rational) man should choose the best" and the parallel statement that "an actual man does choose the best (and if the best is not feasible, the second best, etc.)" are both empty if the ranking order is not supposed to be stable over a period long enough to make the statements of practical relevance. If the ranking order is stable, economics as the study of the best allocation of available resources becomes possible.

The boundary between descriptive and prescriptive economics did not worry early writers. Gresham's law, Ricardo's explanations of rent and of the high postwar price of bullion, and Böhm-Bawerk's theory of interest are deductions from the assumption of consistent ranking of alternatives by reasonable men. But those authors also practiced induction and looked for historical facts that confirmed their deductions. The two approaches are not inconsistent if one assumes that in the cultures considered, housewives and adult, gainfully occupied men have by and large been 'reasonable', at least when deciding not on wars and divorces but on matters of major interest to the economists of the time – for example, quantities such as prices, demands, and outputs, as well as less quantifiable choices such as location and internal organization (division of labor) of a plant. These matters were studied under the assumption of a tolerably well-known future.

The descriptive and prescriptive approaches became more clearly distinguished as more attention was directed to economic decisions under uncertainty (Fisher, 1906; Hicks, 1939; Hart, 1940) and, stimulated by the *Theory of Games and Economic Behavior* (von Neumann and Morgenstern, 1944), to nonquantifiable decisions traditionally assigned to political and military science or to sociology. In search of tools for their descriptive work, economists were also influenced by modern statistical decision theory. It then appeared that the reasonable man was not sufficiently approached even by the *ideal type* of an industrial entrepreneur, who evidently must be aided by a sophisticated hypothesis tester, a statistician, or, more recently and generally, an expert in operations research. As such experts, armed with computers, do indeed progressively penetrate the economic world, predictive and descriptive economics (e.g., the prediction of aggregate inventories) may again become closer to what can be deductively derived from rational decision rules.

To return to the analogy between theories of thinking and of decision, prescriptive theories of thinking and decision are concerned with formal consistency between sentences or decisions, not with their content. If one believes that Los Angeles is on the Moon and that Moon is in Africa, it is logical for him to believe that Los Angeles is in Africa, although none of the three statements is true. Similarly, if a man prefers killing to stealing and stealing to drinking strong liquor, he should prefer killing to drinking, although none of these actions is laudable or hygienic. Hicks (1939) used Milton's 'reason is also choice' as a motto to the theory of consumption. Ramsey (1923–1928) called his theory of decision an extension of logic, an attitude adopted more recently by other logicians, for example, Carnap (1962), von Wright (1963), and Jeffrey (1965). The mutual penetration of logic and decision theory will appear even more founded and urgent when we come to discuss the cost of thinking and deciding (Section VIII).

In Sections I, III, IV and V we shall discuss some prescriptive decision rules and outline some simple experiments whose outcomes determine whether the subject did or did not comply with these rules. Whenever such experiments or similar ones have actually been performed, we shall refer to available descriptive evidence, namely, the frequency of subject's obeying these rules or obeying some other stated behavior patterns, such as the probabilistic decision models of Section II. In Section VI the expected utility theorem implied by the prescriptive rules is discussed. Sections VII and VIII point to unsolved problems on the frontier of decision theory.

I. COMPLETE ORDERING OF ACTIONS

Before we consider the notion of a complete ordering of alternative actions or decisions (we need not distinguish between the two here), it is convenient to restate the *transitivity* of preferences by defining the relation 'not preferred to' or 'not better than', written symbolically as $\leqslant$. If $a \leqslant b$ and $b \leqslant c$, then $a \leqslant c$. It is a *reflexive* relation, i.e., $a \leqslant a$. A relation that is transitive and reflexive is called an *ordering* relation. When $a \leqslant b$ and $b \leqslant a$, we write $a \sim b$ and say that the decision maker is indifferent between a and b, even though a and b are not identical. For example, an investor may be indifferent between two different portfolios of securities. Thus '$\leqslant$' (unlike the relation 'not larger than' applied to numbers) is a *weak ordering* relation. Further, when $a \leqslant b$ and not $b \leqslant a$, we write $a < b$ and say that b is preferred to, or is better than, a.

Shall we say that a reasonable man always either prefers b to a or a to b or is indifferent? Or can he, in addition, refuse to compare them? If he can, the ordering of the actions by the relation 'not better than' is only a *partial* one. This position has been taken, for example, by Aumann (1962), Chipman (in Interdisciplinary Research Conference, 1960), and Wolfowitz (1962). But can one escape choosing? As in Pascal's (1670) famous immortality bet, *'Il faut parier!'* The avoiding of choice itself is a decision. Like other decisions, it is made more or less desirable by the prizes and penalties it entails. If this is granted, the transitive relation '$\leqslant$' is also *connective* and induces a *complete ordering*. Then any subset of actions can be arranged according to their desirabilities (with ties not excluded). Rank numbers, also called *ordinal utilities* (priorities), can then be assigned to the alternative actions provided that certain weak conditions are satisfied (Debreu, 1959, section 4, note 2, and section 4.6).

Tests of transitivity of preferences. As a matter of descriptive theory we ask whether people (of a given culture, etc.) do act as if there exist complete orderings of their actions by preferences. In actual experiments the penalty for refusing to choose was assumed to be strong enough to force subjects to make genuine choices in the form of verbal statements of preferences or, in some cases, actually to stake money on one wager rather than another. With connectivity of the preference relation thus assured and its reflexivity assumed by definition, the transitivity of the relation remained to be tested. The alternative actions were represented by multidimensional objects – a bundle of tickets to various shows (Papandreou, 1957), marriage partners classified by three three-valued characteristics (May, 1954; Davis, 1958), a monetary wager (Edwards, 1953; Davidson and Marschak, 1959), a price policy affecting both the firm's rate of return and its share of the market, an air trip varying in both cost and duration (MacCrimmon, 1965), and so forth. The subject responded by a triad of binary choices – *a* or *b*? *b* or *c*? *c* or *a*? – but in most experiments these choices were separated in time by choices from other triads, that is, '*a* or *b*?' was/followed by '*a'* or *b'*?' rather than by '*b* or *c*?' Moreover, neither of the two actions 'dominated' the other (see Section III), and no subject could use paper and pencil.

In all experiments, the transitivity rule was violated with varying frequencies. The proportion of the number of violations by all subjects to the maximum theoretical number of intransitive triads that were possible in the given experimental designs ranged from .04 in MacCrimmon's tests of business executives to .27 in May's tests of students. Since the experiments record actual choices and not preferences, intransitivity might be exhibited by a person who, although consistent, is strictly indifferent among three alternatives. (To approach, more generally, the case of 'near indifference', the hypothesis tested must be rephrased in probabilistic terms. This will be discussed in Section II.) Thus the outcome of an experiment depends on the nature of the alternatives offered, making the experiments mentioned not quite comparable.

It would also be of great interest to study the effects of the passage of time and the effects of learning, especially if different methods of training are applied, such as 'post-mortem' discussion (a domain opened by MacCrimmon), sequential modifications of the list of choices, etc. In fact, what would be the effect of supplying the subjects with paper and pencil and training them to use these prerequisites of our culture to tabulate the decision problem in an 'outcome matrix' as in Table I (p. 337) below?

It has been suggested (Quandt, 1956; Simon, 1957) that intransitivities of decisions occur when the subject is unable to pay simultaneous attention to the several dimensions of each object of choice. This is somewhat analogous to the psychophysical finding that discrimination is greater between sounds differing in pitch but of equal loudness than between sounds differing in both (Pollack, 1955). This suggests that the probabilistic approach common in psychophysics might be tried in a description of decision behavior. As to prescriptive theory, one may recall Benjamin Franklin's suggestion to score the pros and cons of each decision or the practice of adding scores when grading students or judging young ladies in beauty contests. Again, these or any other ways of overcoming the multidimensionality of decisions through deliberate and simultaneous marshaling of all the dimensions will in general require paper and pencil.

II. PROBABILISTIC ORDERING OF ACTIONS

Since the prescriptive rule of transitivity is often violated, it is necessary to recast descriptive decision theory in different terms. The hypothesis that transitivity of decisions may be achieved by learning or training has already been mentioned. It is also traditional in experimental psychology, especially since Fechner's (1860) studies of perception, to describe behavior by probability distributions. Economists, by contrast, have succeeded in the past in making useful predictions of the aggregate behavior of large numbers of individuals based on the assumption that individuals are, by and large, 'reasonable'. The probabilistic approach is rather new in economics, perhaps as young as the econometricians' attempts to test aggregate economic models statistically and to relate these models to observable behavior of sampled individual households and firms.

Luce and Suppes (1965) have comprehensively surveyed the literature and the experimental evidence relevant to probabilistic orderings. One model that implies all the others suggested so far is that presented by Luce (1959). Fixed positive numbers v_a, v_b, v_c,..., called *strict utilities*, are attached to the alternative actions *a*, *b*, *c*,.... The set of actions includes all alternatives that may ever be offered to a given subject. The strict utilities are assumed to have the following property: if the subject must choose from a particular subset of alternatives, he will choose each with a probability proportional to its strict utility. For example, suppose $v_a:v_b:v_c:v_d=1:2:3:4$. Then, if asked to choose from the subset (*a*, *b*, *c*), the subject will choose *a*, *b*, or *c* with repective probabilities $\frac{1}{6}$, $\frac{2}{6}$, $\frac{3}{6}$; if he must choose from the pair (*a*, *b*), he will choose *a* or *b* with respective probabilities $\frac{1}{3}$, $\frac{2}{3}$. The hypothesis can be tested at least 'in principle' (i.e., assuming that representative samples from the universe of all choice situations can be obtained). One would observe the relative frequencies of choices from various subsets and infer, for example, that the ratio of the probability of choosing a to the probability of choosing b from the pair (a, b) does or does not change if a third alternative is also offered.

In another model, constants $u_a, u_b, u_c, \ldots$, called *strong utilities*, are associated with the alternatives $a, b, c, \ldots$. The strong utilities are assumed to have the following property: in the binary choice between a and b, the probability $p(a, b)$ of choosing a is an increasing function of the difference $u_a - u_b$ (except when $p(a, b)$ is equal to 1 or 0). It follows that $p(a, b) \gtreqless \frac{1}{2}$ according as $u_a \gtreqless u_b$. Note that the case $p(a, b) = \frac{1}{2}$ provides an operational definition of 'indifference' based on actual choices rather than on the verbal statement 'I am indifferent'. This model was used, in effect, in Thurstone's discussion of public opinion and of soldiers' food preferences (1927–1955). It is analogous to Fechner's perception model, which associates a physical stimulus a with a subjective 'sensation' u_a; the subject perceives a to be heavier (or louder or brighter) than b with a probability $p(a, b)$ that increases with the difference $u_a - u_b$ (provided $p(a, b)$ is neither 0 nor 1).

It can be shown that if strict utilities exist, then strong utilities also exist (putting $u_a = \log v_a$, etc.), but not the converse. The strong utility model implies, in turn, the still less restrictive *weak utility* model, which assigns the ordinal numbers $w_a, w_b, w_c, \ldots$ to the alternatives $a, b, c, \ldots$, such that $p(a, b) \gtreqless \frac{1}{2}$ according as $w_a \gtreqless w_b$. Clearly, if the strong utilities exist, so do the weak utilities (putting $w_a = u_a$, etc), but not the converse since differences between ordinal numbers are undefined. Both the weak utility model and the strong utility model can be tested in principle for possible rejection, for they have implications that involve choice probabilities only, avoiding the intervening utility concept. In particular, the models imply, respectively, the *weak stochastic transitivity*,

$$\text{if } p(a, b) \geqslant \tfrac{1}{2} \text{ and } p(b, c) \geqslant \tfrac{1}{2}, \text{ then } p(a, c) \geqslant \tfrac{1}{2},$$

and the *strong stochastic transitivity*,

$$\text{if } p(a, b) \geqslant \tfrac{1}{2} \text{ and } p(b, c) \geqslant \tfrac{1}{2},$$
$$\text{then } p(a, c) \geqslant \max\,[p(a, b), p(b, c)].$$

Of these two forms of stochastic transitivity, the strong implies the weak one: it is, in turn, implied by the exact transitivity rule treated in Section I if the choice probabilities are assumed to take on only three values: 0, $\frac{1}{2}$, and 1, corresponding to the preference relations $a<b$, $a\sim b$, and $b<a$.

Another probabilistic model also implied by, and less restrictive than, Luce's strict utility model is the *random utility* model. It does not imply, nor is it implied by, the strong or the weak utility model. It asserts, for a given subject, the existence of a fixed probability distribution on the set of all preference orderings of all alternatives, so that for a set of N alternatives, a probability is attached to each of their $N!$ permutations. In the nonprobabilistic economics of consumer's choice the (ordinal) utility function that attaches a constant rank to each commodity bundle is a fixed one. In the random utility model this function is, instead, visualized as drawn at random from a set of such functions, according to a probability distribution that is fixed for the given subject. Thus the word 'utility' designates here a random number, not a constant as in the other probabilistic models described.

What relevance do these (and related) models have for a prescriptive theory of decision? Just as not all men are always consistent, not all men are always in good health. Doctors and nurses are busy measuring the temperatures and blood pressures of the sick ones. The probability distributions supposed to characterize a 'stochastic decision maker' may vary in the degree of their closeness to the ideal limit – consistency. For example, consistency is approached in the strong utility model as the values of $p(a, b)$ concentrate near 1 or 0 or $\frac{1}{2}$. We can thus trace the path of progress of learning or training for consistency.

III. INADMISSIBILITY OF DOMINATED ACTIONS

An action's result (outcome) depends, in general, not only on the action but also on the 'state of the world (nature or environment)', which is not in the decision maker's control. For our purposes an action (called an act by Savage [1954]) can be defined by the results it yields at various states of the world. Thus an action is a function from the set of states to the set of results. (This function has constant value if the action is a 'sure action'.) In a decision situation, only some such functions are available; their 'feasible set' (the 'offered set of alternatives' of Section II) depends, for example, on the decision maker's resources, technology, and market as he views them.

An *event* is a subset of the states of nature. In particular, the subset consisting of all states that, for any given feasible action, result in the same outcome is called an *outcome-relevant event*. In a decision situation the set of states is partitioned into such events, with all irrelevant details omitted.

Even if the well-disciplined decision maker can consistently rank multidimensional results according to his preferences, action under uncertainty remains multidimensional because of the multiplicity of events. Actions are bets, or wagers. Yet it seems reasonable to prescribe (as in Section 1) that bets be ordered; indeed, some authors prescribe that bets be completely ordered (Ramsey, 1923–1928; Savage, 1954; de Finetti, 1937). It will be shown in Section VI that a complete ordering corresponds to that of numerical 'expected utilities' of actions *provided* that the decision maker is consistent in the sense of obeying both the traditional rules of logic and certain postulates that are plausible enough to qualify as extensions of logic. These postulates will be discussed in this and subsequent sections, essentially following Savage.

Action a is said to dominate action b if the results of a are sometimes

TABLE I

An outcome matrix (in dollars)

Action	Event	
	Z_1	Z_2
a	1000	1500
a'	999	1500
b	1000	1000

(i.e., when some events take place) better than the results of b and are never worse. Is it not reasonable that you should prefer the dominating action? Any action that is dominated by some feasible action is thus inadmissible. Consider, for example, the actions listed in Table I. If action a is taken and the state of the world is Z_1, a gain of $1000 will be realized; if action a is taken and the state of the world is Z_2, a gain of $1500 will be realized; and so on. Such a table is called an *outcome matrix*.

The inadmissibility postulate would order these actions as follows:

$a' < a$, $b < a$. It does not, by itself, induce complete ordering of the actions. Thus, it is silent about the preference relation between actions a' and b in Table I. The 'expected utility' rule of Section VI will determine this relation roughly in the following manner: depending on the 'probabilities' of events and on the 'utilities' of results, the \$500 advantage of a' over b if Z_2 happens may or may not outweigh its \$1 disadvantage if Z_1 happens. This appeals to common sense but remains vague until, with help of other postulates, we define the concepts of 'probability' and 'utility'.

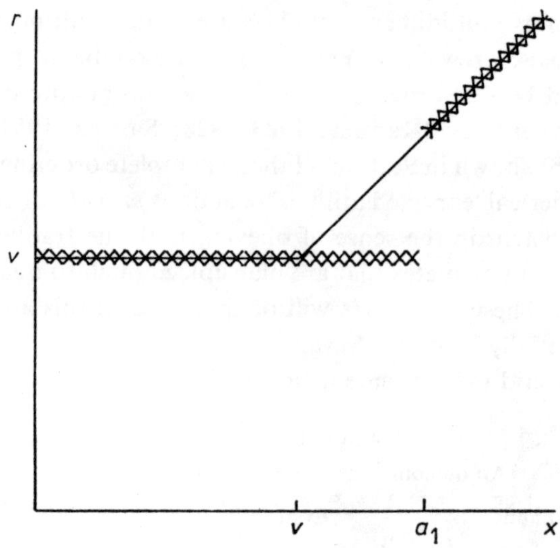

Fig. 1. Result r as a function of bid x when the asking price is equal to v (solid line) and to $a_1 > v$ (crosses).

Does the inadmissibility rule describe peoples' actual behavior? It is difficult to make an individual violate the rule when the decision situation is presented with clarity, for example, by an outcome matrix whose entries have an obvious ordering (sums of money, as in Table I, or good health, light illness, and death). But consider the following experiment. A subject is given an envelope containing v dollars; he is permitted to convince himself that the envelope does contain v dollars. He writes, but does not tell the experimenter his asking price, a, for the envelope and its contents. He will then receive a bid of x dollars. If x exceeds a, he will receive x dollars; otherwise, he will keep the v dollars. There will be no further negotiations.

Subjects often ask more than the true value, setting $a = a_1 > v$. In Figure 1, the stipulated result r of such action is plotted against possible levels of the bid x (state of nature). Comparison with the corresponding plot for the 'honest' asking price, $a = a_0 = v$, shows that a_1 is dominated by a_0. In fact, an asking price $a_2 < v$ (not shown in Figure 1) is also dominated by a_0. Hence the honest asking price is the only admissible one. It seems that some subjects expect further negotiations despite the explicit warning. We surmise that they would waive uncalled-for associations and habits if trained to plot or tabulate payoffs.

IV. IRRELEVANCE OF NONAFFECTED OUTCOMES

Table II presents a matrix of outcomes measured in per cent of return on a firm's investment. We may interpret a, b, a', and b' as the firm's investing in the development of alternative products. The outcomes of these actions depend on the mutually exclusive events (say, business conditions) Z_1, Z_2, and Z_3. Suppose the firm prefers a to b. This preference cannot be due to any difference in the outcomes if the event Z_1 happens, for these outcomes are identically 5. Therefore, the firm's preference of a to b must be due to its preferring the wager '-200 if Z_2, 100 if Z_3' to the return of 5 with certainty. But then the firm should also prefer a' to b', for again, if Z_1 happens, the outcome (-200) is not affected by the firm's choice. Its preference as between a' and b' must depend on its preference as between the wager '-200 if Z_2, 100 if Z_3' and the certainty of 5, just as in the previous case. By the same reasoning, if the firm is indifferent between a and b, it should be indifferent between a' and b'. The rule enunciated here can be regarded as a generalization of the admissibility rule of the

TABLE II

Outcome matrix for the return on a firm's investment (per cent)

Action	Event		
	Z_1	Z_2	Z_3
a	5	-200	100
b	5	5	5
a'	-200	-200	100
b'	-200	5	5

previous section, with wagers admitted as a form of outcomes so that, for example, action a is described as follows: if Z_1 happens, you get 5; otherwise you get a lottery ticket, losing 200 if Z_2 happens and gaining 100 if Z_3 happens.

Tests of the irrelevance rule. Most business executives violated the irrelevance rule when MacCrimmon (1965) *verbally* gave them the choices in Table II – first a versus b, then a' versus b'. However, a large majority of my students, who also never heard of the irrelevance principle but knew how to draw up a matrix of outcomes, complied with the rule. Allais (1953) performed a similar experiment, but instead of describing the three events as alternative business conditions, he gave them numerical probabilities (an extraneous notion in the present context), the probability of one of the events being only .01. Most of his respondents, including some decision theorists, violated the principle (but see Savage's pungent introspective discussion of his own second thought [1954, Section 5.6g]).

The following type of experiment has been discussed widely. Funnel 1 contains an equal number of red and black balls, and the subject is invited to convince himself of this; but he is not permitted to look into funnel 2, which he only knows to contain one or more balls whose colors are either black or red. When a handle is pulled, each funnel will release only the bottom ball. In the following bets, he will win either $100 or nothing:

Bet $1R$: bottom ball in funnel 1 is red.
Bet $1B$: bottom ball in funnel 1 is black.
Bet $2R$: bottom ball in funnel 2 is red.
Bet $2B$: bottom ball in funnel 2 is black.

The outcomes are as indicated in Table III, where, for example, event RB is 'bottom ball in funnel 1 is red, bottom ball in funnel 2 is black'. Suppose

TABLE III
Outcome matrix for the funnel experiment (in dollars)

	Event			
Bet	*RB*	*BR*	*RR*	*BB*
1*R*	100	0	100	0
2*R*	0	100	100	0
2*B*	100	0	0	100
1*B*	0	100	0	100

the subject always prefers to use funnel 1 rather than funnel 2, that is, he prefers bet $1R$ to $2R$ and also bet $1B$ to $2B$. He will thus treat the results unaffected by his choice – namely, those earned when events RR and BB occur – as *relevant* to his choice! Yet similar experiments performed by Chipman (see Interdisciplinary Research Conference 1960) and Ellsberg (1961) suggest that many people do indeed prefer funnel 1 to funnel 2. Some of my student subjects who did so motivated their choice by stating the sharp distinction between 'risk' (funnel 1) and 'uncertainty' (funnel 2), a distinction taught to economists since Knight (1921). Others stated that they could base their bets on more information when using funnel 1 than when using funnel 2. But information, although never harmful, can be useless. In experiments of Raiffa (1961) and Fellner (1965), subjects were, in effect, willing to pay for such useless information.

V. DEFINITIONS OF PROBABILITIES

Having defined events $Z_1, Z_2, Z_3, \ldots$ as subsets of the set X of all states of nature, it is consistent with current mathematical language and current English to require that any numbers, $p(Z_1)$, $p(Z_2)$, $P(Z_3), \ldots$, claimed to be the probabilities of these events, satisfy the following conditions: (1) they should be nonnegative; (2) for any two mutually exclusive events, say Z_1 and Z_2, the number assigned to the event 'Z_1 or Z_2' (meaning the occurrence of either Z_1 or Z_2) should equal the sum of $P(Z_1)$ and $P(Z_2$; (3) $P(X)$, i.e., $P(Z_1$ or Z_2 or Z_3 or...), should be equal to one.

Personal probabilities. The numbers $P(Z_1)$, $P(Z_2)$, $P(Z_3), \ldots$ are an individual's personal probabilities of these events if, in addition to having the mathematical properties just stated, they describe his behavior in the following sense: whenever $P(Z_1)>P(Z_2)$, for example, he will prefer betting on Z_1 to betting on Z_2, assuming he wants to win the bet. This, too, is consistent with ordinary English – he will prefer betting on the victory of the Democrats in the next election to betting on the truth of the proposition that California is longer than Norway if and only if he considers winning the former bet 'more probable' than winning the latter one. Here, 'betting on Z_1' means taking an action that yields a result s (for success) if Z_1 occurs, a result that is more desirable than the result f (for failure) if Z_1 does not occur. The probabilities of events must depend on the events only, i.e., the individual's preferences between bets must be the same for all pairs of results s, f (\$100, \$0; *status quo*, loss of prestige; etc.) provided only that s is better than f. This postulate of *independence of beliefs on rewards* must be added to those of Sections I, III, and IV. Will the subject reverse his judgment about the comparative chances of any two events – as revealed by his choices between two bets – if the prizes are changed? If not, he satisfies the postulate. It seems to be satisfied by practically all subjects asked to rank several bets according to their preferences, the rewards being first a pair s, f, then a different pair s', f'.

Suppose a subject is indifferent to bets on any of the eight horses running a race. His preferences would thus imply that $P(Z_1)=P(Z_2)=\cdots=$ $=P(Z_8)$, where Z_i is the event that the ith horse wins (ties are excluded for simplicity). The nonnegativity property is satisfied if we put $P(Z_i)=\frac{1}{8}$ for all i. What about the other two mathematical properties required? Suppose the subject considers double bets with the same prizes s, f as for single bets. He will prefer every double bet, e.g., the bet on the event 'Z_1 or Z_2', to any single bet (here he has, in effect, applied the inadmissibility postulate), and he will be indifferent between any two double bets (here the postulates of irrelevance and of intransitivity apply). Similarly, he will prefer triple bets to double bets and will be indifferent between any two triple bets, and so on. Consistent with these preferences, we can put

$$P(Z_i \text{ or } Z_j) = \tfrac{2}{8} = P(Z_i) + P(Z_j)$$

for any two horses i and j,

$$P(Z_i \text{ or } Z_j \text{ or } Z_k) = \tfrac{3}{8} = P(Z_i \text{ or } Z_j) + P(Z_k)$$

for any three horses i, j, and k, and so on. In general, we can assign probability $P(Z)=m/8$ to the event Z that one of the m specified horses will win (where $1 \leqslant m \leqslant 8$). Then the numbers $P(Z)$ are the subject's personal probabilities, for they agree with his preferences between bets and also satisfy the three mathematical requirements stated at the beginning of this section.

Instead of a horse race, a subject is asked to imagine a dial divided into n equal sectors. Suppose the hand of the dial is spun and comes to rest in the ith sector. We define this occurrence as event Z_i. If the subject is convinced that the dial's mechanism is 'fair', i.e., that the events $Z_1, Z_2, \ldots,$ Z_n are symmetrical (exchangeable), he will be indifferent among bets on any one of these n events. Following Borel (1939, chapter 5), he can then assess his personal probability of any event T, say, 'rain tomorrow', by finding a number m $(1 \leqslant m \leqslant n)$ such that betting on T is not more desirable than betting on 'Z_1 or Z_2 or ... or Z_m' and is not less desirable than betting on 'Z_1 or Z_2 or ... or Z_{m-1}'. Then his personal probability of T, $P(T)$, satisfies the inequality

$$\frac{m-1}{n} \leqslant P(T) \leqslant \frac{m}{n}.$$

By making n arbitrarily large, one can assess $P(T)$ arbitrarily closely, and by using dial arcs which represent any fraction, rational or irrational, of the dial's circumference, one can define personal probabilities ranging continuously from 0 to 1. Note that such assessments of personal probabilities, when determined in an experiment, are based not on the subject's verbal statement of numbers he calls probabilities but on his actual choices. They may therefore be useful in predicting actions provided that the subject is consistent. If he is not consistent, his violations may or may not be similar in principle to those incurred in any instrument readings – a theme of probabilistic psychology touched upon in Section II.

Objective probabilities. As a special case, personal probabilities of some real-world events may be 'objective', i.e., the same for different people. This is particularly the case when there is agreement that the events come sufficiently close, for all practical purposes of those involved, to fulfilling certain symmetry requirements. Approximate symmetry is assumed for the positions of a roulette dial like Borel's and for the occurrences of death among many similar males of age 20. Such requirements are strictly satisfied only by idealized, mathematically defined events – events that are never observed empirically. *A* 'fair' coin, a 'fair' roulette dial, a 'homogeneous' population of males aged 20 (or a 'random' sample from such a population) are all mathematical constructs. The mathematical theory of probability applies rules of logic to situations in which strict symmetry and the three properties stated at the beginning of this section hold (refining property 2 in order to accommodate the case of an infinite X). If decision makers agree that certain events are approximately symmetric, and if they apply logical rules, then their choices between betting on (predicting) any two events will agree; their personal (in this case also objective) probabilities will coincide with those given by mathematical theory. Clarity requires us, however, to distinguish between mathematical probabilities and objective probabilities assigned by decision makers to empirical events, just as we distinguish between a geometric rectangle and the shape of an actual sheet of paper.

VI. EXPECTED UTILITY

The four postulates discussed thus far – complete ordering of actions, inadmissibility of dominated actions, irrelevance of nonaffected outcomes, and independence of beliefs on rewards – appear about as convincing as the rules of logic (and about as subject to transgression by people not trained in untwisting brain twisters). Together with a 'continuity' postulate (to be introduced presently), they imply the following rule, which is more complicated and less immediately convincing: The consistent man behaves as if he (1) assigned personal probabilities $P(Z)$ to events Z, (2) assigned numerical utilities $u(r)$ to the results r of his actions, and (3) chose the action with the highest 'expected utility'. The expected utility $\omega(a)$ of action a is the weighted average

$$\omega(a) = \sum_r u(r) \cdot P(Z_{ra}),$$

where the event Z_{ra} is the set of all states for which action a yields result r.

The rule is trivially true when the choice is among sure actions; if action a always yields result r, then $P(Z_{ra}) = 1$, so that $\omega(a) = u(r)$.

Consider now actions with two possible results – success s and failure f. This is the case, for example, when actions are two-prize bets (as in Section V) or when the decision maker is a 'satisficer' (Simon, 1957) for whom all outcomes below his 'aspiration level' are equally bad and all others equally good. In Section V we saw that of two two-prize bets, a consistent decision maker prefers the bet that has the higher probability of success. Since s is better than f, we can assign numerical utilities

$$u(s) = 1 > 0 = u(f),$$

and we see that the expected utility $\omega(b)$ of a two-prize bet b coincides with its probability of success $P(Z_{sb})$, since

$$\omega(b) = 1 \cdot P(Z_{sb}) + 0 \cdot P(Z_{fb}) = P(Z_{sb}).$$

Thus the satisficer maximizes the probability of reaching his aspiration level.

As the next step, we compute the probability of success and hence the expected utility $\omega(c)$ of a bet c compounded of n simple two-prize bets or lottery tickets $b_1, \ldots, b_n$ on n different (but not necessarily mutually exclusive) events $T_1, \ldots, T_n$. Lottery ticket b_i is a bet on the event T_i, and the subject will receive ticket b_i if Z_i happens. The events $Z_1, \ldots, Z_n$ are mutually exclusive events one of which must happen, and the events 'Z_i and T_i' (the occurrence of Z_i and T_i) are pairwise independent in the sense that

$$P(Z_i \text{ and } T_i) = P(Z_i) \cdot P(T_i).$$

We can thus regard ticket b_i as the result yielded by action c when Z_i happens. Hence $P(Z_i) = P(Z_{b_i c})$ in the present notation. Moreover, we have just shown that the expected utility of a simple two-prize bet can be measured by its probability of success, so that $P(T_i) = \omega(b_i)$. Clearly, the probability of success of the compound bet c is the probability of the event '(Z_1 and T_1) or (Z_2 and T_2) or ... or (Z_n and T_n)'; by mathematical property 2 of probabilities (Section V), this is equal to $\sum_i P(T_i) \cdot P(Z_i)$. Hence,

$$\omega(c) = \sum_i \omega(b_i) \cdot P(Z_{b_i c}),$$

i.e., the expected utility rule is valid for the special case where each result of an action is a two-prize bet.

To extend this in a final step to the general case, let s be the best and f the worst of all results of an action. In the preference notation of Section I, $f \leqslant r \leqslant s$ for any result r. Consider the continuous range of all bets b whose two prizes are s and f and whose success probabilities take all the values between (and including) 1 and 0. Then, for any b, $f \leqslant b \leqslant s$, and for a given r, $r \leqslant b$ or $b \leqslant r$ depending on the bet's success probability. A plausible *continuity postulate* asserts, for each r, the existence of a bet, say b_r, such that $r \sim b_r$. We can therefore assign to r a utility $u(r) = \omega(b_r)$. A decision maker should then be indifferent between an action a that yields various results r with respective probabilities $P(Z_{ra})$ and a bet c compounded of the corresponding two-prize bets b_r just described entering with the same probabilities $P(Z_{ra})$. That is to say, $P(Z_{b_r c}) = P(Z_{ra})$. The expected utility rule follows, since

$$\begin{aligned}\omega(a) = \omega(c) &= \sum_r \omega(b_r) \cdot P(Z_{b_r c}) \\ &= \sum_r u(r) \cdot P(Z_{ra}).\end{aligned}$$

Some insight into this derivation of the expected utility rule is provided to the trainee in decision making by letting him rank his preferences among the tickets to four lotteries. Each ticket is described by prizes contingent on two alternative events, one of which must occur. An example of such a decision problem is presented in Table IV, where p is written for $P(Z)$ for brevity. If the event Z is 'a coin is tossed and comes up heads' (we refer below to this event simply as 'heads') and the subject regards the coin as 'fair', then $p=\frac{1}{2}$. But Z may also be, for example, "the next sentence spoken in this room will contain the pronoun 'I'." In any case, when the inadmissibility postulate is applied, it is evident from the last column of Table IV that ticket *a* is better than *c* and worse than *b*. Furthermore, the decision maker should be indifferent between tickets *a* and *d*.

Cash equivalents and numerical utilities. Let us define the *cash equivalent* of ticket *a*, denoted $k(a)$, as the highest price the decision maker would offer for ticket *a*; $k(b)$, $k(c)$, and $k(d)$ are defined similarly. If asked to name his cash equivalent for each lottery ticket in Table IV, the decision maker should name amounts such that $k(b)>k(a)=k(d)>k(c)$. If he fails to do this, he is inconsistent, and no scale of numerical utilities can describe his behavior. If he is consistent, and if the event Z is 'heads', the following utilities for some money gains can be ascribed to him:

$$\begin{aligned}
\omega(\$100) &= 1\,;\\
\omega\,[k(b)] &= \tfrac{3}{4}\,;\\
\omega\,[k(a)] = \omega\,[k(d)] &= \tfrac{1}{2}\,;\\
\omega\,[k(c)] &= \tfrac{1}{4}\,;\\
\omega(\$0) &= 0\,.
\end{aligned}$$

Some but not all subjects conform with the required ranking of the lottery tickets. Therefore, in any empirical estimation of a subject's utilities and personal probabilities, one must check whether the subject is consistent, at least in some approximate sense. As pointed out in the simpler context of section 2, probabilistic models of decision and of learning to decide are needed for any descriptive theory, and they too may fail.

Behavior toward risk. Again suppose that the event Z in Table IV is 'heads'. If the subject has named cash equivalents $k(a)=k(d)=\$50$, $k(c)=\$25$, and $k(b)=\$75$ (and similarly for further, easily conceived compound lotteries with utilities $\frac{1}{8}, \frac{3}{8}, \ldots, \frac{1}{16}, \ldots$), we would infer that over the observed range he is indifferent between a 'fair bet' and the certainty of

TABLE IV

Decision problem involving lottery tickets

Lottery ticket	Prize if event Z happens	Prize if event Z does not happen	Probability of gaining \$100
a	\$100	\$0	p
b	Lottery ticket *a*	\$100	$p^2 + 1 - p > p$
c	Lottery ticket *a*	\$0	$p^2 < p$
d	Lottery ticket *b*	Lottery ticket *c*	$p(p^2+1-p)+(1-p)\,p^2=p$

getting its expected gain. We would say that he is 'indifferent to risk'. His utility function of money gain is a straight line. On the other hand, if he has named cash equivalents $k(a)=k(d)<\$50$, $k(c)<\frac{1}{2}k(a)$, and $k(b)<$ $<\frac{1}{2}[100+k(a)]$, his utility function of money gain will be a concave curve (any of its chords will lie below the corresponding arc), and we would say that he is 'averse to risk'. If the inequality signs in the preceding sentence are reversed, the utility function is convex (chords are above arcs), and we would say that over the observed range the subject 'loves risk'. When the utility function is either concave or convex, the decision maker maximizes the expected value, not of money gain, but of some nonlinear function of money gain.

Daniel Bernoulli (1738) pointed out that the utility function is concave in the case of the 'Petersburg paradox'. Marshall (1890) also assumed risk aversion as an economic fact (or perhaps as a prescription from Victorian morals) equivalent to that of 'decreasing marginal utility of money'. Some economic implications of risk aversion were given by Pratt (1964) and Arrow (1965). It should be noted that this assumption is inconsistent with the behavior of a satisficer for whom utility is a step-function of money gain and the behavior of a merchant for whom the disutility of bankruptcy is the same regardless of the amount owed.

The maxmin rule. In competition with the expected utility rule (and the postulates underlying it) is the 'conservative' or 'maxmin' rule, which states that the decision maker should maximize the minimum payoff; that is to say, the maxmin rule proposes that preferences among actions be based on each action's worst result only. Thus in the case of Table I the maxmin rule would prescribe that $a' < b$ even if Z_1 has the probability of, say, an earthquake, and presumably $b \sim a$, contradicting the inadmissibility postulate. However, because of the strong appeal of the inadmissibility postulate, it is usually proposed that the maxmin rule be applied only when domination is absent; this leads to the ordering $a' < b < a$ rather than $a' < b \sim a$. This proposal is not too satisfactory since it violates a plausible continuity principle (Milnor, 1954). A small modification in outcomes – by \$1 in Table I, or by 1 cent for that matter – can make or break domination and thus reverse the preference ordering. Indeed, should we advise people not to live in San Francisco or Tokyo because of possible but not very probable earthquakes? Should we advise pedestrians never to cross streets because of the possibility of being struck by an auto? Such considerations compel us to balance the advantages against the disadvantages of competing decisions, weighing them by appropriately defined probabilities – the expected utility principle.

A historical note. Early theories prescribing maximization of expected utility were confined to special cases. Two types of restrictions were imposed. First, the decision maker was advised to maximize the expected value of his money wealth or gain, i.e., utility was in effect identified with a money amount or some linear function of a money amount. Some other quantifiable good, such as the number of prisoners taken or the number of patients cured, might play the same role as money, but nonquantifiable rewards and penalties of actions were unnecessarily excluded from the set of results. Second, probabilities were restricted to objective ones – a special case of personal probabilities.

It is difficult to imagine that an experienced Bronze Age player who used dice that had 'tooled edges and threw absolutely true' (David, 1962) would bet much more than 1:5 on the coming of the ace. Cardano's efforts in computing the gambler's odds (Ore, 1953) suggest at any rate that by the sixteenth century the rule of maximizing average money gains computed on the basis of objective probabilities was taken for granted.

We have already cited Bernoulli and Marshall as having proclaimed utility a nonlinear function of money, thus lifting the first of the above restrictions. Marshall also applied the utility concept to commodity bundles. Von Neumann and Morgenstern (1944) extended it further to all possible results of actions and derived the expected utility rule from simple consistency postulates. This was simplified by others, especially Herstein and Milnor (1953). All these writers dealt only with objective probabilities, leaving out the important cases in which symmetries between relevant events are not agreed upon.

Bayes (1764) can be credited with the idea of personal probabilities. He thought of them as being revealed by an individual's choices among wagers – not just on cards and coins, but on horses and fighting cocks as well! Thus Bayes removed the second restriction, but he retained the first in assuming that utility was in effect identified with money gains, so that betting 9 guineas against 1 implies a corresponding ratio of probabilities. In 1937, de Finetti provided mathematical rigor for this approach.

In 1926, Ramsey (1923–1928) stated, perhaps for the first time, simple consistency postulates that imply the existence of both personal probabilities (of any events, regardless of symmetries) and utilities (of any results of actions, quantifiable or not). Savage (1954) restated the consistency postulates and, partly following de Finetti and von Neumann and Morgenstern, proved that they imply the expected utility rule. For an original exposition, see Pratt *et al.* (1964).

Reviews of the works of other contemporary authors are found in Arrow (1951), Luce and Suppes (1965), Ozga (1965), and Fishburn (1964). Surveys and bibliographies as well as much original material by 21 leading authors on both the prescriptive and descriptive aspects of decision theory are found in Shelly and Bryan (1964).

VII. STRATEGIES

The existence of numerical utilities describing a decision maker's 'tastes' and of probabilities describing his 'beliefs' has been shown to follow from rules of consistency. To formulate and solve the problem of choosing a good decision, both tastes and beliefs must be assumed fixed over some given period of time (but see Koopmans [1964] on 'flexibility'). In general, the probabilities the decision maker assigns at any time to the various states of nature and thus to the results of his actions depend on his information at that time. New information may also uncover new feasible actions. We shall generalize the decision concept accordingly in several steps.

A *strategy* (also called a decision function or response rule) is the assignment, in advance of information, of specific actions to respond to the different messages that the decision maker may receive from an information source. If, more generally, messages, actions, and results form time sequences (the case of 'earning while learning'), we have a *sequential strategy* (also called an extensive or dynamic strategy). To each possible sequence of future messages, a sequential strategy assigns a sequence of actions (see, for example, Theil, 1964). An optimal sequential strategy maximizes the weighted average of utilities assigned to all possible sequences of results, possibly taking into account 'impatience' by means of a discount rate (Fisher, 1930; Koopmans, 1960). The weights are personal *joint* probabilities of sequences of events *and* messages. This amounts to the same thing as saying that the probabilities of events are revised each time a message is received.

It is still more general to redefine action in order to include in it the choice of information sources to be used and thus of 'questions to be asked' at a given time. The resulting problem of finding an optimal *informational strategy* is a task of economic theories of information and organization and also of statistical decision theory (e.g., Raiffa and Schlaifer, 1961) where events and information sources correspond to hypotheses and experiments, respectively.

Finally, if we allow the decision maker to receive messages about the feasibility and outcomes of actions he has not formerly considered, we obtain the still more general concept of *exploratory strategy*. True, it has been almost proverbially tenuous to assign probabilities to the results of industrial or scientific research; yet these undertakings are not different in principle from many other ventures and bets, such as those discussed in Section V.

The complex strategies noted here are hardly maximized by the actual entrepreneur, although the penetration of industry by professionals may again bring descriptive and prescriptive economics to their pristine closeness. Today many descriptive hypotheses in this field use the concept of aspiration level – the boundary between success and failure. The actual decision maker is said to revise his aspiration level upward or downward depending on whether he has or has not reached it by previous action; exploration for actions not previously considered is triggered by failure (Simon, 1957). The sequence of actions generated by the dynamic aspiration-level model will, in general, differ from that prescribed by dynamic programming. Yet, with utilities assigned to results of actions in a particular way, it is possible that the aspiration-level mechanism is indeed optimal. It has been inspired, in fact, by adaptive feedbacks observed in live organisms; such feedbacks presumably have maximized the probability of the survival of species.

VIII. COST OF DECISION MAKING

One action or strategy may appear better than another as long as we disregard the toil and trouble of decision making itself, i.e., the efforts of gathering information and of processing it into an optimal decision. The ranking of actions may be reversed when we take these efforts into account and deal, in this sense, with 'net' rather than 'gross' expected utilities of actions. A small increase in expected profit may not be worth a good night's sleep. In statistics, we stop sequential sampling earlier the higher the cost is of obtaining each observation. As an approximation to some logically required, but very complicated, decision rule, we may use a linear decision rule (e.g., prescribe inventories to be proportional to turnover) in order to lessen computational costs. The 'incrementalism' observed and recommended by Lindblom (1965) in the field of political decisions corresponds to the common mathematical practice of searching for a global optimum in the neighborhood of a local optimum or possibly in the neighborhood of the *status quo*. How many local search steps one should undertake and how often he should jump (hopefully) toward a global optimum will presumably depend on the costs of searching (see, for example, Gel'fand and Tsetlin, 1962). Indeed, some strategies may be too complex to be computable in a finite amount of time, even though they respond to each message by a feasible action. There is, after all, a limit on the capacity of computers and on the brain capacity of decision makers. Hence, some strategies may have infinite costs.

The net utility of an action is often represented as the difference between 'gross utility' and 'decision cost'. A prescriptive theory would presumably require that personal probabilities be assigned not only to the outcomes of the actions but also to the efforts of estimating the outcomes and of searching for the action with the highest expected utility.

On a more general level, it is not strictly permissible to represent net utility as a difference between gross utility and decision cost. Even if the two were measurable in dollars, say, utility may be a nonlinear function of money gains. Yet the assumption that net utility is separable into these components simplifies the theory – it reduces the cost of thinking! Almost all prescriptive theory to date deals with gross utility only. Little attention has been given to decision costs that might be subtractable and thus definable in arriving at a net utility concept. Still less attention has been given to a net utility concept that cannot be decomposed into gross-utility and decision-cost components.

The elements for a theory of the expected cost of using inanimate computers, given the (statistical) population of future problems, are probably available. However, the current classification of computation problems as 'scientific' and 'business' (differing in their comparative needs for speed and memory) is certainly much too rough. A theory of mechanical computation costs would resemble the theory of the cost of manufacturing with complex equipment and known technology when capacities and operations are scheduled optimally. On the other hand, so little is known about the 'technology' of human brains! If economists would join forces with students of the psychology of problem solving, insights would undoubtedly be gained into both the descriptive and prescriptive aspects of decision making.

BIBLIOGRAPHY

Allais, M.: 1953, 'Le comportement de l'homme rationnel devant le risque: Critique des postulats et axiomes de l'école americaine', *Econometrica* **21**, 503–546.

Arrow, Kenneth J.: 1951, 'Alternative Approaches to the Theory of Choice in Risk-taking Situations', *Econometrica* **19**, 404–437.

Arrow, Kenneth J.: 1958, 'Utilities, Attitudes, Choices: A Review Note', *Econometrica* **26**, 1–23.

Arrow, Kenneth J.: 1963, 'Utility and Expectation in Economic Behavior', pp. 724–752 in Sigmund Koch (ed.), *Psychology: A Study of a Science*, Volume 6: 'Investigations of Man as Socius: Their Place in Psychology and the Social Sciences', McGraw-Hill, New York.

Arrow, Kenneth J.: 1965, *Aspects of the Theory of Risk-Bearing*, Academic Bookstore, Helsinki.

Aumann, Robert J.: 1962, 'Utility Theory Without the Completeness Axiom', *Econometrica* **30**, 445–462. Corrections in Volume 32 of *Econometrica.*

Bayes, Thomas: (1764) 1958, 'An Essay Towards Solving a Problem in the Doctrine of Chances', *Biometrika* **45**, 296–315.

Bernoulli, Daniel: (1738) 1954, 'Exposition of a New Theory on the Measurement of Risk', *Econometrica* **22**, 23–36. First published as 'Specimen theoriae novae de mensura sortis'.

Borel, Émile: 1939, *Valeur practique et philosophie des probabilités*, Gauthier-Villars, Paris.

Carnap, R.: 1962, 'The Aim of Inductive Logic', pp. 303–318 in International Congress for Logic, Methodology, and Philosophy of Science, Stanford, California, 1960, *Logic, Methodology, and Philosophy of Science: Proceedings* (ed. by Ernest Nagel, Patrick Suppes, and Alfred Tarski), Stanford Univ. Press.

Chernoff, Herman and Moses, Lincoln E.: 1959, *Elementary Decision Theory*, Wiley, New York.

David, Florence N.: 1962, *Games, Gods and Gambling: The Origins and History of Probability and Statistical Ideas From the Earliest Times to the Newtonian Era*, Hafner, New York.

Davidson, Donald and Marschak, Jacob: 1959, 'Experimental Tests of a Stochastic Decision Theory', *Selected Essays*, 6.

Davis, John M.: 1958, 'The Transitivity of Preferences', *Behavioral Science* **3**, 26–33.

Debreu, Gerard: 1959, *Theory of Value*, Wiley, New York.

De Finetti, Bruno: (1937) 1964, 'Foresight: Its Logical Laws, Its Subjective Sources', pp. 93–158 in Henry E. Kyburg and Howard E. Smokler (eds.), *Studies in Subjective Probabilities*, Wiley, New York. First published in French.

Edwards, Ward: 1953, 'Probability-Preferences in Gambling', *American Journal of Psychology* **66**, 349–364.

Ellsberg, Daniel: 1961, 'Risk, Ambiguity, and the Savage Axioms', *Quarterly Journal of Economics* **75**, 643–669.

Fechner, Gustav T.: (1860) 1907, *Elemente der Psychophysik*, 2 vols. (3d ed.) Breitkopf & Härtel, Leipzig. An English translation of Volume 1 was published by Holt in 1966.

Fellner, William: 1965, *Probability and Profit*, Irwin, Homewood, Ill.

Fishburn, Peter C.: 1964, *Decision and Value Theory*, Wiley, New York.

Fisher, Irving: 1906, 'The Risk Element', pp. 265–300 in Irving Fisher, *The Nature of Capital and Income*, Macmillan, New York.

Fisher, Irving: (1930) 1961, *The Theory of Interest*, Kelley, New York. Revision of the author's *The Rate of Interest* (1907).

Franklin, Benjamin: (1772) 1945, 'How to Make a Decision'. p. 786 in *A Benjamin Franklin Reader* (ed. by Nathan G. Goodman), Crowell, New York. A letter to J. Priestly.

Gel'fand, I. M. and Tsetlin, M. L.: 1962, 'Some Methods of Control for Complex Systems', *Russian Mathematical Surveys* **17**, 95–117.

Hart, Albert G.: (1940) 1951, *Anticipations, Uncertainty and Dynamic Planning*, Kelley, New York.

Herstein, I. N. and Milnor, John: 1953, 'An Axiomatic Approach to Measurable Utility', *Econometrica* **21**, 291–297.

Hicks, John R.: (1939) 1946, *Value and Capital: An Inquiry Into Some Fundamental Principles of Economic Theory* (2d ed.), Clarendon, Oxford.

Interdisciplinary Research Conference, University of New Mexico: 1960, *Decisions, Values and Groups: Proceedings* (ed. by D. Willner), Pergamon, New York. See especially the article by J. S. Chipman, 'Stochastic Choice and SubjectiveProbability'.

Jeffrey, Richard C.: 1965, *The Logic of Decision*, McGraw-Hill, New York.

Knight, Frank H.: (1921) 1933, *Risk, Uncertainty and Profit*, London School of Economics and Political Science Series of Reprints of Scarce Tracts in Economic and Political Science, No. 16. London School of Economics.

Koopmans, Tjalling: 1960, 'Stationary Ordinal Utility and Impatience', *Econometrica* **28**, 287–309.

Koopmans, Tjalling: 1964, 'On Flexibility of Future Preference', pp. 243–254 in Maynard W. Shelly and Glenn L. Bryan (eds.), *Human Judgments and Optimality*, Wiley, New York.

Lindblom, Charles E.: 1965, *The Intelligence of Democracy: Decision Making Through Mutual Adjustment*, Free Press, New York.

Luce, R. Duncan: 1959, *Individual Choice Behavior: A Theoretical Analysis*, Wiley, New York.

Luce, R. Duncan and Raiffa, Howard: 1957, *Games and Decisions: Introduction and Critical Survey*. A study of the Behavior Models Project, Bureau of Applied Social Research, Columbia University, Wiley, New York. First issued in 1954 as *A Survey of the Theory of Games*, Columbia University, Bureau of Applied Social Research, Technical Report No. 5.

Luce, R. Duncan and Suppes, Patrick: 1965, 'Preference, Utility, and Subjective Probability', Volume 3, pp. 249–410 in R. Duncan Luce, Robert R. Bush, and Eugene Galanter (eds.), *Handbook of Mathematical Psychology*, Wiley, New York.

MacCrimmon, K. R.: 1965, 'An Experimental Study of the Decision-Making Behavior of Business Executives', Ph. D. dissertation, Univ. of California at Los Angeles.

Marschak, Jacob: 1950, 'Rational Behavior, Uncertain Prospects, and Measurable Utility', *Selected Essays*, 1.

Marschak, Jacob: (1954) 1964, 'Scaling of Utility and Probability', *Selected Essays*, 3.

Marshall, Alfred: (1890) 1961, *Principles of Economics* (9th ed.), Macmillan, New York. See especially the Mathematical Appendix, note 9.

May, Kenneth O.: 1954, 'Intransitivity, Utility and the Aggregation of Preference Patterns', *Econometrica* **22**, 1–13.

Milnor, John: 1954, 'Games Against Nature', pp. 49–60 in Robert M. Thrall, C. H. Combs, and R. L. Davis (eds.), *Decision Processes*, Wiley, New York.

Neyman, Jerzy: 1950, *First Course in Probability and Statistics*, Holt, New York.

Ore, Oystein: 1953, *Cardano, the Gambling Scholar*, Oxford Univ. Press. Princeton Univ. Press. Includes a translation by Sidney Henry Gould from the Latin of Cardano's *Book on Games of Chance.*

Oźga, S. Andrew: 1965, *Expectations in Economic Theory*, Weidenfeld & Nicolson, London.

Papandreou, Andreas G.: 1957, *A Test of a Stochastic Theory of Choice*, University of California Publications in Economics, Vol. 16, No. 1. Univ. of California Press. In collaboration with O. H. Sauerlender, O. H. Brownlee, L. Hurwicz, and W. Franklin.

Pascal, Blaise: (1670) 1961, *Pensées: Notes on Religion and Other Subjects*, Doubleday, New York. See especially Section 3: 'De la nécessité du pari'.

Pollack, Irwin: 1955, 'Sound Level Discrimination and Variation of Reference Testing Conditions', *Journal of the Acoustical Society of America* **27**, 474–480.

Pratt, John, W.: 1964, 'Risk Aversion in the Small and in the Large', *Econometrica* **32**, 122–136.

Pratt, John W., Raiffa, Howard, and Schlaifer, Robert: 1964, 'The Foundations of Decision Under Uncertainty: An Elementary Exposition', *Journal of the American Statistical Association* **59**, 353–375.

Quandt, Richard: 1956, 'A Probabilistic Theory of Consumer Behavior', *Quarterly Journal of Economics* **70**, 507–536.

Raiffa, Howard: 1961, 'Risk, Ambiguity, and the Savage Axioms: Comment', *Quarterly Journal of Economics* **75**, 690–694.

Raiffa, Howard and Schlaifer, Robert: 1961, *Applied Statistical Decision Theory*, Graduate School of Business Administartion, Studies in Managerial Economics, Harvard Univ., Boston, Division of Research.

Ramsey, Frank P.: (1923–1928) 1950, *The Foundations of Mathematics and Other Logical Essays*, Humanities, New York. See especially Chapter 7, 'Truth and Probabilities', and Chapter 8, 'Further Considerations'.

Savage, Leonard J.: 1954, *The Foundations of Statistics*, Wiley, New York. Revised, Dover, 1972.

Shackle, L. S.: (1949) 1952, *Expectation in Economics* (2d ed.), Cambridge Univ. Press.

Shackle, L. S.: 1955, *Uncertainty in Economics and Other Reflections*, Cambridge Univ. Press.

Shackle, L. S.: 1961, *Decision, Order and Time in Human Affairs*, Cambridge Univ. Press.

Shelly, Maynard W. and Bryan, Glenn L. (eds.): 1964, *Human Judgments and Optimality*, Wiley, New York.

Simon, Herbert A.: 1957, 'A Behavioral Model of Rational Choice', pp. 241–260 in Herbert A. Simon, *Models of Man*, Wiley, New York.

Simon, Herbert A.: 1959, 'Theories of Decision-Making in Economics and Behavioral Science', *American Economic Review* **49**, 253–283.

Theil, Henri: 1964, *Optimal Decision Rules for Government and Industry*, North Holland Publishing, Amsterdam; Rand McNally, Chicago.

Thurstone, Louis L.: (1927–1955) 1959, *The Measurement of Values*, Univ. of Chicago Press. Selections from previously published papers.

von Neumann, John and Morgenstern, Oskar: (1944) 1964, *Theory of Games and Economic Behavior* (3d ed.), Wiley, New York.

Wald, Abraham: (1950) 1964, *Statistical Decision Functions*, Wiley, New York.

Wolfowitz, J.: 1962, 'Bayesian Inference and Axioms of Consistent Decision', *Econometrica* **3**, 471–480.

Wright, Georg H. von: 1963, *The Logic of Preference*, Edinburgh Univ. Press.

17

THE ECONOMIC MAN'S LOGIC*

(1970)

I

The contributors to this volume want to honour an economist. He is also the author of *Foundations of Inductive Logic*.[1] I shall relate induction to the making of decisions under uncertainty. This will be recognized by economists as a natural extension of the problem facing a producer, consumer, investor (or, for that matter, a government agency) under uncertainty. It is also in the spirit of some modern logicians. Ramsey (1926, 1928) and von Wright (1963) have, in a sense, extended deductive logic by adding axioms of preference. Ramsey has used these axioms as the very foundations of probabilities and thus, presumably, of induction. Harrod, whose preface acknowledged Ramsey's moral support, has gone on to discoveries of his own. But I shall ask later whether Harrod's fundamental principle of 'continuity' of experience is at all related to De Finetti's (1937) 'exchangeability'. This concept is used by some of those working in Ramsey's spirit, in order to understand the relation between the probabilities that the maker of decisions (including predictions) uses, and the frequencies he has observed. Harrod refers at length and, on balance, critically to Carnap's duality of 'probability$_1$' and 'probability$_2$'. The latter is defined as a frequency. The former is closer to, or identical with, the concept to be presented here. This closeness is more evident now than it was at the time of Harrod's writing. For in 1962 Carnap explained some changes in his views, starting with a statement that will be acclaimed by those approaching probabilities via the logic of decisions.[2]

II

Both logicians and economists are wont to distinguish between prescribing and describing. Logic prescribes. Psychology describes. So do other 'behavioural sciences'. To illustrate: if objects x and y are identical, and objects y and z are also identical, the *homo logicus*, obeying the formal norms (consistency rules) of ordinary logic, will recognize x and z as identical too. But the 'brain-twister' puzzle at the end of the weekly paper will present these three objects in such a way that even a well-rested, college-educated reader may fail to recognize the identity between x and z; let alone a tired or sick man, a child, a drunk. And how often does a political speaker conclude in good faith that A implies B when his sole premiss was that A is a necessary condition for B; and how often, and how many people go along with his reasoning! Cognitive psychology[3] or, for that matter, anthropology may study the frequency of such aberrations among subjects with given physical and cultural characteristics, given the type of objects ('stimuli') considered.

Similarly, the consistent decision maker, the *homo economicus*, is not the actual, real man. For example: just like the non-logical (yet real) man may fail to obey the norm of transitivity of the identity relation between objects, the non-economic (yet real) man may fail to conform with the norm of transitivity of the indifference relation between actions: though indifferent between actions a and b, and between b and c, he may prefer a to c, say. And the empirical study may usefully occupy itself with recording the frequency of such behaviour, and its dependence on the characteristics of the man as well as of the actions considered. I say 'usefully' because such records can lead to predictions of practical importance.

It is of some consequence to extend our example of intransitive identity and indifference relations from man to an electronic computer. Because of its limited memory, or its limited speed (and a limited amount of available time), the computer must round off the results of its additions and multiplications. It will happen therefore, from time to time, that although the numbers x and y, and the numbers y and z are defined as pairwise equal, yet the computer's print-out will show x and z as not equal.[4]

Thus, an economic question arises, which I shall not try to answer here. The question applies, in fact, to men and machines alike. How much rationality, consistency, precision can one afford? What price logic? It was Ramsey (1926) who pointed to the 'reluctance to bother about trifles'. Indeed, we are free to proclaim weaker or stricter systems of consistency norms. Some of those which are weaker and which bother less 'about trifles' may turn out to be more 'rational'[5] if, as befits us economists, we take account of cost and limited resources, appropriately defined. The boundary between prescriptive and descriptive studies of human thought and decision is thus fluid.

Whatever this boundary, the study of the choice between conclusions from premises is usually regarded as the business of the logician (if prescriptive) or as the business of the cognitive psychologist (if descriptive).[6] The *description* of choices between actions (or decisions) is also usually regarded as the business of psychologists with their experiments,[7] but also of other students of human behaviour: anthropologists and sociologists with their interviews and questionnaires, economists with their attempts to estimate statistically the effect of various factors upon the (individual or aggregate) demands for goods, securities, foreign currencies....

But what about the *prescriptive* norms, the consistency rules for choices between decisions? In general, action must be decided upon under uncertainty about its results. Or, in an equivalent formulation, under uncertainty about the state of the world, which will affect the action's result. We are led to discussing something called 'probabilities', to be assigned by the decisionmaker to the several possible results of a given action of his, in a manner consistent, in some formal sense, with his preferences between actions. Or, in an equivalent formulation, he is thought to assign appropriate probabilities to the several possible events, each being a set of states of the world that determine the results of actions. In short, we discuss formal consistency rules that lead to judgments which are themselves not judgements about formal consistency but about material truth. And this, I suppose, is the proper domain of inductive logic. But note that, presented here in its relation with decision making, this logic involves, in addition to 'probability judgements' that the decider makes about the world, also his preferences between, his 'utility judgements' about, the compared actions and their results. (Thus both truth and goodness seem to be involved, and the post-Aristotelian wall between logic and ethics seems to be breached. Was not, in Socrates' eyes, the wise and the virtuous the same man?)

III

A set of decision norms or axioms, shaped up by De Finetti and by Savage (1954), is equivalent to the 'expected utility theorem'. We shall give the theorem as a purely mathematical statement. This will be followed by its interpretation, (viz., by translating symbols into corresponding entities relevant to decision making) and by the statement of the axioms.

Define a set A of functions a from the set $X=\{x\}$ to the set $C=\{c\}$. If the binary relation $\succcurlyeq$ on A satisfies axioms 1, 2,..., then, and only then, there exists a probability measure P on X and there exists a real-valued function u on C, such that, for any a_1, a_2 in A,

$$a_1 \succcurlyeq a_2 \quad \text{if and only if} \quad w(a_1) \geqslant w(a_2);$$

where by definition,

$$w(a) = \sum_c u(c)\, p_a(c),$$

$$p_a(c) = P\{x : a(x) = c\}.$$

(X assumed here finite for convenience). This is a purely mathematical statement, and so are the axioms 1, 2,.... But before we talk about the axioms, let us give the *interpretations* for the symbols, and some names:

A = set of *actions* a; X = set of *states* x; C = set of *consequences* (results) c. Thus typically $c=a(x)$: given the state, the action determines the consequence.

$a_1 \succcurlyeq a_2$ reads 'a_1 *is not worse than* a_2'. Depending on whether it is or is not the case that, in addition, also $a_2 \succcurlyeq a_1$, we write, respectively, $a_1 \sim a_2$ ('equally desirable', 'indifferent') or $a_1 \succ a_2$ ('better', 'preferred').

$u(c)$ is called the *utility* of c. P is a *measure* on X, in the usual sense. That is (roughly), P is a real-valued function on the set of subsets Z of X (called events) which is (1) non-negative, (2) additive, i.e., for any disjoint Z_1, Z_2, $P(Z_1 \text{ or } Z_2)=P(Z_1)+P(Z_2)$. Moreover the function P is a *probability measure*, for, in addition to the properties (1) and (2) it has the property (3), $P(X)=1$.

$p_a(c)$, as defined above, is then the probability assigned to the set of all states which make action a result in consequence c; and $w(a)$, as defined above, is the expectation (i.e., the average) of utilities of consequences of action a; in a rather unfortunate abbreviation, $w(a)$ is called *expected utility* of a.

This is, then, the theorem's interpretation. Utilities of consequences and probabilities of events are defined, for a given decision-maker, as numerical variables whose sum of products he maximizes, given the set of actions (decisions) available to him. But these variables exist if, and only if, he is 'consistent', in the sense that his preferences between all conceivable actions (i.e., all functions from the set of states to the set of consequences) satisfy certain axioms.

These axioms need to be stated only because the theorem as just interpreted in terms of decisions may appear less plausible, convincing, 'transparent' (an expression used in just such a context by Von Neumann and Morgenstern, 1947, p. 25) than those simple axioms, similarly interpreted. Mathematically, they are jointly equivalent to the theorem. To a god who sees this equivalence immediately, there is no virtue in the axioms' greater 'transparency': a psychological rather than logical category, a tribute to human weakness. Elsewhere,[8] I have tried to assemble fragmentary evidence on the extent to which responses of some men conform with Savage's axioms, at least when the subject is trained to 'stop and think' (Ramsey, 1928, p. 201): to 'untwist', e.g., to tabulate a verbally confused decision problem. This was followed by a rough outline of the proof (less rigorous than that of Savage, 1954) that the axioms do imply the theorem (the converse is rather obvious); and again, by a proposed test of compliance with the theorem itself.

Axiom 1 asserts that the relation 'not worse than' completely orders the set A of conceivable actions. The economists' well-known partitioning of the set of conceivable commodity bundles, *under certainty*, into equivalence sets called 'indifference surfaces' is a special case. Clearly, there is a 1–1 correspondence between the set C of consequences and that subset of A consisting of 'sure actions' only (i.e., such that $a(x)=c$ is a constant). Hence C itself can be said to be completely ordered by the relation 'not worse than'.

This permits a brief statement of *Axiom* 2: if $a(x)$ is not worse than $a'(x)$ for all x, and is better than $a'(x)$ for some x, then a is better than a'. This principle of 'inadmissibility of dominated actions' has guided statisticians long since (see, e.g., Wald, 1950). As a matter of sheer common sense it surely has guided all practical people who 'stopped to think'.

Axiom 3 can be interpreted as 'irrelevance of consequences that are not affected by the choice between two actions': if, for all x in the subset Z of X, $a_1(x)=a_2(x)$ and also $a_1'(x)=a_2'(x)$, and if, for all x not in Z, $a_1(x)=$ $=a_1'(x)$ and also $a_2(x)=a_2'(x)$, then a_1' is not worse than a_2', provided a_1

is not worse than a_2. I submit that an attentive reader who would care to tabulate a simple example of the premiss of this axiom (with Z and non-Z each consisting just of two elements) might 'convince' himself of the conclusion.[9]

Axiom 4 can be interpreted as 'independence of beliefs on rewards'. Let $a(x)=c=a'(x')$ for all x in Z, x' in Z'; let $a(x)=\bar{c}=a'(x')$ for all x in non-Z, x' in non-Z'; and let c be better than $\bar{c}$. Thus a and a' can be interpreted as two bets, with the same prizes, on the two events Z and Z', respectively. It is a remarkable feature of ordinary English that, when asked why he prefers to bet on Z rather than Z', many a subject says 'because Z is more probable'; and he says this regardless of whether those events are or are not repeatable. Now, Axiom 4 says that this 'belief' (as revealed by preferring a to a', say) remains unchanged when the pair of prizes ('rewards') $c \succcurlyeq \bar{c}$ is replaced by some other pair, $d \succcurlyeq \bar{d}$, say.

The proof of the existence of the numerical utility function $u(.)$ on the set C of consequences is of less interest to us here, than the existence of a probability measure P on X, underlying the 'expected utility' of each action. In fact, Axiom 4 makes it possible to discuss probabilities of events while considering just two consequences, c and $\bar{c}$ ('success' and 'failure'), with utilities 1 and 0 attached to them arbitrarily and with no loss of generality. Then the expected utility $w(a)$ becomes simply equal to the probability with which action a will result in success. In particular, the discussion may be, and is often, confined to the case when the action consists in predicting; its success is 'correct prediction' and its failure is 'wrong prediction'.

This may be also the place to remark that some authors have confined the set of considered consequences to monetary gains and losses only. By tacitly assuming, in addition, a constant marginal utility of money wealth they were able to identify probability with a 'fair betting coefficient'. This is the case with many passages of Carnap and with the original treatment by De Finetti.[10] It seems to me that this approach goes as far back as the Rev. T. Bayes himself![11] The sophistication about marginal utility of money, unleashed by Bayes's contemporary Daniel Bernoulli and taken up by economists, makes the 'fair bets' an insufficient device to reveal the probabilities that guide bettors. A more complicated device, Borel's dial, will be presented in Section V.

IV

Our axioms suffice to prove the existence of a probability measure P on X, such that $P(Z) \geqslant P(Z')$ whenever a bet on Z is judged as not worse than a bet on Z'. Familiar properties such as 'if Z contains Z' then $P(Z) \geqslant P(Z')$' and '$P(Z) + P(\text{non-}Z) = 1$' are then guaranteed.

It is important to note that the axioms also imply corresponding properties of 'conditional probabilities', written $P(Z_1 \mid Z_2)$, read 'probability of Z_1, given Z_2', and defined by considering 'conditional bets'. Such a bet is called off if Z_2 does not occur; and the bet yields c or $\bar{c}$ (where, as before, c is better than $\bar{c}$), according to whether 'Z_2 and Z_1' happens. A conditional bet on Z_1 given Z_2 is not worse than one on Z_1' given Z_2 if and only if $P(Z_1 \mid Z_2) \geqslant P(Z_1' \mid Z_2)$. For a fixed Z_2, the function $P(Z_1 \mid Z_2)$ has again the three properties of a probability measure. Moreover, the axioms entail the following relation between the 'joint probability' $P(Z_1$ and $Z_2)$ (which we shall assume non-zero) and the conditional and non-conditional probabilities:

$$P(Z_1 \text{ and } Z_2) = P(Z_2).P(Z_1 \mid Z_2) = P(Z_1).P(Z_2 \mid Z_1).$$

Consequently

$$P(Z_2 \mid Z_1) = P(Z_2).P(Z_1 \mid Z_2)/P(Z_1);$$

and similarly, replacing Z_2 by some other event, Z_2',

$$P(Z_2' \mid Z_1) = P(Z_2').P(Z_1 \mid Z_2')/P(Z_1).$$

Dividing the last equation by the preceding one (no zeros are involved!),

$$\frac{P(Z_2 \mid Z_1)}{P(Z_2' \mid Z_1)} = \frac{P(Z_2)}{P(Z_2')} \cdot \frac{P(Z_1 \mid Z_2)}{P(Z_1 \mid Z_2')}.$$

Sometimes the events Z_2 and Z_2' are interpreted as two mutually exclusive 'hypotheses', and the event Z_1 as 'evidence'. For later use it will be convenient to denote the latter by E and the two hypotheses by H and H' (replacing Z_2 and Z_2'). We have then

$$\frac{P(H \mid E)}{P(H' \mid E)} = \frac{P(H)}{P(H')} \cdot \frac{P(E \mid H)}{P(E \mid H')}.$$

In this equation, a convenient form of the Bayes Theorem,[12] the ratio on the left-hand side is called 'posterior odds' and is, thus, equal to the product of so-called 'prior odds' to the 'likelihood ratio with respect to evidence *E*'. If you are consistent and if you assign constant marginal utility to money in the range of the prizes considered, these three ratios, as constrained by the above equation, represent the least favourable odds at which you will accept each of the following three bets: (1) the conditional bet on *H* given *E*, against *H'* given *E*; (2) the bet on *H* against *H'*; and (3) the conditional bet on *E* given *H* against *E* given *H'*. If constant marginal utility of money is not assumed, the 'Borel dial' to be described in the next section would reveal, as precisely as it can, that you assign to the six events in question just the probabilities consistent with the equation.

The theorem of Bayes, understood in this manner is, then, along with the expected utility theorem, entailed by the axioms of consistent decision making. The theorem will help us to explain why the consistent decision-maker whose evidence consists of a (properly defined) 'large sample' will (almost) maximize his expected utility if he assigns to a hypothesis a posterior probability equal to the relative frequency of certain observations.

I shall reason on lines consistent with Savage and De Finetti, I believe; and also with Carnap's treatment of the 'estimation' of his 'probability$_1$' (which is logically derived, not from frequencies but from betting decisions), given the observed frequencies. This approach seems to be different from Harrod's for whom (p. 47) 'The probability relation is ... essentially and by definition a relation of frequency', although he does not regard 'probability numbers as derived from or reflections of statistical frequencies in nature.' The difference between the two approaches will turn out to depend on the difference, if any, between Harrod's principle of 'continuity' (Chapter III) and the 'exchangeability' concept which we shall now present.

V

Although I had each axiom accompanied by its interpretation in terms of decisions, they, and the consequent existence of a probability measure on *X*, can be regarded as purely mathematical propositions about a binary relation called 'not worse than'. Now, the properties defining a probability measure form only the beginning of the calculus of probabilities. As pointed out by De Finetti (1937), a further premiss for the body of that calculus is the existence of 'exchangeable' subsets (events) of the set on which the probability measure is defined. For example, let X be partitioned into subsets Z and non-Z such that the decision-maker is indifferent between betting on either: each of these two actions is 'not worse than' the other. The two events are then 'exchangeable' and the partition itself, i.e., the pair 'Z, non-Z' is sometimes called a 'fair coin' (with Z and non-Z then called 'heads' and 'tails'). It corresponds to the gross physical reality of minted coins only in the same way in which the straight line of pure geometry corresponds to the edge of the paper page now facing you, my reader. There may or may not be agreement between people as to how closely this page approximates the ideal rectangle; and similarly, whether one should be indeed indifferent between betting on a particular physical coin's falling heads or falling tails up; or between betting on any of the 52 cards of a given (not necessarily well-shuffled) deck. But if you are indeed indifferent between those 52 bets, and, in addition, obey the consistency axioms, you will be also indifferent between betting on any of the four suits, and on either of the two colours. The probabilities of success in each of these three sets of equally desirable bets will, then, respectively be: $\frac{1}{52}$, $\frac{1}{4}$, $\frac{1}{2}$. It will also follow that you should be indifferent between betting on any specified set of (say) seven cards, the probability of success of any such bet being the same.

Probabilities as revealed by preferences between bets with the same pairs of prizes (c, $\bar{c}$ of our Axiom 4), were so described already by Borel (1924) in his review of Keynes (1921). Accordingly, I would like to call a 'Borel dial' the following device, designed to elicit a man's estimate of the probability of 'rain tomorrow', say. First, ascertain that the subject is indifferent between receiving 10 dollars if the twirled arrow stops within one or another of any two equal sectors of the dial. (This is, itself, an induction on the observer's part, in a sense which will become clear.) Then let him choose between receiving \$10 if it rains tomorrow (and receiving nothing if it does not), and receiving \$10 if the arrow stops between the noon position and the four o'clock position on the dial (and receiving nothing if it does not). If he prefers the former bet, we say that the probability he assigns to tomorrow's rain exceeds $\frac{1}{3}$. We then ask him to choose between receiving \$10 only if it rains tomorrow, and receiving \$10 only if the arrow stops between the noon and the six o'clock position.

If he now prefers the latter bet, his 'personal probability' of rain tomorrow is between $\frac{1}{3}$ and $\frac{1}{2}$. This method of evaluation of probabilities, says Borel (who by the way, uses dice, not a continuous dial) 'has exactly the same characteristics as the evaluation of prices.... If one desires to know the price of a ton of coal, it suffices to offer greater and greater prices to the person who possesses the coal; at a certain price he will decide to sell it.' Economists are aware, of course, that price theory and Walras's '*prix criés ... dans le marché*' idealize gross reality. So does Borel's device, idealizing the consistency of bettors.

VI

Is there any relation between probabilities as revealed by a Borel dial applied to a consistent bettor, and the frequencies of observations in statistical samples, the very heart of scientific induction? To answer this, let us first add another case of exchangeability as a property of certain subsets ('events') of the set X (of 'states' x), on which a probability measure is defined. We shall consider the case called 'repeated and independent trials,' viewed again as a mathematical, not physical object. This case will prove to be much more important than that typified by the mathematical objects called 'fair coin', 'well-shuffled deck', etc. In their physical interpretation the latter objects are those illustrating the 'Principle of Indifference', and I agree with Harrod that it is of little consequence for the understanding of induction. By contrast, the exchangeability of 'repeated and independent trials', should its physical interpretation prove justifiable, would indeed entail important consequences for the problem of induction; and I believe it would correspond to Harrod's[13] weighty 'fair sampling postulate'.

Let, then, the generic element of the set X of states be the sequence (temporal or no, no matter) $x=(x_1, x_2, ...)$. Define the set T_i to consist of subsequences in which the component x_i is omitted. For simplicity let each component in each sequence or subsequence have just two possible values, denoted conveniently by 1 ('success') or 0 ('failure'). Define the event Z_i as the set of all those sequences x in which the ith component is a success: $Z_i=\{x:x_i=1\}$. Suppose a consistent man's indifference between conditional bets (as explained in Section IV) reveals that the conditional probability $P(Z_i|T_i)$ is the same for all T_i and all i, so that we can write

$P(Z_i|T_i)=P(Z_i)=p$, say. Then X is called a set of sequences of repeated and independent trials: the same probability is assigned to each trial, and this regardless of whether any other trial results in success or in failure.

Again, it may be a matter of disagreement whether a particular physical phenomenon has approximately the properties of such a set of sequences: whether, for example, successive experiments performed or to be performed in a certain laboratory under assertedly 'controlled conditions' do indeed possess the property that $P(Z_i|T_i)$ is the same for all i, and for all subsequences in T_i. Will everybody be indifferent between betting on a particular outcome of the first such experiment, given all others, and of the tenth, given all others?

We are now ready to establish a relation between probabilities assigned to given events by a consistent decision maker and the frequencies of those events he has observed. Let the states x in X be sequences he believes (as is revealed by his bets) to be sequences of repeated independent trials. That is, his assignment of probability of success, if evaluated on a Borel dial, will be the same for all trials, $i=1, 2,...$, whether observed or not, and each independently of the outcomes of other trials. Now denote by $Z^{(p)}$ and $Z^{(p')}$, respectively, two subsets of X, each consisting of all sequences x such that, for all i, $P(Z_i|T_i)=P(Z_i)=p$ or $=p'$ (where $p \neq p'$). In the present context, $Z^{(p)}$ and $Z^{(p')}$ are two rival hypotheses corresponding to the H, H' of the Bayes theorem as formulated in our Section IV. If one of them, say $Z^{(p)}$, is accepted by the decision-maker, we say that his estimate of $P(Z_i)$ is p for all trials, viz., for all the (n, say) observed ones as well as for the non-observed ones, $i=n+1,...$. This will be revealed by his betting behaviour; he will be indifferent between betting on the $(n+1)$th trial being a success, and betting on a fraction p of the circumference of the Borel dial. [Moreover, if the marginal utility of money were, for him, constant over the range of prizes considered, he would also accept a bet with odds $p:(1-p)$ or better.]

We shall now define that subset of X [i.e., that set of sequences $x=(x_1,..., x_n)$] which will play the role of 'evidence'. First denote by $f_n=(x_1+\cdots+x_n)/n$ the relative frequency of 'successes' (i.e. of 1s rather than 0s). Now consider the set of all sequences $x=(x_1,..., x_n, x_{n+1},...)$ such that f_n is within a distance δ from p. We can denote this set by

$$Z^{(p,\delta,f_n)} = \{x: p-\delta < f_n < p+\delta\}.$$

The set, $Z^{(p,\delta,f_n)}$, will play the role of evidence, E, in the Bayes theorem which we can now rewrite, for our present purposes, thus:

$$\frac{P(Z^{(p)} \mid Z^{(p,\delta,f_n)})}{P(Z^{(p')} \mid Z^{(p,\delta,f_n)})} = \frac{P(Z^{(p)})}{P(Z^{(p')})} \cdot \frac{P(Z^{(p,\delta,f_n)} \mid Z^{(p)})}{P(Z^{(p,\delta,f_n)} \mid Z^{(p')})}.$$

We shall consider the last of these three ratios: the likelihood ratio of the two hypotheses, $Z^{(p)}$ and $Z^{(p')}$ with respect to the evidence $Z(p, \delta, f_n)$; and shall apply to it the ('weak') 'law of large numbers'. This latter is a purely mathematical theorem. Its premises are the three properties defining any probability measure on any set, combined with the definition of a set of infinitely long sequences, each component of a given sequence having the same probability distribution of its values. The theorem is therefore valid independently of any particular interpretation of the probability concept in terms of natural (including human) phenomena.[14] This theorem says that, for any positive number δ,

$$P(Z^{(p,\delta,f_n)} \mid Z^{(p)}) \to 1$$

as n increases. That is: given that the probability of success in each of the indefinitely long sequence of trials is p, the conditional probability of the average number's f_n of successes in n trials being within an arbitrarily small distance δ of p tends towards certainty as n increases.[15]

Now, the conditional probability just specified is the numerator of the *likelihood ratio* we have proposed to consider. It follows from the theorem just stated that this ratio increases beyond all bounds (that is, towards 1:0) as n increases. What, then, about the *posterior odds*? Provided that the prior $P(Z^{(p)})$ is not zero, which, roughly, means that $Z^{(p)}$ is not impossible – the Bayes theorem as last rewritten and the property of our likelihood ratio as just stated imply that the posterior odds of $Z^{(p)}$ against $Z^{(p')}$ will also increase beyond all bounds. In words (roughly): if, as the number of observations increases, the relative frequency of successes is found to remain close to the number p, then the odds in favour of the hypothesis that this number is the probability of successes in each of the indefinite sequence of trials increase beyond all bounds; provided this hypothesis was not judged impossible to begin with. With this proviso, the effect of prior odds will be 'washed out', 'swamped' by the increasing likelihood ratio derived from observations. On the other hand, zero prior odds will never be overcome.[16]

It must be recalled that we interpret the odds in terms of decision-making. Indeed, one can derive from our premises directly that, for any δ, choices between bets, if based on the estimate $P(Z_{n+1})=f_n \pm \delta$ will yield, as the number n of observations increases, an increasingly higher expected utility relative to other choices between the same bets; where, it will be recalled, $P(Z_{n+1})$ is the probability that the $(n+1)$th trial will yield a success, i.e., that $x_{n+1}=1$.[17] This holds not only for the special case when the decision-maker is a 'predictor' (with utility$=1$ if right, $=0$ if wrong), but also in the general case, with utility depending on x_{n+1} and an action in any manner whatsoever. As before, in the limiting case where a certain value of the success probability is *a priori* impossible, it remains so *a posteriori*.

In addition to the proviso of non-zero prior odds, we must remind the reader most emphatically of a more important one: it has been assumed throughout that all of the indefinitely long sequence of trials have the same probability of success. Without this premiss of 'repeated independent trials' the conclusion of the Law of Large Numbers does not obtain, nor does therefore the conclusion about posterior odds of the considered hypothesis against an alternative.

Let me conclude this section with a side issue which, however, will help us, in the next section, to ask questions about Harrod's position compared with the present one. He rightly declares (p. 59) that the so-called Law of Succession[18] 'is derived from assigning equal prior probabilities' and notes

> that the gross and flagrant fallacies to which the application of the Law of Succession leads, all arise ... in the case of short runs .... If the principles by which the Law of Succession is derived were correct, then it ought to apply to very short runs, as well as to longer runs; no one, to my knowledge, has shown why on these principles this should not be so.'

Harrod remarks that his approach, too, 'does not apply to short runs' and that it has 'some family resemblance to the much abused Law of Succession' although its logical basis is quite different.

Now, we have seen that in the 'long run', that is, with a large number of observations, the effect of *any* prior probabilities, whether assumed equal or not, tends to be 'swamped' by the effects of observed frequencies. Thus the position presented here is consistent with the fact, observed by Harrod, that the applications of the Law of Succession, so flagrantly fallacious in the case of short runs, are less so for long runs.

VII

The reader will have noted that the emphasis on short *versus* long runs when it comes to estimating from observations is common to the present position and to that of Harrod. Now, mark our important provision: the decision-maker was made to assume that the many trials he has observed are 'exchangeable', both among themselves and with future trials. Harrod, on the other hand describes his Principle of Experience (Chapter III) as one of 'continuity' of a path partly traversed and still to be journeyed on. Is there a family resemblance between 'continuity' in Harrod's sense and our (and De Finetti's) 'exchangeability'? At any rate: what is the relation between these two concepts?

To me, this is the most important of all the numerous questions that I would have to answer before being sure that I have understood Harrod's book. Even if I had answered them I could not convey to the reader of this essay the depth, the vigour, and the beauty of Harrod's thought. As one can see by comparing the literature cited in the book and in this essay, the backgrounds are different even though we are both economists. Perhaps just this difference of backgrounds makes a comparison of the two approaches, and thus my main question as just stated, not altogether useless.

For better understanding, it is worth remarking that in most though not all of Harrod's reasoning, the relative frequency of successes in observed trials (f_n in my notation above) is, in effect, equal to 1. See, for example, the description of the continuous journey in the important Chapter III on the Principle of Experience.[19] I do not believe that this concentration on a special case weakens Harrod's argument. What is essential for Harrod is that some features observed during the journey are likely to be observed as the journey continues; the more likely the longer you have travelled.

Nor is it a matter of consequence (it seems to be more a matter of nomenclature) that, like Einstein, Harrod seems disinclined to believe that God plays dice. When Harrod says (p. 242) that 'Most of induction... is not concerned to establish statistical frequencies, but to establish uniformities, laws or particular facts', I infer from the context that he has in mind deterministic laws and that, while he is indeed concerned with evaluating probabilities of hypotheses, these hypotheses are not themselves probability distributions. Modern statistics as a tool of inductive inference, and much of modern decision theory, takes a more general view. One does assign a posterior probability, for example, to the statement that this person has such and such probability of dying within a year if not operated upon, and a different probability if a particular operation is performed. And this may be more useful to the decision-making surgeon than the statement 'the patient has cancer for sure'. I said this approach is more general because 'probability $=1$ for a certain value of the variable' is a special case of a probability distribution. Thus, statisticians are apt to use distribution parameters to describe the 'state of the world'. Again, I do not believe that Harrod's 'deterministic' nomenclature makes a decisive difference.

Mostly, the hypotheses considered by Harrod are statements of the type 'If P is the case, then Q is the case' rather than simply 'Q is the case'. Again, this is not essential for our comparison of the two approaches. Harrod's interest in the conjoint occurrence of two events can be taken care of, in the other approach, by considering some conditional probability of Q, given P, as the hypothesis, and testing it by recording the conditional frequency of observed Q, given observed P.

In trying to establish a relation between Harrod's 'continuity' and the 'exchangeability of repeated independent trials' defined here, it is not decisive, either, that Harrod first proposes (pp. 89–90) a 'sampling postulate' (also called 'fair sampling postulate'), then shows it to be unnecessary for induction, replacing it by a proposition on the properties of our observations, not of nature itself (pp. 116–17). For both interpretations are consistent with the definition of repeated independent trials (observed as well as not yet observed) by stating:

$$P(Z_i) \text{ is the same for } i = 1, \ldots, n, n+1, \ldots$$

where $P(Z_i)$ is the probability of success in the ith trial and n is the number of observations already performed.

Nor does it seem to me that the emphasis on decision separates us Ramseyites from Harrod (and, in this respect, from most of traditional literature on logic) in a really important manner. As already pointed out, prediction is a special case of decision. Harrod's book is full of references to the usefulness of correct predictions, for cavemen and others. To be sure there may be disagreement about utilities in detail but hardly any about the need to survive. Moreover, it is presumed (or alleged) for the case of pure scientists that in their case there is intersubjective agreement about the two-valued utility of prediction (e.g., 1 if right, 0 if wrong). This makes expected utility identical with the probability of correct prediction so that, again, induction logic reveals itself as a special case of decision logic.[20]

What does then make the difference, if any, between the two approaches? In Section II, I pointed out that the boundary between prescription and description is fluid. How relaxed, or how restricted shall be the prescriptive norms of logic including the logic of decision? I have mentioned, for example (in Section II) those who relax the norms by denying transitivity of indifference (between actions, or between their consequences). Others have restricted the norms by prescribing, for example, aversion to risk. As far as I know, even some logicians of deduction are more 'relativistic' than others; although less so than the students of ethics, among whom Natural Right and the self-evident truths of 1776 are in disrepute, merited or not. But this is precisely why Harrod's ideas are so attractive. It is impossible not to share his aversion against 'defeatism' and 'escapism' (p. 20). There must be a fixed point somewhere!

The mathematical deductions – from premisses to conclusions – of De Finetti and others are without blemish. If a given sequence consists of repeated and independent trials, relative frequency approaches probability, and actions should be chosen accordingly. Here the sequences, and the actions themselves, are mathematical objects. But how do we know that a given sequence of actual observations, performed and to be performed in the world of phenomena, can be assumed, albeit approximately, to consist of repeated and independent components? How can we establish intersubjective agreement on these matters (even though agreement on other matters such as prior probabilities is not needed when the sample is large)? Or, in Harrod's language, how do we know that, with respect to a particular physical characteristic of events, we are on a continuous path? In the language of statisticians: how do we know that this and this and another item belong 'to the same population'? Who tells us that, in estimating the mortality rate, separation by age and sex is important but separation by alphabet is less so?

True, Harrod does not answer specific questions like these. But remember: he has not set out to write a treatise for practising statisticians. He has asked the philosopher's question: how has it been, how is it, possible to discover laws of nature? His answer: because the world (or our observation of the world) has regular, 'non-Heraclitean' features – although admittedly it is another matter to specify those features. In another language: yes, indeed, there are sequences sufficiently close to be treated as repeated and independent.

Harrod deplores 'shallow doctrines of a pragmatic kind'. If to be pragmatic is to relate truth to action, the adjective is, to me, a compliment. Separating prediction from decision only makes our thinking more special and thus poorer in results. But 'shallow' is another matter. When Harrod searches for grounds for induction (and thus for decision) he searches in depth.

NOTES

* Acknowledgements to the National Science Foundation and the Office of Naval Research for the support of the Western Management Science Institute, University of California at Los Angeles; and to James McQueen for criticisms.

1 Harrod, 1956, for all subsequent citations of his work.

2 Here is the statement from Carnap, 1962, p. XV:

'A. *The meaning of logical probability* (probability$_1$) was informally explained in ... several ways: (a) as the degree to which a hypothesis *h* is confirmed or supported by the evidence *e*; (b) as a fair betting quotient; and (c) as an estimate of relative frequency. Even at that time I regarded (a) as less satisfactory than (b) or (c); today I would avoid formulations of the kind (a) because of their ambiguity....'

'Although the concept of logical probability in the sense here intended is a purely logical concept, I think that the meaning of statements like "the probability of *h* with respect to *e* is 2/3" can best be characterized by explaining their use, *in combination with the concept of utility, in the rule for the determination of rational decisions* (my emphasis J. M.).... The explanation of probability as a betting quotient is a simplified special case of this rule.'

See also Carnap, 1962a. Carnap's student Jeffrey (1965) proceeded to systematize the approach characteristic of Ramsey (rather than that of De Finetti, or of Savage (1954), which I shall mostly follow here).

3 Abelson and Rosenberg, 1958.

4 Hamming, 1965; Rotstein, 1965. In application to human decisions see Kramer, 1968, and, of course, Simon, 1957, 1959. In application to probabilities, see many passages in Harrod's book. For example on p. 35: 'The reason why we cannot specify... [a precise probability number] is simply that we have not had time, nor, perhaps, inclination, to make the count that would be required for [its] evaluation....' See also his numerous remarks on feasible limits of tolerance.

[5] Indeed, some recent thinking about decision norms (in particular, some yet unpublished work of P. Fishburn and of A. K. Sen) has stated important implications of depriving the economists' indifference relation of the transitivity property usually ascribed to it. This is the very reason why I chose to discuss this property as an example for the (moving) boundary between prescriptive and descriptive theory.
[6] Bruner *et al.* (1956).
[7] Edwards and Tversky (ed.), 1967.
[8] Marschak (1968). See also Luce and Suppes, (1965); Edwards and Tversky (1967).
[9] See, for example, Koopmans (1957), pp. 157–9.
[10] But Carnap's rule R_5 is more general: see the last sentence in the extensive quotation given by me in an earlier note. And De Finetti provides the necessary corrective note, with due reference to Ramsey, in his later, English edition: Kyburg and Smokler 1963, p. 102, note (a).
[11] Bayes (1764), Definition 5 and Proposition 2. See their interpretation in Marschak (1954), pp. 169–70.
[12] In the notation of Harrod (p. 15 footnote), $P(H)=p_2$, $P(H')=p_2$, $P(E\mid H)=q_1$, $P(E\mid H')=q_2$. If, as is assumed in his example, the two hypotheses are exhaustive, then $P(H\mid E)+P(H'\mid E)=1$, hence $P(H\mid E)=p_1q_1/(p_1q_1+p_2q_2)$; the formula he uses.
[13] To quote: 'The Principle of Indifference makes an assumption about nature.... If one defines probability by frequency, this implies that nature manifests each alternative an equal number of times. By contrast, the sampling postulate has nothing to do with the composition of nature, but is concerned only with our investigation of nature. It makes the assumption that the relative frequencies of our observations bear a relation to the relative frequencies of different kinds of observables; this requirement entails no assumption regading the composition of nature itself' (pp. 102–3). This passage is introduced by Harrod's observing 'that the Bayes-type argument would require, *in addition* [his italics; J.M.] to some such assumption as the Principle of Indifference, a sampling postulate'. If so, the argument that will follow in my text is not 'Bayes type'. It will use Bayes's theorem and a premiss akin to Harrod's sampling postulate but it will not use the Principle of Indifference since it will nowhere assume 'equal prior probabilities'.
[14] Therefore the theorem called here (and in textbooks on mathematical probability) the Law of Large Numbers cannot be identical with what Harrod (p. 74) calls the Law of Large Numbers and which he 'cannot regard as a universal law of nature *a priori*'. For the mathematical theorem does not claim to describe nature. It is another matter whether or not a particular interpretation of the theorem's premiss and conclusion, i.e., their translation into terms of natural phenomena, can be accepted with any degree of approximation. The same distinction will be made regarding the theorem we are going to discuss now, about estimating posterior probabilities by frequencies.
[15] The proof given in essence 200 years ago is based on combinatorial arithmetic such as that used by Harrod in a similar context (p. 88, footnote).
[16] The latter is the case of Pigou (1929) and the Archbishop of Canterbury, whom Pigou would maintain to be honest even if the Archbishop had dealt himself in one evening three hands each containing four aces, four kings, and four queens. I owe this reference to W. A. Wallis (1942, p. 236).
[17] See also Marschak and Radner (1972), Ch. II, Sections 8–11.
[18] The premiss of this ancient theorem is, more precisely, the uniform prior distribution on the set of values of the probability of success, i.e., on the interval between 0 and 1. One of its conclusions is that, in our notation, $P(Z_{n+1})=(1+nf_n)/(2+n)$.

This, of course, approaches f_n as n increases. See, e.g. Uspensky (1937), p. 69.
[19] Or, at the beginning of Chapter IV, on Inverse Probability: 'If property Q is not in fact almost always conjoined with property P, is it not a very curious thing that out of all the thousands, perhaps hundreds of thousands, of times that P has been seen, it has *always* [J. M.'s emphasis] been seen in conjunction with Q ' (p. 79).
[20] For a more general view see now Marschak (1974).

BIBLIOGRAPHY

Abelson, R. P. and Rosenberg, M. J., 'Symbolic Psycho-Logic', *Behavioral Science* **3** (1958) 1–13.

Bayes, Th., 'An Essay towards Solving a Problem in the Doctrine of Chances', 1764, now in *Biometrika* **45**, 296–315.

Borel, E., 'Apropos of a Treatise on Probability', 1924, reproduced in Kyburg and Smokler, 1964.

Bruner, J. S., Goodnow, J. J., and Austin, G. A., *A Study of Thinking*, New York 1956.

Carnap, R., *Logical Foundations of Probability* (Second ed.), Chicago 1962.

Carnap, R., 'The Aim of Inductive Logic', 1962a, in E. Nagel *et al.* (eds.), *Logic, Methodology and Philosophy of Science*, Stanford 1962, pp. 303–18.

De Finetti, B., 'Foresight: Its Logical Laws, its Subjective Sources', 1937. Translated from the French and provided with some additional notes of the author, in Kyburg and Smokler (1964).

Edwards, W. and Tversky, A. (eds.), *Decision Making: Selected Readings*, Penguin Books, 1967.

Hamming, R. W., 'Numerical Analysis vs. Mathematics', *Science*, (1965) 473–5.

Harrod, R., *Foundations of Inductive Logic*, London 1956.

Jeffrey, R. C., *The Logic of Decision*, New York 1965.

Koopmans, T. C., *Three Essays on the State of Economic Science*, New York 1957.

Kramer, G. H., 'An Impossibility Result concerning the Theory of Decision-Making', in J. L. Bernd (ed.), *Mathematical Applications in Political Science*, University of Virginia Press, 1968, Vol. III, pp. 39–51.

Kyburg, H. E. and Smokler, M. E., *Studies in Subjective Probability*, New York 1964.

Luce, R. D. and Suppes, P., 'Preference, Utility, and Subjective Probability', in *Handbook of Mathematical Psychology* (R. D. Luce *et al.*) New York 1965, Vol. 3, pp. 249–410.

Marschak, J., 'Probabilities in the Social Sciences', 1954, *Selected Essays*, 4.

Marschak, J., 'Decision-Making: Economic Aspects', 1968, *Selected Essays*, 16.

Marschak, J., 'Information, Decision, and the Scientist', in C. Cherry (ed.), *Pragmatic Aspects of Human Communication*, D. Reidel, Dordrecht, 1974, pp. 145–78.

Marschak, J. and Radner, R., *Economic Theory of Teams*, Yale University Press, 1972.

Pigou, A. C., 'The Function of Economic Analysis', Sidney Ball Lecture, reprinted in A. C. Pigou and D. H. Robertson, *Economic Essays and Addresses*, London 1931.

Ramsey, F. P., 'Truth and Probability', 1926. 'Further Considerations', 1928. Both Papers in *The Foundations of Mathematics and Other Logical Essays* (ed. by R. B. Braithwaite), New York 1950. The paper of 1926 also reproduced in Kyburg and Smokler 1964.

Rothstein, J., 'Numerical Analysis: Pure or Applied Mathematics?', *Science* (1965) 1049–50.

Savage, L. J., *The Foundations of Statistics*, New York 1954. Revised: Dover, 1972.

Simon, H. A., *Models of Man*, New York 1957.
Simon, H. A., 'Theories of Decision-Making in Economics and Behavioral Sciences,, *American Economic Review* **49**, 253–83.
Uspensky, J. V., *Introduction to Mathematical Probability*, New York and London 1937.
Von Neumann, J. and Morgenstern, O., *Theory of Games and Economic Behavior*, Princeton 1947.
Wald, A., *Statistical Decision Functions*, New York 1950.
Wallis, A. W., 'Compounding Probabilities from Independent Significance Tests', *Econometrica* (1942) 229–48.
Wright, G. H. von, *The Logic of Preference*, Edinburgh 1963.

18

ECONOMICS OF ACTING, THINKING, AND SURVIVING*

(1974)

I

The idealist philosophers of some 150 years ago have been accused of pan-logism. Quite likely, they would not mind. The present writer, an economist, will briefly indulge in pan-economism, if only to satisfy the editor of this volume who has encouraged the contributors to be 'as provocative as possible'.

Economics will be understood in the sense in which one speaks of 'Economy of Nature': not in the sense in which so-called 'material' (and sometimes measurable) items – food and shelter, and dollar bills – are contrasted with things lovable and beautiful. "Economics is about economizing" (Charles Hitch). "Economics is about the best use of scarce resources". Better still (because scarcity of resources might, unnecessarily, imply measurability): economics is about the best choice between available alternatives. Prudence would also be an adequate term.

II

These days, journalists and politicians and college administrators talk about 'priorities': we cannot do everything, let us make clear what we should do in the first, second, third place.... Clarity about the ranking of alternative actions is indeed a feature of economic thinking. It is an 'extension of logic' (F. P. Ramsey). Actual men are not 'economic men' nor are they, more broadly, 'logical men'. But illogical thinking can be distinguished from logical thinking. A sequence of choices that are capriciously inconsistent with any ranking can be distinguished from consistent, hence economic, choices.

Ranking, ordering can be applied to any set of possible actions, with the best at the top, the worst at the bottom. Psychologically speaking, to achieve consistent ranking, some soul-searching, some process of trial and error may be necessary.

No numerical characteristics are, in general, needed, to choose, for example, between one menu and another. To be sure some people count their calories. So-called 'criteria' – usually numerical ones – may indeed help. This is simple if there is just one such criterion: more rice is better than little rice. Usually there are several criteria. In a beauty contest, various scores are weighted and added to achieve a convincing ranking. We add, somewhat mysteriously, a student's numerical grades before he gets a *cum*, rather than a *summa cum laude*. The listing of pros and cons by Ben Franklin [5], and on Richard Nixon's pad inspected by Joseph Alsop [1], is of the same nature.

This assumed additivity of numerical criteria is often doubtful, a mere tribute to our weakness or laziness. I understand that some supervisors of airplane designs weigh and add the criteria 'speed, in miles per hour' and 'number of passenger seats'. Yet the airline's profit clearly depends not on the sum (weighted or not) of these quantities but on their product, namely on passenger-miles per hour (or year). Anyhow, additivity simplifies, and thus economizes on our thinking. It is simple, in particular, to think of the result of an action as additively separable into (viz., as the difference between) 'benefit' and 'cost': another current habit, giving some precision to the question: "is this worth while"?

III

I have now touched, in fact, on the 'economics of thinking'; yea, on the prudence of thinking lazily. What's the use of carrying many digits, of paying attention to third-order errors, if the added precision is not likely to cause a shift in the ranking of our actions and to call for a different choice of action.

Perhaps, then, the balancing of benefits and costs is applicable, not only to acting but also to thinking, both inductive and deductive? Recently, some logicians moved in this direction; notably those who tried to clarify and use the concept of probability. The logic of induction has received some inspiration from a new approach to probabilities, which relates statistical inference to the choice of action. And some logicians of deduction have applied probability to the domain of propositions, having been inspired by ideas of communication engineers who have related information to the number of symbols needed to store or transmit it, and thus to the probabilities of alternative occurrences.[1]

IV

The new approach to probabilities is perhaps more in the nature of a revival. For, around 1750, the Rev. Thomas Bayes [2] thought of probabilities as being revealed by the ratio of a bettor's possible gain to his possible loss. Around 1950, Rudolf Carnap [3] took essentially the same attitude. But to bet is to act, is it not?

For reasons to be stated later, we prefer a somewhat different – actually, a less restrictive – approach. Choose between betting on tomorrow's being a sunny day in Cambridge, Massachusetts or in Irvine, California. If you prefer the latter bet and are asked why, you will perhaps answer – and this answer will agree with ordinary English usage: "because a sunny day is a more probable event in California than in the Northeast." Note that the consequences of either bet – your possible gain and loss – need not be sums of money but can be any pair of things of which one – e.g., a vacation – is preferable to another – e.g., a prison term.

Further: are you indifferent, or not, between betting on one or any other particular card being drawn from a well-shuffled deck? And, accordingly, will you not say – again in agreement with ordinary English – that these 52 events are all equally probable? Your belief that a deck of cards is 'well shuffled' (or, for that matter, a coin is 'fair', a pair of dice 'unbiased') is, in fact defined by this, your indifference between certain bets. F. Ramsey [9] the logician, B. De Finetti [4] the actuary, L. J. Savage [10] the statistician, took up this line of thought. They extended the traditional logic of rational thought to include some postulates of rational, consistent action. Consistent preference ranking of actions, of which I spoke earlier, is one of these postulates. All of them are in the nature of plausible logical norms rather than psychological descriptions of actual behavior of hurried or tired men. The postulates imply, it turns out, that the 'probabilities' revealed by those consistent bets (on weather or cards, in our examples) – or, generally, by consistent actions under uncertainty – have about all the properties by which the concept of 'probability measure' is defined by mathematicians. Thus, a consistent bettor will not only, by definition, prefer to bet on those events to which he assigns higher probabilities. His bet will also reveal, for example, that (in accord with the 'additivity property' of the mathematical probability measure) he assigns probability $\frac{3}{52}$ to the event of drawing one of three specified cards, – provided he is indifferent between bets on any one card in the deck.

'Personal' probabilities as revealed by your choice of bets can, then, apply to non-repeatable events. For you can choose, for example, between betting on Julius Caesar's having died on a Monday or during the rest of the week. There would seem to be a gap between the Ramseyan probability and the frequency of successful outcomes of a repeated experiment.

Suppose, however, that you are indifferent between bets on the success of any one of a sequence of repeated trials. That is, you think the experiment is 'well-controlled' (similar to our 'well-shuffled' deck of cards). The following can then be proved from those postulates of consistent action: you will be well advised to assign to the success of any future trial a probability equal to the proportion of successes in a *large number* of already observed trials; and to choose your bets in accordance with the probability thus computed (the 'law of large numbers' is a purely mathematical step in the proof of this recommendation). The so-called 'objective' probabilities based on long-run observed frequencies are thus identical with the 'personal' ones; they presuppose, in fact, your personal indifference between bets on the success of any of repeated trials: your belief that the experiment is 'well-controlled'. See also [8] on the 'Economic Man's Logic'.

V

The consistency postulates applied to bets with just a pair of outcomes (success, failure) entail the existence of 'personal probabilities'. These satisfy the mathematical definition of probability measure and are revealed by the bettor's choices. Applied to any actions under uncertainty, with any number of outcomes, those postulates entail, furthermore, the existence of numerical 'utilities' of those outcomes. These numbers are defined by the following property: Suppose the sum of the utilities of the outcomes of one action, each utility being weighted (i.e., multiplied) by the outcome's probability, is smaller than the corresponding weighted sum for another action; then the latter action will be ranked higher on your scale of preferences. The word utility is borrowed from Jeremiah Bentham but its present meaning is much clearer, and is operational. It is also older. When the outcome is a money amount, its utility is the 'moral wealth' – so called by the founding fathers of probability calculus. They pointed out, in effect, that the risk-averting gambler or investor will not play a game with 50:50 chance (though he might accept a 60:40 chance, say) of winning or losing a hundred *louis d'or*. This is why we have, earlier in this essay, dismissed Bayes' concern with odds in terms of the ratio of money gained and lost. So did, in fact, De Finetti and Carnap when they revised their earlier writings.

We have mentioned earlier the simplifying – though not always justifiable – assumption that the preference rank of an action can be derived as a difference between benefit and cost. Correspondingly, the average utility (the weighted sum of utilities) of the outcomes of an action would be the difference between average benefit and average cost. Prudent laziness in induction, in empirical research, would then prescribe: do not increase the number of experiments unless the consequent change in action will result, on the average, in added benefits exceeding added cost.

VI

If, in matters of deductive logic, we follow J. Hintikka [6], it appears that personal probabilities – possibly again derived from choices between bets – can be applied to alternative possible sentences whose truth values are to be established by deduction. (I was often astonished to hear mathematicians say: 'This conjecture is very probable....") The larger the number of competing sentences, and the more equal their probabilities, the larger is the 'information' that the deductive steps will yield. The number of steps needed (the 'depth' of the true sentence, e.g., a theorem) is said to be a matter of logic, not psychology. This means (I presume) that although the most difficult theorem is immediately obvious to God, there is a minimum number of steps that Man (a logical ideal) must make to prove it. In the language of the present essay, this number might correspond to the 'cost', and the information yielded to the 'benefit' of a deductive job.

VII

I mentioned earlier the Economy of Nature. Ralph Gerard and his fellow biologists who, with this writer and others, want to honor Ralph by their contributions to this volume, will have guessed by now what I am driving at. Economics of surviving, placed along with the economics of acting and of thinking, means this to me: an interpretation of the process of selection as a continuing betting on those organic features that have comparatively great probability to survive in a given environment. A tautology seems to have provided guidance to most fruitful descriptive research. "What has a high probability to survive will survive, with high probability," is a tautology. But it has directed creative attention to the question: why – in terms of known physics and chemistry, say – has such-and-such feature of an organism a higher probability to survive in such-and-such environment, than this-and-this other feature?

As I understand, anthropologists, too, have derived useful insights from the question: what is the 'survival function' [2] of this particular social institution or tribal custom? In my own field – as was pointed out by S. Winter [11] – the description of competing sizes and structures of business organizations is well guided by a similar question. Strictly speaking, the question requires statements in probability terms – unless we are all-knowing. And such statements mean, essentially, comparisons between bets.

I hope – and fear – this essay has become sufficiently provocative without my dwelling further on things I know so little about – be it deductive logic or the theory of evolution.

NOTES

* This contribution to a volume in honor of Ralph W. Gerard was completed in 1970 but was still in press at the time of his death, February 1974.

[1] *Added in 1974*. But see now Marschak [8a].

[2] See Marschak [8b].

BIBLIOGRAPHY

[1] Alsop, Joseph, in *Newsweek*, 1 June 1970.

[2] Bayes, Thomas, 'An Essay Towards Solving a Problem in the Doctrine of Chances', 1764; now in *Biometrika* **45**, 296–315.

[3] Carnap, Rudolf, *Logical Foundations of Probability*, University of Chicago Press (first ed. 1950). In the Second Edition, 1962, see in particular p. XV.

[4] De Finetti, Bruno, 'La Prévision: ses Lois Logiques, ses Sources Subjectives', 1937. Now in English, and provided with additional notes by the author, in Kyburg and Smokler (eds.) [7], pp. 95–158.

[5] Franklin, Benjamin, 'How to Make a Decision', (a letter to J. Priestley), 1772; in *A Benjamin Franklin Reader* (ed. by N. G. Goodman), Crowell, New York, 1945, p. 786.

[6] Hintikka, Jaakko, 'Information, Deduction, and the *a priori*', *Nous*, 1970.

[7] Kyburg, Henry, E. and Smokler, Howard E. (eds.), *Essays in Subjective Probability*, Wiley, New York, 1964.
[8] Marschak, Jacob, 'The Economic Man's Logic', *Selected Essays*, 17.
[8a] Marschak, Jacob, 'Information, Decision, and the Scientist', *Pragmatic Aspects of Human Communication* (C. Cherry, ed.), pp. 145–178. D. Reidel, 1974.
[8b] Marschak, Jacob, 'Economics of Language', *Selected Essays*, 27.
[9] Ramsey, Frank P., 'Truth and Probability', 1926. Now in Kyburg and Smokler (ed.) [7], pp. 63–92.
[10] Savage, Leonard J., *The Foundation of Statistics*, Wiley, New York, 1954. Revised, Dover, 1972.
[11] Winter, Sidney, 'Economic 'Natural Selection' and the Theory of the Firm', *Yale Economic Essays* (1964).

INDEX OF NAMES

INDEX OF SUBJECTS

THEORY AND DECISION LIBRARY

An International Series in the Philosophy and Methodology of the Social and Behavioral Sciences

Editors:

1. GÜNTER MENGES (ed.), *Information, Inference, and Decision.* 1974, viii + 195 pp.
2. ANATOL RAPOPORT (ed.), *Game Theory as a Theory of Conflict Resolution.* 1974, v + 283 pp.
3. MARIO BUNGE (ed.), *The Methodological Unity of Science.* 1973, viii + 264 pp.
4. COLIN CHERRY (ed.), *Pragmatic Aspects of Human Communication.* 1974, ix + 178 pp.
5. FRIEDRICH RAPP (ed.), *Contributions to a Philosophy of Technology. Studies in the Structure of Thinking in the Technological Sciences.* 1974, xv + 228 pp.
6. WERNER LEINFELLNER and ECKEHART KÖHLER (eds.), *Developments in the Methodology of Social Science.* 1974, x + 430 pp.